STAMFORD BRIDGE IS FALLING DOWN

TIM ROLLS

STAMFORD BRIDGE IS FALLING DOWN
Copyright Tim Rolls 2019
ISBN: 978-1081349691
THE MORAL RIGHT OF THE AUTHOR HAS BEEN ASSERTED
Apart from any fair dealing for the purposes of research or private study, or criticism or review, as permitted under the Copyright, Designs and Patents Act 1988, this publication may only be reproduced, stored or transmitted, in any means, with the prior permission in writing of GATE 17, or in the case of reprographic reproduction in accordance with the terms of licenses issued by the Copyright Licensing Agency. Enquiries concerning reproduction outside those terms should be sent to the publishers.

email: enquiries@gate17.co.uk
cover photo: Chelsea manager Dave Sexton & Chelsea chairman Brian Mears in from of the partially demolished East Stand. 13 June 1972 © Getty Images
cover design: GATE 17
www.gate17.co.uk

CONTENTS

INTRODUCTION 1
ACKNOWLEDGEMENTS 5
PRELUDE: At the top of the mountain looking down 9
CHAPTER ONE: 1971-72 – The Cups Run Out 20
CHAPTER TWO: 'We are about to turn our dreams into reality' 73
CHAPTER THREE: 1972-73 – Three Sides, Team Slides 80
CHAPTER FOUR: 1973-74 – The Stars Go Out 129
CHAPTER FIVE: 1974-75 – Empty Seats, Empty Hopes 191
CHAPTER SIX: 'A Monument To Wishful Thinking' 250
CHAPTER SEVEN: In Hindsight 254

APPENDICES

APPENDIX A: Player Profiles 267
APPENDIX B: Total League Appearances And Goals 1971-75 273
APPENDIX C: 1971-75 Season-By-Season Overall Record 274
APPENDIX D: 1971-75 Transfer Activity 275
APPENDIX E: 1971-75 Attendance Analysis 278
APPENDIX F: 1971-75 List of Televised Games 279
          Match of the Day & *The Big Match*

BIBLIOGRAPHY 281

INTRODUCTION

Memory is a funny thing. In football, as in life. What stays in the mind decades later is not always what actually happened. In popular memory, Chelsea Football Club in the late 1960s and early 1970s are associated with success, with winning trophies, with fast-living, glamourous, stylish players linked inexorably with the King's Road.

There is an element of truth in this, but the reality is much more complex and begs one over-arching question. How on earth did a club that won major trophies in 1970 and 1971, that attracted large crowds, possessed a positive public image, featured a number of undoubted star players and a well-respected manager end up relegated four short years later, in a ruinous financial position with most of those star players sold after falling out with that same manager, who himself was sacked as the wheels spectacularly fell off the Chelsea locomotive?

This book explores the causes of the decline in those four seasons, causes that are many and varied. Incompetence, pig-headedness, arrogance, idleness, recklessness, bad luck, bravado, irresponsibility, stupidity and poor communication all played their part. The Chelsea board, their advisers, the players and the manager all bear varying degrees of responsibility for the chaos that consumed and nearly destroyed the club. The events, the personalities and the decisions that together brought a great club to its knees are identified, detailed and analysed.

The idea for the book started when I had a pre-match conversation at the *cfcuk* fanzine stall with fellow Gate 17 author Neil Smith on the subject of the late Keith Weller, as part of a fanzine piece I was writing on the 1970 Charity Shield. Weller was bought from Millwall in May 1970 and sold to Leicester City sixteen short months later having been leading scorer and played a key part in winning the European Cup-Winners' Cup. I could not understand why such a key player had been sold and neither, it turned out, could Neil or any other supporter I spoke to.

After submitting the piece, I researched the matter further and became intrigued. I realised the sale of Weller was actually an early manifestation of the problems that were to grip, and nearly wreck, the club over the next four years. As David Webb, one of the undoubted heroes of this book, has said about the sale of Weller, 'to me, that was the beginning of the end'.

These problems were to manifest themselves in declining performances, diminishing gates, disaffected players and, critically, the delay and scaling-down of ambitious and grandiose stadium redevelopment plans as club finances crumbled. Much of this was played out in the back, and occasionally front, pages of the national press. In 1970 and 1971 Chelsea made headlines because of their football and their trophies. Positive on-pitch headlines ebbed away as less than positive on- and off-pitch headlines became more prevalent.

The more research I did, and the more people I spoke to, the more it became clear that the reasons for the decline and near fall of the club in the early and mid-1970s were complex, the responsible parties numerous. I spent a sunny pre-match in the beer garden of The Cock pub on North End Road in August 2017, with Chelsea official historian Rick Glanvill and Chelsea Supporters Trust board member Ramzi Shammas, bouncing ideas around, ideas that formed the basis of this book.

The 204 competitive matches Chelsea played in those four tempestuous seasons between 1971 and 1975 are covered, but the rationale of this book is to be much more than reporting the displays of a team in decline. The redevelopment of Stamford Bridge, which commenced in 1972, deprived manager Dave Sexton of the cash required to rebuild his team. Star players like Alan Hudson and Peter Osgood became disaffected, openly critical of the manager and, in the end, mutinous.

The team declined just when the board needed it to succeed, to sparkle, to attract supporters. Instead, it became caught up in a vicious downward spiral, a perfect storm of under-achievement that culminated in significantly reduced attendances, relegation and near financial disaster. The matches, the personalities, the decisions, the events, the divisions and the fall-outs are all close examined to try and identify exactly what went so wrong.

As with my previous book, *Diamonds, Dynamos and Devils*, which examined the Tommy Docherty side of 1961-67, I write this as a Chelsea supporter but not one who regularly watched that side. I have seen over 1,450 Chelsea games and been a Stamford Bridge regular since 1976, but in the early 1970s had to content myself with a few games a season. Objectivity is not always easy, especially when human failings are demonstrated, but I have attempted to utilise evidence uncovered rather than emotion aroused.

If your memory of events differs from what I describe then apologies. Events that occurred nearly fifty years ago are almost always opened to interpretation and memory blurring. I have used a myriad of contemporary newspaper reports, articles and interviews as my main source of information, backed up with a series of biographies, autobiographies, Chelsea histories and websites. I accept that newspaper articles are not always accurate, that they are subject to speculation and axe grinding, but by using multiple sources I have hopefully reduced the impact of this. All these sources are credited at the end of the book. I have also picked the brains of several supporters who watched the club in those days. In some cases, there is a consensus about events and individuals, in other cases, a surprising dissension. I have attempted to show both sides of arguments and, where appropriate, to draw my own conclusions. Though I have tried hard to minimise any factual inaccuracies, any which appear are my responsibility and I apologise for them.

Transfer fees are notoriously difficult to report with accuracy, as are payoffs after managerial sackings. Where there is a generally accepted fee involved, I have used that. Often newspapers reported different fees for the same deal, so I have tried to go with the most commonly used. Similarly, trying to get to the bottom of the costs of the East Stand, and of club revenues, has not been easy so on occasions I have had to make a 'best estimate'. Any assumptions have been detailed.

Matchday attendances have been taken from relevant match programmes and cross-checked against the *Bounder Friardale* website and *Chelsea – The Complete Record*.

Tim Rolls
London, August 2019

ACKNOWLEDGEMENTS

I have a large number of people I need to thank :-

My wife Nicki, who had to cope with the frustrations and crises inevitable in any project I get involved in and whose unwavering support is, as ever, massively appreciated.

Gate 17 Books supremo Mark Worrall who, despite suffering my inefficiencies with *Diamonds, Dynamos and Devils*, agreed to publish this piece of work and has been endlessly supportive during its lengthy gestation. He also came up with the book title and cover design.

Chelsea official historian Rick Glanvill and Chelsea Supporters Trust board member Ramzi Shammas for critiquing and fleshing out the original idea, and Rick and Simon Terry for their essential feedback on the first draft.

Chelsea authors including Martin Knight, John King, Clayton Beerman, Mark Meehan, Neil Smith and Walter Otton for their ongoing support and encouragement.

Interviewee John Boyle for his entertaining company, openness and honesty.

Thea and David Sexton (Dave's wife and son) and Dave's son-in-law Matthew Hyams for their time and help. Edward Lishak for setting up that meeting.

Supporters: Terry Cassley, David Collis, Vince Cooper, Tony Foss, Alan Garrison, Brian Gaches, David Gray, Peter Gray, Steve Hodder, Martin Horne, Geoff Kimber, Jonathan Kydd, Steve Lloyd, Allen Mortlock, Richard Pigden, Neil Smith and Howard Sole for sharing their memories of a roller-coaster period in Chelsea's history.

Stephen Holt for providing copies of board notes from his collection. Howard Sole for the loan of his father Gordon's Chelsea scrapbooks.

Rodney George for his help with the listing of televised Chelsea games in Appendix F.

The ever-helpful staff of the British Library newsroom. London Borough of Hammersmith and Fulham archive department. Ally from ColorSport photo agency.

Joe Tweeds, Rod Crowley, Chelsea Daft website, WAGNH website, The Shed chat page, the Chelsea Fancast and everyone who helped me with the hardback crowdfunding process.

All those who bought *Diamonds, Dynamos and Devils* (still available on Amazon…), giving me the confidence to write a second book. Everyone I bounced the idea of this book off who encouraged and supported me. Writing is by necessity a solitary activity, and all decisions made regarding approach, content and emphasis are mine, but moral support and encouragement from so many quarters has been greatly appreciated.

This book is dedicated to Ian Britton, Peter Houseman, Ian Hutchinson, Brian Mears, Peter Osgood, John Phillips, Dave Sexton, Ron Suart, Keith Weller and Ray Wilkins. They all feature in this book but are sadly no longer with us. RIP

PRELUDE
At The Top Of The Mountain, Looking Down

The Team and The Players

It was Thursday 20th May 1971. The previous evening the world-famous Real Madrid had forced a last-minute equaliser, heartbreakingly depriving Chelsea FC of winning their first European trophy, the European Cup-Winners' Cup. The replay was the following day, by when many of the supporters who had travelled out from London would have to had flown unwillingly home. Manager Dave Sexton left the players to their own devices after the massive disappointment the previous evening. How did the Chelsea team lift their spirits? Team talks to boost morale and identify ways to win the replay? Long walks to clear their thoughts and focus their minds? That might have worked for other clubs and would probably have suited Sexton. Instead, three players – Tommy Baldwin, Charlie Cooke and Peter Osgood - spent the afternoon and evening in an epic poolside drinking session.

    Twenty-four hours later all three performed heroically as, against the odds, Chelsea won the replay 2-1 and flew home to parade the trophy to the happy hordes on the Fulham Road. In some ways, this cameo encapsulates the team at that time. Successful and talented yet with a wild, rebellious, Rabelaisian streak evident in certain players. Nearly fifty years later, winning the European Cup-Winners' Cup remains one of the greatest achievements in Chelsea's history and the players were rightly lauded for their display and their resilience in bouncing back from the heartbreak of the late equaliser. This trophy was the club's second in successive seasons, building on the momentous FA Cup Final replay victory against bitter rivals Leeds United thirteen months earlier. Anyone might think that such success would breed harmony across the club and a shared long-term vision. Anyone might be wrong.

    Backtracking eight months, the opening game of the 1970-71 season, the Charity Shield, was played at Stamford Bridge and Chelsea duly paraded the FA Cup, as champions Everton did the League trophy, to the 43,500 crowd who saw the Merseysiders win 2-1. Two days later the *Daily Express* reported, under a 'Sexton Cracks Down' headline, that Osgood, Ian Hutchinson, David Webb, Marvin Hinton and Paddy Mulligan had been ordered in for extra training after a 'pedestrian performance'. The Express also revealed that on the recent pre-season tour of Holland several players had been fined for breaking a late-night curfew, by no means a unique occurrence in Chelsea's history. A week after the Charity Shield, against Derby, Sexton substituted his star player, Osgood, because he thought him 'disheartened'. In retrospect, it seems cracks were appearing in certain players relationships with Sexton, just months after the FA Cup win. Underperformance, clashes between players and manager and what might euphemistically be called 'lifestyle issues' were to bedevil the club in the years ahead.

That 1970-71 season is, rightly, remembered for the trophy-winning finale. What is less regularly brought up is that the team only finished sixth in Division One, compared with third the previous season. For a team with supremely talented individuals like Osgood, Cooke and Alan Hudson, never-say-die battlers like David Webb, Ian Hutchinson and Ron Harris and experienced professionals like Peter Bonetti, John Hollins, Peter Houseman, John Boyle and John Dempsey, augmented by new signing Keith Weller this was underachievement. Inconsistency bedeviled the team and manifested itself in a heavy 3-0 home defeat to Manchester City in the FA Cup Fourth Round, a humiliating way for the holders to go out. This occurred a mere week after a similarly heavy defeat at champions Everton had reinforced the point that Chelsea were not realistic title contenders.

Weller had fitted into the side immediately, ending the season as leading League scorer with thirteen goals but Osgood scored a mere five, compared with twenty-three in 1969-70. This scoring record was not helped by a draconian eight-week suspension from late January 1971, after a series of six bookings in a year.

Typically, though, Osgood did score in both the Athens games. His striking partner, the indefatigable and lion-hearted Ian Hutchinson, suffered a cartilage injury in February that sadly ended his season and forced Sexton to shuffle his forward pack to cover his absence. It was to be hoped, however, that 'Hutch' would be back, firing on all cylinders, for the 1971-72 season and that his return would inspire Osgood to greater things.

The Cup-Winners' Cup run was a glorious distraction from mundane domestic matters, and some European performances were little short of majestic. A 2-0 defeat in Bruges was turned around at Stamford Bridge where a euphoric crowd willed the team to a famous 4-0 victory after extra-time. The next round, the Semi-final, brought an all-England clash against Manchester City and Sexton got it right tactically with 1-0 wins home and away.

So Chelsea went into the summer of 1971 basking in two trophies in two years, and confidence at the club was high that there would be more on-field success to come. It was generally recognised that Sexton, manager since replacing the mercurial Tommy Docherty in October 1967 and a thoughtful, intelligent thinker about the game, had assembled one of the strongest squads in England. That summer he could survey his collection of players and feel confident about the future.

Goalkeeper Peter Bonetti was reliable, experienced, brave, agile and talented. The defence was highly experienced, if perhaps a little short on pace. Ron Harris, his totally committed captain, could play at full-back and centre-back, David Webb, Marvin Hinton and John Dempsey, his centre-backs were cornerstones of the team. Webb's piratical, barnstorming attitude made him a particular crowd favourite. Eddie McCreadie and Paddy Mulligan were very decent attacking full-backs, though the former's pace had been blunted by an increasing number of injuries.

In midfield, club penalty-taker John Hollins was a workaholic, chasing everything and netting important goals. Charlie Cooke, bewitching dribbler and sublime passer, was used out wide or occasionally in midfield. Peter Houseman was a more orthodox winger and the best crosser of the ball at the club. Alan Hudson, at twenty, was tipped to emerge as the great England midfield talent, his football brain and superb passing being widely recognised as something very special.

Up front Osgood, the King of Stamford Bridge and beloved by so many supporters, was supremely talented and on his day the best centre-forward in England, though his temperament was occasionally called into question. Supporting him were Hutchinson, Tommy Baldwin, a hard-working inside forward and Weller, who was used wide but was also effective up front or even as an attacking midfielder.

In reserve were goalkeeper John Phillips, improving and likely to challenge hard Bonetti in the season ahead, who had played much of the season half of the season while Bonetti recovered from pneumonia, though he missed out on playing in Athens, John Boyle, a loyal utility player who could play full-back or defensive midfield, and Derek Smethurst, who had been used up front as injuries took their toll in the latter stages of the European campaign. A few youngsters were starting to press for a first-term place, primarily giant centre-half Micky Droy. It was, though, a concern that only Hudson had come through the club's youth system to cement a first-team place since Osgood and Boyle had done so in 1965.

Osgood had given the *Daily Mail* an interview in the New Year where he talked about how winning the FA Cup was 'the breakthrough for the club and for a lot of the players financially' and looked forward to a glittering future for the club. 'The beauty of it is that we've got a team young enough to enjoy it for at least another five years. Other clubs like Manchester United and even Leeds are starting to go over the top or getting near the day it will happen. Not us'. As this book will show, by summer 1975 only two of the players who started against Crystal Palace the week of his interview were still at the club. Though United were indeed relegated three years later, during the early 1970s Chelsea fell a country mile behind Leeds, and other top sides, in terms of quality of squad and trophy-winning capability.

In *The Bonnie Prince* Charlie Cooke reminisced that 'none of us knew it that close season of 1971, but we were at the top looking down', but at the time, few expected anything other than continued Chelsea success.

The Manager

Dave Sexton had been first-team coach at Chelsea under Tommy Docherty in the early 1960's, his calm, phlegmatic nature a useful counterpart to the mercurial Doc. If Sexton had not left to manage Leyton Orient in the middle of the 1964-65 season Chelsea might well have won the League that season, rather than finishing third. His coaching knowledge, tactical astuteness, willingness to learn and innovative thinking were all recognised throughout the game. There were those, including Docherty, who felt that Sexton might be a better coach than manager, the latter role requiring man-management skills that did not always come easily to an introverted, highly intelligent man.

Ron Suart had been Sexton's assistant since the latter's arrival at the club in October 1967, having previously played the same role to Tommy Docherty. Prior to that he had spent nine years as Blackpool manager, so he was certainly experienced and, for Sexton, a more-than-useful sounding board.

Head trainer Harry Medhurst had played 140 League games in goal for Chelsea after World War Two. He left for Brighton in 1952 and returned to Stamford Bridge as assistant trainer a year later. In 1960, after passing the FA trainers' certificate, the club loyalist became the head trainer, in essence the physiotherapist, responsible for dealing with player injuries and maintaining their fitness. His son Norman had the same qualifications and acted as his father's deputy.

The Board and Club Administration

The Chelsea board in summer 1970 comprised five members. Chairman Brian Mears, his cousin Leslie Juan Mears, George Thomson, Viscount Chelsea and Richard Attenborough, famous as film star and director.

Club secretary was John Battersby. He had joined Chelsea from the FA, where he had worked since 1934, as assistant secretary in January 1949 and became club secretary in Summer 1952. Highly respected across football, his experience, contacts and knowledge had been invaluable to the club for the past two decades.

The Ground

There was little argument that much of Stamford Bridge was old and dilapidated. The lack of cover from the elements for standing spectators, and those at the front of the West Stand benches, was an embarrassment and, compared with many of their peers, the stadium seemed archaic, a poor reflection on the club.

The East Stand, already open when Chelsea FC were founded in 1905, had 4,826 seats and 3,000 standing spectators in the enclosure in front.

In 1930, a new terrace was built on the south side, with only a small part covered to shelter bookmakers and their customers at the greyhound racing which Chelsea shared the stadium with. It became known as "The Shed End", officially named as such following a letter from supporter Clifford Webb, printed in the home programme against Leicester City in September 1966. This became the most favoured spot for much of the loudest and most die-hard support. The total terrace capacity, in The Shed and the North Stand, was 41,500 in 1970.

In 1939, a small two-storied North Stand with 2,244 seats, at the North-Eastern corner of the ground was erected. It was originally intended to span the entire northern end, but the outbreak of World War Two and its aftermath compelled the club to keep the stand small. An architectural oddity and, to some, an eyesore, it looked to the layman as though it was going to collapse at any minute.

Between 1939 and the early 1960's there were no ground improvements at Stamford Bridge. Utter chaos at a Tottenham Hotspur FA Cup replay in January 1964, where three crash barriers gave way in a crowd in excess of 70,000, clearly indicated that improvement work was long overdue. The dilapidated state of much of the stadium, and the inadequate facilities offered to most spectators, added to the need for redevelopment to be carried out.

In early 1966 the West Stand opened, a modest, unambitious structure replacing the enormous West Terrace. There was a roof, although one supported by pillars in an age when other grounds were building cantilevered stands without them, but seating at the front was on benches. Capacity was 6,163 stand seats and 3,360 bench seats. At the rear were six hospitality boxes, making Stamford Bridge the second League stadium after Old Trafford to offer such facilities.

One long-term constraint on the redevelopment of Stamford Bridge had been the fact that the freehold of the Stamford Bridge Grounds was held not by the club but by the J.T. Mears Trust, a family trust representing members of the Mears family. Joe Mears had been chairman of the club until his tragic and untimely death in summer 1966 and, after brief reigns by Charles Pratt and Len Withey, the chairmanship of Chelsea FC passed to Joe's son Brian in 1969.

This ownership of the stadium by the J.T. Mears Trust created a potential conflict of interest, whereby the football club, which included members of the Mears family on the board, paid rent to the Trust whose beneficiaries were members of the self-same Mears family. The possibility of the club buying the freehold had been aired in the 1960s, but nothing concrete had happened. In 1968 the greyhound racing moved away so the situation was, in theory, simplified as the football club were now the only tenant.

Sale negotiations had dragged on for years in the 1960s, and the lease was extended in 1969. The club had used forthcoming ground redevelopment as an excuse for not buying new players as far back as summer 1967, which exacerbated their final falling out with Tommy Docherty, so the issue had been a long running sore. Chelsea had used transfer dealings to recover operating losses for some years, Docherty making a surplus of £150,000 in his six years in charge. Sexton, too, was never in the market for really top players.

As Battersby pointed out, by 1970 the council were very close to closing the East Stand due to its dilapidated nature. Hammersmith Council minutes from April 1972 make this very clear. 'Many of the existing structures are showing signs of obsolescence and the stage has now been reached when the East Stand has been given a "limited" life from the District Surveyor and the license will soon be withheld'.

Chelsea chairman Brian Mears and his board, like Osgood anticipating a silverware-laden future, began to think about creating a stadium to match. Mears and fellow directors Richard Attenborough and Leslie Mears had formed a sub-committee, and started talking about rebuilding, as far back as 1969.

After the catastrophic Ibrox disaster in January 1971 there were increasing concerns about football ground safety, from which Chelsea were certainly not immune. A ramshackle Stamford Bridge was not the arena Mears saw attracting the families and wealthier supporters he dreamt of filling the ground. Dreams of grandiose super-stadium ideas were starting to permeate into the senior club hierarchy, plans that were to fundamentally change the club for many years to come, though not in the way the board imagined.

Stamford Bridge's capacity in 1970-71 was supposedly 60,000 though the Manchester United game in January 1971 had the gates locked with 53,482 officially inside. Despite using crowd packers, the crowd would not move forward, and gangways were blocked, hugely frustrating for the club in terms of the lost revenue and, worse, for the 6,500 supporters who should have seen the game.

To help finance future ground improvement and/or redevelopment, the Derby County home match programme in August 1970 announced the launch of the Chelsea FC Pools Association, or Chelsea Pools as it became known. It cost a shilling (5p) to join and a shilling a week to play, so the revenue per member was £2.60 a season. The Pools Association was actively looking to recruit agents for a scheme that it was hoped would within a couple of years raise £100,000 a season in revenue for the club, a target which would require nearly 40,000 members, the equivalent of the average home gate.

Chairman Brian Mears was photographed with five 'Chelsea Football Club Pools Association' vans, so the club were clearly speculating to accumulate. It seems to have occurred to nobody that spending money on vans, and boasting about it, hardly emphasised to supporters the necessity for them to raise and donate their hard-earned cash. He assured supporters that 'the entire profits will go towards ground redevelopment' and money raised, after administration costs, was to be split pretty much 50/50 between prizes and redevelopment funds. Most of the Chelsea FC board were on the committee, so board support was clear. In addition, that favourite fundraiser, Golden Goals tickets, was to continue, Mears advising that the previous season's profits were used to carry out toilet renovations.

Mears concluded in both realistic and optimistic vein. 'If some of you are wondering why new stands, electronic scoreboards etc. have not shot up since you last saw League football here four months ago, may we say that planning is now at an advanced stage with the architects. We intend to have a first-class job done rather than regret a little more time was not taken in perfecting it, and when the whole vast project is completed you will not be disappointed, we can assure you'.

The reason for the launch of Chelsea Pools became clear when, in the Southampton programme on 31st October 1970 there was an article headlined 'Buying Our Own Ground'. Mears announced at the club Annual General Meeting on October 14th, 1970 that contractual arrangements had been made to purchase from J.T. Mears Trustees the freehold of Stamford Bridge Grounds for £475,000 with completion due not later than May 1974 'although it is hoped to complete the purchase before then'.

The programme article went on to say 'plans are now being drawn up for the necessary redevelopment of the accommodation at the grounds, so as to afford the most up-to-date facilities for the club's supporters, and steps are also being taken to raise the not inconsiderable amount of finance necessary to complete the purchase and pay for the improvements'. The re-development of Stamford Bridge, when purchase price and cost of planned improvements are combined, can be estimated as a £1 million project'. It is unclear where this figure of £1m million came from, given that redeveloping the whole stadium would obviously cost significantly more.

The article concluded 'this is now our No.1 priority and supporters will be kept advised of plans to develop Stamford Bridge into one of the finest club centres – for players and spectators – to be found anywhere in the game'. The clear implication was that stadium redevelopment was more important than strengthening the team, though nobody came out and said so directly.

The *Daily Mail* ran a more detailed story under a 'Chelsea Splash A Million' headline, referring to a £1,000,000 redevelopment to transform Stamford Bridge into the most modern stadium in football. This was to include a new main stand, an indoor training centre, modern restaurant, supporters social centre, sauna baths, an electrical scoreboard, a private cinema, a medical rehabilitation centre and new club offices. Mears admitted they could not yet state a completion date. 'There are so many things which have to be worked out'. They were in the middle of talks with architects and the completed plans would be announced as soon as agreement had been reached. A week after these plans were announced, John Battersby's shock resignation was made public.

The *Daily Telegraph* of 21st October 1970 ran a story that Battersby had sent a letter of resignation to the board two weeks earlier, it had been accepted and he was leaving Chelsea at the end December. He commented 'I am resigning on a question of principles which affect me personally'. He made it evident that he had not fallen out with Sexton, so it was clear where his problems lay. The *Daily Mail*, referring to Battersby as 'one of the most powerful men in football' understood there had been differences of opinion with other officials, underlining the fallout with the board.

In *Chelsea: The Official Biography*, Chelsea Official Historian Rick Glanvill interviewed Battersby, who pointed out that 'they excluded me from the new stadium completely. It was one of the reasons I resigned. (Club Architect) George Skeets had worked wonders in stopping the authorities closing the stadium. The old stand desperately needed replacing. They went to see contractors all on their own – they didn't take me'.

Battersby knew better than almost anyone, and certainly better than the Chelsea board, how a football club ran. It seems astonishing in retrospect that his experience and knowledge was not called upon. The Mail called him 'a key figure in guiding Chelsea from their music-hall image to today's success' and pointed out he had had significant influence on club policy. He had worked well and closely with Joe Mears, and for the club to lose so much experience and football nous, with grandiose talk of redevelopment in the air, should perhaps have set alarm bells ringing. Best intentions do not always lead to the best results, hard realism and hard experience are also essential.

In *Chelsea – The Real Story* Brian Mears made it clear that Chelsea never really replaced Battersby, 'a superb secretary'. Given the way events unfolded, letting him go was undoubtedly a major error. It would have made sense for the board to bend over backwards to mollify him once they knew of his unhappiness at his exclusion. It is easy to be seduced by grand architect plans, and the directors seemed to be like bees round a honeypot with this undoubtedly sexy project, but a cold dose of pragmatism and experience rarely goes amiss. Excluding Battersby from the original project team, and willfully letting him leave, seems in retrospect to be an act of errant stupidity but leave he did. Tony Green, who had been Assistant Secretary, took over from Battersby. Colin Benson, later author of the excellent Stamford Bridge history *The Bridge*, became Assistant Secretary and Chelsea loyalist Christine Matthews, previously Battersby's secretary, became Assistant-Secretary of Administration.

For the club to own the ground meant that, after being tenants since 1905 they would finally be in control of their own destiny. To sell twelve acres of prime real estate in a highly fashionable and expensive part of London for under half a million pounds seems, in retrospect, a good deal for the club and it is to the credit of the Mears trustees that they allowed the agreement to be made. It needs to be pointed out, however, that although the agreement to purchase the ground was in place, the sale never actually happened, which had significant ramifications for the club in later years.

With the freehold would come the freedom, subject to financial and planning constraints, to redevelop the stadium in a modern, forward-thinking way. Only the West Stand was what could be called modern. Arguably worst of all, the pitch was surrounded by the greyhound track meaning the pitch was a long, long way from the stands, making atmosphere creation more difficult.

Having the stands so far from the pitch and with limited cover had long been a problem at Stamford Bridge, relative to other top clubs, since the advent of singing 'ends' such as The Kop, The Stretford End and The North Bank in the mid-1960s. The Shed did their raucous best but much of their noise, their passion, drifted into the Fulham Road air and failed to reach the players. The die-hards in the North Stand suffered a similar problem. Chelsea's support was as passionate as any, their average crowds in the late 1960s and early 1970s were in the top five in the country and their away support was both multitudinous and vociferous. At home, however, the atmosphere was sub-optimal.

In *Chelsea - The Real Story*, Brian Mears reiterated that the local authorities had told the club the old East Stand would not get another safety certificate for the 1972-73 season, confirming what the council minutes said, forcing their hand in terms of the urgent need for redevelopment, urgency caused by decades of under-investment. If the stand had been properly maintained then the redevelopment planning could perhaps have been done in a more measured fashion and, maybe, some of the rasher decisions made would have been reconsidered.

The club did not let the grass grow under their feet and three months later the Manchester City programme on January 23rd, 1971 (three weeks after the Ibrox disaster) contained a full page 'The Chairman writes...' article. In it, Mears advised supporters that the agreement for the purchase of the freehold had just been made so the club were in control of their own destiny regarding the future of Stamford Bridge. 'As you know, your Directors have had many meetings to discuss the future plans for the redevelopment of Stamford Bridge. I am delighted to tell you that we have appointed Architects Darbourne and Darke so that now we can start to place our ideas on the drawing board. Again, this will be a lengthy process and I ask you to be as patient as you have been in the past...Our immediate aim is to ensure that the existing stadium is completely safe. This week our architects have examined every part of the ground, and we are now carrying out alterations as a direct result of their report'

'Your Club has a great deal of hard work to get through in the re-building of the stadium, and a considerable amount of money will be required to complete the re-development. Your directors are giving urgent consideration to the best method to raise the necessary finance, but the day is not too far away when dreams become realities'.

The *Daily Telegraph* reported that the blueprint was apparently expected from the architects before the end of the season. They advised that 'it is estimated that the club will require £100,000 per year for the next ten years', but there was no indication of where this would come from. Builders and suppliers traditionally need to be paid within 30 days, not 3,650 days, so borrowing, or alternative sources of funding, would obviously be required.

The Leeds United programme on March 27th included a questionnaire asking supporters about the comfort and facilities they required in a new stadium. The forms were reply paid, second class, but replies had to be in by April 3rd, only a week away, and would hence need to be posted by the Wednesday, which seemed unnecessarily rushed. There was a near-capacity 58,000 crowd so a fair cross-section of the support was solicited for their views. The information gleaned was designed to help with the improvement plan.

The questionnaire asked for :-

- Postal zone or town;
- Time of journey to ground;
- Time the stadium was entered;
- How the last part of the journey was made;
- Whether the respondent was over 16 or not;
- Male/female;
- Car owner or not;
- Number in car if they drove;
- If you could have driven but didn't, what was the reason? (e.g. parking, traffic, speed);
- How many first-team matches attended at Stamford Bridge so far that season?
- Whether respondents were standing or seated?

Respondents were also asked to rank in order of importance :-

- low-price bench seating;
- all terraces covered;
- more licensed premises;
- restaurant facilities;

- club car-parking facilities;
- other activities (please specify).

There was also a space for suggestions. Although the information to be gleaned was certainly useful, it seemed a wasted opportunity to gather more data, given how little information clubs knew about their supporters, especially non-season-ticket holders, in those days. There was nothing specific on age, occupation, time supported the club, opinion on possible pricing strategies etc.

The average League crowd that season was 39,546, a fall of 800 on the 1969-70 figure but higher than most seasons since the 1955 title win.

In June 1971, the *Fulham Chronicle* reported that the new mayor of Hammersmith and Fulham, Cllr. Tom Morris, wanted to see Stamford Bridge being roofed over and 'turned into an all-weather indoor super sports stadium to serve both professional and amateur interests in Fulham and London'. He reckoned it would cost around £1,000,000 to be jointly funded by the council, the Greater London Council, the Government and Chelsea FC. The idea went nowhere but was certainly an interesting one.

The *Chelsea Football Book No.2*, published that heady summer of 1971, waxed lyrical about the future, talking about 'the stars that will put Chelsea, London's West End glamour club, in a luxurious West End-style setting'. It all certainly sounded very enticing.

CHAPTER ONE
1971-72 – The Cups Run Out

Post-Athens

Following a celebratory night out in Athens, an exuberant, exultant and exhausted Chelsea party flew back to London on Saturday 22nd May. A parade and a second Town hall reception in a year, followed, before the players had a couple of days off. Following a leisurely 2-2 draw at Slough Town on the Monday evening featuring eight of the successful Athens side, the majority of the squad flew out on the Wednesday on a two-week tour with Southampton of El Salvador and Trinidad, sponsored by British-American Tobacco and presumably lucrative for the clubs. For insurance purposes the value of the Chelsea squad on the trip was put at around £2 million, though in retrospect that maybe seems an optimistic figure in terms of resale value.

Four squad members stayed behind. Three were recovering from injury - John Hollins, Eddie McCreadie and Ian Hutchinson, who was running up and down the Stamford Bridge terracing to strengthen his knee after his February cartilage operation. Marvin Hinton, left out of the side since the Manchester City home FA Cup debacle four months earlier, was left behind in anticipation of a possible move.

Before the Latin American trip, Chelsea chairman Brian Mears had a critical task to undertake, the urgency of which at the time, and in retrospect, seemed ludicrous and did not reflect well on the club. It became public knowledge in the days following the Athens triumph that Dave Sexton's contract as manager expired at the end of June and that no new deal had been agreed, let alone signed. Worse, Manchester United had dispensed with Wilf McGuinness's services as manager and were looking for a permanent replacement. Press speculation, unsurprisingly, linked the two, which was certainly not what the Chelsea support, players or board wanted.

It is very hard to understand why agreeing a contract with a trophy-winning, highly respected manager was left to five weeks before he could just have walked into another job, and hence potentially amenable to an approach from another top club. Chelsea, on the defensive and in a weak negotiating position, hurriedly conducted negotiations which were finalised before the party flew to El Salvador, the contract only being signed on June 13th, less than three weeks before the expiry of his three-year contract. The reported salary was £10,000 a year, good but not exceptional money for a manager of his quality. Luckily, Sexton was obviously happy at the club and looked to build on his excellent work over the past three and a half years. Had he known the constraints he was to be placed under in the months and years ahead, his decision may possibly have been different.

The tour involved two games against Southampton as well as matches against the national teams of El Salvador and Trinidad. All four matches were won, Southampton being thrashed 8-3 and 6-2. Derek Smethurst, in the side through injury at the end of the previous season and substitute in the Real Madrid replay, scored five in three games and looked a strong contender for a regular place the following season.

Pre-Season

As the players returned to pre-season training in July after a month off, Sexton was looking to add a forward to the squad weakened by Hutchinson's injury. Weller's thirteen League goals was a decent return, but Hollins was next with six, Osgood got a mere five, as did Hutchinson. Baldwin contributed two. Derek Smethurst's season-end performances showed promise, but Sexton required a proven goal-scorer, to provide competition and to provide cover for Hutchinson. The manager told the *Fulham Chronicle* 'we are on the look-out for a running striker because of our heavy commitments. You cannot relax in this game and, when you play two games in a week...you need all the good players you can get'.

The players and his assistant Ron Suart were interested in were decent First Division strikers but hardly international class. Malcolm MacDonald moved from Fulham to Newcastle for £180,000 in the biggest deal of the summer, without any obvious interest from neighbours Chelsea. John Hickton of Middlesbrough was watched, and bids were made that summer for Coventry's John O'Rourke and Fulham's Steve Earle. Chelsea would not match Coventry's £80,000 valuation for a player who had been at Chelsea as a youngster. Sexton's £80,000 bid for Earle, his third in a year, was again rebuffed.

In the end, Chelsea's only signing that summer was the £2,000 paid for 21-year-old centre-forward Kevin Barry from Hastings United. Gary Locke, a highly promising right-back who had come through the youth system, signed professional terms that summer, aged 17. Energetic Scottish winger Ian Britton did the same. Reserve goalkeeper Tommy Hughes was sold to Aston Villa for £12,500, having been displaced by John Phillips in providing cover for, and challenge to, goalkeeping icon Peter Bonetti.

The *Daily Mail* felt that 'although the depth of Chelsea's first-team pool is the envy of many leading managers, Sexton has been itching to buy even more talent all summer'.

Sexton, a reserved man uncomfortable in the limelight, gave a couple of pre-season interviews. Talking to the *Daily Mail* in mid-July, he stressed he saw winning the League title as his main ambition, the club seeing their sixth place, fourteen points behind Arsenal, as failure. Optimistic about the new season, he was pleased that Osgood, Hutchinson and Hollins had recovered fitness and with Hudson's return to form in the send-half of the previous season. He also praised the mercurial Cooke's 'responsible' efforts in Athens. He wanted Hutchinson to take it easy in training to start with 'but we expect him to be all right'. He stressed the importance of having two big men up front and emphasised the reason for doing so well in 1969-70 was the pairing - Osgood scored 31 goals in all competitions, Hutchinson 22. The importance of a fully-fit Hutch to his hopes and plans was very clear.

Sexton told the *Evening Standard*, just before the season started, that 'we have been in the top six for the past four seasons and it would not take a lot to push us into the lead'. He warned against complacency, and, asked by the *Daily Telegraph* whether winning something had enabled him to be more relaxed, he responded 'I think it makes it harder. We've all got to keep in mind what it could lead to and remember the qualities which won the Cup. Obviously, it helped our self-confidence, but we've still got to keep working'. He pointed out that Chelsea had been among the most consistent sides in the country over the past five years but conceded there had been a lack of consistency within matches, particularly from some of his more gifted players. 'What I want most is to have Hutchinson and Osgood scoring goals as they did the season before last. I want to keep them fit, in form and out of disciplinary trouble'. Indeed.

The side were among the front-runners for the League title when the football columnists filed their season preview pieces. Bernard Joy in the *Evening Standard* thought Chelsea had a real chance if they could get the bit between their teeth and Osgood and Cooke could be more consistent. He praised the strength of the squad, feeling that every player had a challenger for their position. Cooke commented 'I have been doing more positive running ... I have been getting back to do a defensive job, too, when that has been necessary' which will have cheered Sexton, but not necessarily those supporters enthralled by his dribbling and ball skills. In similar vein, the *Fulham Chronicle* felt Osgood, Hudson and Cooke needed to 'turn it on' a little more frequently, especially with Houseman, Baldwin, Smethurst and Hutchinson waiting in the wings. *Goal Magazine* ran a pre-season piece entitled 'Chelsea – The Entertainers' which claimed 'Weller and Houseman look the best pair of wingers in Britain' and recounted how Weller had lost weight, looking to build on his fourteen goals the previous season.

The *Kensington News* saw two problems - appalling inconsistency at home and too defensive a set-up in big away games. 'There is so much ability at Stamford Bridge that one can't visualise Chelsea descending to the mediocre'. They also pointed out that 'another of the trendy London success clubs' had dropped three places last term and lost the title of main London challengers to both double-winners Arsenal and League Cup winners Tottenham. They, too, saw the squad as very strong, when the likes of Hinton, Cooke, Phillips, Boyle, Baldwin, Mulligan and Smethurst were among irregular starters. Interestingly, Arthur Hopcraft in *The Observer*, a serious football writer with a strong reputation, did not mention Chelsea in his preview of the forthcoming season. Ron Harris, in his ghosted *Evening Standard* column, felt 'it's time we won the League title'.

On the money front, on the face of it the situation looked cheering. All 7,600 seat season-tickets had been sold, bringing in £160,000 in advance income, which supporters hoped would provide a transfer war chest. The club announced that League ticket prices for the season would be unchanged at 30p for terrace admission with reserved seats at 60p, 80p and £1.20. This was surprisingly generous given that inflation was running at 7% and the team were having their most successful spell ever. A sliding scale of ticket prices for European games was announced, increasing as the holders went further into the competition. Chelsea had qualified for the European Cup-Winner's Cup as holders, fortunate as their League position of sixth would not have been sufficient to enter the UEFA Cup.

In addition, the Chelsea Pools scheme had raised around £30,000 in its first year, well below the £100,000p.a. target, but a start. It was announced that winning the Cup Winner's Cup had earned the players a £3,500 bonus each (£48,600 in 2018 money). A player bonus system paying £40 a point was implemented, an increase of £10 a point from the club's previous system, already one of the best in Division One. This would mean team members picking up a £160 bonus if they won two games in a week. Not everyone was happy, however. Centre-half John Dempsey and reserve full-back Stewart Houston appealed to the Football League for arbitration on the new deals they had been offered.

Apart from Hutchinson there were other players trying to shake off injury. Eddie McCreadie was fit after a year of almost non-stop injuries and desperate for a decent run in the team. Osgood had been having treatment for a knee injury, training alone to try and get fit. 'It's nothing serious. It's something under the kneecap. I felt it last season. I get it on the hard grounds. It's nagging, that's all'. Aware of need to improve his disciplinary record after eight-match ban the previous season, he explained 'I haven't made any resolutions on the subject. But I shall be getting on with the job and trying to keep out of trouble'.

After a couple of weeks conditioning training, and a knockabout 30-over-a-side game coupled with a six-a-side match at The Oval against Surrey CCC as part of Peter Bonetti's testimonial (in conjunction with Surrey wicketkeeper Arnold Long's benefit), the team flew to Europe for a series of friendlies. Given the competition for places, and Sexton's comments about complacency, they should have been pretty fired up.

The tour was not an unmitigated success. As with most pre-season tours, the manager rang the changes to give all his key squad members match practise. After a 6-0 stroll against Halmstads BK, there was a 1-1 draw against a Stockholm Combination XI, marked by a spectacular display by Phillips, competing hard with Bonetti for a first-team place. Osgood scored. Three days later another 1-1 draw, this time with Oester If Vaxjo. Osgood again netted, leading the *Daily Mail* to exclaim 'Ossie Back In Groove'. The Swedish opposition had only been of a moderate standard, and Bruges promised to be more of a threat. A third 1-1 draw rounded off an unsatisfactory tour.

In terms of results, worse was to follow. Bolton Wanderers, relegated from Division Two the previous season, deservedly beat a strong Chelsea side 2-0. The side looked lethargic, wearied by their recent European exertions. The *Sunday People* headline 'Lazy Chelsea Crash' spoke volumes. Sexton's 'we wanted to play the pretty-pretty stuff' comment did not bode well for some of the more creative team members.

Hudson got married in mid-July 1971. According to *Kings Of the King's Road*, the tour turned into an extended honeymoon and a picture of the squad taken that pre-season shows Hudson with a slight paunch. Not what Sexton would have been looking for. Stories, presumably leaked by unhappy squad members, appeared about Sexton ordering the players into full training on the Thursday morning after landing at Gatwick from Bruges at 1am. The *Sunday People's* observation that 'Chelsea's million-pound team have been shaken by the sergeant-major discipline of frustrated manager Dave Sexton' hinted at a potential fissure between squad members and manager. In *Chelsea An Illustrated History*, Scott Cheshire felt that it was during this pre-season that the first signs of personality clashes between the manager and certain players developed.

Building on this theme, John Boyle recounts one possible reason why the Swedish tour was not a massive success on the pitch. The team traditionally stayed at austere training camps with no distractions, but this time stayed at a hotel in Sweden. The hotel had a large 'DISCO' sign outside and there was a 50-yard queue for the night spot as the coach pulled up. It would be fair to say that the team enjoyed themselves throughout their stay. Dave Sexton did not, and Boyle feels this was the first sign of a split between manager and players.

Analysing the appearances during those five pre-season games, four players (McCreadie, Webb, Harris and Osgood) started every game. Five others (Dempsey, Hollins, Smethurst, Baldwin and Houseman) started four. Their starting places for the opening day visit to Arsenal seemed secure. However, Bonetti, Hudson and Weller only started three, Cooke two and Boyle one. Given the above, it was no surprise when the *Daily Mail* identified five Athens starters as being under threat of being dropped for the Arsenal game - Bonetti, Boyle, Cooke, Weller and, less logically, Houseman. A 'Chelsea Stars Wait - And Wonder' headline emphasised the uncertainty. Webb was recovering from injury, and Hudson was recuperating after tonsillitis. Weller picked up a stomach virus in Sweden which was to keep him out and was also looking for a special boot, a sore heel having troubled him for four months.

Hutchinson was not fit after two knee operations, still experiencing stiffness, and he had pulled out of the Sweden trip to help him fully recover. He came through 20 minutes as substitute for the reserves against Sutton.

The mediocre pre-season rightly concerned Sexton, especially as the first two League games were the trip to Champions Arsenal followed by Manchester United at home four days later. With a visit from Manchester City and a trip to Everton also before the end of August, Chelsea would certainly need to hit the ground running if their season was to get off to a strong start.

Supporter Geoff Kimber sums up supporter feeling post-Athens. 'I think it is fair to say that the mood amongst Chelsea supporters at this time was one of supreme optimism. This applied to both the young and the older followers'. A number of laudatory articles in *Goal Magazine*, under headlines like 'Champion, Chelsea', reinforced the sense of strong optimism, the feeling that winning the title was genuinely within reach.

August 1971

Because of the huge interest, the Arsenal away game was made all-ticket on police advice. Chelsea were allocated 15,000, mainly on the Clock End terrace. To try and beat the touts, both club's tickets were put on sale at same time. In the event, Chelsea returned a large number of unsold tickets to Arsenal. This was perhaps unsurprising as, given the lack a matchday programme to provide the information, how would supporters know they were on sale or even that the game was all-ticket? Only 49,174 entered Highbury, although some 55,000 tickets were apparently sold, disappointing given capacity of well over 60,000. Bob Wall, Arsenal secretary, thought touts must therefore have been stuck with 6,000 unsold tickets. Given the relatively low crowd, press sentiment was that Arsenal would not want more all-ticket games. Few games outside big FA Cup-ties were all-ticket in the early 1970s, clubs finding selling arrangements onerous and supporters disliking having to make an extra trip to the ground to make a purchase.

In the run-up to the game Charlie Cooke opined 'I don't think I will be in the team', having started just two of the five friendlies as Sexton utilised a 4-2-4 formation. In the event his fears were justified, and Derek Smethurst was chosen ahead of the Scot. Alan Hudson and David Webb were passed fit, Keith Weller was unwell, and John Boyle was omitted for Eddie McCreadie. Boyle was philosophical, telling the *Daily Mail* 'obviously it's disappointing for Charlie and I to be left out of the opening game – and particularly because it's Arsenal – but we've got to accept it as part of football. And it always looked as though the team would shape up this way in pre-season games'.

Chelsea's line-up relied heavily on Hudson and Hollins in midfield. Bonetti was chosen ahead of Phillips and commented 'I've been fed up this week with people writing off my career...There's no bitterness between John and I. Whatever Dave decides is what counts'.

The team lined up :- *Bonetti; McCreadie, Dempsey, Webb, Harris; Hollins, Hudson; Smethurst, Osgood, Baldwin, Houseman. Sub. Cooke.*
Chelsea's pre-season had been mediocre in terms of results, but what counted was how prepared the squad were for the rigours of the season ahead. The Arsenal game would certainly be an indicator of that. The match was a showcase, a chance to show millions of Match Of The Day viewers the respective merits of the two most successful English teams the previous season. Its importance in setting the tone for the season ahead was clear to both sides, the two sets of supporters and to the wider football world. Chelsea were notoriously poor starters to the season, but surely this time, on the back of the Athens triumph, they would step up and make everyone take notice?

What the game actually showed was the gulf between the sides. Chelsea were completely outclassed and well-beaten 3-0. The press, who had spent weeks building up the Chelsea team as potential title challengers, went to town. 'Slipshod performance...lethargic incompetence' was the *Sunday Telegraph's* summary of the team's showing. Other observations were 'an abysmal display' and 'a thoroughly disappointing performance'. The energy and spirit of the side was heavily criticised. Dempsey told the *Daily Mail* 'we didn't play well but we weren't allowed to play well.

The defence struggled. The stand-out defender, Webb, was injured and, worse, the over-worked Bonetti hurt an ankle and was set to miss the next few games. Understandably frustrated, he told the *Daily Mail* 'It's a real sickener. I've been choked by many people trying to write me off as it is. Now this happens. My ankle is in plaster'.

Wingers Smethurst and Houseman hardly saw the ball, the forward line was lifeless as Cooke, capable of changing any game, festered dejectedly on the bench. Osgood 'did his level best until he realised the hopelessness of the task in the last half-hour' according to the *Fulham Chronicle*.

Chelsea, not entirely surprisingly, were over-run in midfield, and from a distance of nearly 50 years it is hard to see how Chelsea expected to compete with Eddie Kelly, Peter Storey and George Graham with a two-man midfield. Hollins was praised, as ever, for his energy and effort, but the 'too static' Hudson, 'a shambling spectator', came in for particular criticism. *The Observer* were particularly cutting 'Hudson was depressingly sluggish. Someone said he looked as if he was still on his honeymoon. But surely, if that had been the case, he would have been rather more active'. Ouch. Hudson's comment to the *Sunday People* summed it all up. 'What do you say about it all? Terrible, wasn't it? We've got a lot of work to do'.

The Arsenal fans chanted 'easy, easy', and indeed it was. The desperately disappointing performance, individually and collectively, raised questions about the capability of the Chelsea squad to complete at the highest level. The *Daily Mirror* felt the players did not seem prepared to make the new 4-2-4 system work.

Preparation for the Manchester United game was marred by the desperately sad news that Ian Hutchinson had broken his leg in a reserve game at Swindon the previous day, as he was coming back to full fitness. He was likely to be out until at least the New Year, a dreadfully unlucky setback for Hutchinson and a real problem for Sexton, who was understandably keen to reunite him with Osgood in his first-choice striking partnership. Striking cover was limited, certainly in terms of a 'big man' and his long throws would also be missed.

Sexton required a committed showing against a team with Frank O'Farrell newly installed as manager, containing the classic triumvirate of George Best, Denis Law and Bobby Charlton. Best was having issues dealing with the pressure of being British football's first superstar but was still a great player. Sexton brought in Boyle at left-back, moved Harris to centre-back to replace the injured Webb but left the midfield and forward line untouched, a brave move considering the battering received at Highbury.

54,763 turned out for what was always one of the biggest games of the season at Stamford Bridge, Best in particular adding thousands to the gate. Baldwin gave Chelsea the lead but in a thrilling game Wille Morgan, Brian Kidd and Charlton all scored for United before Osgood netted a late consolation. The headlines the next day were not about the match itself, however. Best was sent off for supposedly arguing with the referee, making United's comeback even more laudable. A highly publicised and controversial referee clampdown on perceived dirty play had begun, and maybe Best got caught up in that. Interestingly, he later got off on appeal, arguing he had been swearing at a team-mate.

Best's dismissal had to fight for back-page space with another sensational development, one which would have long-term repercussions for Chelsea. The defeated team trooped into the dressing room and immediately a furious Sexton confronted Osgood and told him exactly what he thought of him and his showing. He then came out of the dressing room and announced to the waiting press 'I am putting Osgood on the transfer list because I am not satisfied with his efforts or performances. He has been doing less and less and this is not good for Chelsea'.

Cue uproar in the dressing room, in the press and among the support. It was not clear what the outcome would be. Would Osgood, beloved by young supporters, want to stay? Did Sexton really want him to leave, or was this a brutal motivational technique? Was his performance the straw that broke the camel's back, or was the action planned in advance?

Osgood, clearly shocked, stated 'I am stunned. I can't believe it', and probably wisely limited his remarks. He did tell the *Kensington Post* 'perhaps it is the seven-year itch. But a change of club might do me the world of good'. He also told them that if he stayed, he would always be expecting a repetition of Wednesday night's events, and that he had always started the season slowly. Exactly why he had always started the season slowly, and why this should be an excuse for a top professional footballer, were issues sadly not explored.

Sexton's quote to the *Daily Mail* 'He (Osgood) hasn't the same appetite for the game he has for other things' was a clear reference to Osgood's liking for the high life. He went on 'if they (other managers) think they can get the best from him they will make realistic offers'. Osgood was listed at an eye-watering £250,000, which would have been a British transfer record, beating by £50,000 the fee Tottenham paid West Ham for Martin Peters in 1970. This may well have been a ploy by Sexton and Mears to ensure he was not sold, but it confused and infuriated a player who realised there would be no rush from other clubs to commit that scale of funds. The player, years later, still wondered whether Sexton's action was a ploy to get him out of the club, but it was more likely a kick up the backside.

To his credit, Chelsea chairman Brian Mears supported Sexton. 'We shall certainly back the decision of our manager as far as verdicts go on any of his players. These are early days but having lost four points and six goals in our first two games it is quite clear that there is much wrong with our team'.

Liverpool, Derby and Coventry were immediately interested in Osgood, Sexton telling the *Daily Mail* 'Shankly was on the phone so early that I wasn't in the office'. He made it clear that 'Peter knows why he is on the list – for not helping his team-mates. If he improves, we may reconsider the position'. Given Osgood had scored one and made the other against United and was by no means the worst player against Arsenal, the manager's actions were certainly brave and heartfelt.

All this kept the story on the back-pages for days. *The Kensington Post* felt that Sexton did not regret his original decision, which had astonished the football world, but had gone some way to defusing things. The manager told the *Evening Standard* 'the least he (Osgood) can do is run for his colleagues. When you see the fellows up front running their hearts out and he's ...giving them very little support from the running point of view, then I become depressed'. Osgood, perhaps over-estimating his own influence with the hierarchy, was also shocked when Sexton informed him he had the full backing of the board.

Sexton told Brian Moore on *The Big Match* that he was sick of watching Baldwin or Hutchinson doing all the work up front and admitted 'sometimes Osgood disgusts me'. Extraordinarily strong words from a hugely frustrated manager, a cautious man for whom the issue had probably been brewing since pre-season.

The Kensington Post also spoke to a riled Osgood who felt his pride had been undermined. He thought he had been made to look a fool and saw the threat to sell him as an empty one given Hutchinson's injury. They pointed out he picked up a £12,500 signing-on fee if he left. They felt that Osgood, like Best, only had himself to blame and wondered whether clubs would want to take a chance on signing a man transfer-listed for lack of effort.

Hudson, disturbed by the Osgood episode and worried about his own poor form, had a frank discussion with Sexton a couple of days later, the manager persuading him not to ask for a transfer. He was injured for the forthcoming Manchester City home game, but Sexton admitted 'I wouldn't have picked him anyway'. The midfielder later revealed that Sexton gave him a public dressing-down in the dressing room after that United game to try and motivate him.

Osgood's popularity among supporters was sky-high and they duly swung into action to protest about the treatment of their hero. *The Evening Standard* ran a front-page story about an all-night vigil outside Stamford Bridge before the City game and interviewed sixteen-year-old Mandy Brinkley who spent the night outside the ground with fellow supporters. 'Osgood is the best in the world, and we want him to stay at Chelsea'. The *Daily Mail* credited supporter Geoff Paget with organising the protest and petition, which he hoped would attract 20,000 signatures. This level of public support must have cheered Osgood, whose confidence would have taken a knock. As the *Daily Mirror* cheerily put it 'so Chelsea have plunged into a crisis with the season barely a week old' and, indeed, no points from two games, the star player transfer-listed and many supporters in uproar was hardly the start the club expected. Jimmy Hill, close to Sexton, used his *Goal Magazine* column to criticise Osgood's effort and attitude. He sympathised with the manager's 'last desperate effort' to get through to his star forward.

Despite the furore, an ankle injury that required treatment, and a comment to the *Daily Mail* that 'I didn't want to go, but now this has happened I prefer to get away', Osgood was still picked for the City game three days later. Sexton was undoubtedly hoping the shock had giving his errant striker a kick up the backside. He did make other changes. Weller, recovered from his virus, replaced Smethurst who had disappointed in both games that season and had played his last game for the club. Boyle replaced the injured Hudson, stiffening the midfield, and Webb was fit again, allowing Harris to return to full-back.

Chelsea started like a house on fire and were two goals up at half-time. Osgood made both, for Baldwin and Weller. He tired in the second half, Chelsea surrendered the initiative and Francis Lee scored twice to earn City a point. The Shed bellowed their support for their transfer-listed hero before and during the game.

After the game, *the Kensington Post* felt 'a lazy Osgood is better than no Osgood' and pointed out that of four League goals Chelsea had scored so far, he had made three and scored one. 'There is no denying he is unfit and does not work as hard as he might. It is hard to see him leaving, a little less hard to see the differences being patched up'. There was some sympathy for the player, the *News Of The World* pointing out that Osgood was in the same superstar class as George Best and you had to accept frustrating faults with the match-winning magic. A clampdown on dirty play meant bookings for McCreadie and Webb, competitive spirits both, that may have gone unpunished in previous seasons.

One point from three games was a dismal start, not at all what was expected. The Sunday paper back-pages were full of Chelsea stories. Sexton's stance was clear, telling the *Sunday Express* 'we want him (Osgood) to stay and get cracking ... He was keen enough. Now it is a question of picking up his fitness. What I have done I have done for his own sake. He has sufficient talent to play in any company: but you need more than that and we are working for that here. And if we succeed England will gain'.

Osgood on the transfer list, Cooke in-and-out of the side and disappointing against City (*The Observer* wondered whether he was next-in-line for the Osgood treatment), Hudson under-performing. Not what was expected of the club's three most talented stars. It would certainly take all three firing on all cylinders on a regular basis if the club was to have any chance of League success. Ironically, it was expected that they would be among the main beneficiaries of the clampdown on dirty play that had upset tough-tackling defenders and their managers across the English football. Sexton seemed happier confronting creative talents, rather than a defence that had conceded eight goals in three games and looked less than stable.

Osgood and Cooke were retained for the trip to Everton three days later, but Hudson was still injured. On the day of the game the *Daily Mail*, obsessed like the other national papers with the story, ran an 'Unhappy Osgood Gets An Order - Train On Alone' headline. The player was called back for extra afternoon training, Sexton evidently concerned about his fitness. Osgood explained 'I did some extra work, but the real problem is my ankle. I'm fit to play but it hurts most of the time. I've been told the only real solution is an operation but I'm definitely not having one'.

Chelsea dismally underperformed again at Goodison Park in a 2-0 defeat. The *Daily Mirror* were scathing in their criticism. 'Chelsea, so full of talent but so lacking in application, did not reveal any apparent interest in the match until it was too late'. They felt that only Weller made anything happen up front. The 'Holy Trinity' Everton midfield of Howard Kendall, Colin Harvey and Alan Ball completely dominated the game.

Hollins who had started the season well, unlike many of his colleagues, defended the team's woeful start. 'Everybody is jumping on us too much, too soon. Championships are not won or lost in the first couple of weeks of the season. All of us at Stamford Bridge are feeling good. Things will go well. We have no problems'.

The games came thick and fast. Four days later Chelsea found themselves at Huddersfield Town with one point from four games and an embarrassingly low League position of twenty-first, seven points behind shock early leaders Sheffield United. Weller's virus had flared up badly enough for him to have to be admitted to hospital, but Hudson returned. Baldwin and McCreadie were also unfit after going off injured at Goodison Park.

Chelsea went behind at Leeds Road but fought back to win 2-1. The *Daily Telegraph* 'Chelsea Class Comes Through' headline summed up a game Chelsea deserved to win. After Hollins equalised, Osgood rose to head a late winner, acknowledging the travelling support who had chanted his name throughout. However, Chelsea had only scored six goals in five games, whereas Liverpool and Manchester United each had twelve. Ron Harris, always likely to struggle given the referee clampdown, was booked for the second successive match and nearly argued his way to an early bath.

Sexton praised Osgood's performance at Huddersfield as 'the best game he has ever played for Chelsea', quite a statement given some of his displays in the past six years. He felt the star had responded 'magnificently' to the shock of being transfer-listed.

Osgood told the *Daily Mail* 'I have something to prove to Dave Sexton, to a lot of other people and to myself. The only way I can do that is to score goals and play well ... I know I can bounce back. Once I've proved it to Dave, it's up to him what happens and whether I stay at Chelsea. I've always bounced back in the past'. Things were certainly sounding more positive on both sides.

To nobody's surprise, at the end of August Osgood was taken off the transfer list. Sexton was effusive, telling the *Daily Mail* 'He responded so generously in training and playing – he has been coming in twice a day – we had decided to take him off the list. He did more running at Huddersfield than I have ever seen him do, and you can't do that unless you are in peak condition'. Osgood responded in the *Daily Mirror* 'maybe it was a gee-up, but it certainly got me going. I saw Dave after training, and we had a talk. We ended up shaking hands and agreeing the matter was settled'. Their columnist Frank Taylor reckoned Osgood definitely had the talent to be an England regular, but had to harness it to industry.

Osgood later talked to the *Daily Mirror* about that fractious start to the season. Under a 'The Night I Had Hate In My Heart' headline, he opened out about his fall-out with Sexton. 'Nobody will ever know just how hurt and humiliated I was when Chelsea put me on the transfer list. I had hate in my heart...relations between Dave Sexton and myself, right then, were at their lowest. Yet it says much for his decision to sell me that now they have never been better ... His decision, closely followed by comments that I disgusted him, only fired me with a fury to knock them down his throat ... I had no inkling of what was to come when I entered the dressing room after the United defeat. I did not play well but there were not many who did. Dave was angry and said, with fury, that he was putting me on the transfer list and circularising my details ... I was still in a daze when I left the ground.'

'I'll admit Dave's decision was the right one at the time, the way it was made so public was not. I played along for a while, agreeing to questions that a change of club might do me good. I needed to accept a few home truths. I vowed to myself I would never leave Chelsea. There is one thing about Sexton you cannot take away, and that is his ability. You want to please him because he is a great coach, the best. He told me he had put the kind of price on my head that no club in the country could afford. I was greatly relieved. I realised how close I had come to disaster and resolved to always do my best in future'. Fine words, though time proved it was more a papering over of the cracks than a permanent repair.

Selling Osgood would certainly have given Sexton money to spend, though replacing him successfully would have been a tall order. John O'Rourke and Steve Earle's names were again linked, as was Hull City's Chris Chilton, a prolific scorer but in a lower League. Assistant manager Ron Suart made two trips to watch two Dumbarton strikers, Roy McCormack and Kenny Watson, with 62 goals between them in 1970-71. Alun Evans, a flop at Liverpool after his expensive move from Wolves, was also linked with a move to Stamford Bridge. In the end, Chilton, who Sexton was very keen on, signed for Coventry and none of the other proposed deals went anywhere. Chelsea did not seem to be in the market for proven big names, settling for identifying those with promise and hoping to develop them.

Accepting the season was five games old, the month-end table did not make happy reading :-

16th Arsenal	*p5*	*4pts*
17th Nottingham Forest	*p6*	*4pts*
18th Newcastle United	*p5*	*4pts*
19th Leicester City	*p5*	*3pts*
20th Chelsea	**p5**	**3pts**
21st Crystal Palace	*p6*	*3pts*
22nd Huddersfield Town	*p6*	*2pts*

September 1971

After the start-of-season hiatus, it was fervently hoped that taking Osgood off the transfer list would herald a period of calm and stability and a climb up the League table. In an interview later that season, Cooke blamed a lack of concentration after summer breaks for a series of poor season starts but that is no excuse whatsoever and it is hard to blame Sexton for cracking the whip with the unfit Osgood and Hudson. It also begs the question as to whether pre-season training had been hard enough in the past few seasons.

Chelsea had the opportunity to start the month in a positive vein, facing West Bromwich Albion at home. Before the game, Sexton at last signed a forward, something he had been trying to do all summer. In keeping with a number of his other targets it was a Second Division player he bought, paying £100,000 for Chris Garland, Bristol City's England Under-23 striker, who had interested several clubs. Not the major signing some supporters hoped for but certainly a player of promise, a willing runner and scorer of 31 goals in 142 League games for Bristol City. He explained 'the reason I wanted to leave Bristol was because I wanted to be up there with the big boys', and it was certainly a step-up in class for him. He increased Sexton's options, though whether he gave him anything different would remain to be seen.

The *Evening Standard* reckoned the 'Garland deal proved conclusively that Sexton has a lengthy list of Chelsea possibles and once the action cools on one offer, he quickly bounces back for another. It is the type of thinking that must unnerve all his First Division rivals'. Chelsea certainly had a large squad. Whether they had the required quality or strength in depth, time would tell.

It is interesting to read Garland's recollections of the transfer deal, from a 2009 interview with *The Fox* blog. 'When I went from Bristol to Chelsea, I signed a blank contract. I just signed it and said to Dave Sexton, you sort it out. I was on £50 a week and then when I signed for Chelsea it went up to £80. I was happy enough with that until I found out that Peter Osgood was on between two and three hundred a week!'. Proof that not all First Division players were on £100+ a week deals.

Garland was not a direct replacement for the injured Hutchinson, lacking the latter's height and power, and it seemed more likely that Tommy Baldwin or Derek Smethurst would be the squad place under threat. *The Daily Mirror* reckoned that with six forwards (Osgood, Hutchinson, Garland, Baldwin, Weller and Smethurst) competing for three positions 'Sexton may well decide to sell off at least one player'. But which one?

The team line-up was unchanged for the West Bromwich game. Half of Sexton's striking options watched a 1-0 win from the stand – the newly-signed Garland and the injured Baldwin and Hutchinson. A superb volley from Hollins was augmented with a welcome first clean sheet of the season. The absences meant Houseman playing as striker alongside Osgood. The crowd of under 30,000 was a worry. It was an evening game, but so was the United match, and to fall nearly 25,000 in two weeks, admittedly after a rocky start to the season, was a concern.

Three days a later a home game with Coventry gave Garland his debut, playing alongside Osgood as Houseman reverted to his preferred wing position. In a bizarre game, the score at half-time was 3-3, and remained that way. Garland started like a house on fire, creating a goal for Osgood within a couple of minutes. *The Kensington Post* felt they posed a dual threat up front, and praised two-goal Osgood, arguing his recent transfer row seemed to have done him the world of good and 'no-one could complain at any lack of effort'.

Sexton enthused 'I was very pleased (with Garland). He had an especially good first half considering it was his first game'. The player, too, was happy. 'It was all quicker than I've been used to, but Ossie and I can go well together…He supplies the skill and I can provide the work-rate'. Osgood was equally pleased, slightly strangely telling the *News Of The World*, 'I lost a lot of weight out there, so it must have gone well for me'. Evidently his fitness issues had not been completely resolved.

What was less pleasing for the manager, who complained 'we were slack', was the defence, which had now let in fourteen goals in seven games. Chelsea had been 3-1 up but never looked comfortable at the back. As the *Sunday Express* argued, 'might Sexton have been better advised to spend six figures on somebody with poise and authority to hold his defence together?'. This was a very valid point that, in retrospect, looks unarguable.

The *Kensington News* felt that Chelsea had a real problem at full-back. They criticised Harris's distribution, felt McCreadie has lost sharpness since being injured most of the previous season and felt Boyle lacked pace, though would run his guts out. They argued that Mulligan, bought as wing-half and converted to full-back, had plenty of speed and was good going forward but was not a tough tackler, relying on timing, and was often beaten by a clever winger. They thought Sexton was in the market for full-backs Orient's Dennis Rofe or Luton's Don Shanks, and certainly the defence looked as though it required strengthening.

Jimmy Hill, in *Goal Magazine*, wondered why the team appeared to tire in home games, why the defence was inconsistent and sometimes so 'full of holes', and why Cooke appeared lethargic. Having criticised Osgood the previous month, Hill praised the star for putting in more effort and getting taken off the transfer list.

The relentless two-game-a-week schedule continued with a League Cup-tie against Third Division Plymouth Argyle. Marvin Hinton, blamed and dropped after the Manchester City FA Cup-tie in January and not selected since, returned for the injured Dempsey. Garland was eligible as he had been injured for Bristol City's first round game, ironically also against Plymouth. Chelsea won 2-0 but Peter Bonetti was kept in hospital with concussion after playing on after a knock which caused double vision. It was his first game since the opening game of the season, following his ankle injury. Trainer Harry Medhurst sat beside the post talking to him for the last twenty minutes, but in those days before goalkeeping substitutes there was no move to take him off.

Criticism of Harris was strong after Chelsea lost 2-1 at West Ham three days later. The *Fulham Chronicle*, under a "Chopper' Harris May Well Get Chopped Himself' headline, reckoned that as a left-back he was vulnerable to fast or tricky wingers. Clyde Best scored both goals as only a fine goalkeeping display by John Phillips kept the score down. The *Daily Telegraph* reiterated the point, arguing that apart from Webb and Phillips the whole defence looked vulnerable and that Sexton was again upset at the marking. Hollins netted Chelsea's goal, the fifth game in a row he had scored, an incredible record for a midfield player.

Four days later, defence of the European Cup-Winner's Cup began with the easiest possible test, at Luxembourg part-timers Jeunesse Hautcharage. Tony Potrac, an 18-year-old midfield player knocking on the first-team door, was in the party of sixteen who travelled. Bonetti returned from injury. The trip was straightforward on the pitch, Chelsea winning 8-0 with Osgood scoring a hat-trick. Hollins, inevitably, weighed in with another. Cooke was magnificent, though, again, the quality of opposition must be borne in mind. European football was a potentially lucrative opportunity for Chelsea, though as the *Daily Telegraph* pointed out, the size of the win probably spoilt the chance of a large crowd for the return leg.

Garland was ineligible for the Luxembourg trip, where Baldwin impressed sufficiently to keep his place against Derby County three days later, scoring the equaliser. Hudson had another poor game, outshone by £60,000 bargain buy Archie Gemmill, and had not started the season well.

Two days later Sexton entered the transfer market again, buying long-time target Steve Kember, the combative Crystal Palace midfielder. At £170,000 the 22-year old was Chelsea's record signing and an expensive one, especially as it was by no means immediately clear who Kember would replace in the side. The manager recouped £35,000 by selling Derek Smethurst, a Cup-Winner's Cup medalist four months earlier but a long way down the lengthy striker pecking order, to Millwall. Smethurst had made seventeen first-team appearances for Chelsea but had not really taken his chance at the start of the season and the arrival of Garland had severely limited his likely opportunities.

The *Kensington News* reckoned the manager had no idea till the Monday morning (September 20th) that Palace were ready to release Kember, as their manager Bert Head had previously rebuffed him. He bought Garland then when Head phoned him saying Kember might be available, Sexton knew other clubs were interested so immediately said yes. They, and the *Daily Mail*, reported that it took less than 20 seconds for the manager to decide to buy Kember when offered him. They opined that he must have wished he had not bought Garland, as he had now 'overspent his allowance' and speculated that 'he has taken the Blues into the red' and realised he would have to sell at least one forward, in addition to Smethurst, to balance the books. With Hutchinson injured he would surely try to keep Osgood, Weller, Garland and Baldwin until

December, as Kember and Garland were not eligible for the Cup-Winner's Cup until the Quarter-finals.

Chelsea had spent £270,000 and recouped just £35,000 that month. In the *Evening Standard*, the manager, under an unequivocal 'No-one's Leaving Chelsea - Sexton' headline made it clear that 'nobody is leaving the club, including Keith Weller'. Leicester had expressed an interest in the previous season's leading scorer, who was now out with a heel injury having recovered from his very nasty stomach virus, following interest from Crystal Palace earlier in the month. They wondered where Kember would fit in, but said Hudson was told by his manager that the transfer did not threaten him. Replacing Hollins was unthinkable, so they felt 'the player most in danger is flamboyant Scot Charlie Cooke'. If this happened, though, someone would need to move wide, a conundrum that certainly, and rightly, concerned Hudson.

It is likely that Kember was bought partly to give Hudson a jolt, but it was not immediately obvious how his arrival would strengthen the team. Hudson later told *Chelsea's Cult Heroes* that he and John Hollins complemented each other perfectly. Hollins won the ball, Hudson or Cooke used it. It appeared Sexton bought Kember, who he clearly rated very highly, with no clear idea as to his role in the team. Supporter David Gray saw it as 'a really odd buy – although Kember was a good hard-working player he was nowhere near the class of Alan Hudson or Charlie Cooke'.

Chelsea were in a desperately disappointing fifteenth place after nine games, with just two League wins. They had let in seventeen goals, the third worst in the division. The shock table-toppers, who had conceded a mere six goals, were Sheffield United, inspired by hugely talented midfield star Tony Currie. Chelsea's visit there the following Saturday was Kember's debut, but there was again only a place on the bench for Garland, who seemed to be competing with Baldwin for one place in the side. Cooke was left out completely. Kember was the nineteenth player Chelsea had used already that season, hardly a sign that Sexton knew his best side but also an indicator of the level of injuries the side had suffered. As supporter David Gray recalls, 'an ominous sign for the future was that Kember was given Hudson's Number 8 shirt for his debut'.

Kember was hit in the face by the ball after three minutes, bravely playing on though groggy with concussion. Baldwin and Osgood both missed sitters, the latter from two yards, causing Sexton to comment 'we all miss that kind of chance sometimes, even Osgood'. Stewart Scullion scored the only goal. The *Daily Mirror* criticised the defence, adding to the chorus of those who wondered whether Sexton was focusing his attention in the wrong place, as the team slumped to eighteenth place.

A few days later, Weller, apparently categorically not for sale the previous week, was duly sold to Leicester City, after manager Jimmy Bloomfield made an enquiry which Sexton passed on to the player. The feeling that this was a fire sale, that Chelsea had to quickly recoup some of the recent expenditure by reducing the size of the squad, and that the club finances were not necessarily that rosy, was accentuated when it became clear that Chelsea only received £100,000 for the player. This was exactly what they had paid Millwall in Summer 1970, when his value had surely appreciated considerably over the previous season. Was Kember really worth nearly double? Was Weller really only worth the same as Garland? Sexton's comment 'Keith has done a good job for me and I am sure he will do the same for Leicester' did little to mollify concerned and confused supporters.

Weller was popular with most of his teammates and the crowd, had been leading scorer the previous season and improved as a player. He had been used as winger and inside-forward, though he had maybe to find his best spot in the team. He told the *Evening Standard* 'I'm sorry to be leaving Chelsea, but I feel there is a better future for me at Leicester...I'm fully fit and anxious to start with my new club immediately'. Further, he told the *Daily Mail* 'although I realised they might reduce their staff, I didn't think I would be the one to go. But this move suits me fine'. It may have suited Weller but, as supporter Geoff Kimber recalls, it was undoubtedly Chelsea's loss.

Kings Of The King's Road includes strong views from David Webb on the subject. 'Keith was a key player. He gave the team balance. To me, that was the beginning of the end. That make me stop believing in Chelsea as a force that was going onwards and upwards'. He later complained 'Keith was the first to go and everything went downhill from there'. In *Rhapsody In Blue*, Webb told Chelsea Official Historian Rick Glanvill that the club was so short of money and I think the only person they could get cash for was him. I bumped into Bloomfield who told me he was going to buy Weller'. Webb went to see Sexton almost in tears at this news.

Sexton later admitted 'selling Weller was the biggest mistake I ever made' but said he was told he had to sell someone to fund Garland and Kember. In *Football Under The Blue Flag* Brian Mears mentioned rumours that Weller and Harris had a fight in the car park after a bad Harris tackle in training. *Kings Of The King's Road* mentioned a supposed incident where Weller accidentally annoyed Harris with a comment about his wife, got clattered and missed a game. *Foul: Football's Alternative Paper* also referred to Harris injuring Weller. In *The Bonnie Prince*, Cooke implied that Weller and Kember had bruised a few egos among the established players.

Nearly half a century later, it remains a most puzzling move, especially given Hutchinson's injury. On top of the finance issues, Sexton may have felt that with Baldwin on good form and Garland coming through, Weller was dispensable, though that would be a questionable analysis given how the careers of the three developed over the coming seasons. In essence he had replaced Weller with Garland. Not, in retrospect, a shrewd move.

Whatever the motivation for selling Weller, Leicester got an absolute bargain and he became a cornerstone of their team for some years and, unlike Garland and Kember, was capped by England. As Paul Dutton and Rick Glanvill say in *Chelsea The Complete Record*, with the signing of Garland and Kember 'a new, more industrial Chelsea was emerging'.

The return game with Jeunesse was predictably a cakewalk. Chelsea's 13-0 victory was played in front of an unsurprisingly low 27,621. Osgood scored five, Baldwin a hat-trick and, inevitably, Hollins netted another. The players were on a crowd bonus of £5 per 1,000 spectators for European games so earned £135 crowd bonus each for Jeunesse game. A strong run in the competition, with crowds of 40,000 plus, would be a decent earner for the players.

The crowd, presumably bored by the totally one-sided offering in front of them, began to slow-handclap when Chelsea lost impetus in the second half. Houseman was catcalled for passing rather than beating his man, and for ten minutes the crowd roasted him every time he touched the ball. He answered their abuse with a well-taken goal. Often, totally unfairly, the butt of the crowd, his diligent personality and methodical play probably appealed less to the crowd than his more flamboyant team-mates. He told the *Daily Mirror* 'nobody likes that sort of treatment, it's the first time that it's happened to me for years. But I'm only trying to do my job. If the crowd don't like it, they can lump it'.

Supporter David Gray recalls that 'the abuse had been building for some weeks and when he failed several times to outwit his amateur opponent the baying began. Fortunately his performance improved, and he laid on several goals before uncharacteristically flicking a 'V' sign at his detractors in the West Stand'. Geoff Kimber remembers that 'the fact that he assisted for at least five of our goals didn't seem to matter a jot to not just The Shed boys but also the more well-heeled supporters in the West Stand'.

The following month the *Daily Telegraph* ran a feature on Houseman, seeing him as one of the few natural outside-lefts in British soccer and arguing that Chelsea missed him when he was not playing. Leslie Mears, 'a member of Chelsea's lively board', defended him, somewhat bizarrely feeling the crowds get onto local players when things go wrong 'because he reminds them of their own inadequacies'. As we shall see in a later chapter, Leslie Mears was not averse to a bit of direct player criticism himself. Sexton commented 'he knows what we think of him…he is a very gifted player'. Albert Sewell, the programme editor, said most letters he received condemned the barracking. Houseman requested 'don't go too strongly on this because honestly it doesn't bother me. If they didn't go for me, it would be someone else'. Houseman was an invaluable member of the Chelsea set-up and it was good to see the club, and the press, close ranks around him.

Chelsea's inability to climb out of the relegation area was of clear concern, given that the season was already a quarter old :-

16th Huddersfield Town	*p10*	*8pts*
17th Newcastle United	*p10*	*8pts*
18th Chelsea	**p10**	**7pts**
19th West Bromwich Albion	*p10*	*7pts*
20th Nottingham Forest	*p10*	*6pts*
21st Leicester City	*p10*	*6pts*
22nd Crystal Palace	*p10*	*5pts*

October 1971

The *Kensington News* was less than impressed with Sexton's transfer dealings and asked a series of highly pertinent questions. 'What the blazes is going on at Stamford Bridge? Would you transfer list your best player and then take him off the list? Would you buy a Second Division forward for £100,000 and sell a First Division one for the same price? Why not spend a bean on defenders? Why sell Derek Smethurst?'. He already had 'a first-rate forward line', and a defence that up to that point had conceded more home goals than any other side in Division One, yet again focussed his attention further up the pitch. Sexton had not bought a defender since Paddy Mulligan two years earlier. This strange reluctance was to continue, and to limit his defensive options, in the seasons ahead.

To add fuel to the fire, neither Chris Garland nor Steve Kember were selected for the home game against Wolverhampton Wanderers on October 2nd, the match programme for which included perfunctory thanks to Keith Weller. Kember was on the bench and Garland demoted to the reserves. Charlie Cooke reckoned they had had an impact because they had put pressure on others, including himself, but it is hard to believe the board were happy at over a quarter of a million pounds being spent on what were seen by the manager at that point as squad players. Sexton defended Kember's omission 'I bought him because he became available and because he is the kind of player we want. You could say I bought him for the future'. This, despite the fact he was two years older than Alan Hudson. The manager told the *Sunday People* he had bought Garland because Hutchinson was injured, but they were entirely dissimilar types of striker so that made little sense.

A pleasing crowd of over 42,000 saw a comfortable 3-1 win over Wolves. Houseman, butt of the crowd against Jeunesse, silenced the barrackers with his first League goal of the season. Hollins, having a wonderful season in a dressing room riddled with under-achievers, scored yet again, as did Baldwin.

Cooke had been working hard on his fitness since the start of the season, had lost his summer spare tyre and was down to eleven stone.

This might explain his slow start to the season but did not reflect credit on either player or coaches that he was so unfit pre-season.

With Europe and the League Cup in full flow, Chelsea had another busy month of midweek matches. This early fixture congestion was compounded by a 1-1 draw at Nottingham Forest in the League Cup Third Round. Kember was cup-tied, Garland returned after five games out but was injured before half-time. The fact that David Webb had to go up front, and equalised, as John Dempsey was the substitute does not reflect well on Sexton's ambition. As we shall see, Webb's enormous versatility and whole-heartedness meant he was happy to play in any position, often to the detriment of the defence he had vacated.

The Chelsea defence had tightened in recent games but was still finding clean sheets hard to come by and the side languished in fifteenth place, so a trip to Anfield was faced with trepidation. Given this, a 0-0 draw was an excellent result, earning Chelsea their first point there in eight visits. Liverpool boss Bill Shankly praised Sexton's tactics 'they played it just like the continentals, slowing it down to the pace they wanted'. Osgood worked hard in a deeper role in the absence of the ill Hudson.

The Forest replay was moved forward to the Monday, allowing Liam O'Kane and Tommy Jackson to play for Northern Ireland on the Wednesday, a generous move by Sexton and Chelsea, who won 2-1 after going behind, Osgood making one for Baldwin and scoring the other. Garland went off injured and was likely to be out for a while. So Chelsea went through to face Bolton Wanderers, their pre-season nemesis.

Chelsea had an important week ahead. Arsenal at home on the Saturday, a chance to exact revenge for the first-day drubbing, followed by a trip to Sweden for the Cup-Winner's Cup-tie against part-timers Atvidaberg. A near-capacity crowd of 52,338 watched Chelsea employ tactics against the title-holders similar to the predominantly defensive tactics employed at Liverpool the previous week. Missing Houseman with a damaged shoulder, Chelsea were criticised for their glut of midfielders and resultant emphasis on sideways passing, meaning a frustrated and isolated Osgood up front, who scored a consolation goal in a 2-1 defeat but had precious little service.

The *Fulham Chronicle* felt Kember had a miserable home debut. It was obviously going to take time for him to settle into the side, though trying to fit in alongside Cooke, Hollins and Hudson in an overcrowded midfield could not have been easy. He told the *Sunday People* 'people may have been disappointed because the first ball I gave went astray, but after that I can't remember losing possession more than a couple of times…It takes time to settle into a new team…I've just got to do my job in a team of good players'.

Several writers felt the midfield had too many ball-players and could have done with the bite of Boyle, still playing out-of-position at right-back.

Similarly, a lack of fire-power meant Webb being pushed up front late on rather than bring McCreadie off the bench.

Supporters, some of whom had paid touts £5 for an 80p stand ticket, started leaving with fifteen minutes to go, depressed about the team's showing. Those supporters who travelled out to Sweden were hoping for a markedly improved display from a hopefully more coherent team selection. What they got, in the absence of the ineligible Garland and Kember and the injured Houseman, was Hollins playing up front alongside Osgood and Baldwin. Sexton blamed his selections on injuries to strikers, but this entirely foreseeable situation was a by-product of selling Weller and Smethurst, with Hutchinson out with a long-term injury, and replacing them with men who could not play in Europe until the New Year.

In the West Bromwich programme at the start of September, the point was made that 'one of Chelsea's main aims in 1971-72 is to retain the European Cup-Winners' Cup' and the article talked about an 'elite group' of seven clubs who would be the real opposition. Atvidaberg were not mentioned anywhere in the article. A tedious 0-0 draw in Sweden on a dreadful pitch drew more criticism of Sexton for his team selection. McCreadie tore a hamstring, likely keep him out for weeks, bad luck on a player who had suffered a series of cruel injuries. Still, an away draw was not the end of the world. Chelsea were confidently expected to finish the job at Stamford Bridge in a fortnight's time.

A home game against a Southampton side who had conceded fifteen goals in seven away games provided an opportunity to get back on track. Sexton reverted Hollins to his preferred midfield role but played Baldwin on the wing and Kember up front, which surprised the crowd, the press and, presumably, the team.

In the event Chelsea were for the most-part mediocre but more than good enough to beat an abject Southampton side 3-0 in front of an encouraging 38,940 crowd. Osgood 'looked as though he wished he was at the Motor Show rather than playing football' according to the *Kensington Post*, but luckily Hollins scored his habitual goal. Kember netted his first for Chelsea with a twenty-five yard belter, a relief for him and Sexton, and surprise wide-man Baldwin netted the other.

Sexton damned Hudson with faint praise, claiming 'Alan was more like the old Hudson and he seems to be coming back to form, though he is a bit overweight'. So it was clear that Cooke and Hudson had had weight issues and Osgood's season-starting fitness had been poor. The suspicion was that the celebrations that summer had only begun with the victory parade, and it does not reflect well on the commitment of the players involved, supposedly professional athletes.

The relentless nature of the fixture list meant a League Cup-tie against Bolton for the Stamford Bridge faithful three days later. In his *Evening Standard* column Ron Harris felt Chelsea 'should take care' of Atvidaberg. 'Win our next three games (Bolton home, Leicester away and

Atvidaberg) ... and we'll be on our way again'. He told the *Daily Mail* 'there's no hiding it – our First Division results so far have been disappointing. Our target now must be to make amends, not only in the Cup-Winners' Cup but also in the League Cup'.

Hollins again played up front. Going behind to an early Graham Rowe goal, it took until after half-time for Chelsea to equalise through Hudson in a 1-1 draw. The side were criticised for a lack of coherence and urgency. Another game, in an already crowded schedule, was the last thing Sexton needed.

A busy month, with mixed results and a plague of injuries, ended with a trip to Leicester. It took a very late Osgood equaliser to salvage a point in a 1-1 draw. A highly motivated Weller, inevitably, had a fine game. The Leicester goal came after a free-kick following a 'totally unnecessary' foul by Harris on Weller, so maybe there was something in those stories about a fall-out.

The *Fulham Chronicle*, like fellow local paper the *Kensington Post*, never held back in criticism of club, players or manager. They argued that Osgood's appetite for football, his willingness to chase after the ball, his old do-or-die spirit and 'killer' instinct, all seemed to be sadly lacking, and he was also booked. 'He seemed near-enough totally disinterested in Chelsea's attempts. For a number of games he appears to have spent most of the 90 minutes strolling around, with his mind not fully focused on the football field'. Given his early season travails, and subsequent return to form, this apparent reversion to disinterested mode was unwelcome. Ironically, Osgood was voted *News Of The World Goal King of the Month*, based on reader nominations. His goals against Jeunesse undoubtedly had an impact.

Aware that the defence required strengthening Sexton had looked at two centre-halves, though neither were First Division players. Chris Topping, a nineteen-year-old York City defender, was watched and Sam Bartram in the *Sunday People* reckoned Chelsea were after the never-say-die Barry Kitchener of Millwall, with the unsettled Hinton supposedly going in the opposite direction. In the event, the only signing that month was young winger Mike Brolly from Scottish junior side Kilmarnock Star.

One bright spot for Sexton with regard to defenders was Dempsey ending his four-month pay dispute. He had been offered a new contract in June but did not think it was enough. He took it to the Football League who rejected his arguments, the independent tribunal deferring the matter for a month. In the end, the club met Dempsey halfway with 'a reasonable compromise'. Interviewed by *Goal Magazine*, the centre-back, relieved the dispute was over and confident about the season ahead, felt the squad was stronger than ever. Micky Droy told them how effective he felt the Dempsey/Webb partnership was, and what a barrier they presented to him establishing himself in the team.

Hutchinson remained the League's 'highest paid non-player'. Despite his injury, as a squad member he received his normal salary plus £40 a point, though with thirteen points from fifteen games at the end of October, and a mediocre thirteenth place, the £520 point bonus so far that season was probably less than anticipated. Chelsea were already ten points behind leaders Manchester United but only five points above bottom-placed Newcastle United. This under-performance in the League made the upcoming Atvidaberg and Bolton games even more important.

November 1971

Manager Dave Sexton persisted with John Hollins up front alongside Peter Osgood for the Atvidaberg home game. He had little choice as Tommy Baldwin, who according to the *Evening Standard* had spent part of the previous evening taking part in a fashion shoot to launch a new Putney discotheque, missed the game after being injured in training on the day of a match Chelsea were expected to win comfortably. They had to be careful, however, about the away-goals rule, whereby goals scored away from home became worth double if scores were level after both legs.

The crowd, a mere 450 higher than Jeunesse, was a significant disappointment, probably reflecting the complacency surrounding the game. The previous season's second round game, against CSKA Sofia, attracted over 41,600 supporters, despite Chelsea winning that away leg 1-0.

What occurred that evening was like a slow-motion nightmare, what the *Evening Standard* called 'one of the most embarrassing defeats in the club's history'. In reality the match ended in a 1-1 draw, but the impact was the same. Chelsea were eliminated from Europe, as holders, by a team of part-timers. Alan Hudson put Chelsea ahead after half-time, Hollins hit the outside of the post with a penalty fifteen minutes later, afterwards exclaiming 'I don't know how I did it. I just don't know what happened'. Hudson later said that he begged Hollins to be able to take the penalty but was rebuffed. Supporter Brian Gaches remembers the penalty miss as 'the first of a long sequence of penalty misses costing us dearly in an important game'.

Five minutes after that, Roland Sandberg equalised, from the Swedish team's one real chance. Chelsea still had twenty minutes to save the tie but conspired to hit the woodwork and miss a hatful of chances before the final whistle.

The team were booed and jeered off with Osgood, who the *Daily Mirror* felt had a dismal and depressing match, responsible for a string of misses, getting particular flak. Not used to this crowd response, the centre-forward was distraught. 'It was ridiculous…we just couldn't score. They had nine men back on some occasions and about four shots on our goal. I am utterly sick about it. I know the crowd were having a go at us, but nobody misses chances on purpose'. Even for a man of such self-confidence, so beloved by The Shed, getting abuse must have stung. In *The Bonnie Prince* Charlie Cooke remembered that the 'slow handclapping from the seats and booing from The Shed after Atvidaberg was a first at Stamford Bridge that I did not savour'.

Plenty of match reports focussed on Chelsea's complacency until Atvidaberg equalised, about how their part-timers earned £20 a week and received a £45 bonus for knocking out the holders. A mortified Sexton told the *Evening Standard* 'you always have to explain defeat, but victory covers a multitude of sins', advising the *Daily Mail* that 'it is bitterly disappointing to go out the way we did, and we can have no complaints. The turning point was not the missed penalty but all the other chances we missed'. He went on, to the *Daily Mirror*, 'I don't want to hear any talk about our recent form being bad. Just look at the results...they speak for themselves...One defeat in ten games and three in nineteen ... It was very disappointing that we lost, but I am not prepared to say anything more'. The criticism was relentless, widespread, severe and deserved. 'Chelsea shamed themselves and their supporters', 'humiliating', 'a lack of pride', 'a feeble caricature', 'a costly, humiliating and entirely self-inflicted embarrassment', 'a disaster', 'carelessly squandered opportunities' and 'pathetic' were a selection of the scathing comments from across the newspaper spectrum.

The players were mortified. David Webb, moved up front at half-time and creator of Hudson's goal, felt 'we were all to blame...It was a very sad affair'. Dempsey was interviewed by the *Daily Mirror* about 'the night the world seemed to fall in on Stamford Bridge'. He commented 'you don't become a bad side after just one bad result...We should have won out there...Ossie had one of those nights. He could have scored several...We really missed Hutchinson, and Baldwin wasn't fit...I don't think we'll win the League, but we could win one of the cups'...

Captain Ron Harris optimistically, and somewhat bizarrely, felt 'it could be a blessing in disguise. We've been in Europe for a couple of years and we've enjoyed the financial rewards. So now it is up to us to qualify again next season', logic that is somewhat hard to follow. In fact, Chelsea were not to qualify again for Europe for another twenty-three years. Hudson later said that the result 'haunted' the players, who knew the significant damage to their pockets caused by an early exit from Europe. Supporter Terry Cassley, there that night, recalls his 'utter disbelief'.

The *Daily Telegraph* eviscerated the team for their 'casual complacency' and reckoned both team and crowd anticipated an easy win and, when that was not forthcoming, the players could not change gear. It praised the crowd for trying to rouse the team after Sandberg equalised. It seems unarguable that if Hollins had scored, Chelsea would have qualified for the next round and the next few years may have turned out very differently.

A catastrophic night, one that made the flaws in the team's make-up and Sexton's transfer policy very evident. In retrospect, it was an entirely avoidable European exit that can be seen as a turning point in the fortunes, and profile, of what had generally been seen as one of the very best cup sides in the country. Chelsea were still in the League Cup, with a replay at Bolton to follow the following week, and the FA Cup, but their dismal League form meant qualification for Europe was highly unlikely to happen unless the team went on a spectacular run.

Steve Kember remembers his enormous frustration that the team had so unexpectedly been eliminated, as he would have been eligible for the next round and he was desperate to experience European football.

On the Friday a concerned Sexton held a team meeting, demanding harder work, and the following day a chastened Chelsea team took the field against Nottingham Forest. Hollins reverted to midfield, but his replacement was Kember, nobody's idea of a striker. The meagre crowd of 25,812, some 17,000 less than the home game against Wolves a month earlier, watched a mediocre and unconvincing 2-0 victory against weak opposition. Sexton's comment 'let's just say I'm happy with the points', spoke volumes.

Osgood, in his 200th League appearance, made a goal for Cooke and scored the other but the pair came in for some real stick, especially in the *News Of The World*. Under a 'Sexton set to axe the top men' headline, they went to town. 'Half the Chelsea side must be wondering if Dave Sexton's patience is coming to an end ... Osgood and Cooke, despite scoring the goals, must realise there is a limit to what their manager will tolerate. This was another distressing team performance. If Chelsea don't improve...then Sexton, if he is consistent, must take more – and this time collective – action'. What did not help continuity and cohesion was the endless playing of players out of position – Kember, Hollins, Webb, Cooke and Houseman all played as striker at some point that season. Many of the sparse crowd at a 'shapeless slough of boredom' left long before the end, and it was clear that the team must improve considerably if they were to re-attract regular crowds above 40,000. Despite Chelsea being unbeaten in their previous six games, there was the absence of anything approaching a feelgood factor around Stamford Bridge.

The Forest match programme referred to 'Wednesday night's failure here against Atvidaberg in the European Cup-Winners' Cup' and it was clear that it was going to take a while for the team, club and supporters to get that game out of their system. The *Kensington News* reckoned that for the past two or three seasons Chelsea had been better away from home. A lack of atmosphere, pressure from the crowd and an inability to pierce defensive formations were all mooted as possible reasons.

Approaching the potentially tricky Bolton Wanderers replay two days later, The Trotters were top of Division Three and in good form. Sexton was delighted to welcome back Baldwin after injury, especially as Kember was cup-tied. He thrived as Chelsea coasted through 6-0, scoring a hat-trick, making two trebles in six weeks for the hardworking and unsung forward, and thirteen goals in sixteen games. Sexton enthused 'this was more like it' though the *Kensington News* argued Sexton had to ensure it was not a temporary renaissance brought on by the Atvidaberg catastrophe.

In Kember's League Cup absences Hudson enjoyed playing in midfield, as opposed to being shuffled off to the wing when both were playing in League games. Hudson wondered then, and wonders now, why Weller, who was highly effective playing wide, was sold and not replaced if Sexton required width on both sides.

Ron Harris, potentially facing a suspension after a series of bookings that would have meant missing his forthcoming testimonial, received a five-week suspended sentence and was fined £150. A relieved captain commented 'it's up to me to stay out of trouble and keep a clean record'.

Before the trip to Norwich for the League Cup Quarter-final came a potentially tricky game at Stoke but an unchanged side won a tough, physical game, Osgood scoring the only goal. The defence was praised for its efficiency, Boyle doing a fine job in the absence of both McCreadie and Mulligan.

The game at Norwich attracted their biggest crowd for four seasons. A hard-fought 1-0 victory put Chelsea in the Semi-finals, although they were never in total control. Sexton's side had not been beaten since the Arsenal match nine games ago and, further, had not conceded in four games. Osgood's form had improved since the stinging criticism he received after the Atvidaberg debacle and he scored the winner, but he was roundly booed all game after an early clash left defender Dave Stringer with stud marks down his leg.

Crystal Palace were bottom of the table, whereas Chelsea had risen to the dizzy heights of eleventh, so Sexton's team approached their visit to Selhurst Park with confidence. This confidence was justified, Baldwin, Hudson and Osgood all scoring in a 3-2 victory. Hudson, who scored directly from a corner and had an excellent game, suffered a groin strain and was therefore likely to miss a place in the forthcoming England Under-23 squad. In the event, he was, ironically, replaced in that squad by Kember, who substituted for the injured Baldwin. Sexton's striking travails were not going away.

The game showed the two faces of Osgood's complex character. His minute winner was a breath-taking volley, but he was booked for a needless retaliatory foul on Sammy Goodwin and his 'scowling, temperamental countenance' did him no favours. He felt 'as fit as he'd ever be' but the *Daily Mirror* said he felt private hurt at being continually passed over by Alf Ramsey.

A free midweek gave an opportunity for Ron Harris's testimonial to take place, against Glasgow Rangers. A decent crowd of 16,362, who raised over £6,000, turned out to watch the Scottish side win 1-0. Chris Garland made his first appearance in twelve matches, full-back Gary

Locke made his first-team debut and young reserves Micky Droy and Tony Potrac (another debutant) came on as substitutes. Harris released *Chel-sea Of Blue,* a record made with a group of fans from The Shed, for his testimonial. Sadly, it failed to chart.

The final game of another busy month was the League visit of Tottenham, the prelude to an already highly anticipated two-legged League Cup Semi-final a few weeks later. Cooke, who played up front off of Osgood, scored in an impressive 1-0 victory. Sexton claimed it was Chelsea's best home display of the season, telling the *Daily Mirror* 'we have begun to put together a very impressive record, and part of it has been due to the fine form of Hudson and Bonetti. In fact, Hudson is doing as well as I've ever seen him, right back to his best form for the club'. Sexton told the *Daily Telegraph* he played Cooke up front 'because he can hold the ball and make space in the penalty area'. The *Kensington News,* highly critical earlier in the season, headlined the display 'Victory With Style' and claimed every Chelsea player was better than his Tottenham counterpart.

The Observer, eulogising about Hudson, felt that Chelsea could be infuriatingly dull and self-destructive or, as in this exciting game, full of adventurous football, which showed what that Chelsea side were capable of, if only they could add consistency to their undoubted class. The outclassing of Tottenham certainly gave a confidence boost for the key semi-finals to come. In Harris's *Evening Standard* column, he claimed 'we bottled Martin Chivers up once and can do it in the League Cup games'. Chelsea had climbed to ninth place in the table, nine points behind leaders Manchester United and a healthier ten ahead of twenty-first placed West Bromwich Albion.

Long-term neglect of the ground had manifested itself in stories that appeared after the Tottenham game reporting there had been 'shudders' felt by supporters in the North Stand during the match, causing two to complain. The stand backed onto a railway line. One theory was that the shudders were caused by a passing goods train and were nothing to worry about. Supporter Peter Gray was a season-ticket holder in that stand and was at the Tottenham game. He recalls that 'it apparently juddered but I didn't feel it and I was upset when it was closed down. We were later moved to seats that were put in underneath the stand, but it was nowhere near as good a view'. Supporter Terry Cassley was in the stand 'when it shook and shuddered against Spurs. Oddly I believe Allan Mullery of all people was sat just in front of me. Everyone stood up and the stand shook. We all looked at each other and just sat down'.

The 'shudder' story, unsurprisingly, received wide publicity, safety being a hot issue after the Ibrox disaster eleven months earlier. The *Evening Standard*, under a 'Shudders – So Chelsea Stand Is Closed' headline, reported that 'Chelsea will not be using their North Stand, in which 'shudders' have been reported, unless they get a clearance from the architects to do so'. The club architects and the Fulham surveyor were called in, examined the pylons and inspected the foundations for corrosion and engineers drilled down to the foundations. Secretary Tony Green had initially tried to play the matter down, telling the *Sunday People* 'the shudder could mean nothing. The ground is close to the railway and we who work in the offices often feel shudders as though the place was falling down'.

For some reason manager Dave Sexton, whose responsibility the stadium was not, spoke to journalists. 'We have not heard from them (the architects) yet. But we won't be using the stand until we have their report. That applies, of course, to the Leeds match'. All 12,000 seats available for the Leeds match had been sold. Chelsea offered alternative accommodation in the West Stand bench enclosure which held 3300 unreserved seats.' The *Evening Standard* then made an early reference to potential wider ground redevelopment, stating that 'the North Stand is part of the £1.5 million redevelopment starting in April with the East Stand'.

A period of confusion then followed as within a week the stand was closed, then publicly declared completely safe by the club, then closed again, all in the days leading up to the Leeds game. Chairman Brian Mears, quizzed by the *Evening Standard*, explained the latest position the day of the Leeds game. Under a 'Calls For Tougher Tests By Chelsea boss Mears' headline, he announced that the North Stand would be closed indefinitely until further safety checks could be made. The decision came into force only five days after the 'shuddering' stand was supposedly passed safe. Mears stated 'we wanted a cooling-off period. It is still only two weeks since the issue was brought to our notice. Our own consultants carried out remedial work on the stand and gave us the all-clear. We now want more stringent tests. The club has done everything for the best. In these circumstances no chances should be taken...We are not prepared to risk life in any way at all. No-one in his right mind would use a football stand that had anything wrong with it'. As supposedly Terry Cassley observes 'had it actually collapsed, I dread to think of the death toll - me included'.

Though the stand was to be closed, 1,000 fans would still be allowed to stand underneath. It was not anticipated the stand would open again that season, meaning the capacity was cut by 2,244, all seats. The club told the *Daily Mirror* that they lost £1,122 on the Leeds game alone and could in theory cost them over £10,000 over the course of the rest of the season, though that would depend on the stadium being regularly full.

December 1971

A trip to Newcastle, where a scrappy 0-0 draw was fought out, meant an end to Chelsea's impressive run of six victories in a row. Sexton was happy enough 'a point at Newcastle is always welcome' but settling for a draw against a team fourth from bottom of the table hardly proclaimed ambition.

Chelsea started the season 12-1 for the title but had drifted out to 66-1. Manchester United were now 6-4 favourites, five points clear. Leeds were 4-1, with Derby and Manchester City 6-1. The ever-positive Webb felt Chelsea would be back in the race if they could beat Leeds the next week, though they were only ninth, ten points behind United, and five behind Derby, Leeds and City.

Out of Europe and with the first-leg of the Tottenham League Cup Semi-final at Stamford Bridge a fortnight away, Chelsea had a week off to prepare for what one of the most intense and eagerly awaited games of the season, the visit of Leeds. A bitter rivalry had developed between the teams, culminating in the bitterly fought 1970 FA Cup Final games. The teams genuinely did not like each other, and the atmosphere of 'us against the world' paranoia stoked by Leeds boss Don Revie ensured the game would be as feisty as ever. On the eve of the match, David Webb explained to the *Daily Mail* 'beating Leeds is still regarded as the most professional achievement in football. There is a tradition of tremendous battles between Chelsea and Leeds...Chelsea, more than anyone, are prepared to fight it out with them'.

In the event, the game, a 0-0 draw, lived up, or down, to the expectations of the 45,867 crowd. The game was shown on *Match Of The Day*, but the BBC only showed brief highlights of what the *Daily Mail* called 'one of the most cold-bloodedly violent games ever shown on television'. There were three bookings, for Alan Hudson, Allan Clarke and Johnny Giles in 'another brutal encounter between old and bitter enemies'. Very little quality football was played between the feuding and fouling, in the end Leeds settled for a point and Chelsea were unable to break them down.

Chelsea were now unbeaten for twelve games and had six days to rest before a Friday night trip to Coventry, a game moved to allow supporters to go Saturday Christmas shopping. A hard, tense game was made more difficult when Peter Bonetti collided with Quentin Young and had to go to hospital for an ankle x-ray. David Webb, utility man extraordinaire, went in goal and Chris Garland came on as substitute, the first time he and fellow September-signing Steve Kember had been on the pitch at the same time. Given the goalkeeping issue, Chelsea were happy enough with a point.

The League Cup was Chelsea's best chance of European qualification, especially as the other Semi-finalists were West Ham United and Stoke City, neither setting the world on fire. There were five days before the Tottenham home Semi-final. It was clear that Bonetti, who had not suffered a break but still had his leg in plaster, would not be fit, so John Phillips, who had performed admirably when called on the previous season, would get his chance. There was a scare when he needed emergency dental treatment, but he was fit to play. Kember was cup-tied and Baldwin not fully-fit so Sexton brought in Garland in a side that lined up :– *Phillips; Mulligan, Dempsey, Webb, Harris; Hollins, Hudson; Cooke, Osgood, Garland, Houseman. Sub Baldwin.*

The game was not all-ticket, unlike the second-leg. It is a mystery why only 43,330, over 10,000 under capacity and 9,000 less than the League game a month earlier, were recorded as entering Stamford Bridge for what proved to be a night of high excitement, despite Hudson claiming 'Spurs put eight men behind the ball'. Osgood had put Chelsea ahead after goalkeeper Pat Jennings collided with Terry Naylor. Naylor and Martin Chivers put Tottenham ahead. Garland headed an equaliser, a belated first goal for the club some three months after his debut. A Hollins penalty four minutes from time clinched a 3-2 first-leg win against the holders in a defiant comeback which caused a mass pitch-invasion from jubilant supporters at the end. Osgood was booked for kicking Mike England, an old rival, in the chest and could have been sent off. All to play for at White Hart Lane in a fortnight.

The year ended with a home game against Ipswich, remembered by many of the very decent holiday crowd of 43,896 for a highly unusual team selection. Phillips had aggravated a back injury and Bonetti still recovering from his ankle injury so third-choice goalkeeper Steve Sherwood, at home in the Yorkshire town of Selby, was sent for. Sherwood did not leave until 11.00, the arranged police escort missed him and, perhaps unsurprisingly, he only arrived three minutes before kick-off, too late to play. Webb, inevitably, stepped into the breach. Astonishingly, he kept a clean sheet as Chelsea were comfortable 2-0 winners, Kember and Garland scoring in the second half as Ipswich only managed one shot on target. The crowd's cheers for Webb at the end were massive and heartfelt.

Unfortunately, the arrangement whereby the 1,500 North Stand displaced season-ticket holders could be relocated to the West Stand benches had one flaw. The benches were open to the elements. At the Ipswich game, perhaps unsurprisingly, it rained. Because of a short-sighted and penny-pinching board decision in 1965 to leave the front half of the benches uncovered, affected season-ticket holders duly got wet. They were less than happy, especially as away supporters were in covered seats. The club pointed out that away seats had already been allocated, and that they were obliged to give the away team 25% of seats for cup-ties, but that did not mollify angry North Stand season-ticket holders.

A supporter petition was duly organised, which caused the club much embarrassing publicity. One petitioner told the *Evening Standard* 'I appreciate the club were placed in a difficult position with regard to the stand but, after consulting experts, they should now be in a position to decide whether it's dangerous or not'. The club did the right thing by closing the stand but only had themselves to blame, decades of stadium neglect coming to a head. The following month Chelsea made a money-back offer to fans ousted from the North Stand, which took some of the heat out of the matter. Supporter David Gray, a North Stand season-ticket holder affected by the closure, recalls that he ended up sitting in the West Stand itself later that season.

Hudson again played with his old verve and skill, lynchpin in a team that had won six and drawn four of their last ten League games. In a *Daily Mail* feature, a 'slim-line' Hudson claimed 'I'm Back To My Best". He was fitter and had been 'Chelsea's outstanding player for the last month – working prodigiously, creating chances, tackling back and hardly ever wasting a ball'. The ankle trouble affecting him the previous season had cleared up and he again looked a good bet for full international honours.

Positivity abounded in the squad. Houseman, with five goals already that season, told the *Daily Mirror* 'our playing system is not so rigid, and I have much more room and space in which to develop'. A section of the crowd had jeered him against Leeds but, as the *Kensington Post* argued, 'had Houseman not had his confidence sapped by the more moronic sections of the crowd, which seems to want to hustle him out of football, Chelsea might have snatched a win. He is a useful player and it is about time the baiters shut up and let him get on with his game'. Indeed Bonetti, recovering from injury, agreed in the Leeds programme that going out of Europe was 'a real shaker'. Hutchinson was kicking a ball again for the first time since his leg break.

The average home League crowd up to Christmas was down on previous season at that stage from 45,278 to 41,790. Not great, but that statistic should be seen in the context that thirteen First Division clubs had seen a decline in gates.

Chelsea were not active in the transfer market in the run up to Christmas, though the strong run of results had taken the pressure off Sexton in that regard. Two youngsters, Alan Dovey and Kevin Barry were sold for small fees, forward Barry to Margate and goalkeeper Dovey to Brighton. Mike Brolly and youth products Steve Perkins and John Spong were signed as professionals. Highly promising full-back Gary Locke was called into the England Youth team but, unlike a decade or so earlier, he was the only Chelsea player picked.

Chelsea Secretary Tony Green told the *Daily Mirror* that Chelsea had paid the Garland £100,000 fee up front, but still owed some of the £170,000 Kember cash. He pointed out that 'it often suits clubs to spread out a big fee, so they don't lose all that capital in one lump sum. Also, there are cash benefits'. What it also possibly indicated was that funds were tight at Chelsea and, given neither could command a regular starting place, must have made the club hierarchy ponder the wisdom of the signings.

Taking stock at the end of 1971, halfway through the season, Chelsea had had very much a mixed time of it, on and off the field. A disappointing start, with fitness issues affecting key players and highlighted by Osgood's temporary place on the transfer list, culminated in shameful European elimination by part-timers Atvidaberg. Following that fiasco, the team rallied considerably, and entered the New Year undefeated in sixteen games since the Arsenal home game in mid-October. Tenth place in the League an under-achievement given pre-season expectations, although recent form suggested a higher place was there for the taking. They remained nine points off long-time leaders Manchester United but were now twelve points away from the relegation zone, so could look upwards not downwards. With the Tottenham League Cup Semi-final second-leg days away and an FA Cup-tie at Blackpool to follow, 1972 could be looked forward to with some confidence.

January 1972

The New Year started with a tricky trip to Brian Clough's Derby County, fifth in the table and genuine title contenders. Clough publicly castigated his players in the match build-up, accusing them of lacking toughness, thereby guaranteeing they were more fired up than ever. As John Phillips and Peter Bonetti were both still injured, and David Webb was required at centre-back, Steve Sherwood made his delayed debut in goal.

Sherwood performed very impressively and was desperately unlucky to concede the only goal of the game, a late headed own-goal by Webb he could do nothing about. Sexton commented 'Steve did very well...and was unlucky with the goal he conceded'. This was Chelsea's first defeat in seventeen games and, given the nature of the goal and the fact they missed a series of chances, they could consider themselves unlucky to travel back to London pointless.

Looming large was the Tottenham second-leg the following Wednesday, a game that consumed the supporters, the media and the club. Fierce London rivals, an opportunity to exact some revenge for the 1967 FA Cup Final defeat and the chance of another Wembley final. Interest was enormous, touts getting £8 to £10 for £1 seat tickets, with prices expected to increase further on the night. Tottenham assistant secretary Bill Stevens observed 'some of the spivs seem to live in the street outside our ground'. In the event, best seats reportedly went for up to a staggering £25, indicating the importance of the match, a 52,755 sell-out, to both sets of supporters.

Bonetti was fit, great news for the team and no reflection on the inexperienced Sherwood. He was Chelsea's fourth different goalkeeper in four successive games, surely a record. Cooke came in for the ineligible Kember, Eddie McCreadie was fit enough to sit on the bench, after being out since the Atvidaberg away-leg.

Another thrilling game ensued, with Tottenham taking the lead though Martin Chivers before half-time. After the interval Chelsea came out like a team possessed, the *Daily Mail* claiming 'never have I seen 20 minutes of such lung-busting effort and unremitting effort as Chelsea produced'. Garland equalised but a Martin Peters penalty put Tottenham ahead. In the last minute, with extra-time looming, Mike England, not for the first time, fouled Osgood. Hudson whipped in a free-kick from near the left-hand corner flag. Full-back Cyril Knowles tried to clear the ball with his wrong foot, missed it and it rolled into in the corner of the net. Cue bedlam. Tottenham, despite referee David Smith clearly indicating a direct free-kick, claimed it was indirect. It was a freak goal, but it was the winner. Hudson later described the goal as his most important for Chelsea.

The result was a stupendous achievement by Chelsea, whose determination and drive deserved a place at Wembley in March. Even after the game, the hapless England was bleating about how it was an indirect free-kick to any journalist who would listen, but presumably his guilt at conceding the winning free-kick got the better of him.

The whole team deserved enormous credit for a performance up there with any achieved under Sexton's management. Optimism for the final was high, especially as Boyle, Baldwin and McCreadie were all expected to be fit by early March, increasing Sexton's options. Ecstatic chairman Brian Mears claimed 'what a fine manager he is. He must be the best this club has ever had'.

Some Chelsea players celebrated long and hard. At 3.25am, Osgood, still celebrating with Hudson, Garland and others, was arrested with a friend in Royal Avenue, off King's Road on a charge of drunk and disorderly. Assistant manager Ron Suart and club secretary Tony Green accompanied him in court the following morning, where he was given bail in the sum of £5 and told to appear again on February 4th. The story made the front pages ('Osgood Bailed On Drink Charge' being the *Daily Mail's* offering) cementing his status as 'The King' with The Shed. The incident must have given Sexton more cause for thought, however, especially as, on leaving court that morning, Osgood joined Hudson in the Chelsea Bar of the Drugstore in King's Road, close to where he had been arrested hours earlier. Osgood was subsequently found not guilty, but mud had undoubtedly stuck in terms of confirmation of his playboy image.

Three days later an understandably tired team faced Huddersfield at Stamford Bridge. Only 30,800 turned out, despite the feelgood factor from the League Cup heroics. Garland, Cooke and Hudson were injured so highly promising young midfielder Tony Potrac made his debut, with fellow youngster Peter Feely on the bench. Eddie McCreadie, in his first start since October, was completely free of injury for the first time in two years.

A 2-2 draw was a major disappointment, given Huddersfield were fighting relegation. Webb had to go off with a badly bruised arm before half-time, Feely replacing him, and, with Potrac, making a goal for Hollins. Osgood, with a spectacular diving header, scored the other. The

Daily Telegraph, under a 'Chelsea Show Flair' headline, felt 'Chelsea had it in them to be the entertainers extraordinaire of the Football League now that Manchester United are having problems'. Flair was all very well but conceding two goals and a point to a team in nineteenth place was hardly what was required.

Chelsea received 30,000 tickets for the League Cup Final, which, as in 1970, were allocated using the programme voucher loyalty system. The opposition was Stoke City, victors over West Ham in an epic Semi-final after a replay. Chelsea were made clear favourites.

The other route to Wembley was via the FA Cup, and Chelsea's campaign started with a trip to Blackpool, fifteenth in the Second Division. A potentially tricky game was actually fairly straightforward, a 1-0 win understating Chelsea's clear superiority. Dempsey's early header was enough to put Chelsea through to the Fourth Round, where they were drawn against Bolton Wanderers, who they had already played three times that season. They were promptly established as 7-1 joint favourites, with Leeds.

Manchester United were wobbling a bit but still top of the table. For Chelsea to visit the following Saturday and win 1-0 was a real statement of intent. Again, Hudson and Webb, both at the top of their games, came in for special praise, as did Osgood, whose winner was the result of a clever Hudson flick.

The *Fulham Chronicle*, often critical of Sexton's side, saw the display as the 'finest 90 minutes of glory (from Chelsea) so far this season'. Osgood bullishly told them 'we are at the stage where we feel we can beat anybody. We feel so good now that we could play (Semi-finalists) West Ham in the morning and Stoke in the afternoon'. Their words of warning were prescient. 'I would only plead with Chelsea and Osgood in particular not to get too cocky and over-confident. Players can only be made to look foolish if their predictions go cock-eyed'. Hollins, a more measured individual, told the *Sunday People* 'after this victory we feel sure we are going to win something, especially as we are already in the League Cup Final'. Worryingly, Houseman was taken ill and lost nine pounds in five days with possible appendicitis amid concerns he could miss Wembley.

The month ended with a home game against Everton, champions just eighteen months earlier but on the slide, languishing four places below Chelsea in thirteenth place, without an away win all season and having recently sold talismanic midfielder Alan Ball to Arsenal. A comprehensive 4-0 victory was shown to the massed viewers of ITV's *The Big Match* the following day and, looking at the footage, the total dominance of Chelsea, and their ball retention, stand out, the team moving nicely into form for the key cup-ties ahead. All four were scored in the second half including a brace from Osgood, now on 25 for the season, a fine tally given it was still January.

Two key Chelsea players were the subject of profiles in the *Evening*

Standard. Ray Connolly, later the writer of *That'll Be The Day* and *Stardust* films, interviewed Webb in the feature pages, a sign of his growing profile. He called the defender 'The Desperate Dan of Soccer', with scars and stitches all over his face, quietly spoken and a bit shy, a gentle giant, a man who never stops trying. A sauna kept him under fourteen stone. His great friend was actor Michael Crawford and he drove a Mercedes. 'I've got a little business washing football kits'. It remains a mystery nearly fifty years later why Webb never won any international honours, especially when you consider that Larry Lloyd and Jeff Blockley both won full England caps at centre-half in summer 1972.

The *Evening Standard's* feature on 'Sport's 1972 get-ahead people' included Hudson. 'Hudson is happy now – and set for Munich', indicating massive journalistic arrogance about England's chances of World Cup qualification. The player saw 'the end of a family tiff' and shaking off a depressing list of injuries as the reasons for his improvement. 'I was so bad (last season) it wasn't true...I won a Cup-Winner's Cup medal, but you can forget the rest'.

They reported he suffered emotional upset caused by leaving home when his family felt he was too young to marry Maureen, and didn't speak to them for months. 'Hudson usually plays it very tight and occasionally uses the long ball. Like Alan Ball, Hudson's involvement is total. He has to be where the ball is'. Hudson had apparently been on a faddish but effective steak and grapefruit diet to control his weight. Alf Ramsey two years earlier had said 'there is no limit to what this boy can achieve' and at this point that did indeed seem to be the case.

Chelsea were invited by UEFA, as Cup-Winner's Cup holders, to play in challenge matches against the champion club of the Central and North American confederation of FIFA, home and away. Secretary Tony Green commented 'we agreed in principle to them at the beginning of the season and we understood that they would be before Christmas...The fixtures are so congested that it is difficult to say whether we can fit them in'. Sadly the games never took place, as it would have been fascinating for Chelsea to test themselves against such opposition.

In a fascinating *Evening Standard* article, published the same day, highly experienced football writer Bernard Joy eulogised long and hard on why Chelsea would be the Team Of The Seventies. 'Chelsea, already in their third cup final in three years and joint FA Cup favourites, are geared up to take over as the dominant British club in the Seventies. They have possibly the best squad of players, both in depth and quality, in the country, an awakening ambition and Stamford Bridge is going to be rebuilt at a cost of perhaps £5 million into the finest stadium in London if not Europe'. Optimistic words indeed.

David Webb felt 'we weren't a true team when we won the FA Cup and Cup-Winner's Cup. We played in cliques, in fits and starts, we relied on certain players, Cooke, Hudson and Osgood, being on song to lift the whole team. Now everyone pulls their weight ... We've grown up into a manly side with young people in it and are ready to burst forward. We have so many important players. Hudson, Kember, Garland – all eligible for the Under-23s – who are just beginning their careers. No-one has seen the best of us yet'. Powerful stuff, and an indicator of the man's frame of mind. Joy saw Chelsea's 18-strong squad as very adaptable because so many players were able to play in different positions - Harris, Mulligan, Boyle and Houseman (although there was no mention of Webb, the ultimate utility player, or Hollins and Kember, shuttled up front on occasion). He saw able young players coming through – Feely, Potrac and Locke. Of course, adaptability was all very well, but was inevitably disruptive and led to players being less than happy at being played out of their preferred position.

Sexton, questioned about his squad, responded 'they have pride in themselves as professionals and if that pride is hurt the only way to let people know is by asking for a transfer...I understand players becoming upset at not being selected. They all want places...all I can do is pick the eleven I think are the best...There's pride in the club as well'. He pointed out there are players who can do something extraordinary – Osgood, Cooke, Hudson, Webb – dynamos like Hollins, Boyle, Kember and brave strikers Hutchinson, Baldwin and Garland.

All good positive stuff, especially with critical cup-ties on the horizon, and indicative of the feelgood atmosphere in and around the club at that point. More cup success and the Atvidaberg shambles, and early-season struggles in the League, would soon be forgotten. In more good news, Ian Hutchinson had resumed training hoped to be playing again shortly, and to be in consideration for Wembley on March 4th. Mears announced that the squad were off for a break in Tenerife four days before the League Cup Final. 'The players have earned it. We hope to be in the running for the FA Cup and I still have thoughts about the Championship'. Chelsea were still ninth in the table at month end but had closed the gap on new leaders Leeds United to seven points. At this point Chelsea really did look a quality side and, though the League was in reality probably beyond them, confidence was very high.

February 1972

The club announced that full details of the planned stadium redevelopment would be made public on March 6th, with rebuilding to start immediately after the final home game of the season. In a letter to League Cup Final ticket-holders, manager Dave Sexton wrote 'I would like to ask your help towards raising of our plans to make Stamford Bridge one of the finest stadiums in Europe'.

The Bolton FA Cup-tie attracted 38,000 to Stamford Bridge, a decent crowd but well below the fantastic FA Cup crowds of the mid-1960s when 63,000 watched a tie against Peterborough United. Chelsea won very comfortably, 3-0, and, at least in theory, were in for a League,

FA Cup and League Cup treble. The draw took Chelsea to Orient from Division Two, and they were promptly installed 5-1 favourites for the FA Cup.

Bizarrely, it was unclear whether the League Cup winners would qualify for a UEFA Cup place, as such decisions were not made until the end of the season. Mears, understandably, was optimistic. 'As far as we know, the winners will go into Europe. Until we hear to the contrary, we will stick to that assumption'. Of course, thinking the issue affected Chelsea was another assumption, one that would be tested in a month's time.

Ken Jones of the *Daily Mirror* put ten questions to Dave Sexton under a 'One Change Sent Chelsea Soaring' headline. The manager saw team work as essential, and imperative that they operate as a unit. He changed from man-to-man to a zonal marking system two years earlier, where attackers were passed from defender to defender. 'It allows more of our players to get involved in attacking movements…It is part of my job to keep players not in the team happy'. Presciently, even though things were going well, he reiterated that 'there is always a crisis around the corner'. He emphasised the value of accurate passing and ruminated 'Football is the poetry of the masses. They get great joy out of its beauty and style. If you are involved in the game, you have to be involved in that. People weren't put on the world just to work'.

As performances continued at a high standard, awards were flowing in. Webb deservedly won the *Evening Standard Footballer Of The Month* for January. He stated that being 'made to look a clown' by Eddie Gray in the 1970 FA Cup Final convinced him he was not a full-back and he had worked on mastering the centre-back role ever since. He was 'like a magnet' in the Semi-final at White Hart Lane, attracting and destroying all Tottenham attacks. He felt the team were working hard, including Hudson (who was tackling like a tiger) and Ossie (who was doubling back) and praised Sexton for developing his own game, and doing the same with recent signings Garland and Kember. He reiterated his desire to play for England. In addition to Webb's prize, Sexton won the *Bells Whisky Manager Of The Month* award.

Possibly upsetting the harmonious atmosphere, under a 'Chelsea Stars Claim Pay Rise' headline, the *Sunday People* reported that options on Hudson and Osgood contracts ended in a few weeks and they'd be negotiating with Sexton for fatter pay packets. Hollins' new contract apparently made him the highest-paid Chelsea player, with £130 a week plus the normal £40 a point bonus. Given Martin Chivers of Tottenham was on a reported £9,000 a year Chelsea star players must have felt comparatively hard done-by. Kember, interviewed in *Goal Magazine*, felt he had taken time to settle, not helped by having to play wide and up front as well as in his preferred midfield role.

There was a feeling that after all his injury troubles of the last two years, it was great to see McCreadie looking fit and playing so well. In an interview with the *Evening Standard* he admitted there were times he felt like giving up his two-year struggle against injury. 'I've got to admit I sometimes felt like packing it in'. He had a stomach operation two days after the Leeds FA Cup Final, then damaged ligaments, then an injured ankle, then a broken nose then a hamstring injury. He praised Sexton and trainer Harry Medhurst for keeping him fighting'. He was back in the side as Dempsey was injured and intended to keep his place. 'I'm going to be bloody hard to shift'.

Chelsea were apparently interested in right-back Mick Coop of Coventry, who the *Evening Standard* felt would cost 'well within Chelsea's range', though the need for a full-back had lessened with the fine form of Paddy Mulligan. In his column, Harris called Mulligan 'the superb, unsung hero of Chelsea' who never got his share of the headlines, seeing him as solid and reliable with a love of over-lapping.

Leicester City, with ex-Chelsea players Keith Weller and Alan Birchenall, were the opposition at Stamford Bridge after a welcome two-week break. The home team eased to a 2-1 victory that meant an admirable record of one defeat in twenty-four games. As the *News Of The World* put it, 'Osgood, twenty-five that weekend, scored two more goals with that lazy, chilling certainty that must have sent shivers through the watching Stoke spies. He is in the devastating sort of form that can win matches even when his team are not in the mood. Hudson carved the defence to pieces'. The *Daily Mirror* thought Kember gave his best showing in a Chelsea shirt, winning the ball regularly, passing well and getting into scoring positions. Exactly what Sexton had bought him for, making his Wembley unavailability the more frustrating.

Dempsey, demoted to the bench against Leicester, was the latest victim of the 'squad squeeze' also affecting the likes of Garland, Kember, and Baldwin. He was worried about missing the League Cup Final, and angry as he felt he had an excellent understanding with Webb. Keeping squad players happy was a growing challenge for the likes of Sexton and Arsenal boss Bertie Mee, who the *Daily Mail* felt had the strongest squads in the country.

The *Sunday People* reported that when Dempsey was not recalled for Leicester, one of his fellow defenders told team-mates 'if John doesn't play, I want to be left out too'. One star talked about 'the player Dave never drops - no matter how he plays'. This is almost certainly a reference to Ron Harris, whose form had certainly been patchy, though his commitment was never in question.

Chelsea approached the trip to Brisbane Road the following weekend in fine fettle, the team firing on all cylinders. In retrospect, Chelsea were at a pinnacle. In with an outside chance of the League title but within reach of a European place and favourites in two cup competitions.

Harris, Webb and Osgood gave confident interviews in the build-up to the game. Paul Harris, Orient centre-half, retorted 'I'm not afraid of

Osgood...I respect him very much, but he doesn't scare me'. He was to spend the game attempting to intimidate the England star, with some success.

Orient, not for the first time, were in a difficult financial position so saw the opportunity to make some cash by putting ticket prices up to £1, 75p and 50p for terracing (compared with their usual 35p). Chelsea sold their 9,400 allocation but strangely chose not to take the extra 3,000 tickets offered. Plenty of ticketless Chelsea fans went to Orient to get tickets, though had to buy a match programme to get the relevant voucher. In the end, the touts got their fingers burned and were left with scores of tickets. An hour before kick-off, they were selling outside Brisbane Road at face value.

The *Daily Mirror* pointed out that Sexton was keeping players guessing regarding his team line-up, with his squad 'left to wait and wonder in an atmosphere of growing anxiety'. Kember, ineligible for Wembley, claimed 'I'll be choked if I'm not in the team to face Orient'. In the event Kember played and Dempsey was restored to the side, with Ron Harris dropping to full-back and an unfit McCreadie missing out.

The game itself has gone down in the history of both clubs, but for markedly different reasons. Chelsea took a comfortable 2-0 lead after 35 minutes on a mud bath, through Webb and Osgood, and missed a couple of decent chances. All seemed comfortable but, just before half-time, Orient full-back Phil Hoadley hit a thirty-yard screamer Bonetti could do nothing about.

After the interval it was a very different game. Orient fought tirelessly to overcome the gap in class and Chelsea made a series of defensive errors. Mickey Bullock equalised after a mix-up between Webb and Bonetti and, unbelievably, Barrie Fairbrother put Orient ahead with two minutes to go. Chelsea supporters invaded the pitch in an apparent attempt to get the match abandoned and Webb missed a good chance in injury time before the final whistle blew on Chelsea's FA Cup chances. Somehow, the FA Cup favourites had managed to throw away a two-goal lead against a team from the lower half of Division Two. As the *Kensington Post* put it 'it was the FA Cup result that shocked football'.

The result has seared into supporter memories, 47 years later. Supporter Peter Gray recalls the game. 'I still think this was one of the worst results in our history. I thought it was all over at 2-0 up and said to my pal "This is easy". Unfortunately the Chelsea players did the same'. His brother David firmly believes that the start of the downhill slide that resulted in 26 years without a major trophy began that day. Supporter Brian Gaches remembers his 'disbelief' at the surrender, a widely shared emotion.

As with the Atvidaberg elimination four months earlier, criticism was both widespread and justified. The team seemed complacent when two goals ahead, sat back and were unable to step things up when Orient fought back. The *News Of The World* thought 'Sexton must be wondering how his team lost after creating so many chances and pondering his League Cup Final team'. Supporter Geoff Kimber recalls that 'some of our defending was absolutely woeful...we seemed to panic' and certainly the mentality of the side was open to question after such an abject capitulation.

The feeling of relative invincibility in place since the Atvidaberg elimination was washed away and Sexton had but a week before meeting Stoke at Wembley to lift morale. The chastened manager left Brisbane Road without saying anything to the assembled journalists but in the week told the *Daily Mail* 'This will be a normal week for us. We always work hard. And I shall do what I normally do to pick the team up. And that's our business'.

As Webb told the *Daily Mirror*, 'the week ahead is our biggest test of character ever'. He mentioned a sad and almost silent dressing room. 'Right now I'm sick. We're all sick. I'm not making excuses, but the pitch didn't help us'. He told the *Daily Mail* 'luckily Dave Sexton is great at picking us up quickly...We might bounce back and win the League Cup and the Championship. Don't laugh. We've still to play most of the top clubs in the League'. He talked about planning personal stints of extra training all the way to the next Saturday.

Harris's *Evening Standard* column unsurprisingly had a 'Now We Must Get Off The Floor And Start Again' headline that week. 'We gave away a couple of silly goals...We were depressed after the game...We could have kicked ourselves for letting it slip away. We knew we'd let ourselves down and we knew how disappointed our fans were'.

Paddy Mulligan was defiant. 'It's disgraceful - leading 2-0 then losing 3-2 to a team like that ... it will harden us up for the League Cup Final'. Hudson, in *The Working Man's Ballet*, saw the significance of the result, claiming 'a piece of us all died that day when the whistle blew ... It was one of the biggest shocks for years. We had so many chances'. From his perspective he felt that, after that game, 'the team and club were never a force again'. As well shall see, there is more than a grain of truth in that assertion.

There were claims that the crash barrier went on the Brisbane Road terraces, and that was the reason for the pitch invasion. Chelsea supporters were heavily criticised for their actions, though it is not clear whether any actually thought they could force an abandonment. Chelsea Secretary Tony Green made the point that 'all our barriers have been tested and strengthened since the Ibrox disaster'.

A pleasant distraction from the run of matches had been the recording by the squad of *Blue Is The Colour* a song written by Daniel Boone and Rod McQueen and released to mark the team reaching the League Cup Final. Footage of the recording shows a refreshed-looking squad enthusiastically belting out the words. The record entered the Top 20 at the end of February and, the week after the final, reached the heady heights of number five. In all, it spent twelve weeks in the charts, some achievement in those days. The catchy tune caught the mood of the supporters and, nearly fifty years later is still played, and sung, before every home first-team game. Supporter Geoff Kimber remembers the tune being whistled by supporters on the tube to Brisbane Road that fateful day.

Chelsea were tenth in the table, eight points behind leaders Manchester City. The tussle for the title was an exciting one, but sadly Chelsea were too far behind to have a realistic chance. After the Brisbane Road capitulation, the League Cup was now their only chance of silverware.

March 1972

As a chastened Chelsea squad prepared to try and salvage their season by winning at Wembley, newspaper previews felt Chelsea were still clear favourites, possessing too much class for their opponents, whose workmanlike approach was augmented by experience and skill in the shape of Peter Dobing and George Eastham. Stoke City also possessed, in Gordon Banks, arguably the best goalkeeper in the world.

The players made the most of commercial opportunities the week before the game, being photographed in Vidal Sassoon's hair salon and elsewhere, though *Foul: Football's Alternative Paper* later wondered whether these 'mercenary jaunts' affected the teams preparation.

Manager Dave Sexton rejected the almost traditional secrecy and caution over team selection for Wembley. The *Daily Telegraph* saw this as a shrewd move, giving Chelsea 'a lead in the psychological war against Stoke, and preventing public speculation and private misgivings following the Orient defeat'. It was Alan Hudson's first Wembley appearance and Stoke boss Tony Waddington, evidently a fan, pointed him out as the man who made Chelsea tick.

The *Evening Standard* reported that the team, training at Molesey, seemed relaxed and cheerful, rebuilding confidence after the Orient defeat. The banter of Osgood, Webb, Hudson and Hollins was lifting the squad. Sexton argued 'we won't put the Orient defeat behind us until we win again', replaced the cup-tied Steve Kember with Chris Garland and picked the back-from-injury Tommy Baldwin as substitute.

The previous week, the *Sunday Telegraph* had profiled and interviewed Sexton. He felt that Osgood had accepted the role as target man in the absence of Hutchinson and recognised he was a coach not a manager. A private man, they saw him as 'the reluctant manager, knowing he cannot fundamentally ... shield young players from the uncomfortable proximity of the King's Road glitter'.

The *Fulham Chronicle* ran a very positive piece with a 'Swinging Chelsea – The Side To Watch In The Soccer 70s' headline. They referred to 'possibly the strongest squad of players in depth and talent in the League'. Hudson was 'one of the most exciting players in the country...Players like Harris, Mulligan, Houseman, Boyle and Webb are adaptable and able to play in different positions. They have talented youngsters ... I am sure we will hear big things from in the future ... Sexton's chief problem is keeping his reserves from becoming restless'. Moving forward, Sexton must have fervently wished that was indeed his only problem.

The *Daily Mirror* reported that the players were on £2,000 to beat Stoke, plus £250 from the players pool, for each of the twenty-man squad. They argued that Chelsea had made enormous cup profits and would add to them with their cut from the League Cup Final, though of course any reliance on cup revenues was inherently risky.

The *Daily Mail* talked to Osgood about his luxury house, paid for through football. He paid £16,000 for it after the 1970 FA Cup Final and paid for improvements after the Cup-Winner's Cup win. 'Lots of our lads have come to realise what success is all about in the last couple of years. And that makes a lot of good reasons why I think we will beat Stoke'. Whether cash was sufficient motivation remained to be seen. Despite the goals, his form in recent games had been erratic and every Chelsea supporter fervently hoped he would be firing on all cylinders against Stoke.

For their third cup final in less than two years, Chelsea lined up :- *Bonetti; Mulligan, Dempsey, Webb, Harris; Cooke, Hollins, Hudson; Garland, Osgood, Houseman. Sub Baldwin.* Hutchinson and Boyle were injured, McCreadie omitted and Kember cup-tied but it was still, on paper, a very strong side.

There was a full League programme that day, which apparently reduced the demand for tickets from touts, the game kicking off at 3.30pm for no obvious reason. Stoke fans taunted Chelsea with chants of 'Orient' but the blue hordes were in fine voice. The game did not start to plan from a Chelsea perspective. Terry Conroy put Stoke ahead in the fifth minute and made Webb's life a nightmare. The Blues rallied, building up an almost embarrassing superiority and it was no surprise when Osgood equalised right on half-time. Stoke, as usual, were highly physical, targeting Garland particularly. Supporter David Gray, who was at the game, argues that two Stoke defenders would have been sent off these days for hauling him back.

Paddy Mulligan badly damaged his ankle late in the first-half after a dreadful challenge by Mike Pejic and had to go off for ten minutes while it was repaired. At half-time his ankle had to be put in plaster, he could not continue. Sexton brought on Baldwin, moved Peter Houseman to left-back and Ron Harris to right-back. This meant they lost Houseman's accurate crosses and Mulligan's marauding runs up the right, as over-lapping was not Harris's game. Baldwin was also less than 100 per cent fit, hardly surprising given he had suffered hamstring, thigh and Achilles tendon problems already that season. Yet again, the thin attacking options in the continued absence of Hutchinson called into question the sales of Keith Weller and Derek Smethurst.

The half-time changes affected Chelsea's rhythm, key players like Osgood became more anonymous but it was still against the run of play when Eastham netted for Stoke after a goalmouth scramble with seventeen minutes left. Chelsea came again, but chances went begging and a wonder save by Banks from Garland near the end meant Stoke ran out 2-1 winners.

For the second time in eight shattering days, and the third time that season, 'Cup Chumps' Chelsea had underachieved in an entirely winnable cup-tie. Chances had been missed, the defence made mistakes and the lack of urgency was criticised. The *Fulham Chronicle* praised Garland for his 'outstanding maturity', and felt he deserved more support from Osgood 'who seemed somewhat intent on becoming the first-ever League Cup Finalist to be sent off'. *The Observer* felt he 'went from ordinary to worse' despite his goal. He complained 'I thought we were the better side in the final, but we got beaten'. Cooke thought the team were 'cocky and over-confident' and Mulligan later felt 'maybe some of the lads thought it was going to be easy'. John Dempsey argued that Banks won the game for Stoke and certainly he had a majestic match. Supporter Geoff Kimber saw the defending as almost as sloppy as against Orient and losing Mulligan the pivotal moment of the match.

Supporter Peter Gray was at Wembley. 'In the build up to the match it all seemed a bit too friendly between the clubs, every day Stoke were saying 'We haven't won anything for 108 years'. It just wasn't our day, even though we deserved to win'.

As the *Sunday People* pointed out 'now Chelsea are left with only the League. They won't win it this time but might next season'. A remarkably positive spin on as bleak an eight days as the club had experienced in a very, very long time. They still had an outside chance of European football but would have to finish above both Arsenal and Tottenham and hope that the latter did not win the UEFA Cup. They were currently tenth, five points behind Tottenham with three games in hand, four behind Arsenal with two games to spare, so it was a tall order indeed.

Webb, resilient as ever, told the *Evening Standard* 'in eight days all that we have played for in the past three months has gone irrevocably. But don't worry, we'll pick ourselves up. This team has plenty of character'. Harris, in his column claimed 'we know we belong in Europe. We want to make it this season. We think we can'. Their writer Bernard Joy was still convinced Chelsea were going to be one of England's outstanding clubs of the 1970s. All positive stuff, but the team needed to lick its wounds and come back fighting very quickly. For Sexton the reality was that his team had fallen badly short when it mattered most, giving him significant food for thought in terms of both players and tactics.

Chairman Brian Mears remained positive at the after-final dinner.

'There is no need to be downhearted. I know that we will bounce back to win further honours'. From a distance of nearly fifty years, the accuracy of that prediction depends on what time constraints you use when defining 'bouncing back'. Osgood, for example, later opined that 'it all fell apart from then onwards' and certainly if Chelsea had won, picked up a trophy and qualified for Europe their future might have panned out very differently. He also felt that Sexton's willingness to turn a blind eye to the social life enjoyed by key members of his squad ended with that defeat.

Hudson, in *The Working Man's Ballet*, makes the point that in that side there was a lack of continuity and quality supporting Osgood in Ian Hutchinson's absence. A couple of days after the Stoke defeat it was announced that Hutch's plaster had been removed, he was back in light training and could be back playing in late April. This optimism made the news later that week that he had broken his left leg in training, and would be out for at least another six weeks, so desperately sad. The *Daily Telegraph* pointed out that 'this gifted and likeable young man is one of the unluckiest players in modern football history'.

The fixture list was not kind to Chelsea the following weekend, the next game after two shocks defeats being fourth-placed Liverpool at home. The crowd for what was always one of the biggest games of the season was only 38,691, reflecting the sense of disappointment felt by players, club and supporters alike. Both sides missed a hatful of chances in a 0-0 draw, not a bad result considering, but not what was required in terms of points.

Being out of all three cups limited the number of midweek games the side would play, but the following Tuesday Chelsea visited bottom-placed Nottingham Forest. Baldwin was up front on his own as Osgood was injured. The endless team changes, forced or otherwise, hardly helped the team's rhythm or understanding. A dismal crowd of 13,346 saw Chelsea crumble to a 2-1 defeat, a dreadful result against a team that had not scored since January, especially as a Hollins penalty gave Chelsea the lead. Hopes of Europe were fast evaporating.

Something needed to change before the visit to League leaders Manchester City four days later. What Sexton did was probably long overdue and probably deserved, but still a surprise. Two days before the game the *Daily Mail*, under a 'Harris Axed As Chelsea Pick New Skipper' headline reported that captain Ron Harris had been stripped of the captaincy and dropped from the team. Sexton explained 'Ron has lost form recently and I feel it will be best to leave him out of this match and relieve him of this responsibility in future. Ron has been a rock in our cup triumphs, even when playing out of position ... I have made these changes in the best interests of the club and to help Ron get his form back ... He has taken it well, though he is very disappointed'.

Harris had played every League game that season, and been captain since early 1966, but it was an open secret that the rest of the squad had been worried about his loss of form. John Hollins, consistently a star performer that season, took over the team captaincy, with Eddie McCreadie, hoping to obtain his coaching badges that summer, becoming club captain, which 'honoured and surprised' him. Harris's loyalty and commitment were unquestioned, but his form had been erratic, and Sexton was left with little option.

Harris talked to the *Evening Standard* under a 'A Shattering Blow – And I'm So Hurt' headline. 'It has been the most shattering experience of my football life. To lose my place in the team was disappointing enough. To also have the club captaincy taken away was even worse and I wouldn't be human if I wasn't bitterly disappointed', unsurprising after six years as skipper. For the past eighteen months four players – Mulligan, McCreadie, Boyle and Harris – had been chasing two full-back positions and Sexton clearly thought Mulligan and Boyle a better bet. 'You have no idea how shattering these past few weeks have been for me. We had high hopes of doing really well this season.' He vowed not to let it get him down and to fight for his place. Years later, he told supporter David Gray that 'losing the captaincy was one of his saddest days at The Bridge'. John Boyle recently said that Harris was very upset at losing the club captaincy and the Scot felt Sexton struggled to identify a captain in the Bobby Moore and Franz Beckenbauer mould. He did not captain the side again for more than two years and never regularly filled the role again.

Harris's omission meant Chelsea were playing their fifth different full-back pairing in six games, hardly helping create a settled defensive line. The game attracted enormous press interest, and a 53,322 Maine Road crowd, because of the debut of glamourous City signing Rodney Marsh from Queens Park Rangers, a capture manager Malcolm Allison saw as the icing on the cake in their title bid. A Tommy Booth goal gave City the points as Chelsea, again, stagnated in midfield.

Harris's exile lasted precisely one match as the following week, at home to West Ham, injuries to Garland and Houseman caused a reshuffle so he came in at centre-back, Webb moving up front as No.8 alongside Osgood. The fact Webb was chosen ahead of Baldwin, who was on the bench, showed how little faith Sexton had in the latter and the paucity of his options, despite the transfer activity at the start of the season. Five games without a win was the leanest run for three seasons but ended in some style as West Ham were dominated and outclassed. Harris gave 'his most consistent display for many a month' according to the *Daily Mirror*, helping make the first and third goals for Osgood and Hollins. Mulligan scored the second with a piledriver.

With ten games to go, but only three against top-seven sides, tenth-placed Chelsea still had an outside chance of Europe but the inconsistency that bedeviled the side had to somehow be eradicated. Sexton was defiant. 'We needed that win. Our season is not finished. We need every point to finish above Spurs and Arsenal and qualify for Europe'.

Webb rounded off an unusual month, even by his unorthodox standards, by wearing the No.7 shirt and scoring twice as Chelsea beat Sheffield United in front of only 28,444 supporters, nearly 17,000 down on the West Ham game and maybe an indication of the core support. The game had been brought forward two days from Good Friday at the start of the season, in the vain hope Chelsea would still be involved in Europe. Moving the game probably cost the club at least £2,500 in lost revenue as Good Friday was traditionally one of the bigger gates of the season.

Hudson and Kember linked up in the England Under-23 side against East Germany. Hudson dazzled with his precision passing and it was surely only a matter of time before he received full honours. Garland, not in that side, put his recent improvement down to training hard, going back for afternoon individual coaching sessions from Sexton.

Sexton was linked with the vacant job at the ever-ambitious and ever-optimistic Coventry City but, unsurprisingly, that went nowhere. Chelsea were linked with goalscoring winger Ian Storey-Moore of Nottingham Forest but, at over £200,000 he was probably out of Chelsea's price bracket. Reserve full-back Stewart Houston was sold to Brentford for £15,000 in early June, having been on loan there, and two youngsters, winger Jim Davis and centre-back George Price, signed professional forms with the club.

Although Chelsea were in ninth place at the end of March, twelve points behind table-toppers Manchester City, they still had a chance of European football the following season, the only target to aim for in a season that had turned to dust. The thinking was they would need at least twelve points from eight games to qualify for the UEFA Cup, a tall order. The *Daily Telegraph*, noting Chelsea's inconsistency, pointed out 'Chelsea remain an infuriating mixture of promise and banality – a comment that has been made for longer than our fathers care to remember'.

April 1972

April started as March finished, with victories. An encouraging 2-1 win at Ipswich, with their bogeyman David Webb netting twice in a 2-1 win, giving him four in two games, was followed by a turgid 2-1 home win over relegation-threatened Crystal Palace, Hollins and Garland strikes ensuring victory. All that mattered at that stage was the points, though Osgood's fourth booking of the season made the likelihood of suspension high, especially given his track record. A 2-0 win at Wolverhampton Wanderers, distracted by UEFA Cup Semi-final duties, continued the fine run, Garland scoring within a minute, Osgood netting the other as Chelsea dominated.

Five successive League wins meant Chelsea had climbed to sixth place, their best position of the season. Equally importantly, they were level on points with Tottenham, with two games in hand and a point behind Arsenal, having played one game less. The game at White Hart Lane was therefore critical. Win that, have a strong run-in and suddenly European football was a realistic proposition, assuming Tottenham did not win the UEFA Cup and take the London place. This was critical to a club with ambition and would salvage something from the detritus of three crushing cup failures.

The team was unchanged for the fourth match in a row, with David Webb continuing at No.8 and a highly frustrated Steve Kember again substitute. John Boyle and Paddy Mulligan had done sterling jobs as a full-back pairing, Ron Harris and John Dempsey had been solid at centre-back and Chris Garland was flourishing with a regular place. Tottenham had one eye on their forthcoming UEFA Cup Semi-final second-leg in Milan, so it was an optimistic band of Chelsea supporters among the 45,799 White Hart Lane crowd.

The optimism did not last long. Tottenham raced into a 3-0 half-time lead, Harris and Dempsey totally unable to contain two-goal Chivers. Webb was found out up front, Osgood, continuing his feud with Mike England, strained knee ligaments and was out for the rest of the season. Well beaten, indeed 'humiliated' according to the *Kensington Post*, and missing their talismanic striker, Chelsea had to lick their wounds.

Under a 'Dennis Rofe set to join Chelsea' headline, the *Sunday People* reported that Chelsea had decided to pay Orient £80,000 for the in-demand full-back in the summer. Chelsea originally bid £70,000 but Sexton was keen to bid the extra to 'end a defence problem that has been bothering him all season'. In the end the deal never happened, but it showed that Sexton rightly realised that his defence required reinforcing.

Games were coming thick and fast. For the match at Southampton three days later Sexton moved Webb to his natural position at centre-back and brought Kember into midfield. Tommy Baldwin replaced the injured Osgood. Boyle, who had been playing well, was very unlucky to be left out, but never regained a regular place in the side.

A 2-2 draw against a team in nineteenth place was a poor result and it was clear that Europe was increasingly a pipedream unless the team quickly got back to winning ways. Baldwin twice equalised Ron Davies goals.

The following Saturday, an unchanged Chelsea had to beat Newcastle to retain any realistic chance of Europe. Unfortunately, the defence struggled against the Newcastle striking partnership of John Tudor, who scored twice, and Malcolm MacDonald, who netted the other. Chelsea fought back from 2-0 and 3-2 down to force a 3-3 draw in a thrilling match. Baldwin bagged a pair, making it four in two games, Kember netting the other. The inconsistency that had bedevilled much of the season continued to frustrate manager and supporters.

The League table was tight in terms of top London club, as was the real fight, for the title.

1st	Manchester City	p42	57pts
2nd	Liverpool	p40	56pts
3rd	Derby County	p41	56pts
4th	Leeds United	p40	55pts
5th	Tottenham Hotspur	p40	47pts
6th	Arsenal	p38	47pts
7th	**Chelsea**	**p39**	**46pts**

The Newcastle crowd of 33,000 was low but two days later a shockingly poor 23,443, the lowest of the season, turned out to watch a 2-0 win over Stoke City in the final home game. Disillusionment had clearly spread to parts of the support. Those that did make the effort saw a comfortable 2-0 win, Hudson again outstanding and scoring one, Garland grabbing the other. Young centre-back Micky Droy made his first appearance of the season. Supporter David Gray remembers 'at that Stoke game we all took our last look at the old East Stand that had stood for 67 years since Chelsea's formation. Little did we know that the building of the promised 'New Stamford Bridge' would be the burden that would hold the club back for the next generation'.

Chelsea had to win their last two games, at West Bromwich Albion and Leeds, to have any chance whatsoever of European football. West Bromwich had little to play for, Leeds everything. Houseman returned at The Hawthorns after missing nine games through injury but, despite nothing riding on the game for them, the Midlanders won 4-0 against a 'casual Chelsea side who just strolled around' and were 'sagging under the effort of three games in six days'. The *Daily Mirror* called them the 'worst Chelsea side seen in the Midlands for a long time'. Desperately disappointing, as their chance of European football was clearly gone.

Leeds asked to move the game at Elland Road to May 16th, ten days after their FA Cup Final but three weeks after Chelsea's previous game. Chelsea wanted it played on May 1st, five days before Wembley. Sexton explained 'it is out of order that Leeds should expect us to have all this free time before the final match without a game. If the League decide to delay the match until after the final, we will protest'. The club would have had to delay their two-week tour of Barbados, scheduled to start on May 15th.

The game was duly played on May 1st as scheduled. A 2-0 'hard but never ugly' defeat completed Chelsea's season, and meant Leeds only needed to win their last League game, at Wolverhampton, to clinch the title. History records they lost that game 2-1 and Derby County surprisingly won the title. Favourites Manchester City had imploded, with Rodney Marsh unsettling rather than augmenting the side, and Liverpool fell away.

Chelsea finished the season ten points behind Derby in seventh place. In the end they could not have qualified for Europe even if they had won their last six games, as only one side from a city could qualify for the UEFA Cup and Tottenham automatically qualified as holders.

1st	Derby County	p42 58pts
2nd	Leeds United	p42 57pts
3rd	Liverpool	p42 57pts
4th	Manchester City	p42 57pts
5th	Arsenal	p42 52pts
6th	Tottenham Hotspur	p42 51pts
7th	**Chelsea**	**p42 48pts**

Season Review

So a season that promised so much ended in failure. No European football, no trophies, the receiving end of three cup upsets and a sense in some quarters that the team had regressed in the past twelve months. It was obvious to the manager, according to *Chelsea's Cult Heroes*, that his current side were never going to win the League title. As John Boyle says, Kember and Garland 'were lovely guys' but not really of the quality required in Chelsea players and, as a result, the team was weakened. To be fair, Eddie McCreadie reckoned Garland had significantly improved as a player since signing, and his effort was unstinting, so there was hope that he would develop into a very decent player.

Looking at the regular sides put out by the top five teams that season – Derby, Leeds, Liverpool, Manchester City and Arsenal – it is clear Sexton was right, the Chelsea squad was not strong enough for a title challenge. Current internationals abounded in the Liverpool and Leeds sides whereas only John Dempsey and Paddy Mulligan from the Chelsea side won full caps that season. Although the title-winning Derby side was hardly packed with star names, Brian Clough had fostered an extraordinary team spirit and had the knack of making the collective greater than the sum of its parts. These were not claims Sexton could make with any validity that summer. Sexton increasingly preferred, and trusted, hard-working players as opposed to those with flair and a more ebullient approach to life. The upside of that approach is that a team full of such players will be more consistent. The downside is that they will be predictable and probably less likely to win a major trophy.

Supporter Tony Foss remembers 'I still think those two defeats in 1972 League Cup Final and Orient within a week were the turning point for a grim 25 years' and fellow-fan Geoff Kimber rightly calls them 'watershed moments' in club history. Supporter Brian Gaches, 'totally numb' after the Stoke defeat, feels that 'in 53+ years of watching Chelsea this was the most disappointing week I've ever experienced...without a doubt I rate this week as the most significant in the collapse of the great 70's team'.

It is not easy to pinpoint exactly when Chelsea's decline began, but those cup defeats in seven days is one possibility. Another, of course, was the abject Cup-Winners' Cup elimination months earlier by part-time Atvidaberg. Whenever the rot began to set it, it is clear in retrospect that Chelsea blew their chance of honours and, as Kimber recalls from a distance of 47 years, the writing was on the wall.

Between late October and mid-February the side lost just one game in 24. Title-winning form. Sadly, inconsistency, again, bedeviled any title aspirations. The evident need to strengthen the side if a serious title challenge was to be mounted left much for Sexton to ponder, especially with the impending launch of the proposed stadium redevelopment and the economic strictures and imperatives that might cause. A sign of the lack of a settled side was that John Boyle wore seven different shirts in 25 games in that season – the 2, 3, 4, 7, 8, 10 and 11 shirts. Without Hollins' phenomenal eighteen goals, the result of Sexton encouraging him to get forward whenever possible, the side would have struggled further.

Average League crowds fell by 750 to 38,788. Hardly a crisis but when sides like Manchester United, Manchester City, Liverpool, Derby and Tottenham were increasing their attendances still a concern, especially with a new stand to pay for, no European football and a team short of the quality necessary to win major honours.

Close Season

After a testimonial for Brian Powney and Norman Gall at Brighton and a couple of weeks off, the squad unwound on an undemanding trip to Barbados, scoring nineteen goals and conceding just one in three friendly games. In the absence of Hudson, with the full England squad, promising young midfielder Tony Potrac played two games, scoring six goals.

Steve Kember, who had taken time to settle, told the *Evening Standard* 'It feels it is a wasted season. The sooner it ends the better. Just now I don't feel like a £170,000 superstar.' He wanted a regular midfield place next season 'then watch me go'. He rightly felt being cup-tied for the League Cup as well as Europe affected his continuity and 'gave me no chance to become a real part of Chelsea'. The big fee was a problem too. 'When you arrive at a new club it's difficult knowing how to react'. David Webb had a word. 'Take it quiet. Just let things happen naturally'. Kember was disappointed not to be in the England Under-23 touring side but concluded 'I know I can play a bit and all I want is the chance to establish myself'.

There was an over-reliance on the competitive spirit and dynamism of Webb (rightly voted *Player Of The Year*, with Hudson runner-up) and Hollins, the consistency of Bonetti and Houseman and Hudson's bountiful skills. Hutchinson, desperately unfortunate, would be lucky to be playing again by the start of the new season. Cooke and Osgood, despite the latter's 31 goals, were inconsistent, Harris and Dempsey struggled on occasion and Sexton clearly required new blood to compete realistically for honours. The *Sunday People* reported in May that Chelsea were ready to part with Cooke, Boyle, Baldwin and Hinton and, not for the first or last time, were after Steve Earle of Fulham.

The *Sunday People* also advised that Chelsea's shaky North Stand, closed for safety reasons in November, would not reopen. In May, secretary Tony Green said any implementation of the Wheatley Report on ground safety (which required licensing by local authority and had been approved by the government following the Ibrox disaster) would increase prices. He believed spectators were getting their soccer cheap anyway but foresaw no dramatic price rises, maybe the terrace price rising to 50p, and felt increases due to safety work would not cause major revenue loss for clubs. His view was that most clubs were already hot on the question of safety, which showed a sense of optimism, if little sense of reality. Chelsea's own cavalier attitude to supporter safety was to be highlighted three months later.

At the end of May, the *News Of The World* ran a 'Osgood Faces A Pay Battle' headline, revealing that several star players were still negotiating new contracts for the following season, top-scorer Osgood topping the list. 'I gather there is a considerable gap between those new terms Osgood is seeking and what he is being offered' the paper reported, presumably after talking to the star, who would have been conscious of the significantly higher earnings enjoyed by, for example, Tottenham's Martin Chivers.

Hudson did himself no favours internationally when he and Colin Todd withdrew from the England Under-23 touring side for 'domestic' reasons. Hudson's wife was expecting a child, and he spent the week decorating. Sir Alf Ramsey said he had told Hudson on the telephone that he did not accept his reasons for withdrawal, and the Under-23 committee suggested banning the pair for two years. In his defence, he had been chosen for the England squad for Home Internationals and missed Chelsea's West Indies tour as a result, but did not get a game, which aggrieved him. Hudson felt that Ramsey never seemed comfortable with him or Osgood.

In late June the *News Of The World* advised that the 'pay rebellion by seven players' was over. Only Boyle and Cooke were yet to sign, and Sexton expected them to do so when they returned from holiday.

Season Overview 1971-72

League Appearances (inc sub) (top 11 players) – Hollins 42, Harris 41, Webb 41, Cooke 38, Hudson 36, Osgood 36, Dempsey 35, Bonetti 33, Houseman 27, Kember 27, Mulligan 27

League Goals (5+) – Osgood 18, Hollins 11, Baldwin 10
League Clean Sheets – *Home* 10. *Away* 5
Biggest League Win – 4-0 v Everton (H) 29/01/72
Worst League Defeat – 0-4 v West Bromwich Albion (A) 27/04/72
Final League position – 7th

League Record –
Home W12 D7 L2 F41 A20. *Away* W6 D5 L10 F17 A29. Pts 48

Hat-Tricks – (Four).
Osgood 5 vs Jeunesse Hautcharage (H) ECWC 1st Round 29/9/71;
Baldwin 3 vs Jeunesse Hautcharage (H) ECWC 1st Round 29/9/71;
Baldwin 3 vs Bolton Wanderers (A) League Cup 4th Round Replay 8/11/71;
Osgood 3 vs Jeunesse Hautcharage (A) ECWC 1st Round 15/9/71;

Sending Offs – None

Biggest Home League Crowd – 54,763 v Manchester United 18/08/71
Smallest Home League Crowd – 23,443 v Stoke City 24/04/72
Average Home League Crowd – 38,788

Cup Performances:
FA Cup 5th Round.
League Cup Beaten Finalists.
Europe 2nd Round.

Chelsea League Debuts – Chris Garland, Steve Kember, Tony Potrac, Steve Sherwood

Player Of The Year – David Webb

CHAPTER TWO
'We Are About To Turn Our Dreams Into Reality'

The Chelsea Football Book No.2, published in summer 1971, makes interesting reading, going into some detail about possible redevelopment plans, options and ideas. It refers to the possibility of the team playing at Wembley or White City for a season while Stamford Bridge was rebuilt. It did say, however, that the likely flow of funding probably meant it was more sensible to stay at Stamford Bridge and stagger the construction.

It talked grandly about an 65,000 all-seater stadium with double-decker East and West Stands and single decker North and South Stands, which could be converted to double-decker if the need for an 80.000 seater stadium arose. Chairman Brian Mears again made the point, rightly, that supporters would not see progress until the plans were in place and necessary permissions obtained. The point was also made about the waste of a stadium used so rarely, and the idea mooted of a seven-day-a-week social centre for fans.

The August 1971 the Manchester United programme gave an update on the Architects' work. A considerable amount of work had been done and information accumulated, and it was planned that the initial design ideas should be presented to the Chelsea board in September.

The responses from the questionnaire distributed in the March 1971 Leeds programme had been processed and analysed and provided much valuable input. Much of the detail with regard to questionnaire responses was shown in *The Chelsea Football Yearbook No.3* published in Summer 1972.

In order of preference, supporter preference of facility suggestions from the questionnaire were :-

1. covered terraces;
2. more low-cost bench seating;
3. restaurant facilities;
4. club car-parking facilities;
5. more licensed premises.

In addition, the club recognised the need for short-term improvements to current facilities. Work had progressed to improve the toilet facilities and 'had already been carried out in improving safety conditions in the ground'. Other supporter suggestions such as improved entrances and exits, the stands being closer to the pitch, an electronic scoreboard and social facilities would form part of the new stadium.

In terms of travel, 46% of respondents went to games by car, 37% by underground, 8% by bus, 8% on foot and 1% by coach. Car parking in any quantity was never a realistic option for the new stadium, given the lack of available land near Stamford Bridge.

At the end of January, the *Evening Standard* ran a major piece about the redevelopment of Stamford Bridge, the first time most supporters had heard anything specific. The plans were nothing if not ambitious. The club intended to start in April on the first stage of the rebuilding – a new East Stand costing £1,500,000. It would be a double decker, rising to around 120 feet – twice the height of the present stand – and apparently seating a massive 20,000, though this grandiose figure was reduced to 12,000 fairly quickly. Eventually cover would run all round the ground with even more seats. There would be improved dressing and medical rooms, social and refreshment facilities and probably an electric scoreboard. Negotiations were apparently in progress with London Transport for direct access to Fulham Broadway Underground station on match days, significantly reducing congestion on Fulham Road before and after games. The East Stand would probably be moved nearer the pitch and the more compact surroundings would in theory help to lift home performances. They reported that Chelsea already had the best away record in the country, winning 75 and losing 69 out of their last 189 away League games. If Chelsea could improve their home record, the thinking went, then real success was there for the taking. The Chronicle were very positive about the concepts, accepting that more detail would follow. 'With chairman Mears and his board looking ahead today, in such a big way, things look very encouraging at Chelsea for the future'.

Mears, clearly bursting with pride at the plans, stressed 'this is a team effort, a family affair. We want everyone from players to spectators to take part in giving Chelsea the best stadium in the country. We're looking beyond the Seventies into the Eighties ... Stamford Bridge was such an up-to-date ground when it was built in 1905. The playing achievements of the present players and the promise for the future encourage the club to build a stadium worthy of the team'. Redevelopment was certainly needed, though whether it had to be on that scale was arguable. Noticeably, there was no comment regarding how funds to pay for the East Stand, let alone the rest of the redevelopment, would be raised.

The club seemingly adopted a policy of gradual leaking of news about the redevelopment plans, in advance of the formal launch. In February 1972 the *Fulham Chronicle* reported that the club were planning to make an announcement with regard to details of the redevelopment on March 6th, though the announcement was subsequently delayed until May.

demolished and the remainder would temporarily house the press and directors. Crowd safety was a key main consideration. Mears emphasised that 'the Wheatley report on crowd safety has been carried out to the fullest in our plans and even advanced upon'. He stressed that planning permission was still required for the majority of the work. Hammersmith Council had given informal approval, but the finalising body was the Greater London Council, though no difficulty was expected. The possibility of an enhanced Fulham Broadway station linked to the proposed Holborn Line between Wimbledon and Hainault was mooted, though the Holborn Line never got off the drawing board.

In *The Bridge*, Colin Benson recounted how the architects foresaw an increase in female supporters and felt that, given the core support area was South West London and the Home Counties, where incomes were above average, the support would bear premium prices for a high level of comfort. This airy dismissal of the core working-class support pre-supposed, of course, that the team were successful and attractive to watch.

The estimated cost of redeveloping the whole ground was put at £6.25m at 1972 prices. They warned that building costs were rising by 10%-12% p.a. and if this trend continued, then assuming the stadium was finished in 1980 some 40%-50% should be added to the cost, taking it to c£9m. In the event, inflation in the mid-1970s was higher, much higher, and other economic and socio-political factors worked against the club.

The *Kensington Post* thought the design was 'wonderful for the fans and not unattractive for most residents', with careful thought for spectator comfort. Mears announced that the facilities would attract and be available to others for an all-the-year-round service, though went into no details on this. He stressed that 'the planning has been long and thorough because we wanted the end product to be exactly right'.

The *Sunday Express* included a lengthy Danny Blanchflower piece eulogising Mears and the Chelsea board for their vision. He thought there was a missed opportunity at Tottenham, who were refurbishing rather than redeveloping White Hart Lane. He introduced a note of caution, saying that 'some might think it a bit early to crow'. He pointed out that the East Stand was part of a vision to have a grandstand right round the Bridge, 'and might not the present dream also fail to turn the corner in the end?'.

In general, though, Blanchflower thought the Chelsea board deserved enormous credit. 'Of course there will be troubles. There will be obstacles and delays and compromises all along the way, but Brian Mears and his board are young enough to take on the doubts and risks of the future.

They played a 'poker game … setting up the club's future in terms of support and income and development schemes, and eventually they crashed the game…They have still got a couple of aces up their sleeve that it would be prudent not to mention but they have been assured of big money to pay for the scheme. Mears raised the first million and told Blanchflower 'I couldn't quite believe it'. Given the financial problems the stand caused, this seems, in retrospect, a bizarre comment.

'It is a breath-taking venture, the sort we dreamers about the game have been mumbling on about for years ... Brian Mears, you have given Chelsea fans everywhere a cause to be proud of. We hope that you make it and that we are around at the end of the Seventies to help you celebrate the big opening. You are a credit to Chelsea and a credit to the game'. In a cruel and savage irony, six years later Blanchflower became Chelsea manager, working for Mears, as the club struggled in a crippling morass largely caused by the self-same redevelopment.

Dalton, Barton and Company Ltd, were appointed financial consultants to the club and were listed in the programme as such in the early part of the 1972-73 season. They were a secondary bank, owned by controversial financier and property developer 'Black' Jack Delall. Secondary banks, common in the early 1970s, made loans to enterprises that 'normal' banks were reluctant to finance and charged accordingly high interest rates. For Chelsea to be involved with such a company indicates that raising funds was not as easy as first hoped. In the end, no money appears to have been forthcoming from that source, and their name disappeared from the programme.

Goal Magazine, essential reading for early 1970s teenage football supporters, joined in the hymns of praise. 'Stamford Bridge of the 1980s will have the best of everything, for club officials and the architects gleaned ideas from visiting or seeing plans for other grounds, here and abroad. Other clubs may have thought about these things ... Chelsea have taken the lead'. Any 1980s Sheddite would have to laugh on reading those fine words.

A well-respected London football voice expressed concerns. An *Evening Standard* piece by Jim Manning, headlined 'It's Cheers For Chelsea But What About The Town Hall?', thought it a missed opportunity to make the stadium multi-purpose, and urged 'Hammersmith Council to think how the stadium can be used more than 30-40 days a year'. He thought the local authority should insist on a wider sports centre and saw the project as a test of private enterprise and responsibility to the community.

Mears duly responded. 'We thought of this. We are employing our assets to the full and maybe what you say is not ruled out. It is all very complicated, and we cannot say what the final redevelopment of Stamford Bridge will be. We're thinking of starting with squash courts, (they pay for themselves in three years), but the first job is to plan the stadium as a whole and make sure we can finance it. This we have done. We're not jeopardising Chelsea's future with wild dreams'. These words were to come back to haunt the board.

Manning felt clubs should not bear all the risk, and that stadia and facilities should be shared with the local authority. He saw it as a risk for a football club to invest nearly £6,000,000 solely on football, and also felt that, with construction costs being notoriously hard to estimate, that the whole thing could cost £7,000,000. He also concluded that 'not every family would sell twelve freehold acres for only £500,000 to a couple of younger members of the family', highlighting the generosity of the Mears Trust, though it is worth reiterating the point that the sale was never actually made.

The Stamford Bridge land was valued at over £7m but, as *The Bridge* says, was 'hopelessly under-used'. The hugely ambitious plans ignored the reality of fluctuating on-pitch fortunes or wider trends in football and their impact on attendances. A rival consortium pointed out the possibility of falling gates, but this does not seem to have been actively considered by the Chelsea board in their decision making. They did not see the benefits of staging pop concerts or opening night clubs, restaurants etc. or a leisure centre, as alternative sources of income and a hedge against falling football income, as an alternative consortium had proposed.

In a 2015 article on the Chelsea web site, journalist and Chelsea supporter Giles Smith reflected how, as a boy, the 1972 plans for the stadium had dazzled him with its futuristic look and scope and it is undoubtedly true that the plans looked impressive to supporters, who assumed that the club had robust financial backing in place for the redevelopment.

Winning the FA Cup and Cup-Winner's Cup had given Mears the confidence to think expansively. Using a firm of architects who were experienced in major public housing projects but had no previous football stadium experience was certainly a bold move. Using a contract model that seemingly put the impact of cost and time over-runs primarily on the club and not the contractors was also bold. Or possibly reckless. The blithe assumption that the economy would be stable and that the team would continue to win trophies was, at best, naïve. At worst, it was utterly foolhardy.

Looking back, it was never clear where the funds were going to come from to allow such ambitious plans to happen. Architecturally the redevelopment plans looked superb, but what was missing was a cold, hard assessment of the potential downsides.

The stated temporary capacity of 52,000, only 8,000 below the 60,000 capacity when the North and East Stands were open, seemed wildly optimistic given the loss of seats and enclosure spaces, though 1,000 seats had been installed in the lower tier of the North Stand. In addition, the building work limited entrances and, inevitably, introduced an element of chaos. As events soon proved, this was a serious misjudgement by the club.

CHAPTER THREE
1972–73 – Three Sides, Team Slides

Pre-Season

Unlike the previous two close-seasons, the Chelsea squad had little to celebrate in Summer 1972. The previous season had feebly fizzled out, manager Dave Sexton and his squad having much to ponder on their return to training. The season just ended produced no trophies, failure in three cup competitions, the lowest League position for five years, no European football to look forward to and a feeling that the upwards on-pitch trajectory of the club had stalled.

Sexton had spent no significant sums since the purchases of Steve Kember and Chris Garland the previous September. Nor had he moved on any of the first-team squad since the transfer deadline in March. Much of the nucleus of the squad – Peter Bonetti, Ron Harris, Eddie McCreadie, Marvin Hinton, John Boyle, John Hollins, Peter Osgood, Tommy Baldwin, Charlie Cooke, Peter Houseman – had been squad members when he took over in October 1967. David Webb, John Dempsey and Ian Hutchinson arrived within eighteen months, Paddy Mulligan and John Phillips a year or so later, Alan Hudson emerged from the youth set-up in 1969. Only Garland and Kember were relatively new. No defender had been bought since Mulligan in October 1969, no centre-back since Dempsey nine months before that.

No young player had established themselves in the first-team, apart from Hudson, since the emergence of Osgood and Boyle in 1965, though there were high hopes that right-back Gary Locke and centre-half Micky Droy would be challenging hard for a regular place very soon, and that wingers Ian Britton and Mike Brolly, midfielder Tony Potrac and forward Peter Feely would soon be able to step up from the reserves. There were some very promising youngsters who would hopefully be ready in a year or two – midfielders Ray Wilkins and Garry Stanley, full-backs Graham Wilkins (who had recently signed professional terms) and John Sparrow and striker Steve Finnieston prominent amongst them but, in retrospect, the squad required refreshment, especially at the back and up front. Loyalty to players was all very well, but the team had shown itself lacking and, without new blood, was unlikely to improve. The injury-prone McCreadie had signed a four-year contract, taking him up to the age of thirty-six. Tony Potrac, prolific in the post-season tour of Barbados, was sent on loan to Notts County, but returned to Chelsea before the season started.

Statements by chairman Brian Mears, regarding the stadium redevelopment not affecting funds available to the manager available for players, were welcomed by supporters and unchallenged by the press, but if Chelsea were going to become a real force in the land, challenging for the title, now was the time to invest, bringing in a couple of top players to strengthen the squad. This was not done which, in hindsight, begs questions about the priorities, and financial liquidity, of the club that summer.

That pre-season Chelsea only had three friendly matches, one in France and two in Holland. After a 3-0 defeat at St Etienne, results improved with a comfortable 3-0 win at Den Bosch and a 2-2 draw with Go Ahead Eagles. Sexton fielded strong teams in each game, with no youngsters being blooded. Evidently the manager was planning to begin the serious business with his tried and trusted players, despite them being found wanting the previous season. The fixture list had thrown up as opening game what would normally have been an intriguing fixture, a home game against fierce rivals Leeds United. This season the game also became a test of the temporary stadium arrangements and the reduced capacity. It was to be a test that Chelsea were going to fail. Badly.

In the three weeks after Leeds were games against champions Derby County, Liverpool, Manchester City, Manchester United and Arsenal, so it was certainly a fierce start to the new campaign, and Chelsea would need to fire on all cylinders.

Seemingly inevitably, pre-season was disrupted by illness and injury. Ian Hutchinson, who had had a wretched time with injury for eighteen months, would hopefully be fit early in the season. He lost 5lb in three days, 'toughening up' at an RAF rehabilitation centre. Tommy Baldwin had been isolated at home for twelve days with jaundice but had relapsed so had to stay in bed for another two weeks. Sexton explained to the *Daily Mirror* 'he is not at all well and may have to go into hospital'. Hollins, who damaged a knee on the tour of Barbados, was expected to be match-fit for the start of the season. It was also fervently hoped that McCreadie would have a long injury-free run.

In *Chelsea – The Real Story* Mears recounted how Hudson had returned to pre-season training overweight, to the fury of Sexton. Having taken over *Evening Standard* columnist duties from Harris, in an early August piece Hudson said he was feeling the benefit of training and sleeping. The squad had spent the last week at a training camp in Germany, training three times a day and he thought Chelsea must be the fittest team in the League – there was no Swedish disco that summer.

Hudson was working with Sexton on his shooting, the manager stressing that timing and making the connection were more important than power. He had bet Osgood five pounds that he would score ten League goals that season, a challenge given he scored but three the previous season, compared with eleven by Hollins. Mortified at the thought he might miss the 1974 World Cup, Hudson was hugely frustrated with the two-year England ban given to him and Colin Todd for missing the Under-23 tour. Sexton agreed to fight the FA on his behalf.

The *Evening Standard*, in their season preview, listed youngsters Steve Sherwood, Keith Lawrence, Britton, Stanley, Locke, Feely and Potrac as squad members, but it remained to be seen how many, if any, made the breakthrough that season. Sexton claimed 'we've prepared better than ever for the start of a season' and Peter Bonetti argued that he fancied their chances because they could afford to concentrate on the League without too many outside commitments, which was a positive way of coping without European football.

During the East Stand rebuilding, scheduled to take one year, the Stamford Bridge dressing rooms were to be 'luxury' Portakabins (arguably an oxymoron) costing £30,000 and situated near the club offices near the corner of The Shed and where the East Stand had been. To get onto the pitch the players had to walk 75 yards through a building site and down a temporary entrance near the corner of The Shed. They had to pass through ticket-holders heading towards the North Stand, which had been re-named the North-East Enclosure. Half of that architectural oddity had been demolished to make way for the building work, though 1,000 seats had been installed in the lower tier (the upper tier remained closed).

Terrace admission prices rose from 30p to 40p, a very steep rise of 33% at a time of gathering economic gloom. The increase, affecting all League clubs, was made at the Football League annual meeting in June - due to the rebuilding, it was apparently not Chelsea's original intention to increase prices.

With the East Stand gone, this brought the number of seats at Stamford Bridge to around 10,500, with 1,000 in the North-East Enclosure, 6,163 in the West Stand and 3,360 in the West Stand benches. All season-tickets in the North-East Enclosure and West Stand had been sold, and the only seats on general sale were the West Stand benches. The club advised season-ticket holders that one on four would not get their own seat for cup-ties as 25% of seats were designated to the away club, this being done on a rota basis. They would have to sit in the West Stand benches instead, open to the elements.

North-East Enclosure lower tier ticket holders were told to walk along the touchline to reach their seats, were told to be arrive at least fifteen minutes before kick-off, to allow the players to reach the pitch unobstructed, and warned that latecomers may not be admitted. Supporter David Gray, who sat there, remembers they walked past the Portakabin changing rooms then alongside the pitch by the dug-outs. Secretary Tony Green proclaimed that 'anyone who does arrive late will not be let in'. Gray also recalls that the view was nowhere near as good as from the upper tier.

Stamford Bridge looked lop-sided with three sides of stand or terrace and one a building site. In *The Working Man's Ballet* Hudson claimed he felt the dismantling of the East Stand was symbolic of the dismantling of the cup-winning side and, indeed, he has a point. By the time the new stand finally opened the team looked very different and the glory days of 1970 and 1971 seemed a very long way off.

Logic would surely have dictated a home friendly to test the temporary arrangements, or at the very least a discussion with the Football League about a less high-profile game to start. In 1965/66 Chelsea managed to get their less attractive games played earlier in the season as the West Stand was being rebuilt, so surely a request for the likes of Stoke City or Norwich City as an opening fixture could have been heeded.

Chelsea took a more bullish, and possibly foolhardy, approach. Four days before the Leeds game Green told the *Daily Mirror* 'to begin with I thought we could have done with an easier game. But now we feel that this will be the supreme test of our administration. This will be the guideline to future arrangements. They won't come any bigger than this'. Indeed. It almost beggars belief that the club were keen for one of the biggest games of the season to be the test for both the reduced capacity of 52,000 and the new entrance arrangements.

He optimistically claimed 'our biggest headache will be getting the public used to new surroundings'. Being the first game of the season, in those pre-internet days there were very limited opportunities to communicate new arrangements to supporters, except through the pages of newspapers, so many were unaware what to expect. Choosing not to make the game all-ticket may have simplified administration leading up to the game but helped cause total chaos on match day. Chelsea's programme sales were amazingly high but, obviously, they were not much use in giving information about the opening game.

August 1972

Ian Hutchinson and John Boyle were injured but, from the players available, the *Daily Mail* saw two positions in the team against Leeds as uncertain. The more-defensive Ron Harris or the more-adventurous Paddy Mulligan at right-back and mercurial Charlie Cooke or dependable Peter Houseman on the wing. Eddie McCreadie had taken over as team captain from John Hollins over the summer. In the event, Harris and Cooke were chosen, the team lining up against Leeds as follows :- *Bonetti; Harris, Dempsey, Webb, McCreadie; Hollins, Kember, Hudson; Garland, Osgood, Cooke*.

Before the game, Leeds boss Don Revie claimed 'there is too much respect between our teams to turn on the magic', and the thousands travelling to Stamford Bridge for the biggest game of the day no doubt anticipated a highly physical encounter as old feuds were rekindled.

In the match programme, readers received a 'Special New Season's

Welcome from The Chairman'. The East Stand had gone, a start had been made towards 'realising the dream' and, 'stage by stage, we can look forward to the time when all phases of this mammoth rebuilding programme are completed, and the home of Chelsea Football Club takes its place among the very finest to be found anywhere in the game. Inevitably, with a project of this size, there must be inconvenience to everyone while it is being carried out. For this we apologize...but not for the progress which it signifies. Frankly, I have never been so happy to see Stamford Bridge in such a mess, and I hope you will bear with us and be prepared to share our problems during the rebuilding period, particularly this season ... With two Cup triumphs and a League Cup Final in the past three seasons, they have put us among the most successful modern clubs ... I wish Dave Sexton and our Players and Staff good luck in their efforts to bring further honours to Chelsea ... helped by your maximum vocal support from the three sides at present in use at Stamford Bridge'. Inconvenience was inevitable, chaos was not.

That Leeds game is remembered for a number of reasons. On the pitch, it was a great afternoon for Chelsea. They were on top from the start and the supremacy increased when Leeds striker Mick Jones went off injured after twenty minutes. Four minutes later Leeds goalkeeper David Harvey was concussed after a heavy challenge and had to go off, with winger Peter Lorimer going in goal, leaving them down to ten men. Chelsea took full advantage, in the end running out 4-0 winners, with Peter Osgood scoring right on half-time, Chris Garland netting a pair and Cooke also scoring. Chelsea were highly impressive, though the injuries Leeds suffered had a significant impact and, as supporter Geoff Kimber puts it 'this was a totally misleading victory'. Still, so far, so good. On the pitch.

Off the pitch it was a different matter. Work had continued right up to the day of the game to make the stadium ready for the arrival of 50,000+ spectators, but almost everything that could go wrong did.

Hours before kick-off it was clear a massive crowd could be expected. The Fulham Road became rammed and it was clear that the gates would have to be locked. A 52,000 capacity had been set, but more got in because it took twenty minutes to close the gates after secretary Tony Green gave the order at 2.10pm, with the ground jammed and Fulham Road in chaos. He later told the *Evening Standard* 'If the orders had been carried out earlier there would have been no problems. The crowd would then have been around 45,000, which we will probably make a limit while rebuilding is being done. I am responsible for deciding when to close the gates in conjunction with the police. It is their responsibility to close the gates and they do it by radio to the mounted policemen at all gates. There was obviously a breakdown in communications, and it all reflects back at the club'. The mounted police were working on the Fulham Road itself, directing the milling and increasingly frantic crowd, and possibly could not get through the masses behind them for some minutes.

The official gate was 51,102, although some of the crowd got into the ground by storming the gates, the only reason Dempsey and Webb were able to get into the stadium, and gate-stormers were excluded from that figure. An estimated 12,000 were locked out, there were surges, fights and several arrests outside, with some would-be spectators taken to hospital, hurt in the crush. Leeds players had to battle their way through the crowd in the concourse. Space for entering the stadium was inevitably limited by the building work and, entirely predictably, confusion arose from spectators not knowing where to go. Locked-out, crushed or unable-to-see supporters must have read the programmes reference to 'inconvenience' with strong reactions.

The crush and scenes of disorder outside were bad enough, but packed terracing meant severe spectator overcrowding. Supporter Brian Gaches remembers getting to Stamford Bridge two hours before kick-off and only just managing to squeeze into The Shed. He calls it 'the biggest and worst crowd crush I've ever experienced at Stamford Bridge'. The *Daily Telegraph* reported that a Shed End crash barrier buckled, eight injured supporters were taken to hospital and hundreds of youngsters surged out of The Shed terracing onto the greyhound track to avoid the crush. Soon, three sides of that track were packed with young fans. Further pitch invasions followed. Watching highlights from *The Big Match* 47 years later, what stands out is the youth of the vast majority of the invaders. These were boys, early teens and younger, wearing a fine array of fashionable-in-summer-1972 jumbo collared shirts and tank tops. What they obviously were not was an organised gang of hooligans.

A presumably-chastened Green told the *Evening Standard* 'we allowed some of the latecomers on to the greyhound track and when the youngsters saw this, they surged on in the hope of having a better view...we may decide now to put a wire fence around the terracing at both ends'. He said that all-ticket matches for big games would be discussed by the Chelsea board but felt such a step was not likely. 'It may have been a good thing to have Leeds and I hope we have learnt the lesson. We might have been complacent otherwise and been in trouble later on'. This explanation would not have been much consolation to the injured, those who could not get into the stadium, those who got in but could not see and the Police and St Johns Ambulance staff having to deal with problems not of their making. As supporter Brian Gaches says 'somehow disaster was averted that day, more by luck than planning. I always felt it was fortunate Chelsea were fantastic on the pitch thereby avoiding any crowd trouble in the ground, as any surges could easily have led to a Heysel type situation'.

The club's immediate reaction was to blame the young supporters for invading the pitch, and threaten to remove the junior discount, rather than take a long hard look at themselves and the decisions they made. This blinkered inability to take responsibility for their decisions was hardly unique in football. Why blame youngsters many of whom clearly just tried to avoid getting crushed, and only later saw an opportunity to celebrate goals by invading the pitch?

Sensing a shoal of bad publicity about to break, and under severe pressure, the board held an urgent meeting and cut the capacity to 45,000 for the rest for the season, claiming this could cost the club £60,000 (or £100,000 or even £200,000, depending on which paper you read). This assumed, of course, that over 45,000 supporters wanted to see a game. *The Sun* starkly informed its 4.2 million readers that 'Chelsea spent a nightmare 90 minutes on Saturday facing a major Ibrox-type crowd disaster' and, frankly, that comment does not seem very wide of the mark.

Mears, to his great credit, did not hide his concern, stating he was 'worried sick' during the pitch invasions and telling the *Daily Mail* 'we know it could have been a disaster. We're only thankful we saw all the problems come to a head early without a catastrophe. We can put them right ... I nearly died when some fans got up on an excavator on the building site. They got it moving and for a minute it looked as though they would smash straight through the fence into the backs of Revie and Sexton sitting on the touchline'. That supporters were able to approach, climb into, turn on and operate an excavator utterly beggars belief and is indicative of the shambolic, amateurish approach to supporter safety that day.

Mears told the *Daily Telegraph* 'we have got to keep spectators off the tracks surrounding the pitch...We must have more police for big matches ... The club may have to look at making attractive games all-ticket and whether to dig moats or erect wire fences'. With a home game against Liverpool, another game with a tradition of high crowds, ten days away, the Chelsea chairman had to act to prevent any possible recurrence. 'We shall start with the Liverpool match and shall be meeting our architects and the police to discuss other measures being taken'.

Mears explained 'although we are now handicapped by the building strike – Stamford Bridge was being picketed while we held the board meeting – our own maintenance staff will do all that is possible in time for the Liverpool game'. He again threatened to charge youngsters full admission if they invaded the pitch again, despite the clear fact that many were, at least initially, simply trying to avoid the crush.

After the utter fiasco of the Leeds game, the club must have been highly relieved that the next two games were away from home. A visit to Filbert Street to meet a Leicester City side containing old-boys Keith Weller and Alan Birchenall resulted in a 1-1 draw, Garland grabbing a deserved equaliser. Derby County manager Brian Clough opined 'I saw Chelsea at Leicester ... and they confirmed they have the greatest depth of talent in the country'.

The strong start to the season continued when, three days later, the champions were defeated 2-1 at the Baseball Ground, Harris getting a rare goal, only his eighth in 363 League games. Garland hit his fourth in three games, raising hopes that his partnership with Osgood was blossoming. Sexton praised Garland's sharpness, and the forward pointed out he was playing in a different role, making diagonal runs from the right 'and it seems to be paying off', though he joined Hudson as a non-winger occasionally forced to play wide.

The *Daily Mail* got a bit carried away, describing 'Chelsea taking a famous victory by virtue of their superlative range of skills ... Chelsea are on their way...perhaps to the title'. The *Sunday People*, under a 'Chelsea Look Like Champs' headline, suggested 'many people, including myself, see them as possible champions'. They described the midfield of Hudson, Hollins and Kember as a mix of muscle and magic. On his leading scorer, Sexton observed 'I am glad to see he is settling down so quickly'. He had been at the club eleven months, so this is a slightly strange claim. Garland himself was very happy. 'I'm enjoying myself and getting good support from the players around me. I hope I'm in the side to stay'. One black spot was the booking of Osgood for sarcastically applauding a free-kick. Sexton must have been massively frustrated that his star player could not control his emotions, even when the team were doing well.

Talking to the *Daily Mail*, Micky Droy said he was ready to finish with his wild youth and stake a claim for football stardom. The biggest professional in League football, injury to Dempsey meant he was plunged into the defence for the Derby game, performing admirably. 'I'm a big lad and I never had to be afraid of anyone, so I was a bit of a rebel, a bit wild'. Now 21, he had played in the Islington Schools team with Arsenal hero Charlie George.

A couple of squad players were unhappy about being omitted from the team, inevitable when experienced professionals were forced to play in the reserves. Paddy Mulligan was very disappointed to be left out against Leeds. Frustrated, he talked to Sexton about his future, though did not ask for a transfer. When he did get in the side, at the end of the month, he told the *Evening Standard* 'it is difficult to win selection because there is such a strong squad at Chelsea. I'm hoping to hold onto my place until the end of the season'. Reserve goalkeeper John Phillips made a transfer request as he was fed up with reserve football after only 30 first-team appearances in two years.

Despite the off-pitch chaos surrounding the Leeds game, Jeff Powell of the *Daily Mail* wrote an astonishingly laudatory feature on 'The M Factor' – the mutual admiration between Mears and Sexton. 'Chelsea are striving to build a club to totally dominate British football on a foundation of close and permanent co-operation between the two. They hope to wield the stadium and team of the future into an all-powerful force. With one goldmine of a stand pulled down and building work in progress it is costing them another £100,000 in lost customers. 'There is speculation that Chelsea have made Sexton the game's best-paid and most secure manager. If that is so, he will earn not less than £15,000 a year for a decade – by which time Chelsea's destiny will have been well and truly decided'.

Sexton observed 'this club is involved in heavy capital outlay on the ground. I have to consider that and my own balance of accounts in the transfer market when I go for a player'. Powell felt 'Sexton and Mears will look to most punters like a win double for years to come'. Whether the old East Stand was really a goldmine, where the supposed £100,000 in lost revenues came from and how Sexton was supposed to build a wonder-team while balancing the books were questions not asked.

Talk of the title was obviously massively premature, though Hudson optimistically stated 'we can win the title, don't worry', but the team had made what the *Fulham Chronicle* called a 'remarkable, totally untypical, start of the season success story by Chelsea'.

In the Liverpool programme, editor Albert Sewell said the club had received 200 letters of complaint about Leeds incidents. He reiterated that the club view in the summer was that it might be better to meet all the difficulties at the start rather than be lulled through an "easy" opening and come to the major problems later, so did not try to start with an easier fixture. Much of the preparatory work was done by club maintenance staff, due to the builders strike.

The turnstiles against Liverpool opened three hours before kick-off. All very well, but what were supporters supposed to do, especially as the catering facilities were so inadequate? The programme was good, but not that good. The strong start to the season did not last, Liverpool winning 2-1. The visitors took a two-goal lead inside fifteen minutes, Garland pulled one back, but they held on in an exciting game. Droy went off injured. With Dempsey also out, and Hinton out of favour in the reserves, this presented a significant centre-back selection problem for Sexton.

The games came thick and fast and three days later Osgood was back on the scoresheet as Chelsea quickly recovered from the Liverpool setback with a 2-1 win over Manchester City. Houseman came on as substitute for a disappointing Cooke, who had not started the season well, and scored a tremendous late volleyed second goal enjoyed by viewers on *The Big Match*.

In a *Sunday People* interview team captain Eddie McCreadie opened out fascinatingly. 'I've just emerged from two years in hell, but I think I've come out a wiser and better person. I've still got my pride, but I've lost my vanity'. They felt that anyone still believing that old-fashioned idea that all footballers are thickheads who need help to lace their boots could do worse than listen to McCreadie. He had written twenty poems in an exercise book, written at the depths of a depression caused by an ankle injury and other mishaps that kept him out of football for almost two years. He had begun to think he might never play again and felt clubs should have a psychiatrist to help players through times of stress. Now he had his place at left-back back and had been made captain – at 32. Jimmy Gabriel of Southampton had told him writing poetry helped clear his mind.

McCreadie praised Hudson 'one of the most perfect players I've ever seen', Osgood, Kember '(who is) going to be the Billy Bremner of English football' and Garland. On a roll, he told the *Evening Standard* 'I love being captain. I enjoy the responsibility ... I find it's an easy job. It's a team of captains really. I just try and encourage them, and they respond'. Certainly, he was a highly respected player who showed every sign of developing into a very proficient coach. That September he was awarded his full FA coaching certificate.

Ian Hutchinson had been told he could start tackling and training again with the first-team squad after a hugely frustrating eighteen months out and John Boyle had the plaster removed from his injured leg, so the squad would hopefully soon be even stronger. At the end of the month promising young midfielder Bobby Brown signed as a professional.

The month was rounded off with a trip to Old Trafford where Chelsea competed well, achieved a 0-0 draw and ended the month in a creditable fifth place.

1st	Arsenal	p6	10pts
2nd	Everton	p6	9pts
3rd	Tottenham Hotspur	p6	9pts
4th	Liverpool	p6	9pts
5th	**Chelsea**	**p6**	**8pts**
6th	Ipswich Town	p6	8pts
7th	Norwich City	p6	8pts

September 1972

Of real concern to the Chelsea hierarchy was the fall-off in crowds after the Leeds debacle. Under a 'Chelsea woo the missing fans' headline, the *Daily Mirror* analysed why crowds had fallen from 51,100 against Leeds to 35,700 against Liverpool and 30,800 against Manchester City. 'Chelsea suspect they have been deserted by thousands who fear a repeat of the chaotic crowd scenes when they met Leeds on the opening day of the season'. The stay-away support hit the club firmly in the pocket. If the not-unreasonable assumption is that the crowd for each of those two games was 10,000 below that anticipated, at 40p a head that would be £8,000 lost revenue already. 'The situation is worrying Chelsea as they work to overcome the unavoidable inconvenience caused by a bold and worthwhile plan to create a super stadium'.

Concerned chairman Brian Mears told them 'I think we have got to accept that we are suffering a backlash from the Leeds match, when fans spilled onto the running track. Various things went wrong that day, and we are having to learn as we go along. We have taken very definite steps to make life more comfortable for our supporters at a time when they are having to put up with a lot. We saw the need to cut the capacity to 45,000 for the time being - there are now ways we can regulate the flow of people into the ground. I'm confident that what happened at the Leeds game won't occur again. I think that if our supporters understand this then attendances will improve. We certainly need them to improve. Chelsea aren't the sort of club who can get by without revenue. If our supporters can only bear with us for a while we can get through this difficult period'.

Chelsea had large overheads, apart from the massive redevelopment investment, and were relying on a successful team to help maintain stability money-wise. Concern was increased by the knowledge that they had already played three of their most attractive home fixtures. Revenue was well down, and a real test would be their next home game, the London derby against West Ham. More than one rival club, while admiring the boldness of Chelsea's look-ahead redevelopment policy, had apparently already doubted the wisdom of it. *The Daily Mirror* felt 'it would be sad if (the) gamble failed because of inadequate support at a difficult time'.

The club did not try three-year season-tickets, a bond scheme, or similar plans, let alone sell additional shares in the club or attract new board members. Nor did the board pump their own assets into the club. Directors continued to rely on the bank and a hoped-for trading surplus fuelled by transfer profits, plus the Chelsea Pools and Golden Goals income, which was never going to be game-changing. This meant the board retained total control of the club, but at the expense of much-needed finance. A more visionary board may have taken a different approach.

Three days after visiting Old Trafford came a trip to Highbury, to meet table-topping Arsenal. Alan Hudson was injured, a blow, so wide-men Cooke and Houseman played in the same side for the first time that season. Cooke gave Chelsea the lead after half-an-hour. Arsenal equalised through a David Webb own-goal, but Chelsea held on for a well-earned point.

What that game is remembered for, though, is fifteen minutes of madness for which the talented but truculent Charlie George, in dispute with his club and sulking on the bench, was the catalyst. Coming on after 75 minutes of a relatively clean game, he kicked Steve Kember, retaliated when Kember kicked him back then trod on Ron Harris. George and Kember were booked, Harris went to hospital for a chest x-ray. Kember's 'Charlie seems to go beserk' comment summed it up. To be in fifth place, two points off the lead, given the highly challenging opening seven games boded well for the season to come. Consistency had not been a trait of Chelsea's recent seasons and it was hoped that this marked a new dawn.

The midweek trip to Southend for a League Cup-tie should have been straightforward but, in the event, it was a frenetic game that Chelsea were very pleased to escape with a 1-0 victory. Garland scored after fifteen minutes but Chelsea spent the second-half hanging on. The *Daily Mail* phrase 'shaken to the core of their King's Road elegance' said it all.

Southend centre-forward Bill Garner, recognised as excellent in the air but arguably less so on the ground, had scored 47 goals in 100 games for The Shrimpers. He had been watched by Sexton in August but was set to join West Ham for £100,000, though Ipswich, Coventry, Tottenham, Crystal Palace and West Bromwich were also interested. It had been decided by Southend that he would not move until after the Chelsea game. An impressed Sexton drove back to Southend early on the Thursday, talked to Garner and pushed the £100,000 deal through.

Sexton beamed 'I first became interested in him towards the end of last season. It wasn't until Wednesday night that I was able to get permission to offer Southend the money they were asking'. Garner thought it was 'West Ham for me ... I was stunned when I got to the club and found Dave Sexton in the office'. Ron Greenwood, West Ham manager, was apparently fuming after losing the player. The *Daily Mirror* 'Hammers Gazumped' headline hid a sharp piece of business by Sexton. Again, though, a forward had been signed who had no top-flight experience. He did, however, give Sexton options and was obvious cover for Hutchinson. Southend were interested in taking transfer-listed forward Peter Feely on loan as part of the deal, but that did not materialise.

After stealing the player from under West Ham's nose, the fact that The Hammers were visiting Stamford Bridge two days later added even more spice to the London derby. Only 34,392 turned up, compared with 45,137 the previous season, more evidence of a significant fall in attendances.

Garner started on the bench. Chelsea ran out confidently against a team seven places below them in the table but trooped off at the final whistle well beaten, 3-1. The defence had a nightmare, Webb admitting it was his worst performance since the 1970 FA Cup Final. 'Lately I've been below form. And I'm not happy'. Hudson went off with a badly damaged ankle, Garner making his debut out of position on the left-wing. He did not have an auspicious debut. He, Osgood and Webb got in each other's way for high balls, he missed two chances and injured an ankle near the end. Garland's goal was no consolation. The *Daily Telegraph*, concerned about the defence, archly observed 'in this context the £100,000 purchase of Garner seemed as extravagant as a man buying a Persian carpet when the slates were off the roof'.

That month, Tottenham announced a profit of £223,000, thanks largely to their European and League Cup exploits. They had a war chest available should they need to buy players. Having bought Garner, it was evident Dave Sexton had no such funds available. Manchester United announced a loss of £250,000, unthinkable at Chelsea, due primarily to the signings of Ian Moore and Martin Buchan. The thought of a Buchan/Webb centre-back partnership was certainly an attractive one, but Chelsea never expressed any interest when he moved from Aberdeen in February 1972.

Having a free midweek due to failing to qualify for Europe, Chelsea's chastened squad flew off to West Germany for a friendly against Fortuna Dusseldorf. A 0-0 draw was not a bad result, and Feely made a rare appearance, but Chelsea somehow managed to suffer five more injuries, with Osgood and Houseman both out for the Saturday. Add in Garner with his ankle in plaster, the jaundice-ridden Baldwin, injuries to Hudson, Cooke and Hinton, the not-yet-fit Hutchinson and Dempsey's slow return to fitness and Sexton was struggling to get a decent team out.

For the Saturday game at Sheffield United, Sexton wryly observed 'it's not so much who was injured but who was fit'. Brian Bason, a seventeen-year-old winger who had only recently signed a professional contract, was given his debut, unable to play in Dusseldorf as a special license was required for a junior to play abroad. Feely, who the club were happy to let go ten days earlier, wore the number nine shirt. Garland was the latest out-of-position left-winger. It was very much a patched-up team and, inevitably, they struggled. Tony Currie dominated the game , United took a 2-0 lead inside twenty minutes. Garland pulled one back and Chelsea fought hard but could not equalise. So the unbeaten away record had gone, though the press reaction was that Chelsea had battled hard and Bason did well on his debut.

Sexton had a week to try and get as many of the walking wounded on the pitch as possible against second-placed Ipswich, but two defeats had taken the steam out the start to the season and Chelsea had slipped to tenth in the table. Sexton bit one bullet and dropped the out-of-form Webb. In the *Daily Mail*, under a 'My Worst Week' back-page headline, the defender said 'There's no sour grapes from me. I know I've been out of form'. Concussed in the last game against Sheffield United, his wife Jackie had been rushed to hospital with appendicitis, there were problems buying his new house, his friend, Speedway rider Barry Briggs, had crashed the previous week and, to top it all, he was taking delivery of a horse but would not have anywhere to stable it.

Osgood and Cooke returned, Bason dropping out. Osgood and Feely, in his last first-team game, scored in a surprisingly easy win with 'silence on the terraces' according to the *News Of The World*.

Many supporters assumed that the funds to pay for Garner had come from cash in the bank, and it would not be necessary to raise funds to pay for him. It was therefore something of a shock to Chelsea supporters when the following week Mulligan (£75,000) and, twenty-four hours later, Cooke (£85,000), were both sold to Crystal Palace. Mulligan had won back his place in the side but with highly promising Gary Locke ready for the first-team Sexton saw him as dispensable, though an unnamed team-mate called him 'the best attacking right-back in Britain' and the *Daily Mail* reported that some players were 'stunned'. Cooke, a real crowd favourite, was the first of the trophy-winning 'superstars' to leave. His crowd-pleasing ability, on his day, was unquestioned but he had not been at his best that season and, with Garland and Houseman operating wide, Sexton saw the chance to cash in. Cooke and Mulligan realised it was time to go when Chelsea accepted Palace's offers, but neither agitated for a move.

Mulligan told the *Irish Examiner* in 2015 that he had always harboured a suspicion that Sexton didn't really fancy him, but he later regretted leaving. This was a player generally recognised to have had a good previous season and described as 'a bit of a revelation' by defensive colleague David Webb. Cooke had grown tired of playing wide and, at 31, wanted to operate in the middle where he felt he was best suited to play. Interviewed by *Time Out* in 2007, Cooke admitted that he 'allowed the headlines about my being the team schemer and midfield general to get into my head, with the result that I ignored finishing'. He was never a prolific scorer, but his ability to beat a man, to do the unexpected, was lost and not replaced.

The question arises as to why if Sexton sought to play with two wingers, and did not think Bason or Britton were ready, he did not either keep Cooke or buy one, rather than sticking Garland or, worse, wasting Hudson, out there. Selling Cooke only increased the manager's reliance on using Hudson wide. Sexton made £60,000 profit from the deals involving Garner, Mulligan and Cooke so, in theory, money was available.

Another week for the injured to recuperate and a trip to Coventry City. Locke, Webb, Garner and Houseman came in, so a semblance of a first-choice team was on the field, though lynch-pin Hudson was still missing.

Garner scored his first Chelsea goal and, according to the *Daily Mirror* 'showed the type of talents and skills which threaten to cause havoc with defences in top-grade soccer'. They felt he was (unsurprisingly) good in the air, but, less predictably, showed tremendous ball control and speed. He pulled a hamstring in the second-half and was replaced by Marvin Hinton. Sexton enthused 'I was extremely pleased with the way Garner played. He led the forward line well and allowed Osgood to stay back and provide the touches which is his best role. It also enabled us to play with Garland and Houseman on the wings and this type of formation certainly caused havoc'. Houseman, and a Jeff Blockley own-goal were the other scorers in a comfortable victory. The *Daily Telegraph*, getting a bit carried away, referred to their 'wonderful depth of talent despite selling Mulligan and Cooke and missing Hudson'. They felt Chelsea were 'sound at the back, fluent in midfield and thrustful up front'. If only.

Palace, not content with picking up Mulligan and Cooke, were also interested in buying John Boyle, though the move never came to anything. Boyle, like Marvin Hinton, was a loyal squad member whose first-team prospects were limited. He had recovered from long-term injury but was likely to be facing a season of mainly reserve-team football. Apart from Garner, the only player Chelsea were rumoured to be after was Derby full-back John Robson, fancied by Sexton for a long time and recently dropped. Like so many transfer stories, this one went nowhere, and the player signed for Aston Villa the following month.

Stoke expressed an interest in taking reserve goalkeeper John Phillips as cover for Gordon Banks but did not take the matter further. At the end of September, it was happily reported that Hutchinson had played forty-five minutes in the reserves against Swansea. Although Sexton had bought Garner, there was a definite feeling that a match-fit Hutchinson would make Osgood more effective and strengthen the team. Forward Tommy Ord signed as a professional from Athenian League amateurs Erith & Belvedere, following Feely as a non-league signing hoping to follow in the footsteps of Ian Hutchinson.

The month ended with Chelsea back up to sixth, three points behind leaders Liverpool and Arsenal. A decent run in a relatively easy (on paper) October and Chelsea might live up to those pre-season predictions and challenge for the title.

1st	Liverpool	p11	16pts
2nd	Arsenal	p12	16pts
3rd	Everton	p11	15pts
4th	Tottenham Hotspur	p11	14pts
5th	Wolverhampton W.	p11	14pts
6th	**Chelsea**	**p11**	**13pts**
7th	Leeds United	p11	13pts

October 1972

After the previous season's failure at the last hurdle, Chelsea could have done without an away League Cup-tie at champions Derby County, languishing in fourteenth place but still a formidable opponent. Bill Garner was cup-tied, shades of Steve Kember the previous season, so David Webb was forced to play as emergency striker. Webb wore the No.10 shirt at Derby so he only needed No.11 for the full set at Chelsea, a demonstration of his astonishing utility. Worryingly, he was the seventh different No. 10 in the first twelve games that season, showing how hard Sexton was finding it to pick a settled side. In all, an alarming twelve different men wore that shirt that season.

Chelsea's rearguard action in an 'ugly, sterile' 0-0 draw was much lauded and showed a real spirit and commitment to the cause. Peter Bonetti was accidentally kicked in the head by centre-forward John

O'Hare and required three stitches. The goalkeeper was sometimes too brave for his own good.

A trip to lowly Birmingham three days later was a missed chance to put more pressure on the leaders. Chelsea were 2-1 up but a McCreadie mistake let Bob Latchford in for an undeserved equaliser. Webb again played alongside Osgood as Garner was injured, with Garland again out on the wing.

The Derby replay, two days after Birmingham, produced a fine attacking display in an absolute thriller. Webb, for the third game in a row, played emergency striker, demonstrating the impact of injuries but also begging questions about the real depth of the squad. Osgood produced a superb 'mature and magical' performance in front of not only Sir Alf Ramsey but also his England squad, preparing for their friendly against Yugoslavia two days later. After fifteen minutes Chelsea were 2-1 up through Kember and Webb. After half-time Osgood scored one of the finest goals of his career, a 'searing volley from a Houseman cross', and duly fell on his knees and blew kisses at Ramsey. The *Daily Telegraph* headline 'Ramsey Watches Arrogant Osgood Topple Derby' said it all, and it is highly unlikely this behaviour by the striker impressed the taciturn international boss. Chelsea hung on in a frenetic finish for a tremendous 3-2 victory in one of the best games seen at Stamford Bridge in a long time. It was a shame a mere 26,395 saw it.

Osgood's thoughts when he saw that the England striking partnership that week was Mike Channon and Joe Royle, hard workers but not on the same planet as him talent-wise, can only be imagined. The *News Of The World*, dubbing Osgood 'England's forgotten man', reckoned Royle, Channon, Malcolm MacDonald and John Richards were ahead of him in list of prospective strikers, in addition to usual incumbents Martin Chivers and Rodney Marsh. Webb's reaction on seeing Arsenal's very limited centre-back Jeff Blockley capped would have been interesting, too.

Hudson had recovered from his ankle injury but was now ill with a throat problem. A comfortable 3-1 win over West Bromwich, with Osgood (causing The Shed to chant 'Osgood for Chivers'), Garland and Webb all scoring. High praise was offered to Locke, in only his fifth first-team game, helping justify the decision to sell Mulligan. Sexton enthused 'I have been delighted with his progress so far. He has done really well'. Bonetti added 'he's cool and composed and must have a great future'. Supporter David Gray recalls that Locke was very popular with the supporters who felt he was a certainty for England honours. Sadly, injuries and the fact he played for so long in a mediocre side meant that he never won a full cap.

The board had been considering what action to take regarding the pitch invasions against Leeds in August. The action they agreed got them a lot of publicity and implemented, much of it dreadful. At a cost of £1,000, eight-foot high wire mesh fences, topped off with strands of barbed wire, were erected at both terraced ends of the stadium, to prevent supporters encroaching on the pitch and prevent missile throwing being effective.

In the *Daily Mirror*, on the morning of the West Bromwich game, Chelsea 'warned their missing fans that the club's £5,000,000 development scheme could come to a halt unless gates improve'. Secretary Tony Green complained 'the 26,000 attendance for Monday's League Cup replay with Derby was ridiculously poor. If the trend continues, it could be disastrous for the club. Success on the field is an important factor in our scheme for a super new stadium. Manager Dave Sexton is doing his bit, and so are the team, but a lot of supporters have deserted us. If they continue to stay away, it could mean that all of our dreams for a new-look Stamford Bridge will come to a full-stop until things improve'. The assumption that all supporters wanted the stadium redeveloped, especially if it could in theory mean lack of investment in the team (even though this was denied by the club), was never tested.

Green explained the fences. 'We are trying to guarantee the safety of spectators. We understand their fears, and it seems many have stayed away because of the chaos at our opening match with Leeds. With both ends of the ground closed in, we hope the fans will come back. We have done this with some reluctance, but it does stop supporters getting from behind one goal to behind the other. We can now take a crowd of 45,000 comfortably. We have done our best for supporters – we should like them to respond'. The crowd against West Bromwich that day was only 29,000, so early signs were not encouraging. Lecturing supporters on the need to 'respond' by attending games certainly smacked of desperation, another indicator that club finances were precarious.

The day after the game, the club realised there was a downside to the fences. Under a 'Stalag S.W.6' back-page headline, the *News Of The World* went to town. Frank Butler's opinion piece pulled no punches. 'A sad day for British soccer...fences eight feet high topped by three strands of barbed wire...at the home of Chelsea, whose fans were once the fairest in the land'. This was accompanied by a stark picture of the fence, the barbed wire indeed making it look like a POW camp.

In the face of another PR nightmare, Mears defended the board's actions. 'This will be a permanent feature here I am afraid. We must protect the players and spectators from a small minority who just will not behave themselves. We had to do something after the crowd scenes at our chaotic opening game against Leeds. It is not something Chelsea are proud of, but it is very necessary, and I hope will bring back supporters who have not been happy about the behaviour of a small number of people'. The fact that barbed wire fences arguably put off more people than they attracted was not mentioned. It was hardly an image designed to attract the monied, family support Mears hankered after. Indeed, the *Kensington Post* felt that the fences would cut crowds, reporting that supporters thought the fences were too high and the barbed-wire was overdoing things. It felt draconian and it looked dreadful.

In *Chelsea – The Real Story* Mears understandably regretted the barbed wire. He claimed the contractor 'got rather carried away' and that after the 'Stalag S.W.6' headlines the barbed wire was taken down the following day. This does not say much for whoever signed off the work, and the inertia of the board in not realising a PR disaster was inevitable once the press saw the barbed wire.

More welcome news was the appearance of Ian Hutchinson in a testimonial game for Gordon Parr at Bristol City. Twenty long months had passed since his last first-team game. He has broken his left leg twice and had a cartilage operation, spending 'many painful hours battling to regain fitness' but had played in the last four reserve games. 'This means I am really on the way back and I can't tell you how pleased I am...I'm taking each game as it comes', he told the *Daily Mirror*. Chelsea lost 2-1 but all involved were pleased that Hutchinson scored a late goal. New names appeared on that team sheet. Full-back Graham Wilkins, seventeen, and his younger brother Ray, just sixteen the previous month, both came on as substitutes.

The very decent October continued a week later with a battling, high-tempo but low-skill 1-0 win at Tottenham. Webb reverted to centre-back, Garland played up-front alongside Osgood and Brian Bason came back into the side. John Hollins, who had another excellent game, scored the winner.

Sexton had now spent five years in the Chelsea managerial chair. He talked to the *Daily Mirror* about the injury plague and saw youngsters like Locke and Bason as the reason they could sell Cooke and Mulligan. They said that he might have added, but didn't, that Chelsea's admirable, but hugely expensive, ground improvements scheme had made money tight, if not scarce, at Stamford Bridge. Sexton praised Bonetti, Harris, Osgood, Kember and Garland and rounded off 'I'd love Chelsea to take the title'.

Not everything in Sexton's garden was lovely, and the behaviour of certain players was an increasing concern. In *Chelsea – The Real Story* Brian Mears recounted how there were stories of Sexton looking in afternoon drinking clubs for Hutchinson, Osgood, Cooke, Hudson and Baldwin 'a little clique' who had fallen out with him. In *The Mavericks* Hudson recounted how the team used to meet at the Markham Arms after Saturday away games and sort out what had happened on the pitch. Sexton resented this. Hudson reckoned the manager only really got on with McCreadie and Webb, though Hollins was also on good terms. Mears felt a number of the players could not cope with instant stardom, the trap of drink and parties. In retrospect he recognised that the manager gradually became more aloof and drifted apart from the players at a point when firmness was required.

Chelsea had hit an excellent run of nine points from five League games so, in that context, a 1-1 home draw with Newcastle was a disappointment, though in consolation the crowd of 35,273 was an increase of 6,000 on the West Bromwich game. McCreadie scored a rare goal and Garner played ninety minutes for the first time in a Chelsea shirt. This inability to regularly win games against middling sides was a recurrent theme and a concern to Sexton.

The League Cup draw sent Chelsea to Gigg Lane, home of Bury, for the first time since a 2-0 Division Two defeat nine years earlier. Bury were a mix of experience – John Connelly, Jimmy Robson and George Heslop – and promise – Terry McDermott – but were languishing in twelfth place in Division Four. Tommy Baldwin had recovered from jaundice and made his first appearance of the season. In a 'bruising, battering tie' in which Bury gave their illustrious opponents a real scare, Osgood went off with a hamstring injury. Marvin Hinton was substitute so there was no focal-point up front and Houseman's crosses were easily cleared.

Garland netted the only goal, but the game was remembered for a horrific injury to Peter Bonetti after a 53rd minute clash with Connelly, his England 1966 World Cup squad colleague, where he got a kick in the stomach, was left lying 'ominously still' and had to go off. Webb went in goal and the team were down to ten men.

Showing astonishing bravery, Bonetti went back out for the last fifteen minutes. 'It was agony to stand there - let alone play, but I had to get back out there ... I couldn't let the lads down'. Sexton was proud of his team's tremendous win, telling the *Daily Telegraph* 'I was worried about Peter but when the doctor said he should be OK we decided to gamble and risk it'. Bonetti was taken to hospital and had an emergency operation on a torn intestine, was likely to be in hospital for ten days and out for at least two months. In a season blighted by injury and illness this was the most serious. Bonetti's bravery and commitment to the cause can be summed up by his quote to the *Daily Mirror* 'it was a 50-50 ball. If I hadn't committed myself, Connelly might have scored'.

At the end of October Osgood was interviewed by the *News Of The World*. 'Ossie took a look at himself and it seems he didn't particularly like what he saw'. 'The result of this self-appraisal is a new, mature man...The change in him this season is remarkable'. Osgood observed 'perhaps I had the bright lights too soon. I knew I wasn't doing myself justice before this season...Playing behind a target man but ahead of the midfield, I have more space to take on people ... I don't want to sound big-headed but when I'm on song he (Rodney Marsh, in the England team) is not fit to lace my boots'. With just six goals so far that season, he required a prolific remainder of the season to force his way back into the England reckoning. An interview with Sir Alf Ramsey a week later was revealing, the England manager talking about wanting 'further evidence of Osgood's willingness', not a criticism that could be levelled at,for example, Mike Channon.

On 31st October the *Daily Mail* reported that, after six home games, Chelsea had lost 33,697 supporters and an estimated £9,100 in receipts compared to the previous season, despite terrace admission going up to 40p. This despite some of the more attractive home games (Leeds, Liverpool, Manchester City, West Ham) having taken place and the club being in a very healthy fourth place in the League table. Cause for concern indeed. Strong runs in both cups were necessary to boost the club coffers, though it was beginning to dawn on some supporters that funds to pay for the redevelopment could hardly be expected to come entirely from extra turnstile revenue or the Chelsea Pools. Other sources would plainly be required, though it was not made publicly clear which of these would be utilised.

Chelsea ended the month in a creditable fourth place, making competing for League honours and a European place a real possibility.

1st	*Liverpool*	*p15 22pts*
2nd	*Arsenal*	*p16 21pts*
3rd	*Leeds United*	*p15 20pts*
4th	**Chelsea**	**p15 19pts**
5th	*Everton*	*p15 18pts*
6th	*Tottenham Hotspur*	*p15 18pts*
7th	*Norwich City*	*p15 18pts*

November 1972

Another month of fixtures that, on paper at least, looked relatively easy, apart from the first, a trip to leaders Liverpool. The impact of Peter Bonetti's dreadful stomach injury was exacerbated by John Phillips already being out injured with a ligament injury, meaning third-string keeper Steve Sherwood would make his second first-team appearance. Bonetti told the *Daily Mirror* 'it is a frightening prospect for any goalkeeper when they face the Kop for the first time. They are without a doubt the fiercest crowd in football, but this can inspire you too, for The Kop appreciates good goalkeeping. Everyone at Chelsea knows he is a good goalkeeper. There is no better place for him to prove it'. To make matters worse Hudson was still out and Osgood's hamstring had not cleared up, so Garner came in.

With their two most inspirational players absent it is little wonder Chelsea struggled to create chances and were well-beaten 3-1, Baldwin's goal scant consolation as a nine-match unbeaten run ended. Sherwood was applauded by the crowd, and Sexton made it clear he was not responsible for any of the goals. The *Sunday People* reckoned 'Chelsea, surely the biggest team in the League, brought with them a physical approach that led to three bookings and a score of free-kicks'.

To have any chance of competing with the leaders Chelsea needed Hudson and Osgood in the team and on song.

Bonetti left hospital that week but was not expected to return to the team until the New Year. His deputy Phillips had to decide whether to join the Wales Under-23 squad or wait for an England call-up. Probably sensibly, he opted to play for Wales.

Under a 'Sexton To Buy Now' headline the *Daily Mirror* reported the manager may be forced to step up his search for a new defender. Dempsey had been out three months with an Achilles tendon injury and could not start training for at least another fortnight. Trainer Harry Medhurst commented 'we hope John will play again before Christmas'. Reserve Micky Droy was also out injured, so the squad strengthening was necessary, but no signing was made.

A week later Leicester City visited Stamford Bridge, where spectators found the barbed wire had been removed from fencing behind both goals, the dreadful 'Stalag S.W.6' publicity hitting home at the club. The match was a low-key 1-1 draw, an excellent headed goal by Garner equalised by Jon Sammels. What the game, which was shown on ITV's *The Big Match*, is remembered for by the disappointing 28,456 crowd and the TV viewers alike is not the football, however.

Film star and blatant self-publicist Raquel Welch attended the game with Jimmy Hill, ITV football pundit and equally blatant self-publicist, and Chelsea allowed ITV cameras to film her. Welch spent the game howling encouragement from the North Stand and left twenty minutes early, walking along the touchline screaming and waving goodbye at Osgood. The *Daily Mail* was unimpressed and knew who to blame. 'Hill...who might have been expected to know better, aided and abetted the publicity-conscious Miss Welch as she cavorted on the touchline (shouting support for Peter Osgood) ... Hill ... should have been prevented by Chelsea from trying to turn their Saturday fixture into a personal circus ... Having agreed to give Raquel and ITV the run of the place, the club were swept along embarrassingly along on the wave of publicity ... Osgood was too immersed in the game to pay her any attention', though an unimpressed Sexton apparently laid into Osgood about his role in the episode.

Millions watched this sideshow on TV and the papers duly played along. As Ken Jones pointed out in *Goal Magazine*, the charade embarrassed Chelsea, arguing in may have been 'good television, but it did nothing for football'. He also, rightly, pointed out Hill's talent for self-promotion. Hilariously, the ever-pompous Hill, in his capacity as Deputy Controller of Press, Publicity and Promotions, London Weekend Television, wrote to the Mail defending the circus. He argued she had to walk along the pitch as that was the only way out. 'I was as astonished as anyone when she walked onto the grass and shouted encouragement to Osgood and the Chelsea team ... It had become more to her than just a publicity stunt'. It would be fair to say that this was a minority view.

Interviewed 45 years later an unimpressed Charlie Cooke argued that Welch's rumoured romance with Osgood was indeed 'just a publicity stunt for her'. Terry O'Neill, famous photographer and Chelsea supporter, even persuaded Ms Welch to pose in Chelsea kit while filming *Hannie Caulder* in Arizona, the pictures duly receiving a wide circulation.

At Southampton the next week the travelling support were cheered by the news that Hudson was back after ten weeks out, having come through two reserve games unscathed. Confident as ever, he still felt Chelsea could win the title. Sherwood made his third appearance in a row and, early on, it looked like he would have little to do as Osgood scored, hit the bar and had two disallowed within the first twenty minutes. The team dominated but failed to score and Southampton equalised before half-time. Chelsea were again on top in the second-half but could not beat Saints keeper Eric Martin and Ron Davies, a thorn in Chelsea's side for years, netted twice in the final four minutes to give Southampton an unlikely 3-1 win. Sexton was shattered. 'We played some great stuff, Osgood was brilliant, and we should have won by three or four goals'.

Although Hudson had a good game on his return, he had a big fall-out with Sexton who had explicitly asked him to stay out on the wing. He kept wandering into the middle and his manager was furious afterwards. In *The Working Man's Ballet* Hudson described this as 'the start of a bleak time for me...My drinking increased'. Hudson and Sexton never really saw eye-to-eye again.

Three games with seven goals conceded, only one point won and a slide to seventh place. Chelsea had to improve, quickly, if they were to have any realistic chance of qualifying for Europe, let alone winning the title. The squad went on a two-day 'retreat' to Bisham Abbey and came up with the idea of wearing scarves onto the pitch and handing them out to the crowd in The Shed and the West Stand, similar to what Leeds United did at their home games. An attempt to improve the atmosphere and a nice touch, though the crowd against Notts County was small, only 22,500, and many were still stuck in traffic when the teams came out. Chelsea were 3-0 up before half-time and won 3-1, easing up after the interval.

Rather than go back to the dressing room, the players stayed on the pitch at half-time. In a future programme Sexton explained why. 'It is a very long walk now the dressing rooms are so far away. A few weeks ago, someone from The Shed told me 'when the players come out after half-time, they straggle back in two's and threes and it doesn't look good enough coming from Chelsea'. He was right, so I started to think what we could do about it. Now the spectators can see just how we spend half-time, with a few words among ourselves about how things are going in the match and using the rest of the time to show the crowd some of the skills we have been attempting in training. The display helps to keep the fans interested - it's something extra for the money they've paid ... it certainly isn't a circus we're putting on. We'd have no part in anything like that'.

Would they do it in the wet and cold? 'Why not? The crowd stays at half-time so why shouldn't we?'. This initiative lasted a couple of matches before the manager and his team, probably sensibly, retreated to the privacy of the Portakabin. The *Chelsea Yearbook No.4* pointed out that the gimmicks were abandoned little over a month later, having done nothing for Chelsea's gates.

The reward was a place in the Semi-final, the fourth season in a row the club had made that round in a cup competition. They were drawn against Norwich City, well-placed in sixth place in the League, one ahead of Chelsea. This gave Chelsea an excellent chance of another Wembley appearance and they were duly installed as 2-1 League Cup favourites.

Before the excitement of the first-leg at Stamford Bridge, however, there were winnable League games to contest. The visit of Crystal Palace, one point off the bottom, attracted a decent 36,608 supporters, many of them very happy with the news that the hugely-popular and desperately unlucky Ian Hutchinson, after 21 months out of the team, was back in the matchday squad. Delighted, the player told the *Daily Mail* 'I want to begin repaying Chelsea for all their patience'. Garland and Locke were the latest injury victims but, in the end, Sexton put Hutch on the bench and started with Garner. Paddy Mulligan and Charlie Cooke started for Palace and got a cheer, but the crowd only had one favourite. Fans chanted 'we want Hutch, give us Hutch' as early as the twentieth minute as Chelsea struggled, and their frustration grew as Hutchinson stayed in the dugout as the game petered out to a 0-0 draw, Osgood cutting a very frustrated figure at the finish.

Sexton told the *News Of The World* 'the present team has done well for me without a lot of luck. At the moment, I don't think Ian would do any better up front. I named him as sub because you need a bit of encouragement (when recovering from injury). But he would only have come on in an emergency'.

Chelsea's failure to win any of their last three home games had seen them slip seven points behind Liverpool in the title race. In *Goal Magazine*, Jimmy Hill, never short of an opinion, felt that the three-sided stadium ruined the atmosphere at Stamford Bridge and that it was affecting the players. He praised Osgood as 'a complete footballer' but complained about his moodiness and occasional failure to do the necessary grafting.

In the Crystal Palace programme, there was a picture of the demolished East Stand and an update on progress. Groundworkings, foundations and underground services (sewers, gas, electrics etc) had been completed and work on the ground floor was about to start. Pile-driving had begun, and the steelwork was being manufactured. 'Roof erection is planned for the spring and everything is at present up to schedule'. So far, apparently so good. Reserved seats for the January 20th visit of Arsenal had already sold out, showing there was still a strong appetite for attractive games.

At the end of November, a host of stories appeared in the press about George Best, whose behaviour was causing concern at Manchester United. He was likely to be transfer-listed and allegedly seeking a move to London. Chelsea were apparently at the front of the list of clubs interested, and supposedly believed the transfer fee and wages could be met by the inevitable increase in gate receipts. These stories were highly speculative, not least because Chelsea would probably find him out of their price range.

The Best stories continued in early December. The *Daily Mail* quoted Mears 'we are not entirely convinced that the building work ... is the only reason for a decline in our attendances', which suggested a crowd-puller like Best was required to fill the 'splendid new stadium'. As they also pointed out, Chelsea's financial commitment to their rebuilding project was in itself a major barrier to a bid, especially as a figure of £300,000+ was mooted. Additionally, there was the very valid question as to whether Sexton, struggling with the more free-spirited members of his squad, would want to burden himself with Best's much-publicised problems. There was also paper talk about Best being swapped for Osgood and Webb. In the end, though the Chelsea board supposedly discussed the idea, nothing happened.

If Chelsea had bought Best for £300,000 and paid him say £400 a week on a three-year contract (not unreasonable given his profile and pulling power), making the deal pay would have been a real challenge. The total cost of wages plus fee, on that basis, would have been around £360,000. Given the terrace admission price was 40p (the stands were filled with Season-Ticket holders apart from 3,000 unreserved seats in the benches, costing 60p) that would require nearly 900,000 extra supporters over a three-year period, or 300,000 a season, just to break-even. In the short-term, certainly there would have been a huge crowd boost. Sustaining it however, especially given that weaknesses elsewhere in the side meant success could be by no means guaranteed, would have been hard, making the economic risk one not worth taking given exposure elsewhere.

One player likely to be moving on was striker Tommy Baldwin, unhappy at reserve team football, transfer-listed and feeling Sexton disliked his lifestyle. The *Daily Mail*, under a 'Baldwin a £100,000 Snip. Now He's On The Wagon' headline reported that Hepatitis had forced him to give up alcohol. He was told he must not drink for two years. 'I must say I feel better for it...I've lost weight'. Garner, Garland, Osgood and Hutchinson were ahead of him in the pecking order so 'it looks as though there are too many of us and I'll be on the move'. Crystal Palace and Leicester were reported as potentially interested. Peter Feely and Tony Potrac, both of whom had played a few League games without ever clinching a regular place, were also listed. Midfielder Laurie Craker, signed as a professional from the junior ranks two years earlier but never breaking through to the first-team, signed for Watford on a free transfer.

Although fifth in the table at the end of November, Chelsea were now seven points behind leaders Liverpool. Halfway through the season, title contention was already starting to look a bit of a stretch.

1st	Liverpool	p19	28pts
2nd	Leeds United	p19	26pts
3rd	Arsenal	p20	25pts
4th	Tottenham Hotspur	p19	22pts
5th	**Chelsea**	**p19**	**21pts**
6th	Ipswich Town	p18	21pts
7th	Norwich City	p19	21pts

December 1972

Chelsea were desperate to get back to winning ways in the League. For the trip to Stoke on December 2nd, Sexton chose an unchanged team, meaning a forward-line of Bill Garner, Peter Osgood and Peter Houseman, on the basis that the two big men would benefit from Houseman's accurate crossing. The problem was, there was no Plan B, no smaller, quicker player to feed off the front-men. Osgood scored, Chelsea sat back, and Terry Conroy equalised. Chelsea were unable to respond and the *Daily Mirror* headline 'Casual Chelsea Toss It Away' said it all. No win in the League for six games, the team still blighted by a casual manner and an inability to kill games off.

Whether Chelsea were saving themselves for the Norwich Semi-final was a moot point, especially when the first-leg, scheduled for the Wednesday at Stamford Bridge, was called off due to a waterlogged pitch. A quirk of the fixture list meant the next League game was also against The Canaries. When Sexton announced that Ian Hutchinson was in the side, the squad broke into spontaneous applause, testimony to his popularity (John Boyle attests to the affection the squad held for Hutch) and the respect shown for his fightback from serious injury. A forward line of Garner and Hutchinson, with Osgood playing just behind them, certainly had height and power on a heavy pitch. In the event, Norwich were comfortably beaten 3-1 which, as supporter Brian Gaches remembers, raised expectations for the League Cup games ahead.

Hutchinson scored twice to great acclaim from the crowd, also demonstrating that his long throw had lost none of its power or accuracy. Garner scored the other goal, Jimmy Bone netting a consolation, beating four men and showing he would need to be watched in the rearranged first-leg in midweek. Osgood decently hurried off afterwards to ensure Hutchinson got the plaudits. He was duly mobbed by autograph hunters in the queue for Semi-final second-leg tickets in what was rightly a very special day for him, and he duly praised the 'terrific' fans.

Hutchinson admitted he was exhausted in the final half-hour and he hurt his knee, but his return, and the first win in seven League games, gave the club, the crowd, the team and, most importantly, the player a real boost. Supporter David Gray calls it 'one of the most memorable games I have ever witnessed at Stamford Bridge'. He reckons the ovation Hutchinson received from the 30,000 crowd 'was one of the loudest I have ever heard, similar to the one Kerry Dixon received at the 1994 FA Cup Semi-final. I must admit having a tear in my eye such was the outpouring of emotion for this hugely popular player ... I will never forget this game, nor will anyone else who was lucky enough to have been there'.

Chelsea's joy was tempered by the fact that Micky Droy broke his ankle, bravely battling on for an hour as the substitute, Tommy Baldwin, was a forward. The injury was to keep him out until mid-April, causing Sexton a headache as John Dempsey was still not fit and Marvin Hinton had been frozen out in the reserves. Fulham and Leicester were after the transfer-listed Baldwin, but Sexton was unwilling to sell him while his side were still in the League Cup.

For the League Cup game, Hutchinson retained his place despite issues with his knee. Norwich, who had won 3-0 at Arsenal in the previous round, were not to be underestimated but given they had lost seven of their ten away League games, Chelsea were clear favourites. Under a 'Golden Chelsea' headline, the *Daily Mirror* reported that the squad were on a £1,000-a-man bonus if they reached Wembley. Even if they lost the Semi-final, £6,000 was to be spread among the first-team squad.

In the event, the warning Jimmy Bone had given with his goal on the Saturday was not heeded. He and fellow-striker David Cross tore into Chelsea and both scored in the first eleven minutes, silencing the crowd. The central defence was found wanting and a picture of the half-time team talk, given on the pitch, shows a miserable looking bunch of players listening to Sexton's team talk, which supporter Brian Gaches remembers as a 'very public verbal dressing down'. Chelsea created little, Osgood missing a late open goal which would have made the second-leg more interesting.

The *Evening Standard* headline 'Sexton's Sad Men See A Dream Fade' said it all, the report saying he had 'never seen the Chelsea players so glum after an important game'. Osgood, clearly shocked, said 'I'm sick, just sick' and Sexton admitted 'we gave them the first goal, but they played well'. As supporter Geoff Kimber recalls "it was a truly uninspired performance' and he saw the atmosphere for such an important game as 'strangely flat', though the crowd of 34,316 was reasonable.

A massive improvement was required before the second-leg in a week's time so a 1-0 defeat at Wolverhampton was hardly the ideal preparation. Hutchinson, left out as his knee had swollen up, was clearly not yet 100% fit and his return had to be managed.

For the second-leg Hutchinson's knee had not recovered and, with Garner cup-tied, Baldwin came in. Chelsea fought hard, Hudson scoring twice, but were 3-2 down, 5-2 down on aggregate, when thick fog suddenly descended. Gary Locke was injured in an incident hidden from the referee by the fog and was carried off. With six minutes to go, and Norwich trying frantically to play on, referee Gordon Hill took the teams off for twenty-seven minutes. Supporter Brian Gaches remembers the Chelsea support bellowing 'call it off' while the teams were off. Hill brought the sides back on for a futile two minutes then abandoned the match. Cue uproar. Chelsea players 'danced with delight' as Norwich complained bitterly. The fog cleared fifteen minutes later, and as Sexton told the *Evening Standard* 'it was the most bizarre night I can recall in football'. A lucky escape, though whether Chelsea had the wit and ability to make a comeback in the rearranged game, scheduled for the New Year, was another matter.

Chelsea's home League crowds so far were down from 361,246 to 311,056, a concerning trend. In a *Daily Mail* feature on falling crowds, there was a revealing, positive, if arguably naïve, interview with chairman Brian Mears. 'Chelsea are building more than just a new stand at Stamford Bridge, more even than the best stadium in the country. They are laying down the pattern for Chelsea's future'. They saw him as an ambitious young chairman...reluctant to cast himself in the role of pioneer. 'The redevelopment was seen as a great gamble and 'Chelsea … are courageously spending a fortune in order to attract and accommodate a whole new breed of football supporter'.

They continued 'Mears and his fellow directors are committing every last penny, and then some' to a philosophy he aired at length. 'The people who watch the game … have changed. The days are gone in London – at least – when the terraces were filled by people for whom going to a football match was the one highlight of a long and boring working week … They have more diversions...expect greater comfort … we are perhaps able to be the first to do something really drastic about that because of the very situation at the club. Everyone at Chelsea is convinced we can attract a new type of supporter as well as the traditional fan … It is becoming something of the fashion, a bit trendy if you like, to be a Chelsea supporter. But people with a sophisticated way of life need civilized surroundings to become confirmed and regular supporters … Chelsea's football ground has got to become an attractive and welcoming place for a whole young family to want to visit on a match day …. We want to offer facilities for people to use at other times as well because that can only help with the finance … We knew our gates would take an added knock because of the difficulties we have had with the rebuilding … We would not be doing what we are at Stamford Bridge unless the directors were supremely confident that the football which has given us success in the past would give us the basis of more achievement in the future'.

As the *Daily Mail* pointed out, too many English stadia were outmoded and downright uncomfortable. 'It is not easy to undertake a costly project to develop the stadium of the future in the face of dwindling support'. Indeed. This was the first time the risks Chelsea were taking had been laid so bare. Again, there were no questions about the possibility of external funding. The reliance on the success of the team to draw in larger crowds and commensurate gate receipts was worrying indeed, given inconsistent team performances and, arguably, a lack of genuine top-quality in the side outside Bonetti, Webb, Hollins, Osgood and Hudson. The Chelsea board of directors were certainly brave. Whether they were wise, or significantly misguided, to assume that the team would be successful and hence drive the stadium funding would, one way or the other, become clear over the next few years.

Equally, it was unclear whether the aspirational, sophisticated, 'trendy', monied supporters that Mears craved would exist in sufficient numbers to fill the redeveloped ground unless the team achieved consistent, trophy-gathering success. No mention of the loyal terrace supporters who had tolerated substandard facilities for so many years. Mears was right, grounds must be safer. The Wheatley Report, adopted by the government, made this clear. Football clubs, who had got away with under-investment for years, bleated about having to pay for safety work but they could hardly expect the government to foot the bill.

In the programme for the Norwich League game there had been a feature addressing issues of concern raised by supporters.

1. The club accepted they needed more West Stand turnstiles.
2. They asked supporters to arrive earlier. Latecomers to the North-East Enclosure had to walk round the track, which could be distracting to the players and other spectators.
3. They asked terrace supporters not to 'bunch'.
4. The club knew they needed more toilets, were looking into the problem and doing their best to solve it.
5. There were complaints about the ticket office not accepting postal applications for Cup tickets, as had been the practise in the past.

Evidently the 'latecomers will not get in' threat had not been carried out. The lack of toilets had been a disgrace for many years, particularly at The Shed End, and it did the club little credit that they had dragged their heels so dismally on the issue. Given the Chelsea ticket office was now also an agency of Keith Prowse, the less convenient cup ticket sale arrangements, which meant purchasers had to visit the office in person, were both surprising and unacceptable.

Everton at home, three days later and three days before Christmas, drew an abject 23,385 loyal supporters, the lowest League crowd of the season so far. Christmas shopping inevitably intervened for some, but this was a fixture that had drawn crowds of 34,000+ in the past five seasons (in two cases nearly 50,000) so something was clearly up. Everton were not the side they had been two years earlier but, even so, alarm bells must have been ringing long and loud in the boardroom. If the stadium redevelopment was indeed dependent on large crowds, then it looked like problems lay ahead.

One bright spot was the return of John Dempsey to central defence after four months out with an Achilles injury. Garland, extremely unfairly, became the butt of the crowd's frustrations. When Joe Harper put Everton 1-0 up with three minutes to go many supporters left. Those that remained were treated to a double V-sign from a frustrated, angry Garland after he made Hutchinson's injury-time equaliser.

A Boxing Day trip to fourth-placed Ipswich Town saw seventeen-year-old Graham Wilkins make his debut at left-back, but a more experienced player would also have struggled against a rampant Ipswich side. Chelsea created few chances in a chastening 3-0 defeat. Sexton was reduced to taking off the recalled John Boyle, bringing Marvin Hinton on for only his third appearance of the season and pushing Webb up front in desperation. It did not work.

The final game of an increasingly fraught year was the visit of Derby County, a point ahead of a Chelsea side that had slumped to tenth place. The game was shown on *The Big Match* and is mainly remembered for a spectacular last-minute miss by Derby striker Roger Davies after he had rounded Phillips. Osgood's superb curving shot from outside the area equalised a John O'Hare goal. Hutchinson, worryingly, limped off with a swollen knee and was likely to miss the Norwich second-leg in four days' time. Winger Ian Britton came on for a busy debut and his enthusiasm 'sparked Chelsea into action' but it was another disappointing game, yet another point dropped.

In his final *Evening Standard* column of 1972, Hudson felt he would strike his best form in the New Year and that his old appetite for the game was back. He had recovered from ankle and calf muscle injuries. 'I'd lost the taste for the game and it always seems to take me longer to get back into shape...I have big legs and that means I'm carrying extra weight around. But I worked hard, maybe too hard. I'm always the same when I'm training. I sometimes wonder whether I'm too enthusiastic'. Sexton was encouraging him to shoot more, though he had yet to score that season. 'I'm looking forward to the New Year challenge. I've never felt so confident in my life'. Positive words from a man Sexton was desperate to be at his very best, though blaming his 'big legs' for his weight issues was possibly missing the point.

An indication of the impact of injuries and poor form was the fact that Chelsea had used six different full-backs, and six different full-back pairings, in six games which made consistency and understanding almost impossible. It was the same at centre-back, with five different players and four pairings in the same six-match run. Twenty-six players had been used so far that season, an astonishing figure and further indication of the problems the manager had faced. Sexton's key players had to get fit and stay fit.

In the Derby programme Mears wrote a New Year message to the supporters. '1972 was another memorable year for Chelsea Football Club...Reaching a final for third successive season was an achievement of rare merit and worthy of our heartiest congratulations to Manager Dave Sexton, the Players and Staff...We appreciate the patience of you, our Supporters, in your understanding of our problems through these difficult early stages of redevelopment'. A positive message but, by glossing over the League Cup Final and Orient FA Cup defeats, continued underachievement in the League, the lack of European football, the absence of top signings, falling crowds and the utter chaos against Leeds, not necessarily a balanced one.

The team had slipped to eighth place, twelve points behind leaders Liverpool with no realistic chance of catching them. European qualification through League position looked increasingly unlikely, so the cup competitions became even more important. Injuries were a constant problem, but often mediocre performances hinted at a deeper malaise. Five home wins from twelve games was simply not good enough for any side with aspirations for a title challenge. Nobody was scoring goals consistently and Osgood, with ten goals in all competitions, was nowhere near as prolific as twelve months earlier. Hudson, though playing well, had yet to score and his midfield colleagues Hollins, with one, and Kember, with two, were not much better. At this point the previous season Hollins had scored twelve goals. The football was less attractive, the mercurial Cooke had gone. For the board to expect the current squad to play the type of attractive, winning football to turn the decline in attendances round was optimistic indeed.

The Derby programme pointed out that the average crowd after eleven home League games was down from 41,791 to 33,131, a drop of 95,000 (or, at 40p a head, a minimum of £38,000 lost), increasing the pressure on Sexton to pull in supporters through winning matches and trophies. Before the Everton game the manager had held a team inquest into the run of poor results, an 'alarming slump' as the *Daily Mirror* called it.

January 1973

New Year, same old problem. Injuries. Peter Houseman, Micky Droy, Ian Hutchinson and captain Eddie McCreadie were all out of the rearranged League Cup Semi-final second-leg at Carrow Road, in addition to the cup-tied Bill Garner. Peter Bonetti was fit after the awful chest injury he suffered against Bury over two months earlier. Gary Locke, Chris Garland and Steve Kember were only passed fit late on for a game Chelsea had to win by at least two goals to stand any chance of reaching Wembley.

In the event Sexton put out the most attacking side he could :- *Bonetti; Locke, Dempsey, Webb, Harris; Hollins, Hudson, Kember; Baldwin, Osgood, Garland*.

The game was not all-ticket, but over 34,000 filled Carrow Road, for the second time in three weeks. Although Chelsea put everything into the game, in an intensely physical game Norwich managed to stop Chelsea playing. Sexton's men had not given up the ghost until Steve Govier's second-half goal clinched Norwich's Wembley place. Try as they might, the Chelsea players could not repair the first-leg damage. Sexton told the *Daily Mirror* 'I'm proud of the way my players fought' but the fact remained they were well beaten over the two legs and only had the FA Cup to look forward to in terms of possible trophies.

That Semi-final was arguably a defining moment in Chelsea's early 1970s decline. It was the fourth time in fourteen months they had lost a cup-tie when favourites and, as supporter Geoff Kimber remembers, from a Chelsea perspective the tie was a damp squib. It was to be Chelsea's last Semi-final in a major tournament for twelve years, unthinkable at the time. Supporter Brian Gaches saw it as 'another nail in the coffin for the great 70's team, who no longer had that special attacking creativity and flair so often seen a couple of years earlier'.

The next weekend's scheduled game, away at Manchester City, was postponed, giving the players a clear ten days, a chance for some of the lengthy injury list to clear up. The *Daily Mail* reported that eighteen different first-team squad members had been injured at some point in the season so far. The news nobody wanted to hear was that Ian Hutchinson required a second cartilage operation and was expected to be out for at least another ten weeks. He had played just two full games in twenty-three months, having gone off at half-time against Derby. The *Daily Telegraph* worried that he would not be human if he did not experience psychological effects after his long series of injuries. Baldwin, on the transfer list for an optimistic £120,000, had attracted no firm offers.

Chelsea had drawn Third Division Brighton and Hove Albion away in the FA Cup and were sixth favourites for the competition at 16-1, their only realistic chance of winning a trophy. Reaching the last sixteen eight times in the past ten seasons meant Chelsea could approach the competition with some confidence. On the day of the game, the *Daily Mail* put the issues on the line, and more pressure on the manager. They reported 'Chelsea travel to Brighton to face the climax of a crisis, heartened by the unswerving faith of Brian Mears. Defeat would be little short of a financial disaster for Chelsea in the season in which they have launched the building of a £5 million superstadium at Stamford Bridge. The clatter of £50-£100,000 into the coffers from a run to Wembley would be very welcome'. It needs to be borne in mind that even three years FA Cup success, generating say £250,000 plus, would not have made that significant a dent into the East Stand costs, let alone the whole development.

Mears responded 'there is no denying that it is important to us from the financial point of view to do well in the Cup ... However our results go, we have the heart to press on in the way we believe is right. The decision (to rebuild) was based on the tremendous record under Dave Sexton ... (we have been) Semi-finalists four years running ... no team can go for ever without a sticky run ... terribly unlucky with injuries...We have not lost hope of qualifying for Europe with a high League position'. It was increasingly clear that the redevelopment lacked rock-solid funding. Worse, given the builders strike and general industrial unrest, it was unclear whether the new stand would be open for the start of the following season.

Chelsea had won just one of their last ten games, their worst run under Sexton. Brighton were in even worse shape, with ten successive defeats. Chelsea were expected to win comfortably and indeed, after seventy minutes were 2-0 up, thanks to a pair by Osgood. No goals were scored in the last twenty minutes but there were two sending-offs and four bookings in that time, as the game descended into 'Seventeen Minutes Of Madness'. Ron Harris was sent off for allegedly hitting Brighton midfielder Eddie Spearritt in the mouth, though he denied it, and indeed still does. He complained to the *Daily Mail* 'I know I've been in trouble before, but only for dangerous tackles and tackling from behind. I've never chinned anyone or anything like that. That's not me ... I didn't hit Spearritt. He made it look bad'. Sexton backed him up, opining 'I felt Spearritt violently over-reacted' and 'there could have been a bit of acting'. It was Harris's first sending off in England, slightly belying his 'Chopper' nickname, and he made it clear he intended to appeal.

All sense of self-discipline left some players. Brighton full-back George Ley fouled Baldwin and, when Osgood remonstrated, punched him in the face. Osgood's comment to the *Daily Mirror* later hardly covered him in glory. 'What incensed me was his tackle on Tommy. I went over to him and got a punch in the mouth. I shouldn't have gone down really. It didn't hurt all that much and, after all, we are all in this game together'. Ley left for an early bath, but the feuding continued, referee and linesmen requiring police protection as they left the pitch.

A home London derby against high-flying Arsenal would test the team, but also examine the potential for attracting high crowds. Chelsea were eighth, Arsenal second and it must have been a considerable disappointment to the club hierarchy that only 36,292 turned up. Chelsea fielded an unchanged team, a rare luxury that season. Chelsea had eight chances, Arsenal only two, but it was Ray Kennedy who gave the visitors the points on a mud bath. The crowd, not for the last time, chanted 'lucky Arsenal'. The *News Of The World* reported that Osgood had been booked 'by mistake', his third of the season, as it was Garner who actually kicked Alan Ball, as was obvious to millions of TV viewers.

The *Kensington Post*, in a highly perceptive article, felt the team were falling well short of their potential. They noted that Baldwin,

Garland, Hudson and Garner had all been played wide where they were unhappy and, in Hudson's case in particular, were wasting their talents. They saw this as nothing new, as Keith Weller had also been wasted there. 'Sexton is trying to play down the flanks but with only one winger, Houseman'. The only player Chelsea were linked with that month was nineteen-year-old Nottingham Forest winger John Robertson. Given the career he had, including scoring the winning goal in a European Cup Final, it is safe to assume Robertson would have had no regrets staying at Forest. From Chelsea's perspective, though, he would have been a fascinating addition to the team.

Looking at wingers who moved around that time, or would have been of potential interest to Sexton, it is amazing in retrospect that he did not acquire one, by selling surplus existing players if necessary. In addition to Don Rogers, regularly linked with Chelsea, there were the likes of Ray Graydon (Aston Villa), Tommy Hutchison (Coventry), Leighton James (Burnley), Dave Thomas (who moved from Burnley to QPR that season), Dennis Tueart (Sunderland) and Willie Johnston (who moved from Rangers to West Bromwich). All were quality wide men, none were linked with a move to Stamford Bridge.

The *Daily Mirror* identified one reason for the malaise gripping the club. 'I feel the slump has a lot to do with a ground that is currently like a goods yard due to the building operations. There is no atmosphere, little encouragement and a number of the side prefer to play away'. Certainly, having a gaping hole where the East Stand used to be meant the atmosphere was, at best, patchy. No matter how fervently The Shed and the North Stand bellowed their support, much of it disappeared into the Fulham sky. Home League attendances were already down a depressing 20% - 430,000 against 534,000 the previous season - representing a minimum of £41,600 in lost revenue. Worrying, but against a total estimated development cost of £5.5 million surely not in itself terminal?

Regular interviewee Osgood spilt out his heart to the *News Of The World* under a 'How Ramsey Hurt My Pride – Osgood' headline. 'Perhaps Alf thinks my character is a bit dodgy. Yet I've always said that players can lead their own lives as long as they deliver the goods…I'm not among Alf's in-crowd…It hurts'. He failed to grasp that his philosophy on players 'leading their own lives' was not shared by the puritanical Ramsey, who held all the cards. On a positive note, Hollins was back in the England squad, due reward for commanding displays over a period of several seasons.

The month ended with another unchanged team and another defeat, 3-1 at West Ham, Garner's equaliser little consolation. Chelsea had now scored just five goals in nine games, an appalling return, had lost six of those nine games and won precisely two of their last twelve matches. They had slipped to thirteenth, a mere seven points above twenty-first placed Birmingham City.

In *The Chelsea Story*, John Moynihan recounts how changing in a mobile changing room to trudge through a temporary gate onto the pitch began to get to the players, play began to creak, they lost silly matches, lost confidence and morale and the team began to be barracked. By the end of January, pre-season optimism had dissipated.

A sorry end to a sorry month, a decline in performances, goals and results that made the forthcoming FA Cup-tie against Ipswich Town at Stamford Bridge even more important. It was, quite literally, a season-saving game. As Alan Hudson told the *Daily Mail* on the eve of the game 'we can't afford to lose'.

February 1973

The *Daily Mail* laid it on the line, stating that losing to Ipswich would be financially disastrous. 'If Chelsea lost, they would look to spend the last three months of the season in a brutal rebuilding of the team'. How this team rebuilding would be funded, other than by selling the best players, was not made clear. They referred to the 'rapidly emptying building site which is doing service as a stadium'.

The *Daily Mirror* piled in as well with a 'Win Or Bust For Chelsea' headline with a 'Cup Run Their Only Success Hope' sub-headline. Ipswich had lost one game in eighteen and were a heady fourth in the table. 'Chelsea have more to lose than any other team in the Fourth Round. They are committed to a £5,500,000 redevelopment scheme that has left the East side of the ground ... a silent gap. They need a good cup run to retain the interest of the fans they want to fill the £1,500,000 stand scheduled to go up there for the start of next season'.

Even the Chelsea programme that day ratcheted up the pressure on Sexton and his team. 'After three months of low-key League results, we are in urgent need of a performance that, in recent years, has placed us among the most formidable of cup-fighting teams'.

Realising that playing Bill Garner and Peter Osgood together only worked if they had a stream of accurate crosses played to them, Dave Sexton acted. Peter Houseman had been out for five weeks and was barely fit, but the manager rushed him back in place of Tommy Baldwin, desperate to feed crosses to his striking duo.

The Ipswich scouting report, seen by the *Sunday People*, opined that Garner was 'all right in the air but rather useless on the ground'. That scout must have choked on his post-match cuppa when Garner had scored twice, one with either foot, either side of half-time in a hard-fought 2-0 win. Garner's 'exhilarating performance' drew praise from many quarters, the *Fulham Chronicle* claiming he was at last justifying his £100,000 transfer fee. Sexton was enthused. 'Happy? I was nearly deliriously happy to be leading at half-time after Ipswich had played so well.' One negative was the knee ligament injury suffered by David Webb, a cornerstone of the side who was immediately rated doubtful for the fifth-round game at Sheffield Wednesday in three weeks' time. In the event, the injury was more serious than that.

The *Daily Mirror* headline 'Chelsea Save Their Season' was on the button, and a delighted Brian Mears admitted 'the pressure was on. This was a very vital one for us'. Chelsea's monetary challenges were being laid bare in the national press on a regular basis, and it was becoming increasingly apparent to supporters that the wherewithal to buy expensive top-class players was not available, despite assurances the previous summer. Mears celebrating every cup-tie victory so publicly cannot have helped a manager all too aware of the necessity of optimising cup revenues.

Young midfielder Tony Potrac, who had played a couple of games the previous season without establishing himself, moved to South African side Durban City, managed by ex-England centre-forward Johnny 'Budgie' Byrne. Peter Feely, like Potrac given a few games but no more, was sold to Bournemouth for a token £1,000 fee. The number of promising youth players coming through meant the decks had to be cleared. John Boyle, out of the side and with little prospect of regaining his place, talked over his future with Sexton, who commented 'he's the kind of player I could recommend to anybody'. The transfer-listed Tommy Baldwin turned down a £80,000 move to Huddersfield as he wanted to stay in Division One and, ideally, in the south.

Under a 'Chelsea Ban Injury Talk' headline, a frustrated Sexton told the *Daily Mail* 'I want to get away from the image of Chelsea being the Emergency Ward of soccer ... Every time you read about Chelsea it's about who is injured. There has been too much of it. I won't be issuing any more bulletins'. Journalists had still worked out that Webb, Garland, Bonetti, Droy and Hutchinson were all out injured. Webb had an operation and was still likely to be out for several weeks, bad news indeed.

Harris, sent off in controversial circumstances at Brighton, was given a three-match ban starting after the forthcoming Sheffield United game, his 500th League match, and would therefore miss the Sheffield Wednesday cup-tie unless he appealed. Given the absence of Webb, Harris's competitive nature would be sorely needed in what was bound to be a highly physical encounter. The press focus regarding Chelsea was already on the FA Cup-tie two weeks hence, the League season having stagnated.

An embarrassingly small 21,464 turned out to watch Chelsea beat Sheffield United 4-2 in a highly entertaining game, 'riotous, knockabout stuff', as the *News Of The World* put it, so it seemed plenty of supporters were concentrating on the FA Cup as well. Garland, back after five weeks out injured, scored twice, Garner got the other two. An oddity occurred right at the end when United substitute Dave Staniforth took over as linesman for the last two minutes when the official one twisted a knee.

Houseman, apparently essential on the wing seven days earlier, played left-back. Dempsey went off with a thigh strain, adding to Sexton's centre-back injury woes. With Harris due to start his suspension, Marvin Hinton, with just one first-team start and three substitute appearances so far that season, was his only available centre-back. Unsurprisingly Harris appealed, the backlog of cases meaning his would not be heard until after the cup-tie. It did mean though, that if Chelsea went through and the appeal failed, he would in all likelihood be unavailable for the Quarter-final.

Before the cup-tie Chelsea had one more game to avoid further injury. Unfortunately, it was a trip to Elland Road, home of deadly rivals Leeds United. The game was as physical as was expected but Chelsea gave one of their best displays of the season, deserving the 1-1 draw, their first point there for seven seasons. Osgood scored with a fierce volley but, inevitably, was booked, claiming 'I got the usual intimidation treatment and you can only take so much'. Locke picked up an injury which was to keep him out of the Hillsborough clash.

Eddie McCreadie, out for two months, returned at left-back against Wednesday, Harris partnering him on the right, as Chelsea geared themselves up for a very tough game. Kember was optimistic, telling the *Daily Mirror* 'we have more players fit and (increased) determination now and are confident, although Wednesday will provide good opposition...We are all aware that this is the only trophy we have a chance of winning'.

Roy Coyle put Wednesday ahead before half-time, Garner equalised and a wonderful header from Osgood put Chelsea through. Sexton could be very pleased with both result and performance, though neither side ended the game with eleven players. Garner had been kicked all game by John Holsgrove, ending up with heavily bandaged legs. He and Holsgrove were sent off for fighting with two minutes to go.

Holsgrove, nursing a split lower lip, explained 'he butted me, and I hit him'. Garner pointed out that 'Holsgrove kicked my calves and ankles. Eventually I swore at him. He pushed me in the back. I retaliated and he punched me and down I went. I know you are not supposed to retaliate and get involved, but it's easier said than done'. Referee Ken Burns complained 'their behaviour was ridiculous and totally inexplicable'.

So Chelsea, despite ongoing injury problems, a mediocre eleventh place (still only seven points away from the relegation zone), weaknesses at the back, the lack of a second winger and inconsistencies across the team were in the FA Cup Quarter-final where, to massive excitement, they drew Arsenal at home.

March 1973

The Arsenal tie, and all the surrounding hoopla, was inevitably going to prove a distraction for the club but there were three League games to face first. Two entirely winnable home games against Birmingham City and Wolverhampton Wanderers and a trip to bottom-placed West Bromwich Albion. That Chelsea gathered two points from those games spoke volumes about their form.

A drab 0-0 draw with Birmingham was marked only by Ian Britton's full debut, a debut made necessary by an astonishing twenty-five professionals and apprentices apparently being injured. The papers blamed Chelsea's 'timidity' and 'lack of motivation' on the players saving themselves for the Arsenal game.

Sexton appeared on a late-night TV show talking about his love of poetry, which must have bewildered some of his more down-to-earth squad members, who probably thought a stanza was a new Belgian lager. The *Kensington Post* pointed out that 'the poetry has gone out of Chelsea's style but not from Sexton's life'. It was clear that, despite the presence of Hudson and Osgood in the team, flair and pizazz were missing from Chelsea's football, hardly likely to draw in the extra regular punters that Chelsea were so desperate to attract. The Sun, perceptively, noted that Chelsea 'are very much a bunch who need the stimulation of tangible targets' and the frustration in the dressing room that Tottenham met Norwich in the League Cup Final a few miles away that afternoon must have been tangible.

Only 26,259 turned up for that 'ninety minutes of tedium' so it was no surprise that the crowd for Wolves on a Tuesday night three days later was lower. What was a shock was exactly how low the crowd was, a dismal 18,868, starkly demonstrating how fragile the bedrock support had become. A 2-0 defeat, with John Richards and Derek Dougan again demonstrating the potency of their partnership by scoring a goal apiece, making a comparison with Chelsea's pairing of Garner and Garland a stark one and the journey home a depressing one for the loyal supporters who turned out. Sexton had been a long-time admirer of Richards, who would have made a real difference to his side, but nothing ever came of his interest.

The trip to West Bromwich hardly raised the pulse of the travelling faithful, either. A 1-1 draw, with Garland equalizing a Tony 'Bomber' Brown goal within the first seven minutes. The game was unusual in that Osgood was withdrawn to centre-half in the second half to deal with the aerial threat of Jeff Astle, with Hinton, a highly effective sweeper, covering behind him. 'Osgood did us proud' Sexton told the *Daily Mirror*. 'He has never played there before, even in practise. This just goes to show how versatile he can be'. As the *Daily Telegraph* wryly observed, 'switching Osgood to centre-half was like asking Yehudi Menuhin to bang the big drum' but admitted he showed great authority and dominated the penalty box, particularly in the air. Osgood observed 'I enjoyed it, but I hope it's nothing permanent'.

If Dempsey was not fit for Arsenal, Sexton hinted he might consider Osgood at the back, though moving your main striker to centre-half in a critical home cup-tie would hardly be a statement of positive intent. Luckily, Sexton got the call after the game that Dempsey had come through a reserve game unscathed and would be fit for the big game. Harris's appeal was unsuccessful so, as feared, he missed the game and would also be suspended for any replay. The *News Of The World* felt that injury and suspension might force Sexton to pick inexperienced full-back Graham Wilkins.

Chelsea were cursing their luck at hosting London's biggest game of the season with a restricted capacity. The club decided, sensibly, to limit the crowd to 40,000 and make it all-ticket, to avoid potential problems. Mears explained 'I think what happened against Leeds taught us a lesson. People will say we will lose money, but we do not look at it that way. Our first consideration must be safety', a welcome philosophy.

The game could have sold out twice over, and Chelsea were approached by Jarvis Astaire, pioneer of UK closed-circuit cinema coverage of major sporting events with his Viewsport Ltd. company, regarding showing the game in North London cinemas. Both teams were keen, and the FA and Football League were persuaded that the coverage should be permitted because of the 'extenuating circumstances' with the reduced capacity. In the end 12,500 customers paid a steep £1.80 each to watch in one of ten cinemas, with plain-clothes police in attendance to prevent any trouble, and the clubs shared £10,000.

The CCTV coverage did not prevent a thriving black-market operation at Stamford Bridge. In terms of 40p terrace tickets, Arsenal got 4,000, Chelsea around 20,000. Ground receipts were £19,085 from 37,685 fans, though it is unclear why the crowd was not 40,000, unless touts were stuck with 2,300.

Dempsey duly returned, taking his place alongside Locke, Hinton and McCreadie in the back four. Droy had lost more than a stone in weight in three weeks (which does not sound healthy) and was fit, but Sexton decided against bringing him back. Garner was out with a groin strain, but Houseman, out with a heavy chest cold for three weeks, was brought back to stretch the Arsenal defence.

Arsenal were favourites, the atmosphere was tremendous despite the missing East Stand (supporter Geoff Kimber recalls The Shed was 'heaving'), and the game started at a frantic pace. Within 33 minutes the score was 2-2. Osgood's wonderful volley, giving Chelsea the lead, was BBC's Goal Of The Season and is still shown on television 46 years later, as is his celebratory bow to the crowd. Two mistakes by Phillips let Alan Ball and Charlie George score for Arsenal but Hollins equalised with a thumping right-foot drive, his first goal for five months. Locke's crosses helped create both Chelsea goals, but he later suffered a badly bruised toe which limited his effectiveness.

That was the end of the goals but both sides continued to make defensive errors in an exciting second-half and Kember could have snatched a win near the end. Dempsey, not match-fit, struggled all afternoon and Phillips' nerves affected his defensive colleagues. Sexton defended his goalkeeper, who had generally been very solid behind an ever-changing defence in recent weeks, stating he would be selected for the replay. Locke was out, so Hollins had to play at full-back. Garner was fit and was brought back, the feeling being that he could exploit Arsenal's defensive weakness in the air.

The replay, three days later, was not all-ticket. Interest was enormous and a massive 62,746 squeezed into a jam-packed Highbury paying £35,042 for a game forever tainted by controversy in the minds of the Chelsea supporters packed into the Clock End. An estimated 10,000 supporters were locked out of Highbury. Houseman, playing down the middle in yet another tactical switch, headed Chelsea ahead. Kember tackled George Armstrong on the edge of the penalty area. Armstrong went down. TV pictures later showed the foul was in the penalty area, but referee Norman Burtenshaw gave a free-kick. After heated protests by Arsenal players, he was persuaded by Ball and captain Frank McLintock to consult his linesman. He did so and at length changed his mind, pointing to the penalty spot.

Chelsea players, rightly, went beserk, as the clear implication was that Burtenshaw caved in to vociferously complaining players, a point made by commentator Barry Davies on *Sportsnight* and several journalists the following day. Ball duly scored the penalty, Osgood elbowing Kennedy as the kick was taken as the bad feeling simmered. Kennedy headed Arsenal ahead and they held on. Peter Storey appeared to handle a Garland shot but nothing was given. Despite what supporter Geoff Kimber remembers as 'the best performance by a Chelsea team that season' they were out, their season was over, and they were rightly less than happy.

Osgood told the referee to his face that he was a coward and repeated the comment to any journalist that would listen. He was unsurprisingly asked by the FA to explain his 'coward' comments. Burtenshaw did not report the incident as he apparently did not hear it, but FA could still act.

McLintock's comment 'There is no doubt that he (Burtenshaw) wouldn't have given a penalty if I had not protested' did not help matters. Dempsey clouded the water still further, arguing that Burtenshaw originally gave an indirect free-kick for obstruction and even put his arm up to confirm this, though from TV pictures it looked a foul. 'It was ridiculous to change his mind like that when the Arsenal players said it was inside the area'.

An absolutely pivotal game and one the *Kensington Post* felt showed that age had taken its toll on defenders. 'McCreadie's timing was way out, Hinton lost his battles. Dempsey was skillfully tempted out of the middle on one too many occasions'. Certainly, the defence badly needed an injection of fresh blood. Harris's competitive spirit was missed, as was Locke's energy, but the truth was that Chelsea had to significantly strengthen. To do that, of course, they had to spend money, and that was at a premium. Supporter Brian Gaches makes an interesting point, that it was only for these big games that 'the more talented players like Osgood and Hudson who had their battles with Sexton could be really motivated to turn in a big performance'.

Sadly, these big games were becoming less frequent. If Chelsea had come out on top against Arsenal, and reached the Semi-final, events might have turned out very differently. The opposition would have been Sunderland, who went on to lift the cup. A fully-firing Chelsea would, however, have been favourites to reach the final. Cup success, or even reaching the final, would have been an enormous fillip to the club, would undoubtedly have boosted crowds, brought in welcome revenue and, potentially, given Sexton funds to strengthen his squad in Summer 1973. Failure, however, meant an early end to the season from a competitive perspective. The sense of drift began to heighten.

Four days before the Arsenal game Chelsea played a friendly against British Police, at Hartley Wintney, giving Droy his first run-out in four months. Dave Sexton also played in the 1-1 draw, and it was hardly a serious game, being part of the Police College silver jubilee celebrations. Seen by Chelsea as a private game, it was the selection of suspended Ron Harris that attracted the headlines and the wrath of FA disciplinary supremo Vernon Stokes.

The FA got to hear that Harris had played. Stokes, somewhat bizarrely, exploded that it was one of the worst contraventions of the rules he had ever experienced. He threatened to throw the book at both club and player and a full probe was promised. Chelsea claimed total ignorance of the rules, no defence. It was surprising nobody from Chelsea had thought this through, especially as there were spectators (policemen) at the game and a 5p programme was produced. The rule was that suspended players could only play in training matches between players of the same club, which seemed unambiguous. The matter was duly investigated, with the bristling Stokes keeping his beady eye on proceedings.

Three away games followed, though Chelsea's season had stumbled to a virtual halt. Britton, felt to be too inexperienced for the Arsenal games, played in all three. They were not the only side suffering dismal attendances. Under 22,000 at Newcastle and under 24,000 at Manchester City were dreadful crowds, though a derby at Crystal Palace was a much more attractive proposition, drawing 39,325.

A 1-1 draw at Newcastle was notable for the attendance of Prime Minister Ted Heath, not a noted football fan. Garner scored the equaliser in a forgettable match. Houseman badly wrenched his ankle early on and was out for the rest of the season. Equally forgettable was the game at Maine Road three days later, though Osgood's header gave Chelsea a welcome, if surprising, two points. Despite the win, *The Sun* were scathing, dubbing Chelsea 'the First Division dead-end kids' and arguing 'clearly Chelsea could not care less about the game'. Luckily City, whose run had now stretched to nine games without a win, were even worse. A barely troubled Peter Bonetti, in only his second game since October, kept a welcome clean sheet. 'Big Mal' Allison, under-pressure City manager, left for Crystal Palace three days later, so his first Palace game was also against Chelsea.

Palace were in twentieth place, fighting relegation, whereas Chelsea had risen to the lofty heights of tenth, a mundane mid-table position competing neither for European place nor avoiding the drop. Allison, lionised by a wildly enthusiastic crowd, motivated his new charges to a 2-0 win against disinterested opposition. The *Fulham Chronicle's* observation was that 'I have never seen Chelsea play so drably all season', which, given some of their displays, was quite something. The paucity of the Chelsea squad was underlined by the fact that Dempsey had to go up front when Garner was hurt. The youth team reached the Semi-final of the FA Youth Cup for the first time since 1965 so there were promising youngsters ready to challenge the experienced squad members, but they were not first-team material yet.

The latest club to move for Baldwin were Southampton, who agreed a £70,000 fee with Chelsea. He turned it down. The *Sunday People* reported that Chelsea were apparently about to sign John Gorman, attacking Carlisle left-back, for £80,000, but nothing happened. It was clear that the squad required major surgery, but Chelsea were not in the top ten transfer spenders when the transfer deadline passed earlier that month, Manchester United, Palace and Everton topping the list.

April 1973

Seven largely meaningless games to go, for a side in eleventh place, nine points ahead of the relegation zone and eight points off a possible European place. A chance, maybe, for Dave Sexton to blood some youngsters. The Youth Team were knocked out by Ipswich Town but there was growing excitement at the club regarding their future.

The first game in April was Tottenham at home, normally a raucous affair. The level of disillusionment could be measured by the fact that a mere 25,536 turned out to watch Chelsea labour to a 1-0 defeat against a side saving energy for the UEFA Cup Semi-final. Winger Mike Brolly made his debut and at least introduced some width. Britton also impressed, so maybe Chelsea already had some youthful promise to give further chances to. The *Daily Mail* heard an 'understandable ripple of slow-handclapping' in the second half. They reported that this was silenced by fans at each end chanting 'we hate you' at the other.

An even lower crowd, 19,706, yawned their way through a 3-1 defeat by Stoke, the second home defeat in four days. Brolly kept his place, as he was to do for the rest of the season. Another youngster,

Tommy Ord, celebrated his debut with a fine goal ('a missile' according to supporter David Gray) from the edge of the box but there was little else for the crowd to enthuse about. He was the 28th different player to pull on a Chelsea first-team shirt that season and it was Chelsea's first home League goal for almost two months. The *Daily Telegraph* reported that Chelsea fans stayed behind afterwards and 'greeted with rapture' the news of Arsenal's FA Cup Semi-final defeat by Sunderland.

The *Daily Mirror* made a trenchant observation. Under a 'The Dull Blues' headline they argued that 'if Chelsea are ever to recoup the millions of pounds to be spent on improving Stamford Bridge, they will have to concentrate harder on providing better entertainment for the customers'. Indeed. Two crowd favourites, Webb and Hutchinson, were hoping to play in the reserves in the next week but realistically were unlikely to play for the first-team again that season.

Norwich had not won for nineteen League games but a fixture against an 'on the beach' Chelsea side gave them the opportunity to pick up two invaluable points. Droy played his first game since early December but only Bonetti's brilliance prevented a heavier defeat than 1-0. After their fourth defeat on the trot, Sexton took the rare step of 'gagging' his players from talking to the press. Chelsea were only six points off the bottom, their lowest position at a late stage of the season since relegation in 1962.

For their ninth game in thirty-one days, at Everton, Ord came in, replacing Britton. Howard Kendall scored in the second minute and that was almost the end of the entertainment. Chelsea now had a dreadful record of three League wins since late October. With three games left, all at home, Chelsea were still six points off the relegation zone so if Crystal Palace and Norwich won their four remaining games, Chelsea could in theory go down. How the mighty had fallen, and how far below pre-season aspiration the team had slumped.

The first two games, against Southampton and Coventry City, predictably attracted sub-20,000 crowds. Secretary Tony Green had given up berating supporters for their lack of loyalty. What was notable about the 2-1 win over Southampton was the praise meted out by Sexton to youngsters Brolly, Ord and Britton. Brolly, who equalised and made the winner for Hollins, came in for particular mention. Relieved Chelsea chairman Brian Mears beamed 'what a difference a win makes' and, given it killed off any lingering relegation fears, the fact it was an entertaining game was the icing on the cake.

The *Daily Mail* reported that 'Mears ... is doggedly pursuing his super stadium project in the face of falling gates ... count the importance of Saturday's win in a little more cash at the turnstiles'. Mears claimed, bizarrely, 'I was pleased we had nearly 20,000'. He hoped for more against Coventry and a sell-out against Manchester United. 'These are nice thoughts after a traumatic season like ours'. Writer Jeff Powell thought 'the new main stand ... may be open at the start of next season', though given the lack of visible progress this prediction was wildly optimistic.

Chelsea had not won a penalty for sixty-five games until one was awarded against Coventry, in front of the lowest crowd of the season, 18,279. John Hollins duly netted it, doubling a lead given by Hinton in only his fourth goal in almost ten years at the club.

The *Daily Mirror* revived the story about George Best moving to Chelsea that summer, with Rodney Marsh of Manchester City allegedly also a potential target. How these ambitious moves for undoubted crowd-pullers would be financed was never explained, and, needless to say, the deals went nowhere.

The 'Osgood swap for Best' chestnut, allowing Ossie to link up with his ex-boss Tommy Docherty, was floated again, once more with a significant lack of anything concrete happening. Sexton dismissed as 'ridiculous' suggestions they could be involved in an exchange deal. Osgood commented 'you hear things, though I've been told nothing'. The player obviously felt he had an uneasy relationship with his manager, and as they pointed out, 'he has never disguised his admiration for (United boss) Tommy Docherty, who brought him into big football'.

The final game of the season, against Manchester United, was notable for one thing. Won by an Osgood goal rebounding off his knee, it was Bobby Charlton's last League game for Manchester United. Mears presented him with an engraved cigarette case, a somewhat unusual present to give a world-renowned sportsman. The Shed chanted 'We Want Bobby' after the final whistle and he waved to acknowledge their cheers.

The *Daily Mirror* felt that if Best moved to Chelsea his partnership with Osgood could be mind-boggling. 'The Chelsea centre-forward, so spiteful, so brilliant, provided the few memorable moments in Charlton's last match. If only Osgood had the temperament, the character and the discipline of the player whose show he stole'.

Two weeks earlier a story had appeared which concerned many Chelsea supporters, and was to have repercussions over the coming months. The *Sunday People* ran a 'Hudson Wants To Go' headline. He had missed the Stoke game through injury but was told by Sexton he would not have been picked anyway. Dissatisfied with the midfielder's form, Sexton had told the *Daily Mail* 'I don't know what's wrong. He isn't playing very well'. He was then left out of the side defeated at Norwich. The paper felt it unlikely Chelsea would let him go, though they thought Tottenham and Arsenal would be interested, in a bid that would go close to the British transfer record. The same day, The *News Of The World* said Hudson, whose recent form had been poor, had a heart-to-heart with Sexton the previous week, admitted he was unsettled and that a move might be the answer. He had not scored in twenty-six First Division appearances and had clearly lost his pre-season bet with Osgood about scoring ten League goals that season.

A day later, the *Daily Mirror* reported Hudson had put in a written transfer request the previous Thursday, but Sexton revealed 'I shall recommend to my board that it is turned down. There is no chance of him leaving the club'. They reported that the player had asked for a move because of 'family pressures and his disappointing form this season' and may try again.

Evidently well-informed, three days later they ran a 'Hudson Will Ask Again For Move' headline. 'Alan Hudson yesterday began the battle to get away from Chelsea, the club he no longer wants to play for'. He planned to put in another request and seek a meeting with Brian Mears and the board. 'Hudson admits his lifestyle has caused concern at Chelsea, but stresses it is because of his unhappiness with the current situation'. Sexton 'has been concerned about his form and attitude'. Hudson was unhappy about being played out of position, 'but in a season where Chelsea have been cruelly hit by injuries, Sexton has sometimes had no alternative...It appears that breaking point is near between Chelsea and a player who just a few years ago was heralded as the greatest prospect in the country'.

The following week the *Sunday People* ran a feature on Hudson. Sexton enthused 'Alan Hudson is magic at his best – a world-class player. Unfortunately, he's lost a little of his appetite for the game...Change of pace is his outstanding attribute. At the moment he's fighting a psychological block outside the box...He's become a reluctant shooter, preferring to pass', which was presumably an attempt to psych him up. Hudson later told Clive Batty in *Kings Of The King's Road* that 'I stopped caring around then'.

The same week Tottenham bid £300,000 for Mike Channon but Chelsea were not in the market for the Southampton striker or any other top-rated star, though they yet again revived interest in Fulham's Steve Earle, trying to exchange him for Tommy Baldwin.

As the end of the season approached it was clear that the East Stand would not be completed and open for the start of the 1973-74 season. In the Southampton programme the club confirmed that the East Stand would not be all season-ticket when it came into operation and that a proportion of seats would be available to the general public on a match basis. They also advised that the next part of the stadium to be to be developed would be the South End quadrant.

The Manchester United programme advised that as they were unable to give a definite date for the opening of the new East Stand, the club proposed to issue renewing season-ticket holders with their existing seats. Then, when the new stand hopefully came into use early in 1973-74, season-ticket holders wishing to move would be invited to apply for a transfer. They admitted that seat prices for the new stand had not yet been finalised.

Season Review

A worrying sense of drift had begun to permeate the club. Had the team reached the League Cup Final and/or the FA Cup Semi-final then the season who have been seen in far more positive terms but the cup defeats by Arsenal and, especially, Norwich were a hammer blow. Mid-table mediocrity, after the excitements of the preceding seasons, was an additional disappointment in what supporter Geoff Kimber calls 'a nonentity of a season'.

Goal scoring had become a problem, to the extent that Peter Osgood and Chris Garland were joint leading League scorers with just eleven each. The signings over the past two seasons – Steve Kember, Garland and Bill Garner – had hardly set the world alight and the side was losing its reputation as a source of entertainment. The unhappy Hudson's frustration at having to regularly play wide was becoming more evident and his and Kember's inability to score (no goals in 61 League starts between them that season), allied to the previously prolific John Hollins scoring only three, meant that midfield could not be relied on the score in any quantity.

None of the three attacking young players given chances over the past two seasons, Peter Feely, Tommy Ord and Tony Potrac, made a compelling claim for a regular place. Given the mediocre season, it is a great shame that Sexton did not see fit to give them more chances but maybe the reality is they were not quite good enough for First Division football. The emergence of Gary Locke showed the manager was prepared to play youth products and, given the financial strictures at the club he would surely have been delighted to insert more as first-team regulars, had they been on the required quality.

The Manchester United programme referred to 'an injury list without parallel in our history'. While that was true, it did not excuse a swathe of mediocre performances, both at home and away, across the season. The club was forced to use 28 players that season, whereas title winners Liverpool fielded but 16, and the programme opined that no club could expect success when that happened. Only Harris, Hollins, Osgood and Kember played over 30 League games and the Webb injury in February had a huge impact.

The estimate by the Chelsea board, that reducing the capacity after the Leeds embarrassment could cost the club £60,000, was unfounded. Given the only times the reduced capacity was reached was against Arsenal in the FA Cup (when a limit of 40,000 was set) and against Manchester United at the very end of the season (when 44,184 attended), a more realistic loss might be £10,000.

The 23.3% fall in average home League crowds to under 30,000 was a shock to the board. Rather than because of the problems against Leeds, the reason was probably primarily a frustration and disillusionment with the team's worst placing for a decade, allied to the fact that terrace admission had increased by 33% at a time of serious national economic challenge. Whatever the cause, the reality was that, at a time when the club needed every penny it could get, the regular fan base had significantly diminished. The difference between pre- and post-Christmas attendances was even more stark. Averaging 33,100, first half of the season home gates were well down, but the second-half crowds averaged 26,000, little short of catastrophic. *Foul: Football's Alternative Paper* also referred to the board's 'thinly disguised panic' over the falling gates, the necessity to sell Mulligan and Cooke and the 'difficulty' in raising the Garner fee. Team and crowds were both clearly in decline. The lack of atmosphere was a frustration to the extent that Sexton, not a man prone to hyperbole or over-reaction, told an unsympathetic Mears he found it hard to motivate the players at home.

An early season run of nine games without defeat was encouraging, but two later season runs of six or more games without a win, topped off with five defeats in a row from late March to mid-April illustrate the team's decline as the season went on.

Twelfth place was unacceptable for a team of Chelsea's ambition and must have caused significant stress in the boardroom, where the directors were staring at ever-increasing building costs, a series of delays in construction, a failing team and a massive drop-off in support. Any one problem would have been difficult, but to have the lot must have caused serious questions to be asked in private with regard to the future.
Foul: Football's Alternative Paper carried a full-page analysis of Chelsea's season by Simon Holloway. It was not a positive one. He talks about complacent players and issues around behaviour and drunkenness, which were to feature large the following season. He saw the injuries as an excuse and pointed out that only two defenders – Webb and Locke – were First Division calibre but that Sexton was loathe to drop Harris or Dempsey.

The number and seriousness of injuries endured by squad members certainly did not help Sexton, illustrating that although he had a large squad it was not necessarily of the required quality. It was fervently hoped, at least publicly, that the new East Stand would be open early the following season. Whether the current team could produce the brand of attractive, successful football to reverse the trend and fill it was open to debate.

Close Season

Somewhat surprisingly, given he had only scored eleven League goals and had a poor latter part of the season, Peter Osgood was awarded *Player Of The Year* at a packed Supporters Club dance at Hammersmith Town Hall in April. Votes were cast throughout the season to recognise those continually favoured by the members. Chris Garland and Bill Garner were voted second and third. The ever-reliable and loyal John

Hollins and David Webb were, rather unfairly, nowhere.

The Alan Hudson saga continued. The *Fulham Chronicle* anticipated he could be swapped with George Best. Mears again felt Best 'could help return those missing fans to Stamford Bridge'. The rift between club and player grew when he was omitted from the squad on a two-day golfing holiday in Dorset for turning up late for training the day before the trip.

In June, Hudson opened his heart to the *News Of The World*. 'If I'm put on the wing again, I'll ask the chairman to go'. He mentioned a growing split with Sexton, insisting 'I want to play in midfield where I consider I'm most effective. Chelsea are a great club and to even talk of leaving sickens me, but I must get my priorities right…I told the chairman I'd rather play with ten men if it meant I was on the wing. I like to be involved and run at defences'. He claimed he was miserable for most of the previous season. 'Sudden death games appeal to me. It's difficult to get worked up over League matches at the Bridge, where you can't hear the crowd'. Something else for Sexton, Mears and the board to worry about while they recharged their batteries. An obviously unhappy Hudson, who was also refused a pay rise, and a potentially discontented Osgood wondering about a possible move to Manchester United did not bode well for a critical new season.

Chelsea ended the season with a three-match tour of Iran, a somewhat unlikely destination. Sexton took a strong squad who won one, drew one and lost one of the three games, all played in Tehran. Rick Glanvill and Paul Dutton, in their *Chelsea – The Complete Record*, describe the tour as 'a boozy, bad-tempered nightmare for Sexton', a foretaste of what was to come for a manager increasingly struggling to relate to, and communicate with, the more headstrong members of his squad.

More worrying was the lack of progress in terms of completing the East Stand on schedule. In *Chelsea – The Real Story* Brian Mears recounts how at the start of the project the board told the developers the stand must be ready for the start of the 1973-74 season and was told this would not be a problem. As early as winter 1972 it became very likely the stand would not be ready for the following season. Building slowed down almost to a standstill, but the club still had to pay both architect and quantity surveyor fees. There was a fixed contract with the builders, but it contained no clauses about strikes or brick and steel shortages, so the risk sat with the club, and when difficulties occurred and project costs escalated significantly, the club was liable for the extra costs, not the contractors.

By mid-March 1973 the main contractor, W&C French, reckoned they could hand the main structure of the stand over on 28th May for other works to begin. The architects blamed the delay on a wide range of factors - late steel erection, brick and steel shortages, building strikes (at one stage, there were pickets outside the main entrance to stop men and materials getting in), the three-day working week, GLC requirements on emergency lighting and modifications to upper-tier steps.

Delay meant the double nightmare of reduced income and increased costs. New investors could not be found, and inflation continued to spiral. The club was facing potential crises, both on and off the pitch.

Season Overview 1972-73

League Appearances (inc sub) (top 11 players) – Harris 42, Hollins 42, Osgood 38, Kember 35, McCreadie 31, Garland 27, Hudson 26, Webb 26, Bonetti 23, Garner 21, Houseman 21

League Goals (5+) – Garland 11, Osgood 11, Garner 7
League Clean Sheets – *Home* 6. *Away* 3
Biggest League Win – 4-0 v Leeds United (H) 12/08/72
Worst League Defeat – 0-3 v Ipswich Town (A) 26/12/72
Final League position –12th

League Record –
Home W9 D6 L6 F30 A22. *Away* W4 D8 L9 F19 A29. Pts 40

Hat-Tricks – None
Sending Offs
Ron Harris v Brighton and Hove Albion (A) FA Cup R3,13/01/73; Bill Garner v Sheffield Wednesday (A) FA Cup R5, 24/02/73

Biggest Home League Crowd – 51,102 v Leeds United 12/08/72
Smallest Home League Crowd – 18,279 v Coventry City 23/04/73
Average Home League Crowd – 29,739
Cup Performances – *FA Cup* 6th Round. *League Cup* Semi-finalists.

Chelsea League Debuts – Brian Bason, Ian Britton, Mike Brolly, Bill Garner, Gary Locke, Tommy Ord, Graham Wilkins

Player Of The Year – Peter Osgood

CHAPTER FOUR
1973-74 – The Stars Go Out

Pre-season

After a dismal second half of the previous season, and a fractious tour of Iran, the Chelsea squad returned to pre-season training. Manager Dave Sexton's reaction when his unsettled midfield playmaker, Alan Hudson, turned up for the first day of training a stone overweight would have been interesting. Unabashed, the player told the *Daily Mail* he would sweat it off 'as he usually did before the season started', but it was hardly indicative on a honed athlete knuckling down to the rigours of the long season ahead.

Hudson was certainly prolific in his conversations with journalists. He told the *News Of The World* he had patched up his differences with the manager and no longer sought a transfer. He had been back in training a week, had a chat with Sexton and was happy with the situation. 'I'm crossing my fingers that I'll start the season in midfield, which is where I want to play'. He said he was training hard and 'has lost just under a stone already' and nearly fainted in training as he hadn't been eating. He was only 4lb over his best weight and 'eating the right food now'.

The *Fulham Chronicle* emphasised that the 1972-73 season had been a nightmare for Hudson. Banned by England for missing an Under-23 summer tour, plagued by injury, forced by circumstance to play out of position on the wing and plagued by personal problems, he had come through it and faced the new season with growing confidence. 'You can say there's been a reconciliation between the manager and myself'. The lifting of his England ban provided another boost.

The *Kensington Post*, in their season preview, worried that 'this could be the last chance for Hudson to do well in Chelsea colours. For all his promise, he has had a demoralising last eighteen months and if he 'doesn't come in from the cold' Sexton may unload his unsettled starlet'. Certainly, Hudson required a strong start to the season, especially as he and Steve Kember were in reality vying for one place. Sexton's preferred system involved two wingers, leaving only two midfield places, one of which was obviously for John Hollins. Kember could not effectively play wide and Sexton had apparently accepted Hudson's much-publicised plea that wing-play was not for him.

Hudson's crash dieting aside, Sexton had other concerns. His squad was big enough but not strong enough and he had a few experienced squad members he was trying to move on. John Boyle, Tommy Baldwin and John Dempsey were all on the transfer list. Marvin Hinton had been, though he had been back in the side in April. Eddie McCreadie's injuries were catching up with him. Baldwin, who had turned down a couple of moves, interested Stoke City and Bournemouth were keen on Boyle, though, as so often, neither enquiry developed into moves.

Apart from the weight-shedding Hudson, the other temperamental star Sexton needed firing on all cylinders was Peter Osgood. The *Evening Standard* focused on how 'An Eager Osgood Could Spark a Challenge from Chelsea' in their season preview. Osgood felt the easing of the young players into the team 'gave me a sense of responsibility. I think you could say I have grown up now', though he had made similar utterances in previous pre-seasons. He predicted he would fulfil his promise that season if he had a fit Ian Hutchinson alongside him, to recreate the partnership that had been so successful three years earlier. As Hutch had barely played in 30 months, to expect to him to attain his old standards was optimistic. He had not signed a new contract as a government-regulated pay freeze meant he could only get five pounds a week extra and he hoped for improved terms when the freeze ended.

Over the summer Osgood flew to Australia for a showpiece game against a touring Brazilian side. The *News Of The World* claimed 'It's proof that the talented Osgood – though spurned by England – has taken over from George Best as Britain's No. 1 soccer personality'. Osgood beamed 'I'm really flattered…I am being well paid, but I would have gone for nothing. It's nice to think you are highly rated so far from home'. Sexton, struggling on occasion to contain the striker's ego, may have had a different view. The *Evening Standard* even reported that Real Madrid had Osgood and Leeds United's Allan Clarke on their wanted list. His profile was certainly high, even though he had scored just eleven League goals in 38 games the previous season, a poor return regardless of evident weaknesses elsewhere in the side.

The *Kensington Post's* season preview gave some trenchant opinions. They felt Chelsea were unacceptably unpredictable. They could be brilliant, flamboyant and unbeatable, could be sturdy, professional and unbeatable. Too often, however, they were panicky, careless and impossible. At best they were a good bet for a cup. The defence had not been strengthened, they had not had a top centre-half for years, though they argued that David Webb fitted the bill as a second centre-half. These opinions may not have been what Sexton desired to read, but they certainly had the ring of truth. Inconsistency had indeed bedevilled the side for years.

Sexton was indeed faced with a surplus of strikers, especially if Hutchinson, who had played just four senior games in 30 months because of a series of grim injuries, could reach and maintain full fitness. He offered Bill Garner, bought largely as cover for Hutchinson, to Fulham in exchange for long-time target Steve Earle. Their near-neighbours were not interested.

Two youngsters had been released, Jimmy Davis, who moved to Charlton, and John Spong. Several youngsters were added to the professional staff - Keith Lawrence (19), Michael Sorensen (17), Steve Perkins (18), David Lucas (18), Barry Bolton (17) and Alan Taylor (19). Forward Ken Swain, 21, was bought from Wycombe Wanders for a mere £500. Reserve forward Tommy Ord spent the summer with Olympique Montreal, playing sixteen games he hoped would help win him a first-team place in the coming season. Behind the scenes Norman Medhurst was appointed new head trainer with his long-term club loyalist father Harry becoming club physiotherapist.

Sexton admitted he required a right-winger to complement Peter Houseman on the left, though there were hopes that eager youngster Ian Britton could fill that role. The *Evening Standard*, optimistically, felt Chelsea could be London's strongest contenders for a major honour. 'The spearhead of Hudson, who has shaken off the depression of the last two seasons, and Chris Garland has real possibilities'. They also saw giant young centre-back Micky Droy as developing into a regular first-teamer. Sexton told the paper he believed they were unlucky with injuries the previous season, and 'given a break in that direction, we have the players to match the best. Having the new stand open should make a lot of difference in atmosphere compared with last season'. He spoke to the *Fulham Chronicle*, telling them that 'seeing the players train at Mitcham this week, I can honestly say I have never seen the squad so keen and enthusiastic about a new season'. There seems a detachment from reality here, as only a handful of players were top-notch whereas teams like Leeds United and Liverpool had real quality throughout their sides, as well as stronger squad players.

In terms of the new stand, the *Fulham Chronicle* reported that 'The first part of Chelsea's new 'super stadium' is nearly completed. The two-tier cantilever East Stand with 12,000 seats will be open to the public shortly'. The stand showed no signs of being anywhere near finished, so exactly what 'shortly' meant was open to question. Mears admitted there was no firm opening date. It became clear the stand would not open until autumn at the earliest, a significant financial blow to a club relying heavily on income from the new stand. As delay worsened, the Chelsea board made it clear it had to be open by January 1974 for the FA Cup. Players accommodation was not scheduled to be ready until the following summer, but, though less than ideal, this was rightly seen as less important than opening the stand itself. The club had already shelved any idea of linking the new stand with Fulham Broadway station, as they could not afford pay for it.

All 7,000 West Stand and North Stand season-tickets had been sold, and terrace admission increased from 40p to 45p, hardly a surprise given the need for the club to increase revenue and the fact that the inflation rate was spiralling upwards.

In *The Chelsea Football Book No.4*, Mears hoped the 'depression' of the previous season was 'far, far behind us as we begin 1973-74' and implied that the new stand would open soon.

Chelsea arranged five overseas friendlies. Wins over Vfl Bochum, Werder Bremen and ADO Den Haag were followed by draws in Orense and Celta Vigo. Houseman and Britton played on the wing in the first two games, Sexton keen to give them a chance to prove themselves. Hutchinson came on as substitute in the first three games and started the next, looking ready for first-team football. John Dempsey had a toe injury and it was likely to be a while before he returned.

Osgood hurt his knee against Werder Bremen and missed the Den Haag game. He was then sent off against Orense, followed by Kember and McCreadie getting their marching orders against Celta Vigo. They were all unlikely to be reported to the FA, but a frustrated Sexton felt 'the referee was technically correct. It was silly of our fellows to do what they did'.

One legacy from the previous season was cleared up when Chelsea were fined £750 by the FA for playing Harris in a friendly against British Police while suspended. Harris was fined £25, harsh as he can only have been blameless in the affair. All highly embarrassing for FA Council member, and Chelsea chairman, Brian Mears.

August 1973

Ian Hutchinson was selected to play in the opening game at Derby County, his first competitive first-team game for eight months. The *Daily Mail*, under a 'Hutch's Big Gamble' headline, ran a feature about the striker's 'comeback from injury and despair'. Hutch boldly stated 'I'll go in as hard as ever, it's all I know'. He did not have a contract, his old one having run out in the summer, and some team-mates were on nearly double his wage. 'Chelsea have stood by me and I've never had cause for complaint in the whole five years' and Sexton 'agreed to talk money if and when I show him I can do my job for Chelsea once more'. The manager was understandably desperate to keep him fit.

Sexton made a big call, one with repercussions in the coming months, leaving Alan Hudson on the bench, his pre-season form having been indifferent despite, or maybe because of, his crash diet. The player, unsurprisingly, was bitterly disappointed. On the day of the game the *Daily Mirror* ran a 'Crisis for Hudson after 'Axe' shock' headline. They reported he was 'absolutely choked'. 'It seems certain he will seek a showdown with Sexton'. A 'close friend' said 'it was a real blow to him when he heard he wasn't in the side'.

John Hollins was moved to full-back, replacing Gary Locke, Sexton preferring to go with John Boyle and Steve Kember in midfield as the side lined up in an attacking 4-2-4 formation :- *Bonetti; Hollins, Webb,*

Harris, McCreadie; Boyle, Kember; Garland, Osgood, Hutchinson, Houseman.

The manager had his most reliable midfielder at full-back and a reluctant Garland on the wing, putting huge reliance on wing-partner Houseman to feed the Osgood-Hutchinson striking partnership with a stream of crosses. Osgood, by his own admission never started the season well and Hutchinson was obviously not fully fit. Derby were a very good side and expected to beat a bit of a makeshift Chelsea team. The match was highly entertaining for *Match Of The Day* viewers, John McGovern giving the home side the lead after twenty minutes. Derby held on despite Chelsea's endeavours, dominating midfield, which the *Sunday People* put down to the selection of Hollins at full-back. Hutchinson worked hard but was inevitably rusty and, worse, he injured his shoulder and was doubtful for the coming game at Burnley. Osgood, who had tangled with Derby centre-half Roy MacFarland in the past, drew a 'No Tantrums From The 'New' Ossie' headline in the *Daily Mirror*. He was clattered by MacFarland but drew praise for getting up and getting on with it. Whether this newfound maturity would manifest itself through the season remained to be seen.

Hudson was recalled, with Garner, four days later at Burnley, as Boyle was dropped, and Hutchinson was injured. Boyle, a loyal servant for over eight years, never played for the first-team again. Sexton's team, set up to attack, battled hard but were undone by a late Frank Casper goal.

No points from two games, but Sexton pledged to continue to play attacking football. How long that would last if the team continued to lose was an interesting point. Hudson later pointed out that 'after the Burnley game we sat for hours talking it over and realising what we've got to do from now on'. What they had to do was beat Sheffield United at home.

September 1973

Two games a week at the start of the season gave Dave Sexton little time to work out how to avoid the defeats becoming a crisis. Against Sheffield United he retained John Hollins at full-back and dropped Chris Garland for the fit-again Ian Hutchinson. This meant a 'three centre-forward' forward line of Bill Garner, Peter Osgood and Ian Hutchinson. Given Garner was bought primarily as cover for Hutchinson the line-up had a lopsided look, even with Osgood playing behind the burly pair, and put pressure on Peter Houseman to get the crosses in and playmaker Alan Hudson to make incisive passes. Osgood later lamented 'we had a great close-season tour, and everyone was happy. We lost the first two games of the season and Sexton switched from 4-2-4, the style everyone in the side agreed suited us best, to 4-3-3'.

Unfortunately, Chelsea's revised plans did not seem to include marking Tony Currie, one of the great talents of 1970s English football and almost unstoppable that day. He ran the game and his team thoroughly dominated lacklustre opponents. Currie's comments spoke volumes. 'I think Chelsea have too many players who want to attack. They got caught out too often'. Hollins penalty, scant consolation in a 2-1 defeat that could have been much worse, was Chelsea's first goal of the season.

Chelsea, with no points from three games, were bottom of the table and, unsurprisingly, the press went to town. The *News Of the World* was unequivocal. Under a 'Sexton Reads The Riot Act' headline they reported that the squad had been ordered in for extra training on Monday, injured or not…It's foolish to talk about a Chelsea crisis - but the warning signs are flashing…Chelsea were appalling. They knew it - and the thousands who started the slow-handclap 20 minutes into the second half knew it. Currie, with time and room that amazed him, ruined Chelsea'.

The Observer thought 'Kember was so out of touch he seemed like a pen-friend' putting undue pressure on his partner, Hudson, in a two-man midfield. The retention of Hollins at right-back, removing him from his key midfield role, looked more ridiculous by the game. Centre-half Micky Droy was on the bench, hardly a statement of attacking intent. The *Kensington Post* starkly commented 'Chelsea look like its stadium – half-finished, and that's not the way to be after three games and with some of the finest players in the country. The message must be – Wake Up, Chelsea'. Indeed. Other press comments included 'pointless and pathetic', 'lethargic' and 'the worst I've seen for a long time'. Quick, effective improvement was required.

Ironically, the one player to be praised was Peter Osgood, the *Daily Telegraph* claiming that 'so much seems to have gone wrong at a time when Osgood, the former problem child, is going splendidly right that the club needs a fresh approach'.

The Sheffield United match programme contained a Chelsea Pools brochure including an 'Ossie Calling' message. The striker had reassuring, optimistic words for supporters. 'For those a bit disappointed the new stand is not open 'it won't be long now''. Enthusiastic about the atmosphere once the stand opened, he complained that the players found it hard with a stand missing, saying at times it was 'like playing in the middle of nowhere'. Sadly, it was unclear when this less-than-ideal situation was going to end.

The programme also contained a 'The Chairman writes…' piece, welcoming supporters back after the summer break. Brian Mears wrote 'in greeting you at the start of season 1973-74, I feel sure that, as you look across Stamford Bridge, you will share the Club's satisfaction at the rebuilding progress that has been made since Chelsea last played at home little more than four months ago….a striking transformation in the past year…we are more convinced than ever that we made the right decision in embarking on a redevelopment programme of this magnitude...Some further inconvenience, for which we apologise, is inevitable while we finish the East Stand...While we are not able to give a firm date for the opening of the Stand, we look forward to the day, later this season, when it comes into use...It is important that progress is maintained on the field to keep pace with redevelopment off it and I am optimistic that, granted respite from injuries on the scale we experienced last season, we can match the best in the season ahead'.

Optimistic certainly, realistic possibly less so. Steve Kember pointed out that the hold-up in opening the new stand was hugely frustrating. 'It's like playing in a morgue out there. We seem to play better away'. No firm date for opening, no explanation for delay, nothing about strengthening the squad.

The support was unhappy, the manager was unhappy, the board were presumably unimpressed as well. At a fraught team meeting on the Monday, according to the *Daily Mail*, Sexton asked his 'depressed, worried players' to 'say what you think'.

Osgood said 'It's back to the drawing board. When things go wrong, your confidence starts to go'. Chairman Brian Mears stressed that 'we are concerned. It is terrible and most depressing. But we've got time to do something about it'. Sexton admitted that playing three centre-forwards against Sheffield United did not work. 'That was my fault'. He also claimed, slightly optimistically, 'the spirit at the club is the best it's ever been since I became manager'.

Chelsea only had to wait till the Wednesday for their next game, the eminently-beatable Birmingham City at home. They duly went behind to a Malcolm Page long-range shot but fought back to win 3-1 with goals from Hutchinson, Hollins and Kember. The team had better balance after Sexton made changes, the recalled Locke was outstanding, and Hollins looked more comfortable back in midfield. Sexton must have wondered why he started the season with such an unwieldy line-up.

Any chance of maintaining the improvement in results was stymied by the fact that three days later the team were visiting champions Liverpool. The Anfield programme was damning with faint praise. 'Every season, it seems, Chelsea are being tipped to make a bold bid to land the League championship - and this time out there are plenty of people who fancy them again, despite the fact that last May they finished twelfth, and have made a poor start this time'. In a picture of the first-team squad of twenty there were but three youngsters - Droy, Locke and Britton – reinforcing the image of a team getting older together.

Not for the first time, Peter Bonetti had a superb game at Anfield, even saving a Kevin Keegan penalty, but the England star still scored the only goal. Osgood was widely praised for his showing in front of England boss Sir Alf Ramsey but Garner and Hutchinson, not a mobile front two, again struggled to have any impact. Liverpool's 39 attempts on goal, 28 on target, and 20 corners indicated their total domination. Brian Clough joined the chorus of voices demanding Osgood be recalled by England, though Newcastle United's Malcolm MacDonald said he 'wouldn't care to play alongside Osgood for England (as he would not want) to do two men's work'. MacDonald was never a favourite with Chelsea supporters. Maybe that comment helps explains why.

The *Daily Telegraph*, noting the low crowds and low performances so far that season, ran a challenging piece, concerned about Chelsea's future under a 'Chelsea Falter As New Stand Rises' headline. Two points from five games and average crowds 2,000 below the previous season's 29,722. 'When it (the East Stand) opens later this year it will house 12,000. How many fans are fed up with the building site, the constantly incomplete Stamford Bridge? When the project eventually provides London with its best stadium, will it merely be the mausoleum of dead hopes?'.

Arguably very fair questions, and maybe an indication that the days of unquestioning press support for the development were over, drawing a defensive response from Brian Mears. 'I am surprised at the criticism. Surely that is negative thinking at a time where everyone believes that fully-seated crowds are the answer to the game's problems. We are building for tomorrow. We intend to complete the development plan but, for financial and other reasons, we might have to mark time at some stage. We have learned a lot in the last two years and there is a limit to the inconvenience one can put up with. Crowds will come to matches if the facilities are right and we need tolerance and understanding while we try to provide them. But we are investing so much money that playing success is essential. On this, I have been encouraged by our last two performances…They (the players) are aware (of what is at stake), but does it motivate them? One of my co-directors has suggested that the only answer to the effort problem is big bonuses and small wages. There are times I want to ask the players what is going on, but one must observe protocol … I warn everyone about complacency because of the promising youngsters we have'.

The *Daily Telegraph* reckoned Mears was one of those chairmen who made a nonsense of the myth that directors were unprofessional and know nothing of the game. 'I have been steeped in the club all my life'. He talked about working with directors at other clubs to draw up a blueprint for the game's future 'because, in this changing world, serious measures will have to be taken'.

The piece is interesting for a number of reasons. It maintains the fallacy that the East Stand would still open in 1973 when to the casual eye it was clear that would not be the case. It did not challenge Mears on how the stand was being paid for. What it did though, for the first time, was draw an admission that the remainder of the development might be put on hold for monetary reasons, with a dawning realisation that the team was not good enough to draw in his much-desired 'trendy' fans. It also hinted at criticism of the players, their attitudes and motivations.

Games continued apace and three days later the visit to

Birmingham City was a bottom of the table clash with Chelsea in twenty-first place with only their opponents below them. Hutchinson's knee was puffy after three games in eight days and Garland unfit, so Tommy Baldwin, unused that season and on the transfer-list for nine months, came in. In an entertaining game, Baldwin repaid the manager's faith with two goals, Osgood and Hudson also netting in a hugely-welcome 4-2 win.

A second home win of the season four days later, against Coventry City, was equally welcome, though after Osgood netted it took a penalty save by Bonetti from Mick Coop, his second in a week, to cement a 1-0 win. A crowd of 30,593, Chelsea's highest of the season so far, was decent considering the team's erratic form.

As the East Stand construction meandered on, disruption for spectators continued. Ticket holders for the North Stand and North-East Enclosure were asked in a programme to co-operate 'by not wandering into the construction area'. A programme letter was printed from a supporter turned away from the Sheffield United game as he only had a £1 note and the turnstile operator did not have change from 45p. The club response, suggesting everyone arrived at the ground with the correct coinage, showed a breath-taking disregard for their supporters at a time when they should have been actively courting them through exemplary customer service. More reasonably, they also asked supporters to turn up early to prevent turnstile build-up, as happened fifteen minutes before the Birmingham game. The problems continued as many supporters at the Friday night Norwich game the following month arrived after kick-off due to Motor Show traffic and tube problems.

Chelsea had risen to the dizzy heights of twelfth, and after a welcome midweek break approached the trip to Manchester City with some confidence. Sexton fielded an unchanged team for the third match in a row, but City took a 2-0 lead. Baldwin pulled one back, City scored again and, despite Baldwin's second, his fourth in three games, City ran out 3-2 winners. All five goals were scored in fourteen minutes after half-time. The *Kensington Post* praised a 'strong performance by Baldwin, whose only crime appear to be he doesn't get on with Sexton.' They felt their relationship 'needs a little give-and-take on both sides' and certainly, if Baldwin continued to score, the case for him keeping a regular place seemed compelling, especially as he offered something different to his striking rivals.

The final game of a very mixed month meant the visit of Wolverhampton Wanderers. Wolves took a 2-0 lead after half-time. Sexton brought on Hutchinson for Baldwin, a rare tactical substitution by the manager, and Garner pulled one back. Osgood volleyed a stunning equaliser, but the *Daily Mirror's* focus was less positive. Ossie was booked for kicking Mike Bailey, resulting in slightly over-the-top 'Tragedy of Ossie' and 'Moment Of Fury Tarnishes His New Image' headlines. They asked 'can Osgood, in my book the most talented forward in British football today, control his temper when the going gets tough?' Sexton, talking to the *News Of The World*, emphasised 'the game is not to go two down in the first place. We didn't play well at all'.

Terry Conroy of Stoke was a goal-scoring winger who had caused Chelsea problems in the past, whose signing would have made perfect sense and, at nearly 27, was in his prime. Though he was watched, a transfer bid never developed. Another player watched was Exeter striker Fred Binney, free-scoring in a lower division in the manner of Garner, but hardly the classy signing the supporters were desperate for and at 27 hardly likely to significantly improve much. John Phillips, fed up with sharing reserve goalkeeping duties with Steve Sherwood, again asked the board for a move. Displaced John Boyle, with little realistic chance of a return to the side, got married that month and fancied a move to 'interested' Southampton, feeling 'a move like that would be a nice wedding present'.

Osgood was recalled by Sir Alf Ramsey for the game against Austria, England's last before the crunch home qualifier against Poland they must win to qualify for the World Cup. The *Daily Mirror* emphasised what Ramsey's reservations were. 'The big puzzle is Osgood. To put it bluntly, the Chelsea man must recognise that at England level he has failed (to prove) that his marvellous talent and his suspect temperament could ever forge a lasting fruitful marriage. There was always too much of the dilettante playboy in both his attitude and style to ever suit Ramsey, who likes to see the shirts of even the greatest soaked in sweat. At least he knows he is back as a fringe candidate whose approach in preparation will be carefully studied'.

The month-end table was not what Mears, Sexton or the supporters expected to see. Sixteenth place, ten points behind leaders Leeds, was unacceptable.

16th Chelsea	p9	7pts
17th Stoke City	p9	7pts
18th Tottenham Hotspur	p9	7pts
19th Wolverhampton W.	p9	6pts
20th Norwich City	p9	5pts
21st West Ham United	p9	4pts
22nd Birmingham City	p9	3pts

October 1973

Near-neighbours QPR had habitually been in a lower division than Chelsea, indeed they had met just three times ever, Chelsea winning each time. Promoted the previous season, and with an exciting side including Stan Bowles, Gerry Francis and ex-Chelsea captain Terry Venables, they were tenth. Ian Hutchinson was out with a back injury,

Tommy Baldwin keeping his place in the team, and injuries to Chris Garland and Peter Houseman left the side wing-less.

Given this, a 1-1 draw at Loftus Road was arguably a decent result for Sexton's side, though it hinted at a shift in the balance of power in West London. An own goal from Terry Mancini put Chelsea ahead, but Bowles equalised. Chelsea hung on, Rangers manager Gordon Jago accusing Chelsea of playing for a point, though skipper John Hollins argued they did nothing of the sort. 'We did not go out just to do a containing job'. There would have been no shame if they had. The supposedly reformed Osgood was involved in more controversy after a lunging high tackle on Francis, causing the *Daily Telegraph* to point out that 'Osgood several times showed his combative spirit is still not under complete control'.

In the two previous seasons, Chelsea had achieved very decent League Cup runs. An away tie at Stoke two days after the QPR match was a chance for revenge for the Wembley defeat two seasons earlier. The game, unsurprisingly, was highly physical, but Stoke scored the only goal through centre-half Dennis Smith, causing an 'It's Curtains For Chelsea' headline in the *Daily Mirror*. Garner was dropped for Garland, frustrating Crystal Palace manager Malcolm Allison, who went to watch him. He spoke to Sexton about the player but did not pursue a possible transfer. In *Kings Of The King's Road* Alan Hudson recalled that Osgood had a blistering row with Sexton in the dressing room after the match, the manager criticising his effort. Osgood apparently stormed off to a Stoke night club.

Two defeats and two draws in four games was not the improvement in form Sexton was looking for and his concerns grew, along with those of the Chelsea board, when the lowest crowd of the season so far turned up to for the visit of Ipswich. Even given injuries, the front five of Ian Britton, Tommy Baldwin, Chris Garland, Steve Kember and Peter Houseman was an uninspiring and unthreatening one. The return of Houseman after sinus trouble was welcome, but he had nobody tall to cross to. Chelsea were 2-0 down inside fifteen minutes, as Ipswich dominated the game, eventually winning 3-2, their first ever victory at Stamford Bridge. Baldwin and a Hollins penalty kept the score vaguely respectable, but Chelsea were outclassed by a side definitely on the up.

The programme reported that Osgood had won the *Evening News Sportsman of the Month* award, evidence of his continuing popularity and profile. Chelsea were desperate for him to be fully fit, fully motivated and on top form if they were to climb the table, being only four points above bottom club West Ham United. Injury meant he missed the chance to be on the bench for England against Poland. If he had been, and if Ramsey had brought him on, it is quite possible that England's, Ramsey's and Osgood's future could have been very different...

Foul: Football's Alternative Paper had an interesting take on Hudson's absence against Ipswich. Their 'informed source' reported that

Hudson was unhappy Osgood was not playing but also alleged that Harris had 'been mixing in again in the 5-a-sides' and a 'battered and bruised' Hudson was scared 'Chopper' would carry the vendetta into the match. Harris had a reputation for a highly physical approach to 5-a-side training but it was rare to see such stories in print.

Bonetti, Droy and Locke, all injured against Ipswich, were not fit to play at Newcastle. Chelsea's form, and League position, worsened a week later when another defeat dragged the team down a place and only three points off the bottom. Two Malcolm MacDonald goals, one a penalty, separated the sides, as Chelsea were criticised for their negative tactics and physicality. Osgood's control and passing were 'immaculate' but unfortunately Baldwin and Garland were unable to take advantage. Eddie McCreadie started and took over from Hollins as captain. It was to be the club loyalist's final appearance for the first-team, as injuries caught up with him, though he did make nine reserve appearances that season. It was by no means the end of his involvement with the club.

An exposition that Sexton's position might be under threat came in a perceptive, prescient piece by Paul Dobson in the *Kensington Post*. Headlined 'Sexton's Future At Chelsea In The Balance', they felt he could face the axe unless Chelsea's results improve dramatically in the next few weeks. Dobson believed Chelsea would be ready to fire him because the crowds had fallen so badly lately, and that could not all be blamed on the rebuilding programme and the League-wide trend of lower gates. He argued that Chelsea wanted the new stand to be full every other week, not an empty monument to a lean five years.

Dobson believed Chelsea were worried fans may go and watch QPR instead, though that surely was highly unlikely in any significant numbers. 'The directors know the trend must be reversed and for all their debt to Sexton, they are businessmen who realise they cannot be loyal at any price'. They argued that he inherited a 'damned good side' from Docherty and in five years, nobody of note has been introduced to the team. 'Locke is the only youngster to have proved he is good enough for the first-team ... He has failed in the transfer market ... He played Weller out of position, sold him and he has flourished ... All his forward signings have been flops and he has virtually ignored the defence, which is not up to top First Division standard. Worst of all, they have failed in the League ... Seats need to be filled every week, not just for the occasional cup-tie. The sad thing is, Sexton is a nice man. Maybe he is too nice. Chelsea need a dynamo if their new stand is to prove money well spent. Brian Clough, for all his talk, could do the job. So could several other men. Sexton, I'm afraid, can't'.

A harsh perspective, though some of these arguments were irrefutable. To be fair to Sexton, the considerable economic constraints were not mentioned. Also omitted was the growing rift between manager and certain players.

Sexton's fruitless search for a winger continued. He bid for £200,000-valued Don Rogers of Crystal Palace, offering two players, including still-on-the-list Tommy Baldwin. Chelsea obviously could not afford to pay £200,000, so were reliant on part-exchange, and the bid was turned down. Palace were still interested in Garner and keen to take unsettled John Phillips on loan, but nothing happened. Palace bought promising winger Peter Taylor from Southend United for £120,000 begging the question why Sexton made no move for a well-regarded wide-man who would later play for England while a Third Division player. Reserve goalkeeper Steve Sherwood went on emergency loan to Millwall and utility player John Boyle was loaned to Brighton. Centre-back Tommy Cunningham signed professional terms, another promising youngster joining the ranks

The *Sunday People* reported that Sexton had watched Bournemouth five times that season, particularly interested in striker Phil Boyer and full-back Mel Machin. He was also interested in St Mirren forward Jim Pearson who eventually joined Everton.

For the visit of Norwich, the club decided to experiment with Friday night football in an attempt to draw in the missing thousands, also avoiding clashing with QPR v Arsenal the following day. The attempt failed spectacularly, as only 20,953 turned out. Sexton played Graham Wilkins at left back, dropping McCreadie, and on the bench was younger brother Ray, newly signed as a full professional and chomping at the bit to make his first-team debut. The team's form improved, Chelsea winning for the first time in six matches, 3-0. Baldwin scored twice, the *Fulham Chronicle* feeling he had 'burst back into the crowd's affection', taking his season tally to seven in eight games. Kember netted the other and Wilkins came on for the injured Webb.

The *Kensington Post*, which had deconstructed Sexton's failings the previous week, was full of praise. 'A surprise wave of enthusiasm and optimism flowed over Stamford Bridge on Friday as Chelsea turned on one of the most spectacular soccer displays I have seen from them for years ... Vibrancy ... sense of purpose ... Perhaps Sexton realises that unless his side clicks into top gear soon, he may be looking for another job ... Perhaps he has impressed that on the players. Perhaps, too, they were shocked out of their normal casual stride by Sexton's apparent readiness to axe his wayward stars...Chelsea's players can no longer live on reputations gained five years ago'.

Brian Mears and Chelsea Secretary Tony Green visited Real Madrid's Bernabeu Stadium to study the design. Green enthused 'we came to study this terrific ground and particularly the way (there are) hundreds of exits so 125,000 can be cleared from the stadium within ten minutes'. Some of the football played at Stamford Bridge so far that season was equally effective at clearing spectators quickly.

An exhibition by noted photographer Bryn Campbell of Chelsea pictures, entitled 'Come On You Blues' opened at the Photographers

Gallery and later moved to the Chenil Gallery in the King's Road, where, bizarrely, the exhibition was opened by self-appointed anti-pornography campaigner Lord Longford, mockingly nicknamed 'Lord Porn' by the tabloid press.

Chelsea ended October just three points off the relegation zone. The number of promoted/relegated clubs had been increased to three, making it even more imperative that the good form displayed against Norwich was carried into November.

16th Manchester United	*p13*	*11pts*
17th Chelsea	**p13**	**10pts**
18th Stoke City	*p13*	*10pts*
19th Wolverhampton W.	*p13*	*8pts*
20th Norwich City	*p13*	*8pts*
21st West Ham United	*p13*	*7pts*
22nd Birmingham City	*p13*	*5pts*

November 1973

A trip to Tommy Docherty's Manchester United side, one place above them in the table, was a test for a side with only three points from seven away games. Graham Wilkins retained his place, brother Ray again on the bench. Gary Locke returned after a groin strain, allowing John Hollins to revert to midfield but Ron Harris missed a League game for the first time in nineteen months with a damaged rib. Chelsea coasted to a 2-0 lead, Houseman crosses creating goals for Baldwin and Osgood. Garland went off injured, replaced by Ray Wilkins but disaster struck when brother Graham sadly had his leg broken after a 'crunching tackle' from Willie Morgan, an injury that kept him out of the team until late April. Chelsea, down to ten men, conceded two late goals. On the positive side, eight of that match-day squad of twelve had come through the club's junior sides.

No European football and early League Cup elimination meant more free midweeks, but that week a full side, with young left-back John Sparrow making his first-team debut, played Fulham in a testimonial for the ever-loyal Peter Houseman. Only 10,000 turned out so the winger raised about £7,000, nice to have but poor recompense for his hard work over the years. The jeering he suffered a few years earlier had largely ended but his diligence, consistency and loyalty was never fully appreciated by many of the Stamford Bridge crowd.

Crowds remained well below 30,000. The visit of fourth-place Everton, a major attraction even a couple of years earlier, drew in just 26,398 to watch Chelsea win comfortably, 3-1. Osgood netted a pair, including his 100th League goal, the industrious Baldwin scoring the other, giving him nine in ten League games, joint leading Division One scorer with Mike Channon of Southampton. Sexton enthused to the

Fulham Chronicle 'Tommy is playing better than I have ever seen him' but he was still on the transfer list. 'He asked to go on the list, and it is for him to ask to come off'. The *Daily Mirror*, under a 'Baldwin's New Deal is Locked in Freeze', quoted Sexton as stating 'we can't do anything about the contract just now because of the government-imposed pay freeze. Unless the situation alters, we cannot negotiate new terms. Obviously, we want him to stay'.

Marvin Hinton, not a man to throw his toys out of the pram, came in against Everton for his first game of season, having been an irregular starter for the past few seasons. 'You accept these things in football. But it's always nice to be back'. Ian Hutchinson had been scoring in the reserves and was on the bench after recovering from his back injury.

The *Daily Mail* reported 'Strolling Osgood Gives Ramsey a Double Nudge'. The England manager watched Osgood score two brilliant goals but 'not put much work in'. They argued, rightly, that Ramsey liked workers. Osgood was modest 'take those goals out and I didn't have a good game. I didn't show much after half-time. I was nervous knowing that Alf was there'. He bowed and blew kisses to The Shed at the end. 'Why not? They pay my wages and they've been good to me over the years'. Indeed.

Mears produced champagne afterwards, celebrating Osgood's league goal centenary, pointing out that 'those were the kind of goals England could have done with against Poland'. Richard Attenborough, a big fan of Osgood's, brought fellow *The Great Escape* film star Steve McQueen into the dressing room to meet the ton-up hero. In a 2016 interview with *The Scotsman*, Cooke laughed at the memory of the American film star taking out a cigarette in the Chelsea dressing-room and fellow Scot Eddie McCreadie 'jumping up to light it for him like he was a flippin' butler'.

Chelsea now had five points from their last three games. The *Daily Mirror* reported that Sexton had instigated extra training on Monday and Tuesday afternoons in a bid to get more hard work and effort from his side. The manager felt the return to form of Houseman had made a significant contribution, he had made four goals in the past two games, rightly claiming 'he's probably the best crosser of the ball in the country, and yet never really gets much credit'.

Osgood duly played for England the following Wednesday, in a 1-0 defeat by Italy, the winner scored by future England manager Fabio Capello. Supporter David Gray remembers 'there were so many Chelsea fans there it was untrue but despite Ossie having a good game he never won another cap' a sad waste given his huge talent and the workmanlike nature of so many England forwards of that era.

Arsenal, like Chelsea, were on the slide with regard to League position and the sides occupied fifteenth and sixteenth place when they met at Highbury. Sexton's team changes, largely forced by injury, were often hard to fathom. John Hollins turning out at left-back, removed from a midfield already lacking Alan Hudson due to a concerning eye injury picked up in training. Hinton was out injured after his first game of the season, so Harris had to switch to centre-back. The number of team changes, especially at the back, made any sort of consistency and understanding very difficult. In 'a match of dismal tedium' both sides seemed happy to settle for a draw. Britton impressed, again, with his energy and industry but without Hudson Chelsea lacked a conductor, a creator.

It wasn't only Chelsea and Arsenal who were struggling, the whole country was. Due to a national energy crisis, among a whole swathe of restrictions and regulations the government imposed a floodlight ban and decreed midweek games must be played in the afternoon until the energy emergency was over. Only clubs with their own generator were allowed to kick-off after 14.15, which was when Chelsea were forced to start against Southampton.

The energy shortage was not carried over into Chelsea's performance, where the team seemed to have benefitted from a few days golfing in Bournemouth. Britton and Kember, in particular, charged around as Chelsea dominated the game, winning 4-0, their best result since beating Leeds the opening day of the previous season. Kember scored two for the first time in his professional career, Britton's opener was his first professional goal and Garland, despite having to play wide, scored the other on a highly satisfactory afternoon. The *Kensington Post* felt Chelsea had been playing 'winning, glowing football' for the past six weeks, which they felt 'would bring back the missing fans if anything can'. Bonetti, captain for the day, made his 600th appearance for Chelsea in the game. 'A lot of people said I was finished (when out for five months injured the previous season) and it gives me a lot of satisfaction to prove them wrong'.

A happy manager praised Kember and felt if he could maintain his improvement when shooting 'he would be one of the great names of the game'. Baldwin and Osgood did not score but were fulsomely praised by Sexton. 'They are working and combining so well that they are creating large open spaces for others. Things are beginning to come right now and, with these two showing the way, other players are coming through to score'.

The *Daily Mirror* reported that Sexton was grappling with the rare, and positive, problem of having 'too many' players fit for selection. 'We have more players available than at any time this season'. Osgood, Houseman, Droy and Dempsey would all be fit for the trip to Stoke, with Garner due to return the following week after a chest virus.

Coventry were interested in buying several Chelsea players, including John Dempsey, Garland and Garner, who was likely to be frozen out given Baldwin's return to form, especially if and when Hutchinson was fully fit. Garner told the *Fulham Chronicle* he was disappointed about speculation about him being sold. 'I am glad to be back in full training and I want to prove I am good enough for a first-team place with Chelsea'. Hutchinson won £50 in the London long-throw championship that month, with a prodigious throw of 122ft.

Reserve players were attracting interest through the loan system, only introduced that season for top-flight clubs. John Boyle was still at Brighton, Steve Sherwood at Millwall, Tommy Ord went to Bristol City and Orient were trying to get winger Mike Brolly on loan. Brian Clough and Peter Taylor had taken over the managerial reins at Brighton and the *Daily Mirror* speculated they would be likely to sign Boyle for a fee of around £50,000. In the end, he returned to Chelsea the following month after playing ten games on loan.

Chelsea ended the month on a high, though despite improving their position the team were still in a dismally underachieving thirteenth place. They were only six points off likely European qualification, but a significant and sustained improvement was required before such a challenge could be taken seriously. However, with Bonetti as consistent as ever, Baldwin and Osgood working so well together and Hudson fit again, prospects looked relatively healthy for the rest of the season.

December 1973

The scheduled game at Stoke on December 1st was postponed because of snow and ice, so Chelsea had a fortnight off, apart from a trip to Lincoln City for John Kennedy and George Peden's testimonial, which a strong side won 4-2. Returning to League action, a home game against Leicester, with an enforced 14.00 start, was the chance to continue the five-match unbeaten run.

Chelsea fell behind to goals from Frank Worthington and long-time Sexton target (in his Fulham days) Steve Earle in the first two minutes. The situation looked grim but Chelsea, showing a rare doggedness and persistence, turned the game around to leave the pitch exultant 3-2 winners. Two Hollins penalties, either side of another 'superb' Osgood goal, won the game. Hudson was praised, the *Kensington Post* feeling he had returned to his best after more than a year in the doldrums. It was a shame the lowest crowd of the season, a desultory 20,676, braved heavy rain to watch it.

That week Baldwin received another boost when he won the *Daily Mirror Footballer Of The Month* for November, receiving a trophy and cheque for £100. 'That's marvellous. I didn't see myself as a contender'. He had scored nine goals since being called back into the side at Birmingham in September. 'I've grown up. It's as simple as that. I'm a more responsible person now...I'm going to fight to stay in the Chelsea side. I'm still on the transfer list and I haven't signed a new contract but that's because of the pay freeze. I love this club, and I'm happy to stay'.

After another midweek testimonial, this time for Palace goalkeeper John Jackson, Chelsea faced arguably their hardest home game of the season, against a rampant Leeds United. Keeping their six-match unbeaten run going would be a real challenge. Leeds were six points clear at the top of the table, unbeaten in the League with 32 points from nineteen matches.

Chelsea's historic feuding with their Yorkshire rivals was referenced pre-match by Sexton. 'There is certainly something special about Leeds. My players are particularly keyed up, as they always are when we play them'. Talking to the *Daily Mail* about facing Leeds, he stressed 'we are concentrating on the quality of our own play and the attitude of our own players...We have been scoring more goals than anyone in the First Division (only Leeds had scored more but twelve teams had conceded less) ... Of course Chelsea can improve. We have only played one bad match all season'. He refused to discuss whether Chelsea still had an outside title chance, presumably because he was laughing so hard at the ludicrous question, given the fourteen-point gap and the chasm in class. Chelsea actually went into the game with the fourth best Division One disciplinary record, with an impressive seven bookings and no sending offs. Osgood was confident Chelsea could end Leeds' unbeaten record. 'I like playing against them. I am not so sure they enjoy playing against me. Hudson and Kember are playing really well, which has been a tremendous boost to Tommy Baldwin and I'.

Chelsea fielded a side that the *Daily Mirror* saw as their full-strength one, with Bonetti and Houseman back, though Hollins played at centre-back in the injured absence of Droy and Dempsey, not his natural position, diminishing the team's midfield energy. *Bonetti; Locke, Webb, Hollins, Harris; Kember, Hudson; Garland, Baldwin, Osgood, Houseman.*

The crowd of 40,768 showed supporters would still flock to a big match. In a game described by Donald Saunders of the *Daily Telegraph* as 'the most distinguished First Division match he had seen in years' Chelsea worked hard and played intelligently but still struggled. Joe Jordan put Leeds ahead, Osgood thumped in a header for the equaliser, but Mick Jones snaffled a winner. The feuding, inevitably, went on as Osgood and Hunter kicked and squared up to each other. There was no shame in losing to Leeds, given they that day broke a modern First Division record by remaining unbeaten for their first twenty games. According to *The Working Man's Ballet*, before the game Sexton cornered Hudson and told him his breath stank of booze, a portent of things to come.

The programme advised supporters that progress continued on phase one of the redevelopment - the East Stand – but that steel shortages were still causing delays. The club hoped to be able to give a definite opening date soon, but the stand was now four months late, and was still not approaching completion. *Foul: Football's Alternative Paper* reported that the contractors, W & C French, hoped the stand would be ready in the new year but that was not going to happen. It was increasingly clear it would not open that 1973-74 season, an embarrassment to the board but, worse, a heightening of the financial problems, in terms of ever-increasing costs without the cushion of extra income the new stand was supposed to generate.

The key challenge for the team was to bounce back at Wolverhampton the following week and start another good run, but Chelsea were well beaten, two John Richards goals not really reflecting Wolves superiority. Only Bonetti kept Chelsea in the game as Wolves had 26 goal attempts to Chelsea's six. The game ended in lively fashion when Osgood and Frank Munro were booked after a fracas when Osgood clattered Munro, who ran 50 yards to confront him. Osgood's temper had now blown up in two games running, hardly reflecting his supposed maturity.

John Boyle, a loyal squad member for nearly nine years who made 266 first-team appearances and a key member of the League Cup and Cup-Winner's Cup winning sides, was allowed to join Orient on a free transfer, allowing him to negotiate a signing-on fee. Boyle says that his departure to Orient was very sudden, with no real chance to say goodbye. Sexton told him he had never let the team down and had done what was asked of him. Boyle's view is the players were still not really aware of the perilous financial position at the club by the time he left.

Dempsey played in the reserves, his first game for eight months, but hoped to be transferred by Christmas. Tommy Ord and Steve Sherwood returned from loan spells and Eddie McCreadie turned down a month's loan at Bristol City. John Bond of Norwich tried to buy Houseman, but Sexton was rightly not interested, seeing him as a key team member. The only players Sexton was linked with were Cork Hibernian striker Dennis Allen, valued at £20,000, and Orient centre-back Phil Hoadley, who had scored against Chelsea in the FA Cup two seasons earlier. Neither move went anywhere but, anyway, they were hardly the top-class infusions of new blood required.

In a pre-Christmas interview with Brian Mears, the *Daily Mail* felt that 'Chelsea are convinced the (home) games against West Ham and Liverpool will launch them into a prosperous New Year'. The chairman felt 'football will turn the corner in this Christmas and New Year period. We have just got to be optimistic. Things could not be much worse at the moment with virtually all the national circumstances stacked against us. But we are surviving…and if we can survive this crisis, we can survive anything. People will discover in these next few days that a football match is one of the few entertainments which is not at the mercy of power failures or any other emergency'. Events over coming weeks were to demonstrate the danger of optimistic predictions.

He said nothing about the status of the East Stand, now over four months late with no completion date in sight. The Daily Mail analysed the percentage of seats at each First Division ground. Chelsea had around 10,500 out of 45,000, which would rise to 23,500 out of 57,000 when the new stand finally opened. They were criticised for having the fewest bars and snack bars, six, in the division. Manchester City had 36.

Four days after the Wolves defeat, on Boxing Day, a dreadful 26,982 crowd, presumably affected by transport challenges, a petrol shortage, the power crisis and a ludicrous 11.00 kick-off, saw Chelsea take a 2-0 lead at half-time against bottom-placed West Ham, through Britton and Hudson, the latter after beating three men. There then came a turnaround that impacted on not just the match result but the future of a number of star players and, ultimately, the manager. Clyde Best pulled one back. Osgood hit the bar with the goal at his mercy, Mervyn Day saved the follow-up, cleared the ball upfield and Bobby Gould equalised. Chelsea's shoulders slumped as they capitulated, Hollins exposed again at centre-back and the whole defence struggling. Frank Lampard and Best, again, scored as West Ham ran out 4-2 winners, an astonishing turnaround.

The *Daily Telegraph* shared the damning view of many reporters. 'If you hope to win you do not adopt a casual air after half-time as Chelsea did. Best was unmarked at the far post and scored two goals there. Chelsea should have won by a street'. Osgood's 'second-half despondency' was pointed out. The *Kensington Post* made a scathing observation. 'Perhaps a morning kick-off against West Ham had been unkind to those players celebrating until the small hours of Boxing Day'. There may well have been more than a grain of truth in this observation.

In *Chelsea The 100-Year History* Mears says he was in the dressing room after the West Ham game. Sexton accused Hudson of having the smell of whisky on his breath, and criticised him and Osgood for failing to feed Houseman, who had the beating of his full-back. The two blamed the defence and there was a long row, Hudson pointing out he had scored one and made the other. In *Chelsea – The Real Story*, Mears recounted how he rang Sexton after that West Ham game, and Sexton told him how unhappy he was with Osgood and Hudson.

Chelsea were fifteenth after three successive defeats, only four points above 20th placed Manchester United. Sexton, furious, ordered his side in for extra training and, with a hard home game against Liverpool but three days away, made changes. Kember was dropped to substitute, immediately exciting interest from Stoke City. Captain Hollins, reverting to midfield, was defiant. 'We're not talking about relegation because we know we won't be involved'. Fine words, but the fact they even had to be aired said much about the team's decline.

In the Liverpool programme, supporters received a 'New Year Greeting' from Brian Mears. A very positive message referred to 'a mood of greater optimism than ever before at Stamford Bridge. 1974 will bring the completion of our magnificent new stand, and with it fulfillment of the first stage of our ambitious redevelopment programme'. Mears' comment 'with revival evident on the field in the past two months' was unfortunate in its timing three days after the West Ham debacle. Similarly, supporters may well have read his 'I feel that the prospects of Chelsea Football Club are second to none' observation with a jaundiced eye.

Spectator disruption continued. Supporter David Gray remembers that against West Ham they 'were held at the temporary players pitch entrance and had to wait to be escorted around the old dog track, past The Shed, a baying West Stand benches (we were interrupting their vision as we walked past) and North Terrace to get to our seats underneath the North Stand'.

Speaking on the day of the Liverpool game, Sexton, talking about FA Cup chances, felt 'we have been playing well, thanks to individual players hitting form' despite three defeats in a row. Webb talked positively about the three bearded wonders up front - Osgood, Hudson and Baldwin 'they take so much weight off the defence'. Micky Droy was recalled but made the mistake for the Liverpool goal in a 1-0 defeat, 'floundering like a stranded hippo in the build-up to (Peter Cormack's) goal' according to the *News Of The World*.

Under a 'Chelsea Go Down Again' headline, the *Evening Standard* was highly critical as Chelsea were outclassed. 'Little was seen of Baldwin and Osgood – except when Osgood was booked – and Hudson was almost lethargic in midfield. He seldom broke into a gallop'. Supporter Geoff Kimber remembers a conversation with a neutral friend who exclaimed how unfit Hudson looked. The *Sunday People* described how 'Osgood, in his most evil mood, was booked for fouling Callaghan. A minute later he was caught rabbit-punching Hughes'. The *Daily Telegraph* exempted Locke and Britton from criticism but emphasised that 'not all of the Chelsea players seemed to care about the outcome'.

Frank McGhee in the *Daily Mirror* did not hold back. 'Rubbish is a polite description of Chelsea's too cautious, too dull, too unimaginative performance'. Under a 'Skeleton Over Bridge Of Doom' headline, he continued 'The skeleton rattling in Chelsea's closet is made of concrete and steel. It towers into the Stamford Bridge sky and runs almost the length of one touchline – their new, expensive, unfinished grandstand. The danger is if the team continue to play as they did for much of the defeat to Liverpool then too many of its 12,000 seats could remain empty after it is opened. Displays such as theirs bring the prospect of relegation closer than they appear to realise'. Chilling words for the club hierarchy to read.

McGhee felt sorry for Hudson whom several times broke with the ball, but no team-mate was running into space. 'Chelsea's defenders, particularly Harris, failed to appreciate that an ability to win the ball is a wasted asset when the ball is too often promptly given away again'. He described the 'thoughtless, meaningless frenzy of Chelsea's second-half attacking waves...towards the end Chelsea looked demoralised and that is a signpost pointing downwards'.

The *Daily Mail* focused on the wider picture under a 'What's Wrong? Asks Mears' headline. They felt that the chairman had rightly and courageously committed to their expensive rebuilding programme. He anxiously told them 'we need the fans to keep coming and it's a good job our next match is an attractive FA Cup-tie against QPR. That gives us a chance to hold onto the supporters. But what's gone wrong with our team?'. They observed Hudson and Osgood were in the game less than they might have been 'for reasons best known to themselves' and criticised Bonetti's growing reluctance to come off his line for crosses. Sexton had made some blunt points to his side the day before the game but evidently they had not struck home. The *News Of The World* felt that 'many of the side are living in a fool's paradise, believing they can get by on reputations. But they need to snap out of this dreamy attitude before they meet real trouble'.

Key players were under-performing, the team was struggling, crowds continued to fall, the East Stand was already five months behind schedule and there was little New Year optimism amongst team, board or supporters. The unwavering press criticism, of individuals and the team, was damning and there were evident problems on the pitch and in the dressing room Sexton must urgently address.

The manager had three days before the trip to Sheffield United and, clearly, a dramatic improvement in both attitude and performance was required, especially given that the team had slid to down to eighteenth place. Something had to change. It did.

16th Stoke City	p22	19pts
17th Wolverhampton W.	p23	19pts
18th Chelsea	**p22**	**18pts**
19th Manchester United	p22	16pts
20th Birmingham City	p22	16pts
21st West Ham United	p23	13pts
22nd Norwich City	p22	13pts

January 1974

In the 114 years of Chelsea Football Club's history, there have been few months as traumatic as January 1974. The repercussions of the events of that momentous month were felt for years to come by players, manager, board and supporters. Chelsea were the main back-page story most days that month and for several weeks afterwards.

The starting point, the lit fuse, was manager Dave Sexton's team selection for the New Years' Day visit to Sheffield United. After four successive defeats, and chaotic showings against West Ham and Liverpool, changes were expected. What stunned the football world, and the players concerned, was the identity of the four dropped players.

Peter Bonetti, regular first-team goalkeeper since 1960 with over 600 appearances for the club, an England international not dropped because of form for over a decade. Alan Hudson, a supremely talented midfielder with wonderful vision and a slide-rule pass, only twenty-two and widely seen as a future England international. Tommy Baldwin, Chelsea's leading scorer so far that season, voted *Daily Mirror Footballer Of The Month* weeks earlier and, arguably, in as good form as he had ever been. The biggest shock of all, though, was the fourth player to be omitted. Peter Osgood. 'The King Of Stamford Bridge', supremely talented, a huge crowd favourite and in the England team seven weeks earlier.

All three of the 'bearded wonders' David Webb referred to a couple of days earlier were out, though Baldwin did have the mild compensation of a place on the bench. He had particular reason to be unhappy as his displays that season had been widely praised and, after a couple of years in the relative wilderness, he seemed to have found a role in the side that suited him. Given the defence had been utterly hopeless in the second half against West Ham, it seemed clear Sexton had in the main targeted those whose attitude he disliked. Droy and Harris were strongly criticised in the press for their performances against Liverpool but retained their places in an unchanged defence.

Sexton told the *Evening Standard* the day the news was made public that 'none of the four players are injured', under a 'Chelsea Axe Four Stars In Shake-Up' headline. They understood 'the axed players were stunned by the decisions. Clearly Sexton is disenchanted with his team's form and attitude and believes now is the time to act'.

While the discarded stars took stock, the reshuffled side, with Garner, Garland, Kember and Phillips coming in, took the field at Bramall Lane. *Phillips; Locke, Droy, Webb, Harris; Hollins, Kember; Britton, Garland, Garner, Houseman.*

Kember equalised Alan Woodward's opener with a 35-yard belter, Hollins put Chelsea ahead and, as Sexton put it, 'we held on somehow'. A hugely important result for the manager, who would have been under enormous pressure if the side had under-performed their way to another defeat.

Normally, the home FA Cup-tie with QPR in four days would have been the main subject of press comment and, indeed, chairman Brian Mears stressed 'with our rebuilding commitments it is terribly important to us financially to have a good cup run'. Sexton, asked whether the axed stars would return, especially Osgood given injury to Garner, told the *Evening Standard* 'I would rather not talk about team selection. I'll leave that until Friday, when the team is announced. We played well at Sheffield. We worked hard and pushed the ball around well'.

The wheels really began to come off on Thursday January 3rd, two days before the Cup-tie. The *Evening Standard* reported that Osgood and Hudson had categorically refused to train that morning with the first-team at Mitcham when asked by coach Dario Gradi. There were heated exchanges, they were immediately suspended for a week and put on the transfer list, though whether they asked for moves is still disputed to this day. The two left in Osgood's car unaware of this disciplinary action, and apparently spent the afternoon at Sandown Park races.

Sexton explained 'I told them to train with the first-team and they refused and were immediately suspended. I cannot tolerate players telling me what they should do. They are available for transfer at their own request'.

Cue absolute uproar. The fall-out was the main story on every back-page for days. Sexton had the task of trying to pick and coach a team for a critical FA Cup-tie in the middle of a huge press storm. Both players had friends in the press, both, particularly Osgood, were very popular with supporters and, without the pair, Chelsea had very little creative inspiration in the side and even less wow-factor. As the *Daily Mail* said, 'Osgood's extravagant ball skills, his majestic goals and his extrovert nature make him a huge attraction to Chelsea fans'. Chelsea Supporters Club chairman Jack Rosin commented 'I don't think the fans will like to lose Osgood. I can't say what the reaction of the fans, particularly The Shed fans, will be – though as far as I can see, the club had no alternative but to take this action'.

The *Daily Mirror* quoted Sexton 'I'm not disappointed about what happened. In a way I'm glad about Hudson - I was going to put him on the transfer list anyway'. He went on 'Ossie? Well, I've known him a long time. Players don't tell me where they want to train. I tell them. I've no idea whether their refusal was something they'd already decided between them or spur-of-the-moment decisions. I hadn't seen them until this morning (Thursday) after dropping them from the match at Sheffield United on Tuesday. They trained with the reserves on Tuesday and Wednesday'.

The well-informed *Daily Mail* laid out the duo's version of events. Osgood apparently told Sexton 'No, I am training with the reserves' and made it clear he did not want to stay at Chelsea. Hudson allegedly said 'That goes for me too. And I'd like a move'. Sexton then apparently told them 'my pleasure. You can go'. The paper pointed out that 'the pair's social life, which both would admit to being more active than monastic, was a major bone of contention at a team meeting after the defeat by Liverpool, leading to pointed exchanges between the pair and Sexton'.

Both players were the subject of immediate speculation regarding potential suitors and, in Osgood's case, the rumour mill went into overdrive. Some was informed, some was wishful thinking, and some was total fiction. Dave Mackay of Derby was straight in, offering £300,000. Crystal Palace's Malcolm Allison was supposedly keen to offer Don Rogers in part exchange using the press to keep his interest bubbling. Potential swaps with George Best (reviving an old favourite story) and Tottenham's Martin Chivers. Osgood to be sold to Manchester United, no swap involved. Both Osgood and Hudson to go to Southampton with Mike Channon in part exchange. Hudson to go to Norwich. Or Stoke. Or Tottenham, Liverpool, Manchester United,

Arsenal, QPR or Crystal Palace. Take your pick. Pure speculation from supposedly 'in the know' football journalists is not purely a 21st century phenomenon.

Brian Mears immediate reaction was, rightly, to back his manager against this clear challenge to his authority, though he must have despaired at the fact that his two main crowd-pulling stars were in dispute and, in all likelihood, on their way out, Sexton not being a man who would easily back down. The chairman made it clear that if the choice was between Osgood and Sexton, then Osgood went. Sexton preferred player-exchange deals rather than straight sales to bring in the talent necessary to build a championship team of the future. The official valuation of the two errant stars was to be made after the QPR cup-tie, but the general feeling was that Hudson was worth at least £200,000, with Osgood around £100,000 more. The manager told the *Daily Mail* 'the important thing about the win at Sheffield was that the spirit was very good. It was a team effort in which everybody gave everything...and that was the most rewarding thing for me. Every player ran until they dropped. And that's what it's all about'. He also argued that 'you can't defy authority ... No club can tolerate that'.

Hudson explained 'I have felt for some time that my future is somewhere else. Now I know where I stand, and I'll just have to stand back and see what happens'. He was to angrily and bitterly dispute Sexton's interpretation that he had asked for a transfer. The *Daily Mirror* felt there had been simmering unrest at Stamford Bridge and both stars had blamed Sexton for communication breakdowns. It is clear that the relationship between the manager and a number of his squad was less than optimal, but Osgood and Hudson, good friends and confident characters, were particularly challenging to manage. Both players thought others should have been dropped before them, and they definitely had a point, though refusing to train as directed by the manager was totally inexcusable.

If he left the club Osgood would miss out on a testimonial the following year, which could net him at a significant tax-free sum. Club loyalists Hinton and Hollins were both granted testimonials for later in 1974 but Osgood, the biggest name at the club, was in danger of missing out.

David Gray, like many supporters, was deeply concerned. 'I was choked that Hudson and Osgood wanted to leave as it was obvious that they were not going to be replaced in the transfer market. Kember and Garner were never going to be able to reach the heights attained by the flamboyant pair'.

The *Evening Standard*, on the day of the QPR game, under an 'Osgood: I can't respect Sexton' headline reported he, the bigger of the two names media-wise, had told ITV's World Of Sport programme 'I'd love to play for Chelsea, but I just don't respect Dave in the things he does ... He has always had a go at me. That's fair enough. He's the manager. I respect that...I didn't think he was right in dropping me...we would be better off if we just split ... Chelsea have been good to me, but I think I have repaid them for what they have given me'. He had long felt Sexton picked on the flair players never Harris, whose passing was inadequate or, until then Bonetti, whose kicking was occasionally erratic.

In *Chelsea's Cult Heroes* Osgood said he felt he had lost motivation at that point. He did not like Sexton playing him out of position in midfield, much as Hudson was unhappy played wide. He claims he was asked by Sexton in December 1973 if he fancied being captain, then dropped a few days later.

The *Kensington Post* QPR preview demonstrated the perils of early press deadlines arguing that Chelsea would rely on Osgood's insolence and Hudson's zest. 'Without those qualities they are an ordinary side'. 'The six-yard sharpness of the revitalised Tommy Baldwin' was praised. They also made a cogent observation with regard to the retained Harris. 'Harris is left-back, but not by inclination ... (he is) short of speed and sometimes slow on the turn'.

In the middle of this furore, Sexton picked his side for the QPR game, the one change bringing Baldwin in for the injured Garner. The *Daily Mirror* reported that Chelsea were 18-1 for the FA Cup despite a home draw, an indicator of how far the clubs on-field reputation had fallen in the past couple of years. Leeds and Liverpool were 7-1 favourites.

The Chelsea team could have been dispirited at the events of the week but if they were, they did not show it. They picked up four bookings - Webb, Droy and Harris all for fouling Bowles, Garland for dissent – showing a high level of commitment from 'a team of honest triers'. Phillips repaid Sexton's faith in him with a superb performance, including a penalty save from Gerry Francis who, with Terry Venables, complained afterwards about Chelsea's physicality. The home side committed 33 of the 48 fouls in the game, the ex-Chelsea skipper reflecting that there was 'an air of desperation about Chelsea and we understand that they have their problems and wanted to prove things'. The *News Of The World* 'Chelsea Rough Up Bowles In Battle Of The Bridge' headline spoke volumes, as did sub-headings '90 Minutes Of Mayhem' and 'X-Certificate Carnage'.

A disappointing derby crowd of 31,540 turned out, though the off-field problems, and a weakened side, cannot have helped. Houseman and Garland were injured, Ray Wilkins coming on for the former, but Sexton made it clear his suspended, transfer-listed stars would not be considered for the replay, scheduled for the Tuesday. Osgood commented 'I didn't think he would. He's too proud for that'.

Youngsters Brian Bason, Garry Stanley and Mike Brolly were in the replay squad of fourteen, though the game was postponed until the following week, at just a couple of hours' notice, giving Sexton time to get players fit and the off-field shenanigans to continue unchecked.

Sexton told the *News Of The World* 'If it was left to me, I'd insist on players in exchange, but I don't know if the directors will see it that way. There have been several firm inquiries and I will be able to tell interested clubs our valuation on Tuesday, and then things could move quickly'. The paper reckoned 'if there were suitable cash offers the club would forget about part-exchange. They are committed to an extensive and costly rebuilding programme and money is tight at The Bridge. If they lost the replay, the need for revenue would be even more urgent'. Sexton later observed 'this (was) a horrific period for me ... we knew the heart of the club was sound, but people outside must have been wondering what the hell was going on'. Indeed.

Foul: Football's Alternative Paper saw managers like Sexton as 'quite unable to cope with anyone not fitting into their little systems'. They felt that 'authoritarian principles and the lure of two fat transfer cheques' swayed the board and observed how the press ignored crowd reaction when, against QPR, Osgood's name was chanted before and during the game and there were shouts from below the press box of 'Osgood In, Sexton Out'. They saw the press and the board as too close, advising 'keep an eye on attendance figures for a more accurate reflection of 'public opinion''. Indeed, Stamford Bridge crowds continued to fall. The press tended to side with the club, except for those that had 'exclusive' interviews with the two malcontents.

A heated six-hour board meeting was held, and it was agreed in principle that the players could leave if the offer was right, but no public valuation was placed on either player. Sexton was twice called into the meeting for 'a full report and discussion'. Club secretary Tony Green advised that 'clubs who show an interest are being notified accordingly'. The *Evening News* ran a '£500,000 court of King Brian' headline. Mears, trying to offer reassurance to a bewildered fan base, announced 'the supporters have no need to fear that the club is facing a crisis. We survived the departure of Jimmy Greaves and we will survive this'. Cynics might have pointed out that the team finished bottom the season after Greaves departed.

The *Daily Mirror* laid the situation out in stark terms. Sexton had to decide whether to seek a temporary armistice with his transfer-listed rebels, the two most talented players on his staff. Many applauded Sexton's stance in dropping, transfer-listing and suspending them for a week – in theory they would be available for Coventry away the next Saturday. Could he afford to leave them out in the middle of such a predicament? The board might well try and lean on Sexton but he 'isn't a character who bends easily'.

The Cup replay was absolutely vital to the club, so Hudson and Osgood would be of value on the pitch, but cup-tieing them might reduce their attractiveness to potential purchasers. If they lost, club prospects were grim. No chance of a trophy, and a long, hard battle to keep fans they would need to fill the new stand – something that would be an expensive white elephant in the Second Division.

One problem with player-exchange would be if incoming players were cup-tied. The situation was exacerbated by injuries to Houseman, Garner, Hutchinson and Garland, meaning it might be in Sexton's interests to try to patch up his relationships with the rebels, at least short-term. Hutchinson, out with back trouble, was starting another comeback but he had only played four games that season and not started a match since early September. Relying on the ultra-brave striker was becoming increasingly difficult.

The *Daily Mail* reported that a growing lobby of players and others at Chelsea wanted Osgood to make peace with Dave Sexton. The player made it clear it could only ever be a 'temporary truce'. He defended himself against charges of a too-high social life. 'I'm not legless at half-past nine in the evening ... I handle my social life very well. Much better than I used to, I'll admit that...I've got to look after myself...to keep in good physical shape...The odd time I have had one too many, I've always got up and sweated it off. That's more than a lot of players can say. They get their wives to ring in and say they've got a cold or a headache'. He ended, almost wistfully, 'there's so much potential (at the club)'.

There was soon possible progress with regard to Osgood's future. The *Evening News* on January 10th, under an 'It's Up To Ossie' headline, reported that Chelsea had agreed a fee of £300,000 with Derby County. Manchester United, Southampton, Tottenham and Leeds were apparently also keen. After meetings with manager Dave Mackay and other Derby representatives, and some prevarication, Osgood turned them down as he felt the terms were inadequate and he preferred not to move out of London. He was convinced other top clubs would beat a path to his door. The player met with Mears but reiterated that he definitely wanted to leave. The *Daily Mail* reported that director Richard Attenborough approached Osgood and asked if he would stay. The player must have considered the possibility that in the end he would be considered by the club as too valuable to their on-field prospects, and attendance potential, to go.

The *Kensington Post* argued that both players felt they had been scapegoated and that Hudson had been close to his best form since beating Norwich in mid-October. They asked pertinent questions. Did Sexton want to forsake talent for teamwork? Could he have better handled the training ground bust-up when Dario Gradi asked them to train with the first-team? Once the rift became public, they felt it turned a drama into a crisis and that Sexton should have instigated a cooling-off period before accepting their transfer requests. Unlike many national journalists, they felt Sexton's future must be in the balance, arguing that nobody emerged from the situation with credit. Given that Hudson had implied in the summer that all was well between him and the manager, something had gone very wrong somewhere in the past More bad news came with the analysis that Chelsea's av crowds that season were down from 32,800 to 27,400, c concern to the already fraught club hierarchy.

On the Saturday morning, the day of an away game at Coventry, Evening Standard printed two letters regarding Osgood, which are an interesting snapshot of views and make a lot of sense. Colin Brinton of Harwich felt Sexton had no choice but insisted he should buy defenders, not strikers. T. M. Dorsett of Surbiton felt that Osgood was correct when he said 'he always seems to be the one picked on' and referred to several 'regulars' who seemed to be in the team week after week, regardless of form or merit. He worried that Sexton would waste the money raised and said this was one of the drabbest Chelsea sides he has seen since he started going regularly in 1945, that Sexton preferred runners, not those with skills. He argued that the board should have smoothed it all over and worried that Chelsea would open their new stand in the Second Division. It is not hard to imagine that Harris, Droy and Garland might be among the 'regulars' Mr Dorsett was referring to. His point about runners, not flair players, certainly rang true.

While the first-team played at Coventry, Osgood injured his groin after eighteen minutes of the reserve game against Ipswich and was expected to be out for up to three weeks. Nearly 1,000 turned out, compared to average reserve crowds of 150. The player had said he wanted to give his fans a bit of a show and a farewell wave. Little pockets of fans chanted his name and applause rattled round the vast ground when he hobbled off. The dropped Bonetti and the back-from-injury Dempsey also played.

The Coventry away game was a 2-2 draw, Harris and Garland scoring but Mick Coop twice equalising with penalties. Sexton was definitely giving youth a chance, picking Locke, Droy, Britton and Mike Brolly with Garry Stanley on the bench. The *Fulham Chronicle* felt 'gone was the smooth, joyous football, with which one always associates Chelsea', hardly a surprise. Webb, as never-say-die as ever, played on with four stitches in a head wound.

Hudson's path was more straightforward than that of his rebel colleague. Tony Waddington of Stoke City bid £240,000, the bid was accepted by Chelsea, terms were agreed, and the player left for the Victoria Ground. £100,000 was paid up front, the remainder in instalments, which limited Sexton's options in terms of readily available cash.

Most of the noise surrounding the events of that month concerned Osgood, but the loss of Hudson, regardless of his attitude and behaviour, created a huge gap in the squad regarding creativity. He left expecting to get a 5% signing on fee as, in his eyes, he had not asked for a transfer. A happy Hudson, now earning around £200 a week, told the *Daily Mirror* 'it's a great new start for me - and a challenge. Frankly I had my

,oblems in London with this personal thing between me and Dave Sexton. I kept having rows with him and couldn't concentrate on my football'.

That weekend he continued the theme, talking to the *Sunday People*, under a 'I Had Two Years Of Hell' headline. 'Thank god it's all over ... It took only ten minutes of talking to Tony Waddington to convince me...I wanted a club outside London because I am convinced that what I need above all else after my Chelsea nightmare is a completely new environment. I couldn't even move around in London recently without seeming to be in trouble of one sort or another. That's the sort of place it is...I have some fond memories of my early days at the Bridge but in the past two seasons everything has turned sour'. In *Rhapsody In Blue*, Chelsea Official Historian Rick Glanvill called Hudson 'a catalyst for disintegration' and for all his ability it is hard to argue with that description with regard to his later days at the club.

Later that year, Hudson explained to the *Daily Mail* one reason why he left. 'In London, if you're a top player there are invitations from the Playboy Club and all sorts waiting on your doorstep every morning. It's very hard to keep refusing a drink, and there were times when I felt bad about playing on the Saturday because I'd had a drink on the Friday'. Osgood had admitted that Hudson, Baldwin and Cooke used to go to the highly fashionable Tramps discotheque. These tales help explain Sexton's frustration with Hudson and his fellow revellers in the squad. Hudson later said 'to Dave, we had all this talent and we were abusing it'. The manager had a point.

Stoke then promptly put in a £300,000 bid for Osgood. Derby made an alternative bid, offering improved terms to the player and lanky striker Roger Davies in part-exchange, an offer Sexton and Davies were both keen on. The press thought it was a done deal but, eventually, after Osgood strung him along waiting for a more attractive offer, Derby manager Dave Mackay lost interest. The *Sunday People* reported that Osgood, who received £40 a point bonus, turned down Derby because their pay structures heavily relied on bonuses based on League placings. An irony is that Derby won the title the following season, so he could have won a medal as well as earning a very significant sum in bonuses.

Though there was a huge amount of speculation, informed or otherwise, concrete bids for the star were lacking. Maybe Osgood's temperament and perceived arrogance put off top clubs from breaking the British transfer record to buy him, for all his undoubted talent. What was unclear was how much of the funds raised by selling the pair would be given to Sexton to buy attacking replacements, or shore up his creaking defence, and how much would disappear into the black hole of the stadium redevelopment.

Chelsea were still keen for a part-exchange deal, having weakened the squad with the sale of Hudson. Don Rogers of Crystal Palace and Jimmy Robertson of Stoke were possible swap targets. Palace's offer of

Alan Whittle and Derek Possee was rejected, hardly a surprise as neither were exactly top-class players. Arsenal, Tottenham, Crystal Palace and Stoke were apparently all still interested in signing Osgood, who was perhaps wisely given permission to go away for a few days and think things over, elements in the club clearly hoping he would climb down. Manchester United joined Derby County in having lost interest, whereas top clubs Liverpool, Leeds United and Manchester City never expressed any.

Peter Bonetti, a true club loyalist but unsurprisingly unsettled by the upheaval, asked to talk to Sexton regarding his future, adding to the manager's woes. The *Sunday People* reckoned he lost his place as Phillips could kick the ball further, lower and more accurately. Bonetti explained 'it hurt worse than a kick in the head when Dave Sexton told me I was dropped. At my age, reserve football just isn't on...when it comes to saving goals I don't see myself as second best...I am very upset with the way things are going and it's in the best interests of the club and myself to sort them out. If that means putting in a transfer request, that's what I'll do'.

For the most critical game of the season so far, away at QPR, Garner, recovered from a virus, was not risked after only half a game in two months. Webb was moved to centre-forward. Although he had played the role a few times before, Webb hardly justified his place up front in the replay, unsurprisingly lacking positional knowledge. Playing him alongside Baldwin, in front of a midfield of Britton, Kember, Hollins and Brolly, demonstrated starkly how much the errant rebels would be missed. The game was played on the Tuesday afternoon, as QPR were unable to arrange a generator to power the floodlights and government power restrictions were still in force.

Phillips, Droy and Locke were all praised for diligent performances under continual pressure but Stan Bowles, kicked mercilessly in the first game, rose above more of the same treatment by scoring the only goal of the game. Harris was booked for fouling Bowles, who went off near the end with a gashed leg, and was warned he would be sent off if there was any more backchat. The thought occurred that Chelsea had gone from a team with flair to one setting out to kick flair players off the park, inside three years, Sexton's mistrust of flamboyance manifesting itself.

So Chelsea were out of the FA Cup and had nothing to play for in the final three months of the season, except avoiding the drop. With the club in turmoil, gates falling, the new stand already five months late and still not near completion, it was hard to avoid concluding that the club was in real trouble. Something was needed to lift them out of a trough of despond. Under a 'Sexton Splash - Hudson Cash Goes Today' headline, the *Daily Mirror* reported, entirely speculatively, that Chelsea were on the brink of spending the £240,000. 'A big name will stimulate the Stamford Bridge fans' interest'. A club official said 'something is in the pipeline' but if it was, the pipeline was evidently badly blocked. They also ran a story that Chelsea hoped to have peace talks with Osgood to persuade him to stay with the club but, again, there was nothing officially stated.

The endless speculation, much of it without any basis in fact whatsoever, demonstrated again that many football writers were more interested in an eye-catching headline than the often mundane reality.

The club duly made a signing, and it was certainly a popular one, but hardly the expensive deal talked about. Charlie Cooke, a hero at Stamford Bridge until he was sold to Crystal Palace sixteen months earlier, had been languishing in their reserves and was almost sold to Charlton Athletic. Sexton bought him back for £17,000, meaning Palace lost £68,000 on him, and asked him to play on the wing, so Garland could switch to striker.

Sexton told the *Daily Mail* 'life is full of surprises. The fact that Charlie wasn't in the team at Crystal Palace does not concern me. He was always popular here and the crowd will probably welcome him back. It isn't something I rushed into. I've got Charlie back because he can do a job for us on the wing'. He saw Cooke as able to do a special job and give more mobility on the wings. Cooke enthused 'It was a pleasant shock. I had not asked for a move'. It was also likely that Houseman's injury, depriving the side of width, motivated Sexton's move for the Scottish international.

Signing Cooke was undoubtedly a good piece of business, mollifying the crowd and providing an injection of genuine talent. As the *Daily Telegraph* pointed out, 'Cooke is likeable, gifted and articulate. He should attract spectators and draw something out of the youngsters'. His signing reduced the chances for young Mike Brolly, however, and he never played for the first-team again.

The *Daily Mail* ran a fascinating interview with Cooke about lifestyle and alcohol, under a 'Fast And Fit Cooke Takes Teetotal Road To New Soccer Life' headline. The Scot accepted that, until a few weeks earlier, a night out with him was like an action replay of *The Lost Weekend*. He and his American wife won custody of his two daughters from his first wife and he gave up drinking after seeing a questionnaire about alcoholism. As the *News Of The World* put it 'Cooke, like Osgood and Hudson, had a playboy image, and unquestionably at one time could juggle a bottle and glass with professional skill'. Hudson gone, Cooke on the wagon, Osgood on the list, Baldwin marginalised. Maybe the King's Road days were fast drawing to a close.

The match programme for the Derby County home game that Saturday included a whole column on Osgood and Hudson. It was unequivocal in its support of the beleaguered manager. It referred to a clash of personalities and reiterated that 'the board felt they had no alternative but to make them available for transfer...The relationship between manager and playing staff is an absolute prerequisite for the ultimate success and happiness of a club...Our principal emotion is one of distress and disappointment that these events should have happened, but in the taking of all decisions the long-term future of our club must come above all other considerations. We have backed Manager Dave Sexton 100% in this matter and believe that, with the same backing our Players, Staff and supporters we shall be able to look back on recent happenings, unhappy though they have been, as a point in Chelsea's history from which we grew in stature'. Fine words, but whoever drafted the final sentence had obviously been drinking deeply at the optimism well.

The manager rang the changes again against Derby, with his side still languishing in eighteenth place, four points above the relegation zone. Cooke was straight into the side with fit-again Garner and liberated-from-the-wing Garland also selected, Webb reverting to centre-back. Hinton, Brolly and Baldwin were left out, the latter very unhappy at being dropped, refusing to be substitute and not staying for the game. He told the *Sunday People* 'I had a row with Dave after he announced the team. I'd been named as substitute but told him I wouldn't be turning up. When asked why I'd been dropped, he said that I'd been playing well but he wanted to try a new system. It's always me that gets the chop when he tries new systems. I've been on the transfer list since the end of last season so there's no point in asking again for a transfer, but I desperately want to get away'.

The match itself was a drab affair. The crowd of 27,185 was boosted by the return of the prodigal Cooke but still below the board minimum target of 35,000. All three sides of Stamford Bridge cheered the returnee to the rafters, and he put on a polished display of dribbling, passing and crossing from the left wing, giving the crowd, and his teammates, a much-needed lift. Garner headed Chelsea ahead before half-time, but Jeff Bourne equalised after the interval and neither side could find a winner. Hollins, in his 500th first-team appearance, was once again man of the match.

Baldwin's walk out in a huff seemed to seal his lack of future at the club. Crystal Palace were ready to pay £70,000 for the unhappy striker, though Sexton was no keener on taking Possee and Whittle, who Palace had in mind for part-exchange, than when they were mooted in an Osgood deal. Sexton was still interested in their team-mate Don Rogers, but Palace were not prepared to lose him. Bournemouth revived their interest, amid talk of a part-exchange with Phil Boyer, but to no avail.

Hudson may have moved to Stoke but the controversy continued. Under a 'Hudson Cash Starts Row' headline the *Daily Mirror* reported Hudson claimed he never asked to leave and was therefore entitled to 5% of the pre-VAT and transfer levy transfer fee, about £10,000, as a signing-on fee. Chelsea maintained he asked for a move. Tony Waddington of Stoke was trying to clear it up. Hudson understandably complained 'I am very concerned about the prospect of losing this money. I never asked Chelsea for a transfer - in writing or verbally. Now it looks like I might have to go to an independent tribunal to get my money'. Waddington stated 'as far as Alan and Stoke are concerned there is no disagreement'. Brian Mears diplomatically commented 'I don't think Chelsea should be involved in any slanging match'.

Hudson told the *Daily Mail* he believed Sexton had told Stoke that he had not officially asked for a transfer. He admitted that in a row with Sexton he had said 'what are the chances of me getting away now'. Sexton replied 'you can go with pleasure'. From the player's point of view it was a year's wages and worth fighting for. From Chelsea's perspective, funds were very tight and there were in no frame of mind to be accommodating to a player they had fallen out with. Hudson claimed to the *Evening Standard* that Sexton told Waddington the player had not asked for a move and it was OK to give him the 5%. Five days later he was told they had changed their mind. A messy business that did not reflect well on any of the parties involved.

A *Sunday People* interview was revealing in terms of Hudson's frustration with his role at Chelsea. He had spent two years trying to convince Sexton he was best used moving 'forward with the ball and to sense instinctively where it should go'. When Kember was signed, Sexton had told him it wouldn't affect him at all, then stuck him out on the wing 'because no-one else likes to play there'. In the FA Cup game with Arsenal in March 1973 he was told to stay on the right and stop Peter Storey breaking through, a ludicrous waste of his talent. He asked for a transfer then, but Sexton would not let him. Mears had told him 'this is a great club. We are building a great new stadium, we'll have a great team and you are a great player'.

In late 1973 Sexton told Hudson that he was under pressure to sell players but that he (Hudson) would only be sold over his dead body. He said the manager had him and Osgood in his office after the Leeds game in mid-December. 'Are you looking after yourself? You've got a big influence on the other players. I don't want you leading them astray'. After the Liverpool defeat first Osgood, then Hudson were called into Sexton's office and told they were dropped for Sheffield United. Hudson blamed Sexton's fixation with wingers for Chelsea failing to be one of the top clubs and did not understand why he didn't buy one rather than play strikers and midfielders there, a view shared by many and, in hindsight, irrefutable. Sexton had told Mears he saw Hudson as 'the real problem boy' and a stronger character than Osgood. Whatever the truth, at Stoke Hudson lost weight, moved back into his much-preferred central midfield position and thrived.

Frank Butler, authoritative *News Of The World* columnist, reckoned several players and Attenborough had spoken to Osgood to get him to try and change his mind. 'For him and Sexton the chemistry was so difficult, it was hard to see how they could honestly enjoy each other's company. When Osgood hits a good day, he's the best striker in the world, but he lacks application. He is unreliable, forgets appointments or turns up late'. The transfer speculation surrounding the player continued.

Crystal Palace manager Malcolm Allison visited Sexton to discuss the latest position regarding him and Baldwin, and Osgood excited comment when he went to watch Hudson play at Stoke.

The *Daily Mail* put the boot in nicely with an 'Osgood...The Great Unwanted Talent' headline, pointing out that the star was both astonished and bitterly disappointed by the lack of reaction to his transfer-listing. His theory that top clubs would enter a lucrative bidding war for his services was in tatters.

Chelsea even sent a circular to clubs reminding them that Osgood, Baldwin and Dempsey were on the transfer list, a humiliation for the trio. Fulham were interested in the latter pair and Bonetti, Dempsey having started his career at Craven Cottage. The *Evening News*, trying to coin a nickname to rival 'The Busby Babes' and 'Docherty's Diamonds', could only come up with the frankly feeble 'Sexton's Shavers' for the group of youngsters, led by Ray Wilkins, who it was fervently hoped by the club would be strongly challenging for first-team places within months. On the downside, the *News Of The World* reported that the club were preparing to part with four teenage professionals - Keith Lawrence, Tommy Cunningham, Alan Taylor and Tommy Ord of whom only the latter had played first-team football. Third-choice goalkeeper Steve Sherwood went on loan to Brentford, staying there for the remainder of the season.

Bonetti, unsurprisingly still unhappy, preferred to train with reserves than the first-team. He was asked to join the senior squad under Sexton but chose to continue with the group he had been with all month. He had lengthy talks with Mears and Sexton about his future. He was 32 and wanted to be released if it would benefit his career, telling the *Evening Standard* 'I am not jumping on the bandwagon. I want to do things in the nicest possible way so that all parties benefit. I have been thinking about my future for a few days now. I didn't think I was playing badly when I was dropped'.

The *Daily Mirror* thought they had identified a major Chelsea signing. Under a back-page headline 'Chelsea In For Boyer', they said Sexton was set to make a £100,000 bid for the Bournemouth striker and might offer Baldwin in part-exchange. Boyer, a decent striker but probably not a top-class one, eventually moved to Norwich for £145,000, a sum Chelsea did not have to hand. Chelsea also apparently sought Stoke's full-back Mike Pejic and forward Jimmy Greenhoff in part-exchange for Osgood, but Tony Waddington was uninterested in swapping. Pejic played for England and the highly talented Greenhoff later moved to Manchester United, so they would certainly have been interesting signings. As it was, Chelsea did not pay for a striker until they the hardly earth-shattering sum of £45,000 was paid for the hardly earth-shattering Jim Docherty from East Stirling some four years later.

Despite the chaos enveloping the club, the *Evening News* faithfully reported that Chelsea remained committed to the £5.5m stadium redevelopment. They estimated that the cost 'may rise to £7m by the end of the decade when the work is finished...The scope and vision of this all-embracing Chelsea project is almost breath-taking'. Again, no questions were raised as to the funding of the redevelopment or the financial state of the club.

The game at Stoke, giving an early reunion with the departed Hudson, was moved to Sunday 27th January because of the energy crisis and resultant three-day week. The law dictated that admission could not be charged on a Sunday, so spectators had to pay for a team sheet. If the Sunday games were a success, there were stories Chelsea could switch their home games from Saturday while the emergency continued. Chelsea competed hard, but captain-for-the-day Hudson won a penalty after a tackle by Locke nine minutes from time, Geoff Hurst converting it.

So a traumatic month that began with four established stars being dropped and included walkouts, transfer-listings, a refusal to sit on the bench, a major transfer, a returning hero, an FA Cup elimination, four points from four League games, endless transfer speculation and a torrent of negative headlines came to a welcome close. The club were still in eighteenth place, four points above the relegation zone but the threat was still very real and, to the Chelsea directors trying to fund the East Stand, let alone the redevelopment of the rest of the ground, a nightmare that must have given them sleepless nights.

16th Wolverhampton W.	p26	24pts
17th Tottenham Hotspurp	26	24pts
18th Chelsea	**p26**	**22pts**
19th West Ham United	p26	18pts
20th Birmingham City	p25	18pts
21st Manchester United	p25	17pts
22nd Norwich City	p25	14pts

February 1974

A tough February on the pitch, with away games at Leeds and Ipswich and visits from Manchester City and QPR, coupled with trying to resolve the unsettled player issues, was a chilling prospect for a manager under pressure on several fronts.

The Leeds away programme on February 2nd asked the pertinent question whether the stadium redevelopment, with the crowd on just three sides, was responsible for Chelsea 'not ... doing well enough in the League'. It also contained a revealing interview with Dave Sexton, that deserved wider coverage. 'Plans were announced more than a year ago for a new ground that would be as futuristic as it would be possible to be. Entirely new stands, covered underground concourses linking us to local tube stations, family enclosures, private boxes ... My enterprising directors have incorporated practically all the suggestions ever made for making the football ground a place for the family'. He believed Sunday football could help fill the new stadium, as the club need to fill the seats if the capital outlay is not to be in vain. He did not want grounds entirely seated as there would always be many people who preferred to stand and saw the need to strike a balance. He could see family season-tickets being introduced in the future. 'No-one knows how successful we will be on the field. The pressures on me as a manager to keep the team in a successful vein are therefore even greater'. A man expected to produce a side capable of filling Stamford Bridge but who seemed, at least publicly, to have 100% bought into the board's plans.

Chelsea had not won at Leeds since 1936 and, given their unbeaten record and the unyielding bitterness between the clubs, would do well to avoid comprehensive defeat, especially with a front five of Ian Britton, Chris Garland, Steve Kember, Bill Garner and Charlie Cooke hardly promising goals, so Garner heading Chelsea ahead before half-time was not in the script. Chelsea defended heroically and, though Trevor Cherry equalised, stout defending gained a deserved, and totally unexpected, point. Sexton was unsurprisingly delighted, beaming 'they have been battling hard in away games like this recently'.

Webb was certainly battling, having three stitches over his right eye after a clash with Joe Jordan. He had four inserted in his left one two weeks earlier after a clash with Colin Stein of Coventry. 'It's getting worse for defenders ... managers are geeing up forwards'. Sexton praised his bravery. 'He never comes off. He keeps going'. The player denied to the *Daily Mirror* that he had asked for a transfer. 'It's just not true, I am a Chelsea man through and through. My future is at Stamford Bridge. All I want to do is help them get clear of relegation trouble'. The departure at that point of Webb, a loyal, committed team figurehead, would have been calamitous.

The *Daily Mail* reported that Osgood was winning the fight against his groin injury and may play in the reserves shortly. Sexton was clear. 'If he is fit and Chelsea are still paying his wages then he is available for selection'. They reported what was becoming a widely held opinion, that 'Chelsea's talented rebel may have to make his peace with Sexton', though the *Evening Standard* reported that chairman Brian Mears had put the brake on speculation that Osgood could stay. This type of partially informed, partially speculative reporting was a daily feature at the circus that was Stamford Bridge that winter. It kept Chelsea in the headlines but supporters in the dark as to what was really happening at their club.

Dave Sexton gave a revealing interview to The *Daily Mail's* Jeff Powell, opening his heart about the Osgood affair. 'Maybe it would have been the best thing for Ossie if he and I had sorted it out quickly between the four walls of a locked room'. He complained that 'anything said to Osgood gets out to the press ... Ossie's basically alright. He doesn't know whether to be a good lad or Jack The Lad ... there's bravado ...

he's got a good football brain. He's well liked...He has got to be more of a team player ... What's the point of scoring 25 goals a season if you're not up there holding a cup or a medal ... you must strike the right blend and balance, so the players aren't falling out with each other'. Valid points.

Sexton stressed the need for trust and belief. 'A manager's job is to create the right circumstances and atmosphere in which players can work, in which they can do what they do best...The problem comes if the player won't do the little extra you ask of him in addition to his own thing', presumably a reference to Osgood. He praised Webb, Harris, Hollins and Droy for stepping up while the club was in turmoil.

Sexton, in a clear message to the board, emphasised to the *Evening Standard* that the first-team squad must be brought up to strength, the return of Cooke being the only signing since Hudson and Osgood were transfer-listed. Young striker Steve 'Jock' Finnieston hit a hat-trick for the reserves against Swansea, and there was speculation he could be called up.

Seven days after the highly encouraging result at Leeds, with a scheduled midweek home game with Burnley postponed when a thaw flooded the pitch, an unchanged team took on a Manchester City side struggling, like Chelsea, to reclaim the glories of a few years earlier. Heavy rain may have kept the crowd down, given how little of the stadium was under shelter, only 20,206 turning out to watch Chelsea take a lead through Webb, playing with stitches over his eye, then hold on. Droy, who had struggled at times that season, was praised by the *Daily Telegraph*, who said he had 'richly rewarded Sexton's faith by this display, a mix of discretion, well-balanced tackling and passing'.

Paul Dobson of the *Kensington Post* gave one of his occasional club critiques, astutely deconstructing the team. 'Chelsea's new stand, which grows a little every week, already seems a monument to wishful thinking. Chelsea very definitely lack star quality. They have no single individual able to entice the crowd into an excited murmur. Sexton's insistence on his two passions, work-rate and wingers, will need a lot of luck unless it is to backfire seriously. The club's, as well as his own, future hangs dangerously in the balance. Locke had a fine game. Britton has improved immeasurably in the past two months...but he is essentially all bustle. Droy is immense...but his range of skills is severely limited and, like most of the others, he lacks the charisma to appeal to spectators. Garland, Kember, Garner and Hollins have all just missed becoming crowd-pulling stars. The youngsters seem likely to miss it, too. The only present team member who has it is Cooke, but age has taken its toll despite the sentiment that still surrounds his every swivel and turn'.

Dobson saw four possibilities, in order of merit. 1) A successful side with stars like Osgood. 2) A successful side without stars. 3) An unsuccessful side with stars. 4) An unsuccessful side without stars.

'Three months ago Sexton had the third option. Now he has the fourth. Time waits for no-one and it is not on his side. He had better hurry up or the fans will drift, one by one, to QPR. Chelsea cannot afford that'. Hindsight makes this a highly perceptive analysis, except he under-estimated the youngsters due to come through to the first-team over the next year or so and massively over-estimated the pull of QPR. Any board member reading that piece can only have shuddered at the perspicacity and relevance. Chelsea had indeed become an unsuccessful team with no stars.

Foul: Football's Alternative Paper was a deeply cynical, well-informed sort of 1970's *Private Eye* about football. They, too, saw Hudson and Osgood taking on authority but supported their actions. 'When everyone is crying out for entertainers, it isn't the entertainers who are punished - Cooke, Hudson and Osgood (are) all gone'. As Cooke pointed out in *The Bonnie Prince*, the unravelling of the side happened disturbingly quickly.

The crowd chanted errant star Peter Osgood's name towards the end of the Manchester City match, but he was not there, as he and Ian Hutchinson, the pair of them recovering from injury and due in over the weekend for treatment, were 'playing truant' in Spain, disappearing for a long weekend without permission.

This trip became public on the morning of the City game, the *Daily Mirror's* main back-page story being headlined 'Ossie Mystery. Chelsea Striker In Flight To Spain'. Mears and Sexton had no comment to make at that point. Osgood's agent, Ken Adam, said he (Osgood) had gone away (to Alicante) for a couple of days to get away from all the phone calls. Fevered, wildly optimistic, speculation that he might be signing for Real Madrid was denied.

A certain amount of supporter sympathy for Osgood must have dissipated, as he was openly defying club rules. He was doubtless hugely frustrated at not being courted by a string of top clubs, but leaving the country was hardly the best way to handle that. Hutchinson's behaviour, too, was disappointing, given how the club had stood by him during an injury plagued three years.

The *Evening Standard* reported on the Monday that Hutchinson and Osgood had flown in that morning from Alicante. They had committed 'a breach of contract' as 'neither had permission to leave the country' according to Sexton, had reported for treatment and were 'expected to meet Sexton tomorrow'. The trip to Spain was apparently arranged by Hutchinson's friends as Osgood was thinking of buying a holiday bungalow. The matter was to be discussed at the next board meeting.

A couple of days later the *Daily Mail* ran a 'Chelsea Cool The Osgood Climate With Token Fine' headline. Osgood and Hutchinson were fined but neither Sexton nor Mears would reveal the size of the fine, which was assumed to be tokenistic, maybe £50, rather than draconian. Hutchinson's previous behaviour had been exemplary, which was presumably a factor in his case. Osgood indeed bought a holiday home in Alicante on the trip. The *Daily Mirror* reckoned the meeting with Sexton lasted less than fifteen minutes and thought Chelsea would have sanctioned the trip if permission had been sought.

The squad went to Malaga for a three-day break after the Manchester City game. Sexton hoped it would boost his players in the fight to stay out of relegation trouble. Being out of the FA Cup, Chelsea arranged a friendly at Scottish First Division side Aberdeen for their blank weekend. There was much speculation as to whether Osgood would make the trip. He was in the party of thirteen, which also included youngsters Brian Bason and Ken Swain, the former coming on as substitute. Osgood played in a 2-1 defeat but made little impact. It was to be his last appearance in a Chelsea first-team shirt for over four years. Sexton said after the game there was no chance of an immediate League return for the transfer-seeking star, and that Garland would get preference.

Sexton appeared on a London Weekend Television programme 'It's Worth Reading' broadcast after midnight, discussing poetry and a Robert Frost poem about fireflies which 'glow like stars at the start but have not the heart to sustain the part'. He stressed he was trying to mould a team which, unlike the fireflies, glowed brightly without diminishing.

Second Division Aston Villa were interested in buying Garner, but Chelsea preferred to keep him with Hutchinson still not fit and Osgood in the departure lounge. The *News Of The World* thought highly rated Villa right-winger Ray Graydon could be offered in part-exchange for Osgood with a balance of £175,000 paid, and though Sexton had been interested in the player for a while, Osgood was keen to stay in London and in Division One. Opening out the speculation internationally, AEK Athens were thought to be another potential bidder.

Osgood was selected to play in the reserves at Crystal Palace. If he came through that test and into the first-team reckoning, the *Daily Mirror* reported that he planned a meeting with Sexton. The same paper, 24 hours later, took a different perspective. Under a back-page headline 'Ossie: I've got to go' the star was unequivocal. 'The talk about me staying is rubbish. I know I could never see eye-to-eye with Dave Sexton while he's manager. There's no doubt in my mind that my future lies with another club ... I want to get away as quickly as possible and will talk to any club'. So much for building bridges.

In the QPR League programme, the club, which had previous sold reserved West Stand benches seats until the end of March, announced they were available for games up to the end of the season, a quiet admission that the new stand was not going to open until August.

The derby game drew in 34,264 spectators for a thrilling game. Chelsea were unchanged for the fifth successive game, a welcome change from the last couple of injury-ridden seasons. The team lined up *Phillips; Locke, Webb, Droy, Harris; Hollins, Kember; Britton, Garland,*

Garner, Cooke. Not an exciting team, for sure, but a hard-working one, probably what Sexton most required at that point of a desperately disappointing and frustrating season.

Garner scored twice, both headers from Hollins set-pieces, working to prove that Sexton would be wrong to sell him. Cooke volleyed the other. Unfortunately for Chelsea, QPR's flair and creativity meant they were on the scoresheet three times as well in a thrilling 3-3 draw. Bowles, mercilessly barracked by The Shed, capped a superb display by scoring twice.

On the day of the QPR game, the *Daily Mail* reported that Hutchinson and Baldwin had been dropped from the reserves, Sexton confirming reserve coach Dario Gradi desired to play some of the youngsters. Hutchinson was upset. 'I was making a bid for a first-team comeback. This will put me back at least a fortnight as I need the match practise...It's a sickener...It makes me wonder what my future is'. He was still not on a contract. Baldwin, bitterly disappointed to be left out of the first-team in the shake-up, complained 'I'm sick. I'm still on the list and I now see that I'll have to get away this time'.

Unhappiness duly manifested itself in absence. The pair faced fines of £50 for to failing to report to training on Monday 25th. Hutchinson apparently had a sore throat and Baldwin had 'gone missing', believed to have taken an unauthorised weekend away. They were joined in their displeasure by fit-again John Dempsey, unable to regain his first-team place from Micky Droy and also dropped from the reserves.

A Chelsea spokesman claimed there were no plans to fine Baldwin and Hutchinson for missing training on the Monday. However, under a 'Chelsea Put Rebel Hutch On List' headline, the *Evening Standard* reported he had been listed after talks with Sexton, who was taking a hard line to halt the recurrent incidents of indiscipline. Baldwin, already on the list, was suspended for two weeks for missing three days training that week visiting Spain. It meant a loss of wages of around £200 and accelerated his desire to leave the club.

The duo had to be disciplined if the manager was to retain any credibility but arguably, Sexton should not have let things reach this state. Hutchinson sought match fitness, which he could only get from playing. Baldwin felt he was being victimised and, given he had scored nine goals in eighteen games whereas Garland had netted two all season, he had a point. The *Kensington Post* comment 'there is a strong wind of change blowing through Chelsea Football Club at the moment, and I don't think it is a healthy one' was close to the opinion of many supporters who wondered what the hell was going on at the club. Hutchinson told the *Daily Mail* 'it's up to the manager to make the next move. I'm probably in breach of contract for talking to the press. I could be suspended - but I'm not worried'. He complained that Chelsea would not tell him what they thought he was worth.

Amidst the chaos, a decent month in terms of results was rounded off with a 1-1 draw at fifth-placed Ipswich. A rare Garland goal was equalised by Mick Mills. Another fighting performance delighted Sexton who smiled 'we battled well at the back'.

Long-serving reserve centre-back Marvin Hinton was granted a free transfer as part of the policy to give youngsters more opportunities. Portsmouth, Huddersfield and Swindon were interested but, in the end, he was to stay, play three more games that season, and indeed, remain at the club the following season. Young centre-back Keith Lawrence went on a month's loan to West Bromwich.

Off the field, the month ended with yet more negative Osgood stories. He walked out of a training session after a row with Gradi during a five-a-side match in the gym. With Sexton away scouting in Aberdeen, Gradi objected to some tough tackling and ordered the players to 'cool it'. When they failed to do so, he gave Osgood an ultimatum 'go away and get changed and leave'. They had another heated argument outside. Hutchinson walked out in sympathy. This latest row further stiffened Osgood's resolve that he would never play for Sexton again, and the only solution was a transfer, though interest in him seemed to have evaporated. It must have been tough for the coaching staff, and the other players, with tense confrontations taking place so regularly.

So the month ended with massive challenges up front. Osgood, Baldwin and Hutchinson were all on the transfer list, Garland had three goals all season and Garner seven. If a clear-out took place, decent new striking blood was absolutely essential. To Sexton's credit he had developed a settled side, who worked hard for each other. Chelsea had slipped to seventeenth place, only six points away from the relegation zone. The improvement over the previous two months was noticeable, but the side had still only won once in nine games.

16th Southampton	*p30*	*28pts*
17th Chelsea	**p30**	**27pts**
18th Arsenal	*p31*	*27pts*
19th West Ham United	*p31*	*26pts*
20th Birmingham City	*p29*	*21pts*
21st Manchester United	*p29*	*19pts*
22nd Norwich City	*p30*	*18pts*

March 1974

Manager Dave Sexton woke on Friday March 1st to see that two of his unhappy players had given detailed interviews to the *Daily Mail* regarding their discontent, under a 'Hutchinson For Sale And Baldwin Banned' headline. The paper referred to 'Sexton's purge of the gifted but volatile old guard'. Ian Hutchinson complained 'that makes half the cup-winning side who are gone or going ... I don't want to leave Chelsea. I don't think any of us do. But we're all at odds with the manager, so it looks as if we're on our way'. Hutchinson received no further punishment for missing training and walking out in sympathy with Osgood.

Tommy Baldwin complained about his fine. 'It seems tough to me to lose that much when Ossie and Hutch only got fined £50 each for flying off to Alicante a couple of weeks ago. But I've got used to being the scapegoat at the Bridge'. Told he would be training alone for a fortnight, he replied 'that suits me. I hope I'm sold in that time'. No regret for disappearing without permission for three days, but a complaint that his punishment was more severe than the, admittedly soft, fine meted out to his wayward colleagues.

Sexton called in Osgood and Hutchinson, ordering them in for solitary training the next afternoon. Then he phoned Hutchinson back and told him he was on the transfer list. In Osgood, Hutchinson, Baldwin and John Dempsey, Chelsea had around £500,000 worth of senior players for sale. Sexton optimistically claimed 'I hope there will be moves for all of them before the deadline closes in two weeks...Our supporters need have no fear ... Chelsea will be all the better for sorting out these problems'.

The club seemed to be in anarchy. Players sent home from training. Walkouts. Unauthorised holidays. Fines. Suspensions. Transfer requests. Incessant negative stories in the press. Whatever the rights and wrongs, for senior players to behave in such an unprofessional manner was indefensible and Sexton was right, the club seemed to have little option but to sell them.

The day after that latest story broke, Sexton had to field a side at relegation-threatened West Ham. In their matchday programme, Sexton was crystal clear regarding his stance on the lifestyles of certain players. 'I can't understand that Friday night out business. A player's career is so short that I can't understand how one can throw away his talent, the honours, the money he can earn, the pleasure he can take from playing. Yet some do ... perhaps they are unlucky in their friends', a frustrated barb aimed at Hudson, Osgood and Co. As Hudson put it in *The Mavericks* 'a few went off the rails'. There was a clear split in the squad between the socialites and the quieter ones family ones such as Bonetti, Hollins and Houseman, though, as John Boyle points out, Osgood lived in Windsor, Boyle in Thornton Heath and plenty of other players in the suburbs, so the stories of half the team drinking in the King's Road every night were a myth.

The programme informed the West Ham fans that the visitors had 'playing-staff difficulties which seem to be an inevitable part of "the soccer scene" these days'. This was presumably a barbed reference to the great Bobby Moore, who had fallen out with the club and left for Fulham a fortnight later.

An unchanged but uninspired side were heavily beaten 3-0, battling midfielder Billy Bonds getting a hat-trick. The *News Of The World* seemed to hit the nail on the head. 'Sexton has had a week of bitter internal strife and it looked as though those battles behind closed doors have sapped the club's strength...Players in key places were short of concentration and spirit'. An unnamed player observed 'tactically we were all wrong. I think the troubles we've lived with are affecting everybody'.

Chelsea had won two of nine games, but Sexton snapped to the *Sunday People* 'how can you say we're going through a bad run? We only lost one of our last seven games before today'. Brian Madley was highly critical. 'Seldom have I seen a First Division side turn in such a lacklustre performance ... Players wandered round aimlessly wondering what to do next (with) a complete lack of co-ordination or method'. After a game like that, against opponents below them in the table, relegation suddenly seemed a genuine threat. As the *Fulham Chronicle* put it, 'a triumph of mediocrity over mere inefficiency as two clubs fought to stay clear of the chasing pack at the foot of the League'.

After the distraction of a football match, back to the bickering, infighting and anarchy. Even by the dismal standards of the past two months, the following week was a debilitating shambles, almost unparalleled in the history of the club and, indeed, any club.

Opinion was mixed as to who was to blame for the chaos and what course of action should be followed. Frank Butler, in the *News Of The World*, was very clear in a 'You've Got It Right, Sexton' opinion piece. 'The Bridge of Stamford is becoming the Bridge of Sighs. Osgood, Hutchinson and Baldwin have joined the confrontation with manager Dave Sexton. Hudson waged war and has switched on all the old magic again since joining Stoke ... Chelsea can't allow this player rebellion to spread ... Highly paid soccer stars no longer respect authority. Osgood is brilliant, unreliable and has some of Best's 'couldn't care less about anything' attitude. The Chelsea board must stick by Sexton. But even Dave knows that directors practise what they preach only when the going is good. What happened to Drake and Docherty (i.e. the sack) could happen to him ... Chelsea must stand firm and insist their highly paid stars obey the rules'. Butler, a respected writer, seemed to hit the nail on the head.

Reports also appeared that weekend that two senior players, Hollins and Houseman, were unhappy with the chaos at the club and had sought meetings with Mears. The *Daily Mail* also reported that some of the players were locked in conversation with him at the PFA Awards dinner on the Sunday night, which Sexton left early. Which players, and what they said, is unclear, but when even loyalists like Hollins and Houseman were unsettled, Mears clearly thought action was necessary.

On the Monday an under-pressure Sexton attended a Chelsea board meeting, the directors terrified by the economic impact relegation would have and deeply concerned about Sexton's disagreements with senior players. In *Chelsea – The Real Story* Mears said the manager spelt out to the meeting why Osgood should go, explaining that he did not play or train properly and was a bad influence in the younger players.

That night's *Evening Standard* cleared the front page for a 'He's Out. Sexton Leaves Chelsea' story. They revealed that the Chelsea board had sensationally decided to part with Sexton and keep Osgood. He told Houseman, Droy, Webb and Harris, all Sexton loyalists, that he was leaving. The manager made it clear to them that Osgood would be taken off the transfer list and would not be leaving Chelsea. Sexton was driven away from Stamford Bridge, grim-faced, at 3.25pm. In a bizarre twist they reported that Bristol City manager Alan Dicks, once a Chelsea player, was believed to have driven into the Stamford Bridge car park, seen the photographers, reversed and sped away. A senior player said 'Osgood has proved to be greater than the club – and Dave Sexton'. The assumption was he had refused to take Osgood off the transfer list.

The following day, the *Evening Standard* followed this bombshell up with a gloriously contradictory 'Sexton Stays As Chelsea Manager – Official' headline. Secretary Tony Green made it clear that 'Dave Sexton isn't resigning, nor is he leaving the club. He will remain as manager. There has been no dispute (with Sexton). Osgood is still on the list...We hope this is the end of the matter'. Chaos. Utter chaos.

Mears, in a statement raising optimism to new heights, told the *Evening Standard* 'we all hope that we can now pull together this season, and in the years ahead, and must step up the drive for points...I can categorically deny that he (Sexton) has been sacked or has resigned'. He advised the *Evening News* 'as far as I know things are as normal'. He did not define what 'normal' was given the continual hiatus of the past two months. He continued 'it is essential that the atmosphere becomes happy and harmonious again...In view of our tremendous commitment to the redevelopment of Stamford Bridge, it is vital to make a big effort on the field to maintain our status ... I want to make it quite clear, he (Sexton) will take training on Tuesday and continue as usual'. He told the *Daily Mirror* 'We back Dave all the way and are behind him 100 per cent'.

Mears refused to comment about Osgood and the other rebel players. In *Chelsea – The Real Story* he told how after the meeting he saw the *Evening Standard* headlines, rang Sexton and cleared up the 'misunderstanding'. He also pointed out that Sexton should have shared his problems with the errant duo with the board much earlier.

The players were amazed by Mears' statements. One, unnamed, confirmed to the *Daily Mirror* 'Dave came out of the boardroom and shook hands with about five of us. He told us he was leaving, thanked us for our support and wished us good luck. It was quite obvious to everyone that he had walked out. He was close to tears, pale and very upset. Half-a-dozen players and office staff confirmed this'. In *The Special Ones* Osgood recounted how he thought, wrongly, that player power might win in the stand-off against Sexton. 'We had the champagne out when we heard he had been sacked but he was back the following day'.

Two days after the infamous board meeting, the manager was interviewed by the *Daily Mirror* under a 'Sexton: Why I'll Stay' headline. 'I was wrong – now we need stability…I misunderstood something that was said at the board meeting and was under the impression that the club wanted me to go. I was wrong, as a call from Mears proved later that evening. I was not asked to resign, did not offer to and have no intention of doing so. We realise we are too close to the bottom of the table for comfort. in view of our position at the moment it is essential we have stability…The lads in the team have been nothing short of heroic. That's why I must choose players I know I can rely on. Baldwin has been on the list for a year, has had only two offers and he turned both down. Derby are the only club to make an offer for Osgood. I would have been prepared to have him back if he had proved he was willing to buckle down and work for the good of the team'. The *Daily Mirror's* view was that Chelsea had acted swiftly, and commendably, in coming down on the side of the manager, 'and the (board) believe now their troubles are behind them'. The journalist must have had a choking fit writing that last sentence.

Columnist Frank McGhee, in the same paper, went to town. 'Chelsea players have nicknamed Stamford Bridge 'Colney Hatch', once a well-known lunatic asylum. Chelsea lost a lot of credibility when they appeared to be in the lunatic position of either a team without a manager or a manager without a team. The club belongs to the supporters. Why didn't anybody tell them what was going on. Osgood has been gathering allies in team and boardroom (and) a number of players (are) dissatisfied with Sexton. Chelsea's League position precipitated this crisis for Sexton. Directors are worried about …attendances (and the possibility of) relegation'.

Getting to the bottom of what happened is not straightforward. Sexton undoubtedly though he had been sacked. It seems clear there was a faction within the board who wanted Osgood to stay and that the manager was given a very firm message by a board member, or members, to patch up his differences with the dissident players, and took it as an ultimatum. It was apparent he did not have the unanimous support of the full board. The *Sunday People* later reckoned he had only survived that crisis board meeting on a split vote by directors.

Mears told the *Daily Mail* 'There appears to have been a misunderstanding. I spoke to Dave and told him he had been under a misapprehension about a point which had been strongly put during our board meeting'. The *Daily Mirror* felt that without doubt Mears had steered his five-man board through a red-hot meeting and into hard-line support for the authority of the manager against a revolt by some players. Sexton, half-way through a five-year contract, told the *Daily Telegraph* 'the situation which only came about because of the big stadium investment and anxiety over our League position'. It also begs the question as to exactly why board members thought Sexton had left the meeting.

The *Daily Telegraph* pointed out that it appeared the board had eventually decided to support the manager and keep Osgood on the list. Whether the directors' action came before or after Sexton had left the meeting is a matter for conjecture but in the end, Mears was very clear in the board's support of Sexton. 'If they do not wish to start the new season with supporters in a brand-new grandstand watching a Second Division programme, the rot must quickly be stopped where it started – in the dressing room'. They rightly pointed out that 'any attempt by players to oust the manager, for that is what happened at Chelsea, could do the club and the game irreparable harm'.

In *Ossie, King Of Stamford Bridge* the player insisted that Sexton said he would talk to Mears about a new contract but failed to do so. He also felt Richard Attenborough had told Mears not to let Hudson and Osgood go. Sexton insisted there was no pressure on him to compromise in his attitude to Osgood, Baldwin and Hutchinson. 'Their behaviour does not encourage anyone to buy them' he argued, which was certainly true.

Even by the dreadful standards of Chelsea that season, a manager leaving a meeting under the impression he had been sacked when others at the meeting supposedly thought he had not was abominable and reflects no credit whatsoever on the board. The chairman's backing for Sexton was to his credit, as was his management of the board to, eventually, support the manager.

Manchester United boss Tommy Docherty enquired about Ian Hutchinson, was quoted £150,000 and felt that was too much given his injury record. This certainly seemed a very optimistic valuation for a player who had only been able to start eight first-team games in three years, so it is hardly surprising The Doc turned him down.

While all this managerial chaos was at its height, Osgood was, for once, quiet. Once it was clear the manager was staying, the player having been quite possibly tipped off by one or more board members in advance of the board meeting that Sexton's days were numbered, he suddenly announced he would rather retire than stay with the club. To the astonishment of everybody he asked for his cards, in effect quitting. He put out a statement to the effect that the sooner the club part company with him the better. It is hard to escape the conclusion that he was shocked by the lack of interest in buying him, and, realising the manager was going nowhere, sulked and threw his toys out of the pram. For all his talent and popularity, it seems he was badly advised and maybe, as Sexton unfairly went public on, he was indeed depressed.

The *Daily Mirror* reported that Osgood had indeed asked for his cards and, further, would retire unless another club came in for him before the March 14th transfer deadline. 'The last few weeks have been agony. I have asked for my cards to give me peace of mind'. If another club didn't come in for him, he would go back to the bricklaying and building trade, as he owned a building business with his brother. He was clear he would not go to Stamford Bridge again, unless it was to ask for a transfer, he had seen Mears and made it clear he sought no peace pact. Chelsea Secretary Tony Green explained 'he is fed up with football and disillusioned that only one club has come in with an offer. If he insists on having his cards there is nothing we can do'. The club were apparently looking to do a quick deal for maybe £200,000. It would have been financially calamitous for both club and player if he had walked away from football.

It was the turn of the *Sunday People* to buy Osgood's views on the increasingly-tangled situation. 'I've taken my biggest gamble by collecting my cards'. He said he did it to end the deadlock with the club and blamed the lack of communication at Chelsea on Sexton. He reckoned at least four clubs had been in touch with Chelsea, not just Derby. 'The problem with Chelsea is that no-one, from the chairman down, is prepared to make a decision. They're all waiting for someone else to do it. Sexton and I have crossed swords many times. More than once he's asked me outside to settle a row, but we never actually landed any blows. He's the hardest man in the world to hold a conversation with'.

Osgood felt that by wanting a move he would be losing about £30,000 from the testimonial due the next season, and though that seems an optimistic figure he would certainly have earned a significant sum. 'I'm doing it all for a principle, not for fun'. In terms of other interest, Stoke and Crystal Palace had certainly been interested but Stoke did not want a player-exchange deal and the players Palace offered were not what Sexton required, so neither were followed up. The transfer deadline was looming, and it is entirely likely clubs were holding off, or planning to put in ridiculously low bids, as they suspected Chelsea would be forced into a malcontent's fire sale.

Osgood was photographed working at his building business. Hutchinson had already been fined, put up for sale, sent home from training and ordered to train alone. Baldwin had also been fined, was still suspended by the club and was training alone. An utter shambles. Peter Bonetti, still unhappy at being dropped, was ordered to rest for two weeks after receiving delayed concussion playing for the reserves, but his future would need to be resolved at some point.

Baldwin turned down a move to Sheffield United after a £55,000 fee had been agreed. A frustrated United manager Ken Furphy revealed 'the player wanted financial assistance with a private problem - and we were unable to help him'. He had also turned down Bournemouth, Newcastle United and Huddersfield Town. It was hard to unload a player who kept turning down opportunities to move.

The *Kensington Post*, in a stinging article, blamed both manager and board for the mess, saying there had been no communication between the parties. They argued that board allowed the rift between Sexton and Hudson / Osgood to drift on, with no firm action taken. 'Monday's board meeting...had a touch of black comedy...No wonder the players wanted to leave and say they have no respect for the men running the club. Players need firm leadership and direction. They are not getting it at Chelsea...Sexton is putting principle before practise and may be an idealist, but Chelsea are a business and cannot afford to go down with £5 million of new stand going up...Board, players and manager have all made mistakes. Sexton has stirred up more than he can handle and should go. If he goes now, they can escape relegation, which would be ruinous', one of the few calls for Sexton's head in the media that season.

A trip to bottom-placed Norwich was a welcome distraction for the beleaguered manager and an opportunity to pick up two much-needed points. Despite taking a two-goal lead through Houseman and Kember, Chelsea only drew 2-2. Afterwards Sexton opened out to reporters. He told the *Sunday People* 'it has been a lousy week working in this atmosphere - the worst week of my life. I have been quite heartened since the beginning of the year when we won at Sheffield United and have been beaten only twice in League games since ... the relegation situation is very tight ... nobody from halfway down the table can afford to relax. The target is 10 points out of our last 10 games. I am more than satisfied that these fellows can do the job. I have faith in them ... There is no chance of reconciliation between Osgood and the club'.

The *News Of The World* felt that the past week had taken the Chelsea situation beyond the stage where a compromise between Osgood and Sexton was possible. They saw the director-inspired attempt at a truce as well intentioned but hopelessly naïve, a repeat of the August 1971 fall-out where hands were shaken but issues lingered. Sexton confirmed 'I wasn't joking when I listed Osgood then. It was a climax to several indifferent displays, not just the result of the way he played in one game against Manchester United...There comes a time when you have to act the way you feel is right, regardless of whether it's popular or not'. Many supporters idolised the journalistically well-connected Osgood, and Sexton did not like airing his views in public, so there was only one likely winner of the public relations battle. Osgood was the only player on the books with the star appeal to fill the seats.

One bit of apparent good news the Monday after the Norwich game was Hutchinson changing his mind and being happy to stay. The club announced he was off the transfer list but later in the week the player said 'it's news to me that I'm off the list - I just don't know what's happening'. Sexton attempted clarification. 'I've talked things over with Hutch and he assures me he wants to stay at Chelsea'. This sort of confusion could only happen at a club that bordered on the systemically dysfunctional.

Interest in Osgood inevitably rose as the Thursday transfer deadline approached. Stoke and Southampton both agreed with Chelsea a £240,000 fee, plus 10% transfer levy and 10% VAT, and were given permission to talk to the player. QPR also made a late bid, with Crystal Palace, Birmingham City, Leicester City and Arsenal (in a part-exchange with Ray Kennedy) also mentioned in dispatches. Sexton refused to countenance Osgood going to Palace on loan, understandably preferring to sell him and hopefully use funds raised to strengthen the team.

Chelsea had given up demanding a part-exchange deal, they were looking to sell him for the best price. There was less hubbub around Baldwin, though Tommy Docherty of Manchester United made an enquiry before losing interest.

The only quality player Chelsea had been linked with was goalscoring right-winger Dennis Tueart of Sunderland, who would almost certainly have been an excellent signing, and they were keen to offer Baldwin in part-exchange, but Manchester City bought the player for £275,000 and Chelsea were not able to spend on that scale, especially as they had only banked £100,000 of the Hudson money so far. Interest was expressed in 19-year-old centre-half Steve Wignall from Doncaster Rovers, but that would have been a signing for the future and did not happen anyway.

The day before the deadline the inevitable happened, as Osgood moved. He chose relegation-threatened Southampton for a cash fee of around £275,000 (including transfer levy and VAT). The star's parting shot to the *Daily Mail* was less than gracious. Under a 'Who Is Going To Watch Chelsea Now Sexton Has Sold all The Stars' headline he asked 'Who have they got now? They might pick up a few points with hard graft from the youngsters but that's not the way to win anything, and Chelsea have got used to being among the honours. They ought to be a really great club ... Chelsea were selling so many good players and an ambitious club does not do that'. Good points and fair questions, ones that supporters were certainly asking.

So Osgood and Hudson had gone, lancing the boil but leaving the patient considerably weaker. How Chelsea proposed to fill the new stand with the two most attractive, crowd-pulling, headline-grabbing stars gone was an interesting point. Chelsea spent nothing before the transfer deadline, despite raising around £450,000 through sales. It is interesting that Osgood and Tueart went for similar fees, despite the Chelsea star having a much higher profile. Maybe managers had indeed been put off by his attitude and reputation.

The same day Osgood moved to the South Coast his ex-teammates were facing Burnley on a Wednesday afternoon due to the power restrictions. As most supporters were at work or school, the opposition were not particularly attractive, the most popular player was off and the club was in turmoil, a low crowd was no surprise. The actual turnout, 8,171, the lowest League attendance at Stamford Bridge since 1938, was still a shock. Left-back John Sparrow, only sixteen, made his first-team debut, in for Harris. He made a goal for Houseman with Kember and substitute Hutchinson in his first first-team appearance for six months, getting the others in a surprisingly comfortable 3-0 victory.

The win sent Chelsea up seven places to twelfth and largely banished relegation fears. The game almost seemed a distraction from the circus of the past ten weeks and Mears, as ever, tried to reassure the support, telling the *Daily Mirror* 'it is the end of a chapter. But it is the rebirth that is the hard thing to do. The last few weeks have been very unsettling. We are now interested only in the future'. Sexton felt 'Osgood's move is best for both of us. I'm sure we feel much freer in our minds'. They also reported that, two days earlier 'a cluster of first-team colleagues' persuaded the player to re-think his future. He was prepared to apologise to Sexton and meet him for talks, but the manager refused, ending hopes of a reconciliation. Whether this was true, or mischief-making, is unclear. What was clear is that one of Chelsea's greatest, and most popular, players had left the club, leaving an aching void it would be very hard to fill.

In terms of loan deals, Steve Sherwood stayed at Brentford for a second month and Keith Lawrence similarly extended his loan at West Bromwich. Tommy Ord, available for transfer and keen to return to part-time football, joined Southern League Chelmsford City on a month's trial. Three youngsters who had come through the club youth system, goalkeeper Derek Richardson, midfielder Ray Lewington and Striker Teddy Maybank signed as professionals and the club also signed 21-year-old striker Alec Jackson from Dulwich Hamlet. Peter Feely and Ord, signed from non-league clubs, had not come off but Sexton was obviously hopeful of another Hutchinson-style success.

The day after the Burnley game, and hours before the transfer deadline, under a 'We Shall Re-Build Chelsea – Mears' headline, the chairman 'today pledged that the money received in transferring Osgood and Hudson, nearly £500,000, will be ploughed back in building the first-team squad up to strength'. Many supporters complained that the sale was to help finance the rebuilding of the ground while Osgood criticised Chelsea as 'being unambitious' by selling 'their good players'. The chairman assured supporters that the fees would remain in the transfer fund, even though 'the rebuilding meant a loss of £100,000 in income last season'.

Mears pointed out that the loss would be increased by government-imposed power restrictions in the current season, which contributed to the club's worst crowd for 36 years against Burnley. Mears went on 'even when the rebuilding programme began nearly two years ago, we made it clear that money was available to buy players. If manager Dave Sexton recommends going for a player, he has the money to do it. He stipulated at first that we should have players in exchange for Osgood and Hudson. It didn't work out that way and we have to use the money to bring new players in. Sexton did not attempt to beat this deadline but would postpone his business until the end of the season or the summer, 'when prices are more reasonable'. That interview and others like them, laudable in intent in trying to reassure anxious supporters, were to become albatrosses round his neck. There was no mention of the East Stand, but most supporters recognised that the delays, with an almost total lack of visible progress, meant it was highly unlikely to be opened until the following season, twelve months late.

Three days later another home game, against Newcastle. Being on a Saturday the crowd was bigger, though still only 24,207. Hutchinson scored the only goal of a nondescript game, but Chelsea were happy to take the points. On Hutchinson, who had scored two in two games, Sexton tried to clarify the situation. 'Ian has had a chat with me about his contract and he is definitely off the transfer list. He will be staying at Chelsea'. Ken Swain made his debut, coming on for Garland.

The Newcastle match programme reported that 87% of respondents to a request for programme feedback were against the permanent introduction of Sunday football. Manager Dave Sexton was in favour as he reckoned it would bring in more spectators, but evidently many regular supporters preferred Saturday afternoons. Forty-five years later, as Chelsea play just four or five home League games a season on a Saturday afternoon because of the demands of television, mid-1970s supporter opinion can only be wistfully looked at. Apart from the FA Cup Final, the only club football televised was highlights. The Crystal Palace programme reported that Chelsea had been on television thirteen times so far that season, the seventh most.

As part of the Peter Houseman testimonial programme, for a game at Basingstoke that midweek Sexton took most of the first-team squad. Hutchinson started, Baldwin came on as substitute and youngsters John Sparrow, Brian Bason, Ken Swain, Steve Finnieston and Ray Wilkins each featured.

A midweek trip to Everton earned another point in a 1-1 draw. Garner equalised in injury-time as Chelsea consolidated a top-half position. The manager was relieved and bullish, proclaiming 'mathematically we can still finish high enough to qualify for Europe' (they were in tenth place, five points behind fifth-place Ipswich) … 'We've lost just two League games this year. Since I made the changes and we had the troubles we've been very consistent. We've brought in youngsters and that must pay off for the future'.

A horrendous month for the club ended with a home game against Manchester United, seemingly heading down. Only 29,602, the lowest Stamford Bridge crowd for that fixture for many years, turned out. The fact that at least three different journalists used the word 'pathetic' to describe Chelsea's performance emphasises the depths of a dismal 3-1 defeat. 'Lifeless', 'lethargic' and 'shameful' were other adjectives used as Chelsea, seemingly safe from the drop, sleepwalked their way to defeat.

Garner's goal was little consolation. The *Daily Telegraph* called it 'the worst Chelsea display I can remember since they returned to Division One more than a decade ago'. Stewart Houston, United's ex-Chelsea defender, scathingly commented 'they weren't worth a carrot'.

So a month that involved two wins, two draws, two defeats and a welcome climb to eleventh place was over, though the results seemed inconsequential compared with the seismic ructions, the anarchy and chaos taking place off the pitch. It was to be fervently hoped that Chelsea could round off the season in reasonable style, retrench, rebuild the side over the summer and turn the corner. The worry was that the falling gates, the delay in opening the new stand and clear squad weaknesses would, taken together, mean more struggles ahead.

April 1974

With the two most high-profile malcontents sold, the transfer window closed, and relegation almost certainly averted, Dave Sexton could hope for a quieter month with six games to blood a few youngsters and make his mind up on the future of some longer-established squad members. Apart from Ron Harris, John Hollins, Peter Houseman and David Webb, there were few experienced players who could be certain of their place the next season. Sexton, therefore, was unsurprisingly staggered when Webb, one of Sexton's staunchest supporters, asked to leave the club, having 'lost heart' playing for Chelsea, with all the disruption and loss of key players. Webb explained to the *Daily Mirror* 'I have been reluctant to take this step but see no alternative in the current situation. It's been boiling up for months. My game has started to suffer and against Manchester United I played without heart'.

'Unhappy Webb must stay, says Sexton' was the *Daily Mail* headline. 'The latest player to become disenchanted will be told he must stay, at least until the close season. Webb said publicly he wanted a transfer and Sexton acted quickly'. Webb was dropped for Tottenham away, replaced by Marvin Hinton. Sexton explained 'I am replacing him with someone who wants to play for the club'. The manager continued 'we had a private conversation last week … I was surprised to hear Webb had gone public…I can't see that we can (let him go)'. Webb and Hollins had been the bedrock of the side for the past few years and his loss would surely be unthinkable. In *Chelsea – The Real Story* the chairman recounted that he was horrified that other players, like Webb and Hollins, were unhappy. Webb, who had been with Sexton at Orient, told Mears he could not understand what the manager was trying to achieve.

The *Daily Telegraph* felt the news of Webb's disenchantment – he had even considered giving the game up – was a real blow to a club emerging from the shadow of Hudson and Osgood. Webb spoke of a 'personality clash'. The paper argued that 'Webb, in common with many with Chelsea's interests at heart, is concerned that two players of their quality were allowed to leave ... and expects Mears and the board to investigate what has gone on. Webb has never been difficult to handle and there is considerable sadness in his confession that he played against Manchester United 'without heart".

Mears spoke to the Daily Mirror, making it clear Webb would not be allowed to depart. The paper argued the situation 'inevitably put a question against Dave Sexton's future' following the series of upsets. 'With Webb, regarded in the past as a Sexton disciple and the club's most loyal player, Chelsea are obviously drawing the line...Webb, it seems, has become increasingly disillusioned with the direction the club is going, a feeling, I understand, shared by at least one other senior player'. Sexton, unconsciously confirming communication issues, stated 'I don't know what Dave's difference of opinion is'.

Alan Hudson failed in his bid for a £10,000 signing-on share of his transfer fee after a 150-minute tribunal case, commenting 'I'm disappointed too, but I didn't expect anything different'. Evidence, including newspaper articles, was presented to the tribunal. The Football League ruled that a spoken request carried as much weight as a written one, so he was not entitled to the 5%. He is still angry about this perceived injustice forty-five years later. It was not to the credit of the club that this issue was not finalised to the satisfaction of all relevant parties before the transfer was completed.

Chelsea's crowds were indeed poor, but this was a wider problem across football, as evidenced by the laughably small crowd of 26,258 at White Hart Lane for the Tottenham v Chelsea derby on Wednesday April 3rd. Ken Swain made his full debut. Ray Evans put Tottenham ahead, but an inexperienced Chelsea side fought back, and the unlikely pair of Micky Droy and Harris gave Chelsea an unlikely, and welcome, 2-1 victory. Tottenham boss Bill Nicholson summed the game up. 'They were bad in the first half, but we were even worse in the second'.

Although hardly on the scale of the Webb upset, reports that Sexton could do without appeared that Steve Kember was unsettled after the sales of Osgood and Hudson and might be seeking a move. Nothing happened but Sexton must have been all too aware that several of his experienced players were less than content.

A visit to relegation-threatened Southampton the following Saturday was spiced up by the inclusion in the Saints team of Peter Osgood. The *Kensington Post* summed the game itself up nicely, saying it had as 'much passion and drama as a typical episode of *Crossroads*'. The match mattered to Southampton, desperate to get away from the bottom three, but did not seem to inspire them. Osgood, totally dominated by Droy in the air, had a poor game and was even slow-handclapped by their supporters at one point. His comment 'it's different from Stamford Bridge' were hardly the words of a man happy in his new surroundings. He had obviously hoped to go to a bigger club but, having made his bed, was having to lie in it.

The 'Webb unsettled' story rumbled on. The *Daily Mirror*, well informed of developments, reported that Chelsea would want written a transfer request from Webb before deciding if he could leave. Mears stated that 'the board talked about Webb's desire for a move but did not make a decision. We shall probably let it ride for a while and in any case, we would want a written request. There's nothing I can say about the matter, we just want a happy Easter at the club, with no more disturbances'. The thought of a Webb-less defence must have kept chairman, manager, teammates and supporters awake at night. Harris was short of top class, Hinton and Dempsey were past their best and Droy too inexperienced, so they could ill-afford to lose Webb's abilities, his buccaneering spirit, or the versatility which had seen him wear ten different shirts in his six years at the club.

Webb, again underlining the systemic failures in communication at the club, complained 'I have not been informed of the club's decision. Nobody has told me a thing'. A few days later, Sexton said 'he has (still) not made any written request for a transfer'. Mears should have told all parties to get in a room to either sort things out or at least agree a way forward, but for whatever reason he did not.

Webb was not picked for the Easter Saturday home game with Arsenal, where his experience and commitment would certainly have come in useful. A young side, unchanged for the third game running, struggled from the off against an experienced opposition languishing in seventeenth place and were well beaten 3-1. Swain scored his first first-team goal but there was precious little else to celebrate.

In the Arsenal programme a full-page article, entitled 'The Heart That Is Chelsea Football Club', gave extracts from a speech Mears gave to a Chelsea Supporters Club dinner-dance. It was a much-needed rallying call, an attempt to reassure concerned supporters that the club was striding towards a confident future. Whether it achieved that aim was debatable. Pointedly, it barely mentioned the redevelopment, either in terms of the delayed East Stand or the wider project. No mention, either, of the farcical phantom sacking of Sexton or the fact that the club was a laughing stock within football. Neither did it give any reassurance that funds raised by the two sales would be spent on much-needed squad enhancement.

'With Alan Hudson and Peter Osgood leaving the Club, you are all obviously thinking: How ambitious are Chelsea? I can dispel any doubts – a club without ambition does not spend two million pounds on a new stand, and you would be right in thinking there would be no point in rebuilding if we did not have ambitions on the field'.

'But for those to be achieved, an important quality is discipline and respect within a club, for without such qualities, no club can achieve real distinction. I feel confident that the future will prove we are stronger for the events of the past few months. The way our players have responded to the Club's recent problems reflect the heart that is Chelsea Football Club, with senior players drawing on their experience and helping young players to do extremely well during difficult times. All have been magnificent. Remember, it is the Chelsea players of today and the future who matter most, grateful though we are for the efforts of all those in the past'.

'I reaffirm our belief and confidence in Dave Sexton as the man to bring Chelsea through this team rebuilding phase. I thank everyone connected with the Club – Players, Management, Staff – for the way they have coped and drawn together during the difficult weeks past, and I thank all our supporters, who may not have always understood what was going on but who gave us encouragement when we needed it most'. The supporters who continued to go to games had not turned on the board, despite the gathering storm clouds, and their loyalty was commendable.

Baldwin was still on the transfer list and out of the team. A front-page *Daily Mirror* story on his divorce probably explained his enthusiasm for a signing-on fee in any move, as a judge had ordered him to pay his ex-wife £3,000 plus £30 a week.

29,152, another crowd below the 30,000-minimum target, watched the Arsenal game but, worse, 26,258 turned out at Stamford Bridge for the 'dreadful' goalless return game against Tottenham two days later. Historically the two most attractive London derbies played in front of a total crowd under 56,000. A sad indicator of the reduction of the club's crowd pulling ability.

The Leicester away programme made the perceptive point that Phillips had played so well since replacing Bonetti on New Years' Day that the latter had had to take a back seat. Ironically, Phillips had to pick the ball out of his net three times as Frank Worthington and ex-Blues Keith Weller and Alan Birchenall tore Sexton's team to shreds. Fit-again Graham Wilkins played alongside Sparrow in the youngest full-back pairing Chelsea had fielded for many a year. Sexton complained 'I'm just bitterly disappointed with the way things went…Overall, an abysmal display'. Birchenall rubbed salt in the wound, telling the *Daily Mail* 'We are playing the kind of creative football Chelsea were playing five years ago … their play was obvious. It was easy for me to pick up in midfield'.

The season ended, limply, a week later with a 1-0 home defeat by Stoke City. Alan Hudson had never been quite as popular with Stamford Bridge crowd as Osgood but the boos he received when he led Stoke out, and every time he touched the ball, were harsh and unjustified. He, inevitably, scored the winner and took the opportunity to dash across to the West Stand, where a fight broke out between his detractors and his supporters, with his fists raised delightedly in the air, his answer to the loudest of the boo-boys. He joked afterwards that 'that goal was worth the £11,000 transfer cut I never received!'. David Gray remembers being surprised to hear that Stoke were paying for Hudson in instalments 'a further insult (given that) he had already won Stoke two games against us'.

The match programme was as upbeat as ever about prospects. 'We believe that, starting in August, we shall go forward again - particularly with our magnificent new stand coming into operation from the opening home game of 1974-75. The £2 million East Stand is fast approaching completion. It will come into use at next season's opening home match'. At last some confidence about when the stand would open.

Only 17,150 turned out to watch Chelsea's eighth home defeat of a dreadful, debilitating season. Almost everything that could go wrong, had, though at least relegation was avoided. A final placing of seventeenth, one point above doomed Southampton, was deeply concerning.

16th Coventry City	p42 38pts
17th Chelsea	**p42 37pts**
18th West Ham United	p42 37pts
19th Birmingham City	p42 37pts
20th Southampton	p42 36pts
21st Manchester United	p42 32pts
22nd Norwich City	p42 29pts

Season Review

Sexton had much to ponder over the summer. The youngsters were promising but play too many, too quickly and the team would surely struggle. He had to replace the star quality of Peter Osgood and Alan Hudson to attract crowds, which the club required to fill the new stand. Gary Locke and Micky Droy had won their spurs, the latter effectively replacing John Dempsey in the first-team and making 30 League appearances. Locke made 31 appearances and deservedly won *Player Of The Year*. Ian Britton had done well in the seventeen games he had played that season, but other youngsters like Peter Feely, Tommy Ord and Mike Brolly had fallen by the wayside and the likes of the Wilkins brothers, John Sparrow, Ken Swain and Brian Bason had yet to be given real opportunity to prove themselves.

The defence was still regularly porous and the leading scorer, Tommy Baldwin with nine, did not score after November or start a game after December. Chris Garland, Bill Garner and Ian Hutchinson scored just thirteen League goals between them. Without new blood, there was no reason to expect the next season to be anything but another struggle. The cup magic had disappeared as well, unwelcome early elimination in both competitions significantly reducing supporter excitement, as well as cash flowing into the club coffers.

John Hollins was the only League ever-present, making it four ever-presents in five seasons for the ultra-loyal midfield dynamo. He had played every game since missing the Cup-Winners' Cup Final replay in Athens three long years earlier. He rightly described it as 'the most disappointing season since we were relegated twelve years ago'.

It was a strange season all round. Manchester United went down, Leeds won the title comfortably (as opposed to suffering their usual late implosion) and Ipswich, Stoke and Burnley all finished in the top six. Finishing over ten places below those three clubs, whose playing strength, revenue and ambition should have been well below that of Chelsea, was a clear indication of how far the club had fallen, and how quickly. Relegation looked possible until worryingly late in the season and to be a point away from the drop at season-end was not acceptable to board, supporters or, equally importantly, the bank manager.

The decline in League attendances at Stamford Bridge was becoming critical. A further 12.6% fall in the average, to 25,983, compared desperately unfavourably with 39,500 three seasons earlier. Only one gate, against champions Leeds United, exceeded 40,000. Manchester United, Arsenal and Tottenham all drew under 30,000 to Stamford Bridge whereas a few years earlier crowds of 50,000 plus when those sides visited were the norm. All the fine talk of 40,000 crowds was crumbling to dust.

The average home League gate before Christmas was almost 27,000 but in the second half of the season fell to 24,900. This despite many of the most historically well-attended games, against Liverpool, Manchester United, Arsenal and Tottenham being after Christmas. This seems a clear sign that apathy and disillusion set in during the season, not helped of course by the Osgood/Hudson imbroglio in January.

A historic analysis of the number of cup-ties the team played in is another indicator of the growing lack of success and the commensurate fall in income.

1969-70 12; 1970-71 17; 1971-72 16; 1972-73 12; 1973-74 3.

Much to worry about for the board and the manager. Success, and attractive football, was the only way to bring back the crowds and fill the new stand. Looking at the squad that summer, it was hard to be anything other than pessimistic about the future, on or off the field.

Close Season

With a display of abject pettiness and spite that shamed the club, Chelsea refused to let Peter Osgood play in Eddie McCreadie's testimonial against Manchester United four days after the season ended. Chairman Brian Mears explained 'it's too soon to have Ossie back at Stamford Bridge. It's partly in everybody's interest that he doesn't play. There was, after all, a certain amount of feeling when he left, so we all felt it would be better if he did not come back to the club'. Osgood rightly argued 'What harm could it do? I just want to play for Eddie ... (it seems) very petty ... Brian Mears won't let me play but Sexton said I could turn out with his blessing'. Insulting to McCreadie, insulting to the supporters and blinkered in the extreme, assuming the 'we' was the Chelsea board, they would have been better employed working out ways of raising finance to stave off impending emergency than arrogant acts of stupidity.

McCreadie could have expected a bumper gate with the return of Osgood but in the event only 6,437 turned up so he only received just over £3,000, poor recompense for 400 first-team games and captaincy for two years. A wet night and United's recent relegation did not help the size of crowd, so the enforced absence of Osgood was even more unforgivable.

Tommy Ord was released and signed for Rochester Lancers in the North American League, having been given a couple of first-team chances but never getting a regular place. Keith Lawrence, recently on loan to West Bromwich, moved permanently to Brentford and Steve Sherwood returned from his loan spell there. That summer Mike Brolly, given a run in 1972-73 but used only once in the following season, moved to Bristol City. Peter Bonetti almost moved to Fulham, and both clubs were keen for the deal to happen, but it broke down.

Chelsea were supposedly interested in goalkeeper Bryan King of Millwall and Fulham winger Les Barrett, though neither move developed. Certainly, if Sexton was to persist playing two men wide, he must buy a right-winger, as Kember and Garland were not comfortable playing there. The manager actively pursued winger Alex Cropley of Hibernian and bid £150,000 but the player turned the move down after a public courtship and ended up at Arsenal. Manchester United paid Hull City £200,000 for Stuart Pearson, a prolific scorer at Hull City who went on be a major success at United and to play for England, a centre-forward with talent, personality and energy. Chelsea were not even mentioned in such transfer speculation, despite their clear need for a goal-scorer.

Webb refused to sign a new contract, asked for his wages to be doubled (according to Sexton) which was unsurprisingly unacceptable to the board, and was therefore granted his wish to be placed on the transfer list. Sexton had said it was one of the worst moments of his managerial career when the player originally asked for a move earlier in the year. He had asked for a wage increase, but Sexton had thought it was out of order to make an issue of wages so far in advance, though you could hardly blame the player for wanting stability, given the chaos enveloping the football club.

A deal was agreed with Arsenal to swap Webb for experienced centre-half Peter Simpson, and again both clubs were keen, but Simpson turned Chelsea down. Mears lamented 'It's a let-down that in the past week Simpson and now Cropley have declined to join us'. Cropley was highly promising but Simpson was nearly 30 and could not get a place ahead of Jeff Blockley in a mediocre Arsenal defence, so would hardly have been a marquee signing.

Shortly after the season ended, the *Daily Mail* reported a 'Chelsea

Row Over £2 Tour Expenses'. The players complained about their tiny daily allowance for the forthcoming Australian tour, and the fact they would have to pay tax on it. Skipper Hollins made representations to the board, but this is another example of the club's dirty linen being aired in public, when to double the allowance would have cost £32 a day, or well under £1,000 for the whole trip. More pettiness from a board who failed to recognise the need to improve team spirit.

The tour to Australia only involved sixteen players, and only added Hutchinson to the party at the last minute. Ron Harris did not tour, recovering from injury and neither did experienced reserves Tommy Baldwin, John Dempsey or Marvin Hinton, or indeed first-team regular Steve Kember. Graham Wilkins, John Sparrow, Ian Britton, Brian Bason, Ray Wilkins, Steve Finnieston and Ken Swain all went, so Sexton rightly had youth firmly in mind.

While Chelsea were touring Australia, the transfer-listed Webb moved to QPR for a surprisingly small £100,000 (plus levy and VAT). He had already turned down Birmingham City, Arsenal and Crystal Palace and admitted the past few months at Chelsea had been the most miserable of his career. His boots would be particularly hard to fill, and the club had now contrived to lose three of their best players inside five months, severely weakening an already sub-standard squad. As supporter Terry Cassley points out, David Webb was 'the sort of player the club desperately needed at the time to help steady the ship and give some leadership and direction to … a team in transition'.

A struggle the following season seemed almost inevitable. Webb, in *Rhapsody In Blue*, confirmed 'I only left because Sexton had allowed the team to be broken up…The players coming in weren't the Chelsea players I thought they should be' and, as supporter Geoff Kimber points out, 'none of Garland, Kember nor Garner had that "star dust" element that could have kept the trophy laden run going'.

The Australian tour, with four wins in five games, was reasonably successful, though the *Sunday People* felt the tour did little to settle the problems between the players and Sexton. The players went off on holiday knowing that a repeat of the finished season was not acceptable, and the manager with a lot on his mind.

On the basis that it never rained but it poured, a potential players' mutiny - with at least seven of the squad refusing to sign new contracts – was probably not a surprise. Having sold Osgood, Hudson and Webb after bitter internal rows, it transpired that Kember, Garner, Garland, Hutchinson, Houseman, Droy and Phillips (most of the experienced core of the side) were refusing new terms and Dempsey, Baldwin and Bonetti were hopefully set for moves soon.

The *News Of The World* broke off from its World Cup coverage to cover the latest ructions, reporting that Garland and Hutchinson had had no pay rise for three years. Droy's contract had run out and he would not sign a new one unless it was satisfactory. 'If Chelsea want to keep their players they will have to pay more' he argued. Hutchinson added 'I played last season without a contract because I wanted better terms. Obviously, there are problems'. Garland had a lot to say. 'My contract ran out at the end of last close season. I refused to sign a new contract which meant continuing with my old wages. What's more I don't want to be a makeshift. I've already played on the right wing and at centre-forward and on the left wing. And on our tour of Australia I was given a new midfield role. I want a settled position'. Sexton looked like facing another period of discontent and confrontation.

Given that inflation had risen by over 25% in those three years, it is unsurprising there was so much discontent. The club was undoubtedly tightening its belt, but this latest pettifogging row was hardly going to motivate the players.

The £2 million East Stand, now nearing completion, towered over Stamford Bridge like a huge question mark. It was a year late and a huge drain on resources. Season-tickets for the new stand were on sale but it remained to see how full it would be once the initial novelty had worn off. To make Chelsea's ambitious project pay, the seats in it would have to be regularly filled in the seasons to come.

Season Overview 1973-74

League Appearances (inc sub) (top 11 players) – Hollins 42, Webb 39, Kember 37, Harris 36, Locke 31, Droy 30, Garland 26, Houseman 25, Garner 23, Phillips 22, Osgood 21

League Goals (5+) – Baldwin 9, Osgood 8, Garner 7, Kember 7, Hollins 6
League Clean Sheets – *Home* 7. *Away* 2
Biggest League Win – 4-0 v Southampton (H) 24/11/73
Worst League Defeat – 0-3 v West Ham United (A) 02/03/74; 0-3 v Leicester City (A) 20/04/74
Final League position – 17th

League Record –
Home W9 D4 L8 F36 A29. *Away* W3 D9 L9 F20 A31. Pts 37

Hat-Tricks – None
Sending Offs – None

Biggest Home League Crowd – 40,768 v Leeds United 15/12/73
Smallest Home League Crowd – 8,171 v Burnley 13/03/74
Average Home League Crowd – 25,983
Cup Performances – *FA Cup* 3rd Round. *League Cup* 2nd Round.

Chelsea League Debuts – John Sparrow, Ken Swain, Ray Wilkins

Player Of The Year – Gary Locke

CHAPTER FIVE
Empty Seats, Empty Hopes

Pre-season

After the extended debacle of the previous season, both on and off the field, Chelsea desperately sought a lift, something to excite the supporters, strengthen the side and help fill the new East Stand, which, they were assured, would finally be ready for the opening game against Carlisle on August 17th.

David Hay was a star of Scotland's World Cup campaign. There had been a lot of interest in the Celtic midfielder, who could also play centre-back, the previous season, with Tottenham, QPR, Arsenal and Manchester United keen and he almost moved to White Hart Lane. Given his increased profile post-Germany, Chelsea moved quickly and on July 3rd, while other clubs prevaricated, bought him for a club record £225,000.

'Hay looks at Chelsea's super-stand and decides 'This is the club for me'', the *Daily Mail* enthused. Chairman Brian Mears set up the deal while Sexton was in West Germany for the World Cup. 'David was impressed by the scale of our ambitions. A player of his talents will help us match these ambitions on the field ... This is a major breakthrough for us. It is a new era as far as I'm concerned in Chelsea history and the supporters will see something they deserve next season, a brilliant exciting player in the club colours'.

Hay headed for Cyprus for a much-needed holiday, not starting training until July 25th, eight days after the other players, though his holiday was disrupted when his family were caught up in the civil war which broke out that summer. He was definitely a marquee signing, strengthening and adding personality to a team who had earlier that year lost Peter Osgood, Alan Hudson and David Webb. He had a similar never-say-die personality to Webb, though it was a great shame that Webb's differences could not have been settled, as seeing the two together in Chelsea shirts would have intimidated many an opposition.

That summer the club reorganised their back-room staff. Dario Gradi was made first-team coach after three years in charge of the reserves, though Ron Suart was still assistant manager. Eddie McCreadie, plagued by injuries, was made player-manager of the reserves though he was still officially a member of the first-team squad. In the end he played for neither and retired as a player. Ken Shellito continued as youth team coach. John Hollins was made club captain, in succession to McCreadie, after two years as vice-captain.

The contract rows of the previous month were gradually getting resolved. Chris Garland and Steve Kember had already signed new deals and Ian Hutchinson, Bill Garner and Micky Droy were offered new terms. A resolution for Hutchinson, unable to get a new deal the previous winter because of the government pay policy, was welcomed by both parties and it was fervently hoped he would be able to shake off his appalling litany of injuries and make a fresh start.

A few players moved on that summer. In addition to Webb, three youngsters who had not made the grade were released. Bobby Brown went to Sheffield Wednesday, Alan Taylor to Reading and Barry Bolton to Dordrecht. Youngsters added to the first-team squad were goalkeeper Derek Richardson, centre-backs Tommy Cunningham and Steve Perkins, full-back Mike Sorensen and forward Alec Jackson. Full-back John Sparrow, who had made his first-team debut the previous season, signed professional terms in June, having reached the age of seventeen.

Three pre-season games were arranged for early August. The first was a tough game in Rotterdam against UEFA Cup winners Feyenoord, who had beaten Tottenham in the two-legged final. Hay made his debut in a 3-1 defeat. Taken off after 79 minutes, he told the *Daily Mirror* 'Dave was quite right to take me off. It didn't upset me. I've only trained for two days since the World Cup. It's going to take time to settle in, but I'm happy the way things are going'.

Sexton told the *Sunday People* 'David has had a difficult time settling in. It will take time for us to get used to him, and him to us'. Sexton had already told the *Fulham Chronicle* 'Hay will play in midfield and I shall start the season with my senior players in the other key midfield positions – Kember and Hollins'. He stressed that the highly promising Ray Wilkins would be making a strong challenge. 'He is going to be as good as Alan Hudson. Already he is in the mould of Johnny Giles and Johnny Haynes. I'd never worry about putting him in the side'. A 1-0 win at Borussia Moenchengladbach and a 3-1 win at Wuppertal rounded off the friendlies. Hay started all three games in a defensive midfield role.

Between the two friendlies Chelsea made an unlikely signing, paying £50,000 to Norwich City for reserve left-winger John Sissons, hugely promising as a West Ham youngster a decade earlier, but whose career had stalled and who seemed increasingly injury-prone. There was a feeling that Chelsea had bought Sissons because he was cheap, as funds to buy the required quality were not available. Nobody would have guessed at the time, but Sissons was to be the last player Chelsea spent money on for four years.

Sexton had long been looking for a winger and tried to buy Mike Summerbee from Manchester City and Don Rogers from Palace that summer. Peter Houseman was the natural left-winger in the squad, but

Sexton had been playing him at left-back pre-season and presumably intended to keep that switch going. Sissons played, and scored, in Wuppertal.

Bill Garner, who started the last two friendlies, turned down a move to Tottenham after a £200,000 fee had been agreed, hopeful of a Chelsea first-team place. Whether Sexton was pleased at this development is unclear, given it was a lot of money for a man who scored just seven League goals the previous season and was unsure of a regular place. The long-time-listed Tommy Baldwin was for sale for only £35,000, £40,000 less than at the start of the year. There was no interest, so he realistically had nothing but reserve football to look forward to. Goalkeeper Steve Sherwood, on loan to Brentford for the second half of the previous season, signed a full-season loan deal with the same club.

Crystal Palace made a bid for Hutchinson, but Chelsea turned it down. The *Evening Standard* thought Sexton might look to trim his 'powerful' first-team squad and that Kember might be on the move, especially with the signing of Hay. Peter Bonetti, who interested Sheffield Wednesday, had spent the second half of the previous season in the reserves but was hopeful of regaining his first-team place. This was the first season where top-flight clubs could borrow players.

The board clearly thought money was one way to motivate the players. The *Daily Mirror*, under a back-page '£100-A-Point - That Is Chelsea's Incentive To Reach The Top' headline detailed the new bonus scheme. They saw the 'lucrative' bonus scheme as an enormous incentive for the players. They could in theory earn up to £200 a week extra if they emerged as championship contenders. In addition to new contracts, they got £45 a point and £100 for every point over 50, though whether the club would need to pay out under the latter criteria was arguable. Chairman Brian Mears enthused 'the players stand to make a lot of money if they are successful. They are very good incentives which are spread across the board'. They were indeed.

Sexton had smoothed out the contract rows that had blown up at the end of June, presumably helped by the bonus announcement, and said only Micky Droy and Marvin Hinton were still to sign. He saw Sparrow as competing with Houseman for left-back and the centre-forward spot being between Garner and Hutchinson, with Garland, Steve Finnieston, Charlie Cooke and Baldwin also competing for a place.

Talking to the *Daily Telegraph* in early August, Sexton felt Osgood, Hudson and Webb leaving 'in some ways...has been a blessing. It gives me a chance to develop the younger players. I think we have a useful blend of youth and experience and I feel more optimistic than for some time... I won't use the building works as an excuse, although they detracted from the match-day atmosphere. The reasons went much deeper than that'. The *Daily Telegraph* were duly impressed. 'Certainly no-one could miss the changed atmosphere at the training ground yesterday. There was an air of dedication and contentment with Hay a happy participant'.

In the *Chelsea Handbook*, programme editor Albert Sewell shared the positive attitude surrounding the club. 'Hay brings skill, experience, maturity and character to Stamford Bridge...He also brings with him a reputation as a footballer who is willing to take responsibility and no club can have too many players with this quality; it was one of Chelsea's deficiencies last season'.

Headlined 'The Season When Chelsea Go Forward Again', Sewell's article made some very salient points. 'Having built a £2 million stand that is nothing short of breathtakingly spectacular, (the club) now find themselves in the position of having to build a team worthy of the new superstructure and, equally important, capable of filling it'.

John Hollins enthused 'It will be nice to walk out on to the field from the tunnel instead of through a builders' yard. It will be good to wallow in the bath afterwards, to linger a bit and talk about the game...You couldn't help notice a difference, having to change in temporary dressing rooms these past two seasons: we'll feel different again – in the changing room as well as on the field – with our new stand open'. His reaction on discovering it would be at least another month before the dressing rooms opened was sadly not recorded.

Chelsea featured prominently in season previews, as much because of the new stand as the team. The *News Of The World* reported that the plan for a £5 million, all-covered 60,000-seater stadium with heated seats, dining service and car parks was a year behind schedule. 'In these days of inflation, the original estimate cost is probably now well over £10 million...Sexton knows relegation for Chelsea would mean the sack. A super stadium without a super team is the kiss of death'.

There were 11,280 seats in the new East Stand (5,413 upper tier, 2,116 middle tier, 3,751 lower tier). The lower tier of the North-East Stand was closed that summer, meaning that whole stand remained empty. The overall seating capacity of Stamford Bridge was now 21,305, and the overall stadium capacity an estimated 55,000.

East Stand seats ranged in price from 80p to £2.50, in the West from 80p to £1.20. Terrace admission was 50p and, as in previous seasons, there were no terrace season-tickets. Season-tickets included League, Football Combination (reserve) games and four possible FA Cup-ties and were priced from £20 to £62.50.

When it opened the East Stand loomed large over the rest of the stadium, which looked even shabbier by comparison. It brought fans closer to the pitch than ever before, covering the old dog track, and the sightlines from the middle and ultra-steep upper tier were superb. It has lasted 45 years and, at the time, was state-of-the-art. Whether it was worth it, given the near-calamity it caused at the club, is arguable but it was rightly lauded as a stand to be proud of.

As an example of the chaos enveloping the club, in *The Bridge*

Colin Benson recounts how the delay in appointing Trust House Forte as catering contractor caused a delay in finalising the kitchen design, created extra building work and meant the 250-seater restaurant did not open until early 1975. When the stand did open against Carlisle, there was still significant interior work to be completed. The club had looked at the possibility of a leisure centre behind the North Stand including a restaurant and cinema. This would have cost around £750,000 but was reckoned to be self-financing and would produce a predicted net profit to the club of £150,000 per annum.

Sexton, demonstrating the pressure he and his and players were under because of the redevelopment, commented 'the team have got to do better to support the very brave venture by the directors. We've all got to see it through...I sold Osgood and Hudson for around £500,000. We've a new star in David Hay and I still need one experienced forward'. Sexton believed, at least publicly, that this could be Chelsea's year, though it was hard to expect Hay to transform the team on his own.

As the Carlisle game approached, the *Evening Standard* reported that more than 300 men were still finishing and clearing up the East Stand. Mears was relentlessly positive. 'Tomorrow we open one of the finest stands in world football. It is the day we have waited two years for. Although there is still a lot to be done in the weeks ahead, the important thing is that the fans will be sitting in this new stand for the first time tomorrow. The staff have worked day and night against the clock to have it open on time'.

On the day of the game, the *Daily Mail* introduced a note of caution, an antidote to the cheerleading. They asked a very pertinent question. Could the club draw up to 40,000 supporters for each game in the face of increasing public disenchantment with football? Mears admitted the need to make the new stand pay for itself increased the pressure on Sexton and his team to achieve success. 'The pressure is on us all and it's not a bad thing for the team to feel it...We need to average 30,000-40,000 fans at each League game to pay our way with this new stand. We hope to do well in the cups to help us press on with the next stage of the redevelopment next summer...The team have got to accept their share of the pressure. They know they must grow with the stadium if Chelsea are to be above the ten or a dozen clubs around whom football will revolve in the future'. There was no timescale given publicly for the payback of the East Stand debts, but for the purposes of this book 35,000 will be used as the average attendance necessary to breakeven and meet repayments on the stand for the foreseeable future.

The chairman continued 'If we don't get break-even gates it will be serious, and we will have to take a close look at the situation at the end of the season. We can be the first all-seater stadium because we are lucky enough to be in an area where people pay £50-£60,000 for a mews cottage'. Whether the local mews cottage residents were, or were ever likely to be, football supporters in the mid-1970s is surely open to question.

Season-ticket sales were slightly down in the wake of the previous season's upheaval. It was now clear that the board were to a large extent relying on gate income to pay for the stand, which was a remarkably optimistic, some might say foolhardy, stance to take and in indicator of how rickety club finances were.

In the Carlisle programme, in one of his occasional 'The Chairman writes' features, Mears continued in positive mode. 'More than the start of a new season, it is the beginning of a new era in the history of Chelsea Football Club, marked by the opening of our magnificent new East Stand'. He pointed out that inevitably a 'settling down' period would be required. He expressed gratitude for supporter patience during 'the past two difficult seasons' and asked them to 'bear with us a little longer over any snags that come to light'. The question was, how many supporters had been lost during those two unsuccessful and fraught seasons of transition?

In *The Chelsea Story* John Moynihan recounted the mood of optimism when Mears revealed the new stand to the press. What was not apparent to press and public at the time was the fact that the costs had soared such that the stand was in danger of bleeding the club to death.

August 1974

It was crucial for Sexton to start the season strongly and apart from injuries to reserve centre-half John Dempsey and striker Ian Hutchinson, he had a full squad to choose from. The side he put out against Carlisle, newly promoted and playing their first ever top-flight game, was relatively experienced and contained one surprise, Peter Bonetti being recalled at the expense of John Phillips. The team lined up :- *Bonetti; Locke, Droy, Harris, Houseman; Hollins, Hay, Kember; Garland, Garner, Sissons.*

Compared with forward lines of recent vintage it looked weak and, without Webb the defence looked less than formidable. Garland was again stuck out on the wing, Sexton having failed to buy the right-winger he sought. Peter Houseman was left-back, which the manager hoped to make a permanent switch, though it meant losing much of his ability to put in accurate crosses, despite the intention that he over-lapped whenever possible, with Cooke only on the bench. Against Carlisle, though, surely those concerns would be irrelevant. The crowd was 31,268, within the 30,000-40,000 target set by Mears if the stand was to be paid for and the redevelopment of the rest of Stamford Bridge paid for, but still a disappointment.

The game kicked off and ninety seconds later the first goal of the entire Football League season had been scored. Unfortunately for Chelsea supporters, it was scored by Carlisle centre-half Bill Green after errors by Bonetti and Droy. A shocking start, but the game got progressively worse. Les O'Neill scored a second after another mistake by Bonetti. East Stand supporters, including some in the best seats, joined their cohorts in The Shed in a bout of slow-handclapping and cries of 'what a load of rubbish'. The game ended in a 2-0 defeat and the team left the pitch stunned. As supporter Geoff Kimber recalls, 'in what seemed typical Chelsea fashion we completely blew it letting in two really soft goals'. Fellow supporter Terry Cassley felt the team were complacent, had the 'wrong attitude and got found out'.

A similarly stunned Mears was angered by the crowd's reaction, calling their actions 'totally unnecessary', though he did express disappointment at the result, venturing optimistically that 'we did not play badly in the first half. The press had a field day, the *Daily Telegraph* worrying about the character of the team. The *Kensington Post* caught the mood with a 'Chelsea And The Slow Handclap Shame' headline. They criticised Droy, who they described as 'as cumbersome as a tank in a Grand Prix'. On Sissons, describing him as 'more of a Woolworth's than a Gucci' they said he 'had a fair game. I doubt he will ever do much better'. Summing up a 'doleful' performance, they said 'the half-empty new stand hung remorselessly over the proceedings defying the players to justify its existence'.

Supporter David Gray remembers being so impressed by the new stand. 'I had purchased my season-ticket in the Upper Tier, level with the penalty area line at the Shed End, and was immediately astounded by the magnificent views afforded. All the talk was true, it truly was a magnificent structure and years ahead of its time'. Supporter Brian Gaches remembers feeling 'disappointed that the much-promised great atmosphere from the stand being near the pitch didn't materialise, in a shocking display which was the pattern to come for most of the season'. Most of the noise came from The Shed, which was still far away from the pitch, so a truly fervent atmosphere would have to wait for the promised further development.

Millions of viewers saw the embarrassment on *Match Of The Day* and the missing thousands were hardly inspired to attend the next home game, against Burnley four days later. Seven and a half thousand supporters were lost in those four days, a paltry 23,745 turning out. The match kicked off at 7pm as the club were uncertain as to the state of their floodlights.

Chelsea started like a house on fire and at half-time it looked as though Sexton could relax. His side were 3-0 up, Houseman, Garner and Cooke all netting. Burnley pulled one back, the defence got anxious and conceded two more as Chelsea's confidence wilted. The *Daily Mail*, reflecting on the crowd reaction to the collapse, thought 'a sad, slow handclap was unwelcome evidence that last night's gathering was not completely placated by the excitement'. Two home games against moderate opposition, five goals conceded, two slow handclaps, one point.

Sexton, on the face of it, was unperturbed, telling the *Evening Standard* 'what a shame, we threw it away. It's not good to give away a three-goal lead but, nonetheless, I was encouraged by some of our play'. The switch to full-back of Houseman certainly worked going forward but he was not a natural defender and the defence lacked reliability.

Chelsea had long been rightly proud of their match programme, which had won awards, and was traditionally ahead of the competition in terms of content, information, action photographs and design, despite having no advertisements and being priced at a very competitive 5p. That was to change.

In the Carlisle programme, there was a boast that the club had introduced a 'larger new look programme, complete with colour ... (we shall) endeavour to make it the best in the field'. They had also doubled the price to 10p. A flick through revealed it had far less photos than the previous one, there was less information, no action photographs, advertisements featured heavily, and it had the same cover every week. This was a depressing regression from the days when most attendees bought a programme.

In the Newport programme a month later the club responded to criticism that supporters were paying double for an inferior product. The club pointed out, fairly, that the price had been held at 5p for seven seasons. They also claimed they had planned to have more pages, but the price of paper had doubled. Supporters were paying more for a worse quality programme and more to watch a sub-standard team. Supporter David Gray feels 'the doubling of price and inclusion of adverts for the first time were probably the first indications that the club was facing financial troubles and every penny counted' and Supporter Geoff Kimber reiterates that point. 'It had always been a cracking good read in the late 1960's and early 1970's but by the 1974-1975 season it seemed like it taken ten minutes to produce and even less time to read it...It seemed to sum up our newly impoverished position'.

Two away games followed, a chance for Sexton and his team to improve away from the remorseless shadow of the East Stand. In the first, at Coventry, Sexton bravely kept the same side that had capitulated against Burnley. Cooke and Sissons operated as orthodox wingers, trying to provide regular stream of crosses to Garner. The tactic worked a treat. Cooke, Garner and Locke, with his first League goal, netted in a 3-1 win that brought much-needed relief to the manager. He told the *Daily Mirror* 'Charlie has certainly taken on a new lease of life. He is having a big influence again. He has taken his chance magnificently'.

For the visit to Burnley's Turf Moor three days later, Phillips came in for Bonetti, who had damaged a finger against Coventry. Hutchinson was on the bench after four goals in two reserve games. Leighton James gave Burnley the lead, Hutchinson came on for the injured Cooke,

Garner equalised and Hutch, in his first appearance of the season, hit the winner.

Away programmes that season had plenty to say about Chelsea, on and off the pitch. In the Burnley one, manager Jimmy Adamson refers to Chelsea as 'one of the most progressively managed clubs in the country...Like ourselves, they have spent a considerable sum of money on massive ground developments and improvements'. Burnley had built two stands in five years and, given they went down the following season there is an argument that they, too, over-extended themselves.

So after four games Chelsea had five points and were in tenth place. Early days, but a reasonably encouraging start. The first big test of the season, Liverpool at home, loomed large, the fifth game in fifteen days against an opposition that had started the season by dropping just one point.

A crowd of 39,461 was disappointing given the capacity of around 55,000, but gross receipts (excluding season-tickets, boxes and the Executive Club) were £34,150 – a record for a Chelsea home game. The East Stand was full, apart from some £2.50 seats in the centre of the middle tier, as the crowd waited expectantly to see how a side lacking the injured Cooke, with Hutchinson up front alongside Garner, would fare against a Liverpool side lacking suspended talisman Kevin Keegan. The answer, sadly, was very badly. Very badly indeed.

The result, 3-0 to the visitors, was bad enough. The way Chelsea were totally outclassed was far worse. Limitations in every department were there for all to see. Abject defending, with Droy and Harris regularly exposed, and Houseman's lack of full-back experience exploited on his 250th League appearance. The midfield was dominated by Liverpool while an immobile striking partnership of Hutchinson and Garner cut no ice. Only Phillips saves avoided humiliation.

The *Sunday People* made some self-evident points. 'Stamford Bridge has a magnificent new stand to make Chelsea fans the most pampered in Europe. But those fans still haven't seen a home win to make them happy. They gave them the slow handclap'. For the third home game running. A dreadful start to the home season.

Under a 'Scared' Men Of Chelsea' headline, the *Daily Mirror* had a field day. 'A tragedy for Mears and his board...the worst display of the season'. Liverpool captain Emlyn Hughes was scathing. 'Too many Chelsea players just didn't want to know'. Mears tried to put a brave face on events. 'I am very disappointed but not as disappointed as I was this time last year. Then I could foresee troubles ahead but now I think we can only get better'.

A worried Sexton ordered two full days of training. Like his chairman, he tried to put a positive spin on things, saying 'we stuck to it well under the cosh, but gave the ball away at the wrong time. That's five points from six lost at home - the lads seem to be nervous, knowing that so much is expected of them at the Bridge'.

The *Kensington Post* took a more reflective view, but still savaged team, manager and board. 'A big man at the back and two big men up front is not the way to woo back the public...Droy doesn't have enough skill to fill an egg cup ... Devastating lack of pace ... Houseman is defensively a disaster...Sexton must be criticised for buying Sissons as a replacement before Houseman had proved himself at full-back ... More than the stand needs re-building'. Other papers carried similarly damning critiques.

It is possible to see that Liverpool game as the day the dream finally died, the day the men who ran Chelsea realised how poor the team were and how their hopes of an all-conquering team playing in a full 60,000 all-seater stadium were likely to bite the dust and bite it hard. Not one of the Chelsea players who turned out that day would have got into the Liverpool side, except possibly a fully on-form Hay. Those who had left in the past three seasons – Weller, Osgood, Hudson, Webb – were superior to their replacements. Others were getting older. None of Phillips, Harris, Houseman, Hollins, Kember, Garner, Garland, Hutchinson or Sissons were likely to improve as players and a number of them were arguably short of Division One class.

Many of Chelsea's eggs had been placed in the Hay basket but though everyone expected him to come good in the months ahead, there were clear limitations all over the team. The side were in thirteenth place and, though the board, at least publicly, expected the side to be higher placed than that, the fear was that it was actually a false position and the team was likely to spend the next eight months fighting relegation.

The sale of Osgood, Hudson and Webb raised nearly £600,000 but only £300,000 had been spent on Hay and Sissons. Even if Hinton, Baldwin, Dempsey (a target for Southampton) and other fringe players were sold they would be unlikely to collectively raise more than £100,000 in a deflated transfer market, though such disposals would also reduce the wage bill. The maximum Sexton could therefore have expected to have had available to strengthen his side was around £380,000, assuming there was nothing else in the kitty. Despite Mears' fine words it was by no means clear whether that money was actually available or would be spent propping up the funding of the East Stand, especially if crowds were below target, a highly likely scenario. It was hard to see the players available to Sexton making a realistic challenge for any title or trophy and youngsters in the reserves and youth team could hardly be expected to come straight in and turn things around. Much to ponder for manager and board.

September 1974

After the salutary lesson meted out by Liverpool, there was, unsurprisingly, press talk about the need to strengthen the squad. Mears, more aware than his questioners of the predicament his club were fast getting in to, denied to the *Evening Standard* that the club were on point of buying new players. 'I was asked at the weekend whether the club had money available for players. I said we were always on the look-out for new men, but it was inferred we were about to go out and sign three or four. That suggests major team surgery - and it is not the case'. How desperate the situation would need to be before he allowed expenditure on, for example, a centre-half, a left-back, a right-winger and a centre-forward who could score goals is sadly not recorded. This lack of transfer activity, early enough in the season to have a transformative impact on that season, was to come back and haunt the club and severely limited manager Dave Sexton's options.

A week later, Sexton took his team to Middlesbrough. Charlie Cooke and Chris Garland returned to the side in place of Steve Kember and Bill Garner, as Sexton abandoned his failed 'dual big man' tactic of seven days earlier. There was a sense, though, of rearranging the deckchairs on the Titanic.

Chelsea's efforts were considerably improved on the previous week. After going behind to a Willie Maddren goal, fashioned a fine equaliser through Ian Hutchinson and they could have won, though were happy enough with a draw. One worry was the form of David Hay, who *The Observer* felt had 'yet to justify his hefty fee'. Sexton observed 'it's funny how we get good results away and yet struggle at home'. Cooke's return made a big difference in terms of control and creativity. By some distance Chelsea's best player so far that season, he was playing further upfield, not as involved in defence as he used to be. He had been training hard and evidently feeling the benefit.

Cup revenue had been publicly identified by chairman Brian Mears as a critical source of income and a home League Cup-tie against Newport County was welcomed in terms of likely progression but not in terms of attraction. Newport, allocated 3,000 seats, sold 57 in advance. Only 13,222 die-hards turned up to watch Garland score a hat-trick and Cooke, bizarrely wearing the No.9 shirt, net the other in a 4-2 win. Hay was rested, the concern was that he was still tired after the World Cup, the problems experienced on holiday in Cyprus and his short pre-season. Chelsea's reward for going through was a home tie with Stoke City, who had knocked them out of the competition in two of the previous three seasons.

The *Evening Standard* ran a feature entitled 'How Do Chelsea Look After Their Fans?'. The East Stand facilities, unsurprisingly, were seen as excellent – the bars, toilets and public telephones. The rest of Stamford Bridge was, starkly but rightly, seen as 'abysmal' with one snack bar and one toilet for the whole of the Shed End. There was criticism as the pitch was miles away from the two ends. The turnstile queues for the East Stand were criticised, the box-office seen as inefficient.

There was a clear feeling that the other three sides were not fit for purpose. This criticism reinforced Mears' dream of a shiny new stadium but did not help pay for it. The chairman, vested interest shining through, complained that 'it is quite wrong that major developments should be taxed, whereas money spent on buying players is not'. Manchester United received a large rates increase after opening a new stand and Mears feared the same.

Chelsea had failed to win any of their three home League games so far, but a game against twenty-first place Arsenal was surely a chance to remedy that. A game that used to attract 40,000 crowds a few years earlier drew in just 34,596, nearly 5,000 below the Liverpool crowd and another sign disillusionment had set in. A dull 0-0 draw between 'cautious, tense teams', with a 'slumbering second half' was unlikely to attract new supporters. Hay returned but still he struggled.

John Dempsey played his first League game for seventeen months, replacing the much-criticised Droy, and had a fine game. He sought a bigger pay rise than Chelsea were prepared to offer and had a difficult relationship with the manager. In another example of the shambolic communication at the club, Sexton said he was off the transfer list, but the player thought he was still on it, at £35,000. Mears was adamant 'there is no way he is going to leave. I thought he was tremendous today'. Dempsey told the *Daily Mirror* 'I'd like to thank reserve manager Eddie McCreadie for all the encouragement he has given me. He has known what it is like to be constantly injured'.

Crystal Palace tried to sign Hutchinson in exchange for Don Rogers, but Mears said he was definitely not for sale and 'we are not interested in Rogers'. Sexton admitted 'there is no way I can play both Hutchinson and Garner in the same team, they are too similar' after the Liverpool humbling, but obviously did not want to lose Hutch.

The *Daily Mirror* reported that Kember had been told Chelsea would listen to offers and believed they would be looking for close to £200,000. Dropped for Middlesbrough, recalled for Newport then omitted again, he was becoming frustrated at being unable to seal a regular starting place. The Mirror also reported a club fine of £25, devised by Mears and Sexton, had been introduced for players booked for dissent. Kember had already been fined once, though the departure of Osgood probably reduced the potential for revenue from that particular scheme.

Captain John Hollins told the *Evening Standard* 'We have been keen to do so well at Stamford Bridge that I suppose we have become too nervous and tense. Our performance against Arsenal proved we are overcoming this, and as soon as we start producing our 'away' form at home, then I think we will earn everyone's respect'. The *Daily Mail* pointed out that 'as the years catch up, Hollins is running less…and thinking more…He used to be action man, now he runs less but directs more. He enthused 'we are playing a new system and I'm doing my bit in organising it'.

STAMFORD BRIDGE IS FALLING DOWN

New England manager Don Revie invited eighty-four players to a get-together, including anyone with presumably even the remotest chance of being selected for their country. Garland, Garner, Hollins and Kember were invited, though it would take a real leap of imagination for any of them, except possibly Hollins, to think they were anything approaching international standard. Peter Osgood, languishing in Division Two with Southampton, was not among those invited.

Ipswich Town were top of the table, with twelve points from seven games and ran out easy 2-0 winners at Portman Road. As TV highlights made all too clear, Chelsea were outclassed, had only two chances, and the back four looked uncomfortable. Chelsea had now scored one goal in four games and were looking nobody's idea of a top team. Only Cooke looked like a quality footballer. The programme argued that Garner, Garland and Hutchinson were 'dogged by injury last season but now look like regaining their previous confidence and ability'. That was a very optimistic stance given the team's dismal scoring record and, for all their effort, the lack of quality up front.

Visiting the Baseball Ground a week later, Chelsea recalled Droy for the injured Dempsey, but it made little difference. He was promptly run ragged by the Derby forward line of Kevin Hector, Roger Davies and Francis Lee, who made the Chelsea front three of Garland, Hutchinson and Sissons look the relatively mediocre outfit they, sadly, were. Hutchinson did score but the 4-1 scoreline in no way flattered Derby.

The home game against Wolverhampton Wanderers on September 28th was beginning to take on seismic importance for the manager. Two points from four games so far in September, a slump to fifteenth place and no home League wins so far. Not good enough, and vultures were starting to circle round Sexton. Their opposition had not won in eight games and had a home UEFA Cup-tie against Porto the following Wednesday to distract them, so this was an entirely winnable game. The new dressing rooms were finally open, boosting the morale of a squad fed up with twenty-five months in a Portakabin.

The manager made a bold decision by resting Hollins who had been nursing a knee injury. He missed a game for the first time since the replay in Athens over three years earlier, replaced by Kember. Sissons had a bruised ankle so Ray Wilkins was brought in. Hutchinson was left out for Garner, who was seen by Sexton as having the edge in control and holding play together, to link up in a striking partnership with Garland.

Garner, having missed five games, had been busy telling the *Evening Standard* that he wanted to talk to the manager, under a 'Garner Will Tell Sexton: I Want To Go' headline. Hutchinson told the *Daily Mirror* 'I'm sick of the whole situation and think it would be best if I left Chelsea. It really hurts being dropped. There certainly doesn't seem to be much future for me at the Bridge'. He did not watch the game. Two more issues for the under-pressure manager to deal with, in a painful echo of the previous season's travails. They joined Kember and Dempsey in being discontented at not having a regular place.

Sexton hoped this shake-up would get the weight of the new stand off the back of his team. He told the *Daily Mail* 'the stand is marvellous...but it can be a stick to beat you with because you are under more pressure to produce a team and results to go with it. Now we are able to use our new dressing room in the body of the stand it should be a help...It was not desirable to mingle with the crowd on the way out to play the match'. Indeed.

Only 23,073 turned up, hardly a ringing endorsement of the beleaguered manager or his team, and there were shoals of expensive empty seats in the East Stand middle tier. For what supporter David Gray recalls as 'possibly one of the poorest games ever seen at Stamford Bridge', those who turned out watched John Richards, who had an excellent scoring record against Chelsea, net after five minutes, taking advantage of a collision between Harris and Phillips which summed up Chelsea's performance. That caused chants of 'what a load of rubbish' to break out, followed half-an hour later by the slow handclap, which must have sounded like a death knell to Sexton. Chants of 'Sexton Out' followed as Chelsea only had two shots on target all game, both from Cooke, who with Wilkins gave a decent showing in a sea of mediocrity and incompetence. The Garner/Garland striking partnership was a resounding failure, as all the others that season had been.

In five League games at Stamford Bridge so far that season, Chelsea had failed to score in four of them. They had conceded eighteen goals in ten games, equal worst in the division. They were in seventeenth place, looking a million miles away from competing for honours. Sexton optimistically and defiantly told the *Daily Mirror* 'there were some good things in our game ... We played patiently, and we worked at it. You can't afford to get depressed when you're on a run like this. If you do you might as well give up'. Or have others give you up. When the crowd turns on a manager there is usually only one outcome.

'The Bridge Of Sighs' headline in the *Evening Standard* summed up much of the press coverage. The *Daily Telegraph* gave a stark view. 'Many more displays like this and the new stand could become the biggest white elephant in football...Even in 1974, spectators still put results and entertainment above comfort'. Sexton was now under enormous pressure. He knew it, the Chelsea board knew it and the supporters knew it. On the Sunday and Monday after the game, press speculation was relentless.

The *News Of The World* 'Now Sexton's On The Brink' headline, with a 'Crisis For Chelsea Boss' sub-header, summed up the widely-held view. 'The terrace customers, who have yet to see a home win, had groaned a blood-thirsty chant of 'Sexton out''. Sexton admitted 'I don't blame people screaming for my head. They've paid their money and they're entitled to shout what they think. You have to accept it in this job'.

The article ended 'one can understand a board who have invested so heavily becoming uneasy...but one hopes and trusts that Sexton can put things right and that he will be allowed to'.

Mears, hardly effusive in his support of Sexton, opened out to the *Sunday People*. 'We are very concerned about the crowd's reaction and the team's performances. It's a situation no-one likes but we are faced with it and we shall be thinking of ways of remedying it...I'm thinking about it right now'.

The Monday papers were no kinder. Mears told the *Daily Telegraph* 'we are in a very difficult situation and with money heavily committed on our future we cannot allow let things drift on. As long as Dave Sexton is Chelsea manager, he gets my full support ... The slide has got to be stopped somehow. It is essential we all take stock and we are giving the matter very deep though this weekend'.

The *Daily Mail* went further, running a fallacious 'Sexton Is All Set To Quit Chelsea Today' back-page headline. Mears was becoming more open with every interview. 'We simply have not won a game at home. And with our ground development we cannot afford that. We have got to do the right thing...For the last two years we have very little to show for a lot of hard work except a lot of heartache'.

The *Daily Mirror* reported a board meeting would discuss the 'Chelsea crisis' on Wednesday week, but it was hard to see how they could leave things that long. Mears was becoming ever more unequivocal. 'We will examine every aspect of the situation. Obviously, I am concerned. If changes need to be made, we will make them...This club has got to have success – the next few matches will be critical. I know what must be done and we are thinking about it right now. I don't want to talk about Sexton's future now. We stood by him last season over Osgood and Hudson. With that episode behind us, we felt we had sorted ourselves out as a club for this season but now we are asking ourselves 'what's gone wrong'. Over the weekend, Mears' stance seemed to have hardened to the extent that Sexton's departure was fast becoming more a matter of when, not if.

Gates had been dismal, the Wolves crowd being 10,000 below the 35,000 subsistence target the board had identified. The home record had declined over the previous three seasons – 1971-72 31pts, 1972-73 24pts, 1973-74 22pts – though it was impossible to identify what impact, if any, the building work had. The average League crowd over that period was down from 39,545 to 25,983, so expecting a 9,000 per game uplift in that economic climate was, frankly, ludicrous.

The month-end League table underlined the poor start Chelsea had suffered. It also highlighted the problems London clubs were having, filling four of the bottom five places.

16th Leicester City   p9 7pts
17th Luton Town   p10 7pts

18th Chelsea	*p10*	*7pts*
19th Leeds United	p9	6pts
20th Arsenal	p9	6pts
21st Tottenham Hotspur	p9	6pts
22nd QPR	p10	6pts

October 1974

In the absence of any definitive announcement by the Chelsea board regarding Sexton's future, speculation continued, as did public pronouncements by an increasingly publicity-happy chairman. It took three more days of press speculation, rumour and innuendo before a decision was made public.

After the two met, Brian Mears duly reported what was covered to the *Evening Standard*. 'We sat down and asked ourselves where we are going. It is not use just scrambling to avoid relegation season after season. Our whole purpose is winning something, like the League Championship and the FA Cup. It is time we won a major honour, but we seem to be on the wrong lines…He was not asked to resign. We had a frank conversation about what had gone wrong and what remedies we could take. I will be reporting back to the other directors … We shall be making our decision as soon as possible'.

This quotaholism was grossly unfair on an anguished manager waiting for the axe to fall, reflecting badly on a board that had only allowed the expenditure of half of the funds raised by selling three of his best players earlier in the year, leaving a side composed largely of journeymen footballers. To talk about winning a major honour given the lack of quality in the squad seemed wildly optimistic, and the chairman cannot have possibly thought it a realistic perspective.

Sexton made his position clear, telling the *Daily Mail* this is the showdown. If they want me out, they'll have to sack me…Why should I resign?' He had two years of his contract to run, though figures given in the press on the value of his contract vary wildly. Before meeting Mears, Sexton interviewed the unhappy John Dempsey, Ian Hutchinson, Steve Kember, Bill Garner and Tommy Baldwin and told them he was prepared to let each of them go. The *Daily Mail* felt that Brian Mears and fellow-director Richard Attenborough had always supported Sexton. Vice-chairman Lord Chelsea, an irregular attendee at the club, had apparently backed Sexton when it was a choice between selling players or dispensing with him earlier in the year. It is therefore not an unreasonable assumption that the other directors, George Thomson and Leslie Mears, did not support the manager.

Sexton was highly thought of in the game and by journalists. Many thought the problem lay not so much with him but with the board, who had commissioned and built a stand when at least part of the investment should have been used to revitalise and rebuild the team.

The *Daily Mirror* reported, on the Tuesday, that Mears 'feels (there is) a lack of motivation at the club and feels only way to inject enthusiasm is to appoint a new manager'. That presumably came from the chairman or someone close to him and made it clear exactly what the end game was.

Mears took soundings from the other board members on the Tuesday and Wednesday and, sure enough, on Thursday October 3rd the inevitable happened and, to the surprise of nobody, Dave Sexton was fired from his position as Chelsea manager after almost seven years in the role, the most successful ever at that point. A tawdry end to his time in charge.

The board painted themselves into a corner regarding the replacement, Mears announcing the same day that 'we would like a young manager who has proved himself – preferably with a Chelsea background, but not young enough to have played with the current staff'. That cut the field realistically down to two. Frank Blunstone, whose Chelsea credentials were unchallengeable after twelve years on the playing staff and another five on the coaching staff, youth team coach at Manchester United under Tommy Docherty, who we can safely assume was not on the Mears shortlist. Blunstone had played with Bonetti, Harris and Hollins but that had been a decade earlier, and he was an older generation to them. The other was potential candidate who met the criteria was Alan Dicks, manager at Bristol City. Ron Greenwood, ex-Chelsea centre-half and now West Ham United manager, was hardly likely to leave for a club with, it was rapidly becoming clear, little or no money and a mediocre squad. Despite the self-imposed restriction, the press listed a lot of talented non-Chelsea individuals who might fancy the job including Jock Stein, Gordon Jago, Bobby Robson and Sir Alf Ramsey.

Mears spoke to the five unsettled players trying to persuade them to stay and see the club through their current problems. He certainly could not afford to let them all go, as he would them be left with the less-than-prolific Garland up front on his own, but certainly one way to reduce costs was to offload squad players with little future at the club. One of Sexton's last acts was to fine Dempsey for talking to an Irish paper about wanting to leave the club.

Immediately Sexton had gone, the 'Osgood to return' rumours inevitably began. His fall-out with Sexton had undoubtedly been terminal but with him gone, Mears' thinking was that Osgood was the man to fill the empty East Stand seats.

Every paper had their theories about what had gone so wrong, and the *Daily Mail* was no exception. Under a 'Osgood Row Was The First Bad Sign For Sexton', they said that his transfer-listing of Osgood three seasons earlier was the beginning of the end. They felt his failure to communicate with some senior players finally brought him down, including the currently unsettled five. Others complained about being left out or played out of position. As supporter David Gray remembers, Sexton seemed to have lost the ability to motivate his experienced players.

Sexton was immediately courted by QPR, whose previous manager Gordon Jago had recently left the club, and it was clear he was not going to be out of work for long. Under a 'Sexton: I Don't Blame Anyone for This' headline, it was described as football's most drawn-out sacking. Sexton left with dignity – he knew on Monday he would be asked to go, and blamed nobody, not even player-power. He admitted that player unrest contributed to his dismissal, wryly commenting 'you don't get good team spirit when players are chatting away to the press all the time'. He was dead right when he talked about players speaking to the press, but that was out of his hands. He praised loyalists Harris, Bonetti, Hollins and Houseman, all 'sturdy as oaks'.

Mears explained 'I telephoned Hollins and Bonetti, the senior professionals, and told them the news. I will be speaking to the players tomorrow ... I shall expect their full support'. A more diplomatic individual might have spoken to the players first but, the increasingly under-pressure chairman seemed to use the press as a means of unburdening his frustrations.

Having waited three days to announce publicly what he had already told Sexton (apparently, and utterly ludicrously, because he thought it would be 'more humane' to delay the announcement) Mears acted quickly, and sensibly, appointing Sexton's assistant Ron Suart (who he saw as 'Chelsea's Mr Reliable') as Caretaker Manager, with Eddie McCreadie as his first-team coach. Dario Gradi, appointed to the first-team role only in the summer, was back working with the reserves. Some senior players had apparently been unwilling to accept Gradi's advice that season because of his background of amateur football, so the change may have suited everybody (except presumably Gradi). McCreadie had focused on discipline and skills with the reserves, losing just one game so far that season, and had impressed the club hierarchy in doing this.

In *Chelsea – The Real Story* Mears recounted telling Sexton it was time to go was 'the most distressing thing I have had to do in football...Fortunately he took it well and we parted on good terms...I know he found it extremely difficult to operate when there was a big restriction on money' as any manager would when faced with a signal lack of quality in his squad.

The *Daily Mirror* pointed out that Sexton had spent £1,006,000 in his seven-year reign, but recouped £1,216,000, a surplus of £210,000. Tommy Docherty, his predecessor, had similarly turned in a transfer profit during his time in charge. Chelsea were a selling club but, despite this, Sexton had won trophies. He was a victim of Chelsea's ambition as well as their impatience. The board had eventually decided he could no longer produce the players or play to fill the new stand. They thought

Chelsea required a glamourous team and a concerted attempt to bring style and appeal to the club. Apart from the veteran Cooke and (hopefully) Hay, however, there was nobody with those skills or charisma, and no funds to bring high-end talent in. Whenever players like Frank Worthington, Stan Bowles or Malcolm MacDonald moved, or were unsettled, Chelsea were never mentioned.

Mears apparently did not want an outspoken manager like Brian Clough or Malcolm Allison who might create a buzz around the club. Suart was a decent man and an experienced football man, but charismatic he was not. The *Daily Mirror* reported that 'Suart, who reluctantly takes over caretaker duties, said "Dave is a wonderful man and a brilliant coach. Everyone had the greatest respect for him". They reported that Sexton's contract would apparently be paid up, around £35,000, as he had three years of a five-year contract to run.

Sexton talked to the *Daily Telegraph* about how players, fans and the board all had power. 'It is how you use that power ... You don't get good team spirit if everyone is talking to the press. I am very sad, but I have no complaints ... Chelsea have been very good to work for and the staff have been terrific. It is good underneath too. There are many good young players coming through'.

Mears denied the pressures of financing the new stand were the cause of the dismissal. 'The stand is no excuse for lack of success. If we have a new stand then we have to have a team to go with it. We have to think of the supporters in terms of success. We have to look beyond survival or a place in the middle of the table. The object is to win the championship. The board felt we had no chance of doing this and it was our job to do something about the situation'. How the current, mediocre squad was supposed to challenge for the title given the lack of funding available for major surgery was not explained. It is surprising, in retrospect, that the interviewer did not challenge this wildly optimistic view.

Donald Saunders from the *Daily Telegraph* doubted crowds would flock back even if Suart got more from the players. He argued that 'it is Chelsea's misfortune to have opened their expensive new stand at a time when crowds are generally dropping below what used to be considered subsistence level'.

Suart was a real football man, who prior to joining Chelsea under Tommy Docherty in 1967 had been manager of Blackpool and was caretaker manager when Docherty was sacked that October. Appointing McCreadie as coach was a smart move, as he was popular in the dressing room and ambitious to make his way in the coaching and managerial world, with FA badges to prove his prowess.

Two days after his appointment, Suart had to field a team at second-place Manchester City, no easy start for the caretaker. Mears spoke to the senior squad the day before the game. His message was 'tomorrow's match is the beginning of Chelsea's future, and I am asking you all to give the club 100 per cent support. If everyone pulls together, as we must, I am certain we have a great future and are bound to be successful'.

The failed experiment of playing Peter Houseman at left-back was summarily ended, Harris moving there, Droy partnering Dempsey at centre-back, Hollins coming in for Ray Wilkins in midfield and Houseman reverting to his favoured wing position. Hay and Garland were unfit, so Hutchinson played alongside Garner, a pairing that emphasised Suart's limited options. The team, functional but hardly flair-ridden, lined up :-
Phillips; Locke, Droy, Dempsey, Harris; Kember, Hollins, Cooke; Garner, Hutchinson, Houseman.

The new managerial duo tightened up the side's defensive play, and the side played with plenty of steel and commitment, but very little spark. Chelsea took the lead after an hour with a superb volley by Hutchinson. Colin Bell equalised, and the game ended 1-1, a satisfactory point for Suart's side. Hollins went off injured, holding his throat after a clash with City midfielder Asa Hartford, who was sent off. Kember went for an early bath too, after a clash with Bell which ended with him hitting the England star. Kember commented 'City got angry because we stopped them playing...they started all the niggle in the game because we played the best football and took the lead'. Rodney Marsh, a frustrated figure, complained 'Chelsea were so defensive it was ridiculous'. They travelled north for a point and they got it, in a good start for the new partnership. Chelsea were in the bottom three, needing a boost. They were no nearer appointing a new manager, though one obvious possibility was to appoint Suart and McCreadie on a permanent basis if they did a solid job on a caretaker basis. Afterwards Brian Mears applauded how the players put spirit and sweat into the game.

The Osgood rumour mill was working overtime. Under an entirely speculative 'Osgood's Coming Home' headline, the *News Of The World* reported that Chelsea wanted Osgood back, and looked to clinch a deal before the Tottenham game on Saturday. Mears and his directors, conscious of the mood of the fans and desperate to fill the new £2 million stand, were apparently even prepared to plunge further into the red to sign him, and Sexton's dismissal cleared the way. There was little doubt about the feeling of the supporters, and a 'Bring Back Ossie' petition was duly circulated.

Osgood was surprisingly gracious in an interview on Sexton's sacking. 'I'm sick for Dave. I like him, and I'd never have wished that on him...I've never hated him and, at this moment I feel full of sympathy not revenge ... The early days with Dave were great ... he had bright ideas and we were winning things ... (he was a) fantastic coach ... Then gradually things began to change with us. I believe he started to listen to others instead of pushing his own ideas. He began to demand more of me, and he let others get away with it ... Then he sold Keith Weller, who really didn't have much of a chance to prove himself. I was sorry to see

Keith go'. Given the public criticism Osgood had given him in the past, that interview must have had the ex-manager choking on his Sunday morning cornflakes. It is unclear who Ossie had in mind regarding the 'others' Sexton started listening to.

Southampton gave a provisionally favourable reply when approached regarding selling Osgood, and the *Sunday People*, interestingly, thought this 'may have clinched the fate of Dave Sexton'. Osgood's position was clear. 'I never wanted to leave Stamford Bridge in the first place. It was a clash of personalities that forced me out'.

Jimmy Hill's *News Of The World* column pulled no punches and must have caused significant discomfort among Chelsea Board members, as it certainly had the ring of truth. Headlined 'Guilty – The Men Who Signed Hay' he argued that 'Chelsea took the first step towards self-destruction when they signed £200,000 David Hay in the summer. I believe he was not the choice of Sexton. If that was the case, the Chelsea board undermined Sexton's authority. The players who later asked for transfers instinctively knew it was possible to drive a wedge between Sexton and the board. Towards the end, his position was made untenable. On the face of it, it was the selling of Osgood and Hudson that started the rot for Sexton. Replace them with others of equal skill was necessary to retain the balance in his team. Hay in no way fills the creative hole they left. My inquiries reveal that although the board's intention has been for the best, pressure that the costly new stand put on them seems to have led them to make mistakes as to the way a football club should be run. But it's Sexton that has shouldered the blame'. Logically argued and, very likely, an accurate reflection of the situation given that his friend Sexton was away at the World Cup when Hay was signed.

Hugh McIlvanney, arguably the finest British sportswriter of the 1970s, had plenty to say in *The Observer*. 'It was a shock to see him (Sexton) looking drained and almost skeletal. He appeared more like a man who had been shot than one who had been sacked'. He continued 'there was a damaging gulf between a number of senior players and Sexton, a gulf that left the team with a vacuum where its heart should be. It may be unjust but given the fact that Chelsea's performances of late have been so dishevelled and spiritless, so obviously indicative of a fundamental weakness that only the most drastic changes could rectify, it was inevitable that when the storm clouds burst, Sexton would be the one left out in the rain. Much has been made of the effect of Chelsea's huge and expensive new stand in intensifying the pressures at Stamford Bridge and ... there is obviously a sense in which it is a symbol of many of the ills that now afflict English football'.

John Moynihan, an erudite writer close to Chelsea, wrote in the *Sunday Telegraph* that, for Mears, the dismissal was a particularly sad occasion. He had stood by Sexton during boardroom rumblings, particularly during the Osgood and Hudson affair. But after the 'rotten display' against Wolves and the 'sickening jeering' from the home supporters, he and his directors felt they had hardly any choice. The writer thought they were unlikely to appoint 52-year-old Suart as full-time manager and were looking for a younger man of Bobby Robson's quality. Jock Stein, George Petchey, Terry Venables and Frank Blunstone were all named as possible contenders. The 'Chelsea connection' stressed by Mears days earlier was not mentioned. Venables, who had captained Chelsea under Docherty but then fallen out with him and been transferred to Tottenham, was a bright, confident, opinionated thinker about the game and an intriguing possibility. Possibly he was too bright, too confident and too opinionated for Mears.

Sexton was highly respected by the players as a forward-thinking, progressive coach. Where many of his charges felt he fell down was in man-management and communication, and in the end that is probably what did for him. Chelsea official historian Rick Glanvill succinctly put it in *Rhapsody In Blue*, 'it's still hard to forgive a man who traded Osgood, Webb and Hudson in their prime for Kember, Garland and Garner, who never had one'. Harsh but fair. Hudson felt Sexton 'started to tinker with the team as anxiety consumed him' and that 'it was a case of finances starting to hit home'. Certainly, if Sexton had been given funds to spend that he had required since late 1971, when weaknesses in a number of positions became apparent, the team could only have improved.

John Moynihan also had opinions on other events in the club's recent history. He reckoned that Keith Weller, who Sexton wanted as his own Jairzinho, never settled in on the right wing. David Webb, loyal to both club and manager, left because communication with his manager had broken down. Sexton seemed to draw more and more into himself, he did not have the success with new players like Garner that he did with the old guard and he showed weakness at man-management. Starkly, Moynihan ended with the warning 'Chelsea face one of the biggest crises in their history'.

The costs of operating a First Division club had been laid bare when Manchester City, in their match programme, detailed some of their operating costs. It cost City around £500,000 a year to operate. Police costs were £30,000, rates £18,000, electricity £7,000, travel and hotel costs £40,000. Chelsea's operational costs would have been similar, though their average crowd that season was 5,000 below City's. Additionally, of course, there were the cost, repayments and interest for the East Stand to factor in.

Those players who had fallen out with Sexton seemed keen that Suart and McCreadie were given the job on a permanent basis. Under a 'Make Ron The Boss' back-page headline, the *Daily Mirror* reported the pair had clear popular support from the players. Dempsey felt 'if Ron got the job, I think I'd be prepared to stay' and Garner added 'Ron is a player's man, and Eddie is a very good coach and very popular. It's a partnership that could work well'. Suart had not applied for the job but was delighted with the players' response and attitude at Manchester City. The directors were to meet to consider club policy and have preliminary talks on a successor.

Four days later the League Cup, for the third time in four seasons, pitted Chelsea against Stoke City. A sub-20,000 Stamford Bridge crowd was disappointing but hardly surprising given poor results and the turmoil the club still found itself in. Hay was out with a badly gashed shin, desperate luck for player and club as he was still trying to recreate his World Cup form. He was to be out for six weeks. Chelsea fell behind but Hutchinson equalised in a typically hard-fought draw. Hutch now had six goals in eight appearances, and Suart rightly praised him to the *Daily Mirror*. 'Our spirit was terrific ... In the end we nearly won it ... what a fellow this Hutchinson is. He is all heart'. The team were certainly showing spirit, though the flair Mears was looking for was hardly in abundance. Still, the most important thing was that the team improved their results and that seemed to be happening, reflecting well on Suart and McCreadie, who had certainly improved the side's robustness, commitment and physicality.

In the Stoke programme, the club explained Sexton's departure. 'After seven years as Manager of Chelsea Football Club Dave Sexton was released from his contract last Thursday. This was felt to be in the best interests of all concerned and we wish Dave every success in the future'. After this graceless thank you to a man who won two major trophies and has been operating under almost impossible constraints for more than two years, the explanation continued. 'The position of team manager has been advertised and in the interim Ron Suart is in charge. In winning the FA Cup and Cup-Winners' Cup we reached high points of success during the period of Dave Sexton's management and it is to a comparable level of application and achievement that we must again aspire so that we may fulfil on the field ambitions that are the equal we have shown in our rebuilding plans off it'. Given the front five that evening was Kember, Garland, Cooke, Hutchinson and Houseman it is unlikely many supporters could see the chairman's aspiration becoming reality any time soon.

The board wanted the question of a new manager settled as quickly as possible, hoping to be able to announce something the following week. On Saturday October 12th, the day of the Tottenham home game, the *Daily Mirror* ran a headline 'Chelsea's Choice - Blunstone Ready To Take Charge - Suart To Step Up As The Supremo'. Manchester United youth team coach Frank Blunstone was well-liked and well-respected at Chelsea and seemed a logical choice. It was planned that he would meet Mears before the Tottenham game to discuss the appointment. Blunstone's boss Tommy Docherty was philosophical. 'Mr. Mears has asked to speak to Frank and we have agreed. Reluctantly, we feel we cannot stand in Frank's way'. The plan was that Suart, who had a good relationship with Blunstone, would become general manager with

McCreadie as assistant manager. Mears, anticipating a positive response, said 'I'll be making an announcement on Monday' and 'I'm expecting a phone call from him (Blunstone) and we should complete matters over the phone'. Despite this, the *Daily Mirror* felt that Suart deserved the chance to be Number One.

The team's improvement continued when the visit of Tottenham was marked with a 1-0 victory. The defence had certainly tightened up under the new managerial duo. Hollins scored the only goal, a penalty. The crowd, though, was 32,660, over two thousand below the break-even figure. If they could not reach that target for a London derby against fierce rivals, what hope was there?

Baldwin came in for the injured Garland, for his first start for nine months. He was still on the transfer list and sought a new contract. 'It's up to me now. I don't really want to leave Chelsea; the problems have been more financial than anything else'. Suart enthused 'I'm lucky we have a striker of his calibre to be able to call on.' Well down the striker pecking order, and on the transfer list for a significant period of time, only Baldwin's refusal to agree terms had stopped him leaving on five separate occasions, but he was still a useful option for the caretaker manager to turn to.

After Mears had gone so brazenly public on his preferred new manager, the outcome of a phone call from Blunstone on the Sunday night must have come as a hammer-blow. He turned the job down out of loyalty to United, who had kept his job open when he was hurt in a car crash and also offered him a pay rise. Docherty was delighted, Mears aghast. The chairman promptly announced that Suart and McCreadie would carry on, with the chance to become full-time appointments, but they knew they were not first choice. Mears stated 'there is no need for us to go running round in circles' but admitted his disappointment. Another poorly handled affair at a club specialising in them, openly talking to the press before Blunstone made a decision.

The *Kensington Post* argued that Blunstone, 'a man whose honesty and happiness outweigh his ambition', was right to reject the Chelsea managership. They thought him a fine coach but without the fire in his belly a top manager needs, whereas McCreadie was certainly providing drive, fire and passion. The paper thought he and Suart deserved the chance to prove themselves at least until Christmas.

Three games, two draws and a win. This after three successive defeats ended Sexton's Chelsea career. So far, so good. The League Cup replay at Stoke four days later was another physically demanding one. Ian Britton came in for his first game of the season and gave Chelsea the lead. They battled hard to hold on, but Jimmy Greenhoff equalised, extra-time brought no further score, so it was back to the Victoria Ground six days later for a third go.

McCreadie was interviewed at the Mitcham training ground that week by the *Daily Mirror*, in dark glasses and puffing a cigarette under a

'Eddie Chases His Dream' headline and an 'I'm Going To Make Chelsea The Greatest' sub-header. He knew he was on trial and would stand or fall by the results over the next few weeks. 'I know I am capable of doing this job. I'm a qualified FA coach and ambitious. I'm a person who must have something to aim for in life...I want the best from the players...I'm also lucky to have Ron Suart to help me. We work so well together. First, we have to get a dedicated Chelsea again, a Chelsea as dedicated to succeed as I am. I don't just want a very good team, but a great one. My own discipline for this is total honesty and respect. If what I say hurts, okay, I'll take what's coming back ...This is a tremendous opportunity for me, I never dreamed it would come so soon'.

Suart responded 'you can't help but be impressed by Eddie ... very knowledgeable, confident and positive ... the players have responded because they respect him. After all, he was club captain. The influence he had then has carried over. They like him and want him to carry on. What bigger testimony can a coach have?'. McCreadie's positivity, after the reserve and reticence of Sexton, must have given the squad a tremendous lift.

Sexton, interviewed after taking over at QPR, was magnanimous. 'I've no complaints over what happened at Chelsea ... I'm a bit philosophical about things like that ... The question of my compensation has been settled amicably. The taxman has won as usual'.

An away game at Everton was not expected to be particularly highly charged. From a football perspective it was a 1-1 draw, Cooke putting Chelsea ahead, Gary Jones equalising with a penalty. What took the game out of the ordinary was the booking of six Chelsea players and trainer Norman Medhurst, and the sending off of Dempsey after the final whistle.

Four men – Hollins, Houseman, Cooke and Baldwin - were booked by referee John Yates for not retreating ten yards when forming a wall at a free-kick. Garner and Droy were also booked. The hapless Medhurst had his name taken for treating the injured Dempsey, who later required two stitches, without permission. Dempsey's sending off was for commenting 'it's about time you gave us some decisions' to Yates after the final whistle. Suart backed his players. 'There is no question of the club disciplining the players because of their behaviour. It wasn't a rough match'.

Mears, a member of the FA Disciplinary Committee and therefore hugely embarrassed, did not back his players, telling the *Daily Mail* 'I'm very unhappy about this. Eight players being booked in this way is a club record, a most unenviable record'. He said he would study the referee report and decide what action to take. The fact that four of the bookings were for one minor offence, an offence committed by every team in every match without punishment, seemed to pass him by. There were even noises in the press that the disciplinary issues might deprive the new managerial duo of the jobs on a permanent basis, which would have been grossly unfair. Later that week Chelsea announced they were to fight six of the eight Everton bookings, including all the 'defensive wall' ones and Medhurst, who was to write to the FA. Yates was later suspended for allowing his notebook to be photographed and published in the *Daily Mirror* after the game.

All this nonsense distracted from the fact that Chelsea were now unbeaten in five games under the new regime and had played with a tactical astuteness that was unlucky not to win both points.

With confidence in the side increased with the unbeaten run and Hutchinson back in for Garner, the team headed to Stoke for the League Cup second replay in positive mood. That positivity did not last long. By half-time Stoke were 4-0 up, their direct football tearing the heart out of Chelsea, with Droy and Harris both scoring ludicrous own-goals. Stoke scored two more and took their feet of the pedal, letting Hollins and Baldwin give a smidgeon of respectability to the scoreline.

This was, though, a thrashing, a wake-up call to Suart that his side was simply not good enough. He was defiant to the *Evening Standard*, stating 'it's amazing. We did so well for five games, especially defensively, then this happens'. Alan Hudson, who must have thoroughly enjoyed himself, assured journalists 'I'm not gloating. I feel sorry for them'. In *Chelsea: The 100-Year History* Brian Mears reports how his cousin Leslie Mears verbally abused the players after the game, outrageous and embarrassing behaviour from a Chelsea board member which can only have undermined Suart. In *Chelsea – The Real Story* he mentions that one of the directors, presumably Leslie, told the players to their faces that night 'you are an absolute disgrace'. In *Kings Of The King's Road* John Phillips recounts how that night one director, again presumably Leslie Mears, told the players they were overpaid.

That Friday (October 25th), Suart was appointed permanent Chelsea manager and McCreadie first-team coach, with contracts to be drawn up at a November board meeting. The Board unanimously decided over lunch to make the appointments as 'they have been doing so well' despite the Stoke humiliation. McCreadie was 'knocked out' by the news. He felt the Stoke display wasn't as bad as had been made out but showed things could not be put right overnight. Given the improvement in results, the 6-2 thumping notwithstanding, and the clear popularity of the pair with the squad, it was a sensible appointment. The thought occurs that the top names linked with the job in the press would have been put off by the lack of budget available for new players, and quite possibly the salary on offer, so keeping the job internal made sense for more than one reason.

The board were apparently initially concerned that McCreadie might be too close to members of the squad, but as he told the *Daily Mail* 'I'll treat all the players the same...I don't have any special friends' and the board were certainly impressed by his energy and positivity. Dempsey enthused 'I'm enjoying my football for the first time in nearly two years'.

The managerial duo was under no illusions as to the criticality of Chelsea staying up, having a decent FA Cup run and improving crowds.

A quirk of the fixture list meant the final game in yet another tumultuous month was Stoke at home. The crowd, only 24,718, saw a thoroughly entertaining 3-3 draw, Chelsea equalising three times through Droy, Garland and Hutchinson. Hudson was persistently fouled as grudges from the recent League Cup games played themselves out. The *Daily Mirror* ran a 'Chelsea are a disgrace says Hudson' headline. He complained bitterly about Chelsea tackling and lack of referee protection. When he complained to referee Derek Nippard he was 'warned if I didn't keep quiet, he would send me off...What Chelsea got up to must have been condoned by Suart and McCreadie. They have played like that in all our four games with them recently. I spent most of the game jumping out of the way. That's not football'. Suart dismissed it 'you inevitably get situations like this when two team play each other so often in such a short space of time'. In seven games under Suart there had been fourteen bookings, a sending off and a technical dismissal. Red-blooded stuff, certainly, but evidence he and McCreadie had got the players totally committed.

Hudson gave a two-fingered salute to the crowd at the end, a crowd that had been chanting for the return of Osgood. There was no official comment from the Chelsea board on their interest, but Ron Suart observed that 'Osgood is obviously popular here. You heard the crowd chanting for him today'. Hutchinson on fine form, made two goals with his long throws and scoring one. The *News Of The World* eulogised that he was back to his form of four years earlier, pre-injuries, when an England place looked likely. There was even talk of Stoke putting in a £250,000 bid for him. Droy was at fault with two of the goals, the *Kensington Post* observing that 'one can never quite decide whether he's hopeless or just inexperienced'. His commitment was unchallengeable, however, and he was still young. With no transfer funds available, Chelsea needed him.

Cooke was interviewed by Barry Norman in *The Observer*, noted film critic but not usually a sportswriter, an indication of what an interesting character Cooke was. He told Norman he 'used to occasionally get legless' but the conditions that caused it, including a marriage break-up, no longer existed. He admitted he used to be neurotic. Norman thought him an intelligent, thoughtful and sensitive man, who had knuckled down when Sexton threw him a lifeline. 'There's not much time left, so I might as well use it properly'. He later said that '(signing for) Charlton would have been Endsville'. He felt embarrassed by the £68,000 Crystal Palace lost on him. A loner with few friends, the people he admired were writers. He had written a film script called 'Keeping Up' for David Puttnam, largely autobiographical by nature. Norman ended 'Chelsea fans have got their occasionally irritating but essentially beloved Charlie Cooke back'.

In a quiet month for transfer activity, young striker Steve Finnieston went to Cardiff on a month's loan. So a traumatic month, even by Chelsea's recent standards, ended with a new manager and coach and a mollified bunch of rebels. After fourteen games, a third of the season, Chelsea only had twelve points and were two points *above the* relegation zone. Stability, of a sort, had been created in the managerial dugout. A sustained run of improved results, and crowds, were required. Quickly.

16th Leicester City	p13	12pts
17th Chelsea	**p14**	**12pts**
18th Leeds United	p14	11pts
19th QPR	p14	11pts
20th Tottenham Hotspur	p14	10pts
21st Arsenal	p14	9pts
22nd Luton Town	p15	9pts

November 1974

November started with a trip to Birmingham City on the back of four League games without defeat. Hutchinson was out injured and Bonetti recalled for the first time since August. Objectively, the Chelsea team of *Bonetti; Locke, Droy, Dempsey, Harris; Kember, Hollins; Britton, Garland, Baldwin, Cooke* was a limited one, but there was optimism that they could compete against a Birmingham side two points above them in the table. Apart from Locke, Droy and Britton the team looked like an 'All Our Yesterdays' XI.

In the event Chelsea were outfought, out-thought and outplayed, losing 2-0 to the frustration of the loyal band who had travelled to St Andrew's. Suart blamed two defensive errors, but the *Daily Mail* reckoned 'there was much more wrong with Chelsea then their defensive mistakes'.

In midweek John Hollins had his well-earned testimonial, against Arsenal. It was his bad luck that his match coincided with diminishing crowds generally, and an unexciting opposition, as less than 10,000 turned out. Osgood refereed, and Sexton played in, an All-Star game before the main match. The former was cheered, the latter booed. Three youngsters, striker Tommy Langley, centre-back Steve Wicks and midfielder Garry Stanley, all played for the first-team for the first time. The board's pettiness towards Osgood was over, perhaps a sign the player was wanted back at Stamford Bridge.

Suart was given the authority to talk to Southampton and make a firm bid for Osgood. The *Daily Mail*, pulling no punches, reckoned 'Chelsea are in dire economic need of a big-name personality to fill their new stand. Osgood…is the easy answer to that problem'. It was hard to see how Chelsea would be able to pay for him, although Southampton were still paying for him by instalments which could, in theory, have made the deal easier. Chants from The Shed of 'Oh bring back our Ossie to us, to us' made it abundantly clear that many supporters would have welcomed back their departed hero.

The *Daily Mirror* thought that Hutchinson, Garland, Garner and Baldwin could all interest Southampton, though presumably not all of them, and certainly any of them would have been an asset in the Second Division. Suart said preliminary talks had been held, though Southampton did not want to release Osgood while they were still in the League Cup. Boss Lawrie McMenemy did not want him to go, though he confirmed a bid had been made.

The match programme for the Leicester City home game confirmed that it was a unanimous board decision to confirm the two appointments after 'doing well in an acting capacity...With the situation now resolved we look forward to everyone responding with 100 per cent endeavour towards producing the results that are essential to securing Chelsea's First Division future. Clearly there is much to be done, with dedication and concentration demanded of everyone in the weeks and months ahead'. These rallying cries increasingly began to resemble school reports from a despairing schoolteacher months before important exams.

John Dempsey was suspended, the almost-forgotten Marvin Hinton coming in for his first game of the season. Ian Hutchinson and Chris Garland were injured, and Bill Garner was also suspended, so Suart was forced to put out a striking partnership of Tommy Baldwin, who had not scored for the first-team for a year, and Tommy Langley, a sixteen-year-old £8 a week apprentice. Desperate days indeed.

Langley missed a couple of chances early on but showed willing until he understandably faded. Hinton was praised for a polished display and Kember, on the transfer list two months earlier, shone. 'Before I was never encouraged and operated in a restricted role'. Apart from them, though, the team were criticised for lack of ideas and energy in a thoroughly dismal 0-0 draw. Old boy Alan Birchenall's comment 'we were bad, but luckily my old club were even worse.' rang all too true. He added that the plight of Chelsea was 'sad and difficult to understand...something seems to have gone wrong somewhere'. Quite.

The Leicester crowd of 23,915 was disappointing. The midweek crowd against Coventry City four days later was little short of catastrophic. In heavy rain and high winds, against uninspiring opposition, a tiny crowd of 11,048 turned up, with vast empty spaces in the albatross-resembling East Stand and the crowd sheltering under any available cover. Mears, seemingly unperturbed, retorted 'I'm just grateful that so many turned out in such weather to watch us'.

The two crowds added together still didn't reach the 35,000 per match target if the the board had said was necessary if the East Stand was to be paid for. This was desperate stuff indeed. Though they had only lost one of the last six League games they had only won one of their last twelve, so there was little feelgood factor among the support.

Hay was welcomed back after being out since the City game six weeks earlier. Hollins was out injured so Kember, on good form, was made captain. The 3-3 draw may have entertained the wet and cold crowd but meant Chelsea had now won one of thirteen League games and were only two points off the bottom three.

Supporter David Gray remembers it was a foul night, and the 'mud-bath only emphasised the sheer brilliance of Charlie Cooke skipping over the surface whilst playing in the centre of midfield. I can still see him in my mind now, gliding along whilst others slipped and skidded. He was truly magnificent in this dire season'. Indeed.

A trip to mid-table Newcastle three days later was never going to be easy, but a disciplined performance would have given the chance of at least a point and a goalless first-half underlined this. Unfortunately, in the second half Chelsea imploded as Newcastle ran riot, scoring five times including a brace from Malcolm MacDonald. Suart told the *Daily Mail* 'I can't remember such a Jekyll and Hyde game' and added 'there is no point in going mad to get various players just because we have had a bad run of results. It is important to stop giving away so many silly goals away from home, but I am sure we have the players to do the job.' Captain Kember was equally puzzled. 'We weren't that bad. It's hard to explain'. The game was shown on ITV and the highlights show dreadful defending in front of a less-than-commanding Bonetti.

Suart's defiance was laudable but the fact was the club simply did not have the wherewithal to buy the new players required. Worse, it was unlikely there would be any cash available for the foreseeable future unless crowds significantly improved. A chicken and egg situation – what came first, the new players or the bigger crowds?

The *Kensington Post* interviewed a group of supporters after the match. 'We don't blame Ron Suart. We like him. But he just hasn't the players. They have sold the best, Ossie, Webbie and Hudson'. Unarguable logic.

Hollins faced a knee operation and it was feared he could be out until the New Year. Hutchinson was fit again and had scored a hat-trick in the reserves, but his appalling luck with injury after injury meant relying on him was becoming increasingly difficult. The scheduled game the following Saturday, against Sheffield United, was postponed due to a waterlogged pitch, giving Suart and McCreadie time to try and drill the defence and work out the most potent attacking force.

Baldwin went on a month's loan to Second Division Millwall. He was valued at around £30,000, a massive fall from the c£75,000 talked about at the start of 1974. New Millwall boss Gordon Jago hoped to make the move permanent, and the player was on loan while they tried to sort out a permanent transfer.

The month ended with a not-exactly-easy game at Leeds United, now under the stewardship of Jimmy Armfield after the short, chaotic reign of Brian Clough. Two Bonetti mistakes gifted goals to Allan Clarke and Trevor Cherry, and Chelsea had no answer. Again the partnership of

Garner and Hutchinson was tried and again it failed. Britton again gave a spirited display until he was injured. His form gave some hope for the future but the mediocrity of a number of the experienced players was going to drag the team into Division Two unless things changed drastically. No win in nine games and twentieth place at month end, meaning a berth in the relegation zone.

16th Tottenham Hotspur	*p19*	*17pts*
17th QPR	*p20*	*17pts*
18th Arsenal	*p19*	*16pts*
19th Leicester City	*p18*	*15pts*
20th Chelsea	**p19**	**14pts**
21st Carlisle United	*p20*	*13pts*
22nd Luton Town	*p19*	*9pts*

A leaky defence, a lack of creativity and a lack of proven goalscorers. One would be troubling, to have all three was a nightmare. There was too much reliance on veteran Cooke to make what chances were created, chances that were usually not taken. A grim end to a tough month for manager, coach, team and, especially, Chelsea board.

December 1974

There were only two teams below Chelsea in the League table, Luton Town and Carlisle United. They were Chelsea's next two opponents, and victory in both games was essential if the club were not to sink into a pre-Christmas morass of total despondency.

Luton were a poor side and were already six points from safety so if Chelsea were going to play anybody at home after their recent poor run, The Hatters were probably an ideal opponent. Suart decided to make changes. Out went Bonetti, increasingly error prone. Out went Marvin Hinton and Bill Garner, with one goal since August. Ian Britton was out injured. In came John Phillips, the Wilkins brothers, Chris Garland and John Sissons. Ray Wilkins, hugely promising, had not started a game since the Wolves debacle that precipitated Sexton's departure. Garland had only two League goals all season and Sissons had only fitfully impressed since signing in the summer, so it seemed another case of Titanic deck chair shuffling.

The crowd, predictably given the team's form, the quality of the opposition and the proximity to Christmas, was a mere 19,009. Chelsea's tactic of high balls to Hutchinson fell down because there was nobody to feed off the knockdowns. Despite this, Chelsea eked out an uninspired but vital 2-0 win through goals by Hutchinson and skipper Kember. The latter linked up well with Ray Wilkins, and the youngster was to keep his place during the months ahead. It was to be Sissons last League appearance for the club, a signing that looked uninspired in the summer and now seemed pretty pointless.

Ron Harris caught Phillips' knee in his ribs and was coughing up blood and vomiting at half-time. He played the second half despite Chelsea Doctor John Vyse telling him at the interval 'if you go back you are taking your life into your hands'. It was a suspected punctured lung, but an x-ray showed it turned out to be deep chest bruising. Harris's commitment and bravery, again, shone through.

Suart, accepting financial realities, told the *Daily Mirror* 'we've got to stay in the First Division ... I've got absolute confidence that our present squad of players can keep us there. I think you can rule out any signings in the weeks ahead'.

Mears gave a wide-ranging interview to the *Daily Mail* before and after the Luton game. Asked about the meagre crowd, he bullishly and wildly optimistically responded 'we will never put up with scenes like this again.' His vision remained a perfect stadium thronged with a fashionable crowd watching a glamourous team. He was in a 'tense mood' when dining with fellow directors Leslie Mears and Richard Attenborough before the game.

He drove his silver XJ6 to Stamford Bridge and said 'the future is in our own hands, just as it was when we had to reach our decision about Dave Sexton. After our commitment on the stand we cannot admit the possibility of relegation'. He went to the dressing room to see the team. Back in his seat, he said 'It's inhibiting (sitting) here. You're not supposed to cheer and shout'. He and his wife June sang under their breath in unison with The Shed 'give us a goal'. 'My son, Chris, would be with the lads in The Shed if he was back from school'. He felt the future of the club lay with youngsters like Ray Wilkins.

After the match, he offered the Press a drink and joined in banter. He spoke to Attenborough and planned to go to the ground the next day to discipline Garner for attacking the club in comments in a newspaper. He concluded, even more bullishly, 'nobody is going to get in the way of this club's progress. We know what we must do and where we are going'. The more powerful floodlights were finally turned on, 60 lamps in a gallery under the East Stand roof.

The relegation-fight double was pulled off the following week with a 2-1 win at Carlisle, Hollins scoring both goals after a four-game layoff. Scottish team manager Willie Ormond went to the game looking at young players but enthused that 'Cooke was the best player on the park. He looked as good – if not better – than anyone I've got in the team at the moment'. Cooke had been a revelation since his return, one of the very few bright spots in a sea of mediocrity.

On the morning of the West Ham game, Mears told the *Daily Mirror*, somewhat obviously, 'it was vital to beat Luton and Carlisle...Nobody will know the inner agony I went through...We've still got a long way to go and we're under no illusions, but I'm now convinced we're heading in the right direction'. He hoped the East Stand would be almost full against West Ham despite the rival attraction of Christmas shopping.

The chairman also confirmed what had seemed obvious for weeks, namely that Osgood would not be re-signing. Mears explained 'the whole thing seems to have fizzled out. They don't seem particularly keen to let him go and we are not particularly keen at this time to become involved...We must rely on the players we've got. We have a good squad of senior professionals and a lot of good youngsters coming through'. The article pointed out the funds shortage was another, primary, reason.

A match programme letter complained about 'groans, complaints and witty remarks – and no shouting FOR the team...The inane chanting for Osgood does not help the team either, we have the players...all we need now is some luck and some *support*. So let's hear cheering and not groaning all the time'.

The West Ham game drew a very decent 34,969 crowd, the biggest of the day, despite being four days before Christmas. Hay started in the back four, moving to midfield when Kember went off injured. He had struggled so far that season but was widely praised for his performance that day. Bobby Gould equalised a Hutchinson goal in another physical encounter, not a bad result against a team sixth in the table, though another point dropped. Suart and McCreadie had certainly toughened up the side, and the players were very happy to mix it. Even Garland, not recognised as a hard man, got involved in a televised punch-up with Tommy Taylor.

In the match programme, editor Albert Sewell made a few salient points. The average age of the side against Coventry in August was 28. He felt Sexton should have tested more young players in the past two or three years, which seems unarguable. He also made the point that of the first 21 League games, no forward had played in more than twelve, so achieving continuity was impossible.

Hay was still not regularly showing his World Cup form, dogged by injury, still living in a hotel and apparently finding it hard to settle in London. Before Christmas, he did a revealing interview with *The Observer's* Hugh McIlvanney. He came back 'shattered' from his holiday after civil war broke out in Cyprus. He felt he had started the season less than 100% fit, had played poorly and had been playing catch-up ever since.

He lacked the capital to buy a house and had experienced a 'misunderstanding' with the club over the amount that he felt had been promised for a mortgage, but which was not forthcoming. He had spent ages talking to mortgage brokers. His family were left in Lanarkshire, so he would visit them for 24 hours after matches. The club booked him into the West Centre hotel near the ground and paid his travel to Scotland plus accommodation for his family when they could come down. Mrs Hay was, unsurprisingly, finding the situation difficult. He was praised by

Suart for his 'fearlessness, positive attitude and fact he always looks for the forward ball'.

The mortgage issue was finally sorted out, so his family could move down to Epsom. The whole affair has got him down, though he tried not to let it impact on his play. 'As things get better for David Hay, they are bound to get better for Chelsea' surmised McIlvanney. For Chelsea to treat such an important player in such a way beggars belief. No wonder he was unsettled and underperforming, if his family was in Scotland and he had to rush up and seen them after matches. The club had a long, inglorious record of failing to quickly find suitable family accommodation for big signings, Derek Kevan and Tony Hateley being two other examples.

Two more games that year, and two more London derbies. A trip to Arsenal and a home game against QPR. Arsenal were level on points with nineteenth placed Chelsea and QPR only had two more, so both games were critical. The Boxing Day game at Highbury was low on quality but high on competitive spirit and Chelsea came out on top 2-1, an excellent result. Garland scored twice in the first half, welcome goals for a man who until then had only scored two League goals that season and struggled to hold down a regular place.

Three wins and a draw took Chelsea into the QPR game full of confidence, and they were backed by a 38,917 crowd, the second-best home crowd of the entire season and, to the joy of Brian Mears, with the East Stand sold out. Dave Sexton brought a team full of creativity and excitement back to Stamford Bridge, including Don Masson, recently bought from Notts. County for £100,000, a midfielder with the flair and vision Chelsea were crying out for. Going in at the interval reasonably content with a 0-0 scoreline, Chelsea were duly torn apart after half-time, Don Givens scoring twice. A chastened Chelsea trudged off, totally outclassed in a humbling 3-0 defeat, the run of seven points from four games ended abruptly.

At the end of December it was reported that an Osgood deal might be back on if player-exchange deals could be worked out, given that Southampton were still paying for the star by instalments. Osgood, showing little loyalty to his current club, stated 'a move back to Stamford Bridge would be magic for me'. Steve Finnieston returned from his loan spell at Cardiff, where he played nine games, scoring twice and looking ready to challenge for a first-team place. Baldwin's proposed £30,000 transfer to Millwall hit a snag as the clubs could not agree who should pay the signing-on fee, this despite Millwall boss Gordon Jago being happy with his loan displays.

On New Year's Eve the *Daily Mirror* reported Osgood had indeed asked Southampton for a transfer and his request had been granted. 'I've never adjusted to Second Division football or to my move from Chelsea'. They reckoned the deal was dead as 'Chelsea …would have to offer midfield stars Hollins or Kember in exchange, and they won't do that'.

The suspicion remained that the club made the enquiry, and kept the story bubbling, to try and keep the crowd on board, but were never in a position to seriously bid for him.

So a dreadful year for the club ended in grim fashion. The manager had gone, three star players had left, the team had declined, and the side were in eighteenth place, out of the bottom three by four points but still under real threat of relegation. The position at the club was clearly desperate though, unsurprisingly, little information on the finances was made public. In *The Bridge*, Colin Benson noted that £346,000 was due at year end, to clear commitments to the builders and the bank.

The club could not afford new players and the current team was not good enough. The challenge for Suart and McCreadie, to bring talented youngsters into the first-team whilst at the same time staying up, remained. The end-year table made stark reading :-

16th Birmingham City	*p25*	*22pts*
17th Tottenham Hotspur	*p25*	*21pts*
18th Chelsea	**p24**	**21pts**
19th Arsenal	*p24*	*20pts*
20th Carlisle United	p25	17pts
21st Leicester City	p24	16pts
22nd Luton Town	p24	15pts

January 1975

The FA Cup was always a welcome distraction for relegation-haunted teams, and there was an added incentive for Chelsea in terms of the imperative of increasing revenue. The *Daily Mirror* reported that the interest payments on the new East Stand were around £2,000 a week and that was before the actual debt was repaid to the banks. Chairman Brian Mears, in positive mood, proclaimed 'the spirit at Chelsea now is tremendous. A good cup run could get us moving forward in a big way'. He admitted that failure in the Third Round would cost Chelsea the chance of collecting up to £100,000 from a good cup run.

A home draw against Sheffield Wednesday, twenty-first in Division Two, was surely winnable. The crowd of 24,679 (paying £20,493) were duly stunned when Wednesday took a 2-0 lead, a lead they still held with fifteen minutes left, Hollins hitting a penalty high over the bar and the crowd, unsurprisingly, slow handclapping. Only Cooke, as ever that season, was able to step above the mediocrity and incompetence. An unlikely hero then stepped forward. Micky Droy, the subject of criticism for his lack of mobility and finesse but certainly a whole-hearted player, pulled one back. In an atmosphere of increasing excitement Chris Garland equalised then, with five minutes left and with a seething crowd backing them, Droy converted a Cooke free-kick for an unlikely winner. The match-winner was booked, meaning a two-match suspension and a selection headache for manager Ron Suart, but would at least give him a chance to rest his injury. Mears, hugely relieved, commented 'like a drowning man, the thoughts going through my head were horrible'.

That week the *Evening Standard* carried out an analysis of the fights against relegation by Arsenal, Tottenham and Chelsea – the sides were in seventeenth to nineteenth place and it was unheard of for London's three premier teams to all be struggling so ignominiously. They pointed out that Chelsea's only signings in the past four seasons had been Kember, Garland, Garner, Cooke, Hay and Sissons whereas Weller, Smethurst, Mulligan, Cooke, Boyle, Hudson, Osgood and Webb had all been allowed to leave, a stark decline in quality. Mears went over old ground, determined to remain, at least publicly, positive. 'With the £2,000,000 new stand only just opened, it is absolutely essential we stay in Division One. I accept we are not out of the wood yet. But I can see a way now – I really can. A good FA Cup run is very important to us, particularly for our gates. I can honestly say I am looking forward to the rest of the season'. The last sentence may well have had an element of artistic license, as the next four months could easily turn into a nightmare.

One bright spot was the regular inclusion of Ray Wilkins in the side in the past half dozen games. The *Kensington Post* was duly impressed in their assessment of him. 'Wilkins could be the young midfield revelation Chelsea have sought since Alan Hudson first flopped and finally left the club'. Playing in the centre of the midfield trio he was confidently directing colleagues, keen to be involved, happy playing the ball with both feet, unafraid to risk long passes and happy to shoot. A real prospect.

Back to League action and a trip to Luton Town, still rooted to the bottom of the table. The *Fulham Chronicle* described Chelsea's approach as being 'so scared of losing that they settled for caution and the point which would keep them from losing too much sleep'. They woke up after Jimmy Husband put Luton ahead and Kember snatched a late equaliser, but it was another scuffling performance against a mediocre side and did not bode well for the tougher tests ahead.

The seemingly never-ending 'will Osgood come back?' saga gurgled on. At the start of the month Mears, again changing his stance, had said 'it is up to the two managers to sort something out ... Given enough time, I am reasonably confident something can be sorted out. But whatever happens we are not sitting on the fence'. The reality was that Southampton still only wanted Hollins or Kember in exchange, and Chelsea still could not afford to lose either. There was also concern as to whether Chelsea could afford an 'adjustment fee' to balance off any exchange. After the Luton away game the Mirror reported on a possible Osgood deal with Garner plus £35,000 going the other way. That must have been wishful thinking, as Garner's performances that season simply did not want a valuation of £200,000 or anything similar. In the end, Suart was forced to admit that Osgood would not be returning, to the frustration of many supporters.

Concerned about Phillips' reliability, and with Bonetti marginalised, Suart expressed an interest in highly rated Millwall goalkeeper Bryan King, rated at more than £150,000 even in those days of a contracting transfer market.

One move that did happen was Tommy Baldwin going to Manchester United on loan, linking up with manager Tommy Docherty, who had brought him to Chelsea back in 1966. If he proved his worth, £25,000 would seal the deal. 'I don't know what went wrong at Chelsea' was his comment. The *Daily Mail* ran a piece on the player under a 'Baldwin: My Long Fight For this Comeback' back-page headline. The player explained 'I've not only seriously limited my drinking, but I've been going back in the afternoons for extra training. Most days I was on my own but sometimes Charlie Cooke was with me'. He also observed 'there are a lot of social distractions around Chelsea', reiterating a point made by Alan Hudson.

A home game against Leeds was never easy, despite their relatively lowly tenth place. Osgood's name was still bellowed by the supporters, even though any possible deal was dead. The game was less physical than almost any game between the sides in the past decade, possibly because many of the main protagonists, like Osgood, McCreadie, Johnny Giles and Jack Charlton, had moved on, though the crowd of 34,733 showed interest in the game was still high. Chelsea competed hard and gave a decent, spirited account of themselves, but were outclassed and a 2-0 away win was deserved. Hay and Hinton was, ludicrously, the eighth centre-back partnership of the season but worked well together, Hinton's coolness standing out.

The match programme pointed out that there were five points between Chelsea and the three clubs below the 'relegation line'. 'Not that we can ever be complacent about a position of nineteenth. Equally, it would be a case of dangerous delusion to believe that Carlisle, Luton and Leicester are cut off at the bottom'. Complacency would have been insane given the club had the worst home record in all four divisions with just two League wins. This would need to improve, and improve quickly, if catastrophe was to be avoided. They had two cup wins at home, against Newport County and Sheffield Wednesday, and were desperate to make it a third the following Saturday against Birmingham City in the Fourth Round of the FA Cup. This was a massive game in terms of the season and, arguably, the club's future. Win and a lucrative Fifth Round tie could be anticipated. Lose, and the season would consist of a relegation fight.

Hutchinson had arguably been Chelsea's best striker so far that season, not that hard given the competition was Garner, Garland and the loaned-out Baldwin. He had started eight of the last nine games and was in line for his first FA Cup-tie since the Fourth Round four seasons earlier. It is testament to the man's tremendous bravery and spirit that he had fought so hard to get back in that position. The tactic of pushing the giant Droy forward for Hutchinson's long throws had got Chelsea seven goals, not a pretty tactic but an effective one. Droy said because of injuries they had not played together much but 'nobody seems to have an answer to us'. Suart revealed to the *Daily Mirror* 'what surprises me is that the play never fails to upset defences. It is something that has now become a vital part of our thinking'. Droy was back after suspension and the plan was evidently to use the tactic against Birmingham.

A training injury to Cooke was a massive blow, Sissons coming into the side just an hour before kick-off for only his second first-team game in four months, weakening the side's creativity. For arguably Chelsea's most important game of the season so far, a very decent crowd of 35,450 turned up in anticipation. The side lined up :- *Phillips; Locke, Droy, Hay, Harris; Hollins, Kember, Wilkins; Garland, Hutchinson, Sissons.*

Birmingham were a physical side and displayed a highly committed approach to the match. Chelsea had two tactics. Long balls to Hutchinson, which Birmingham's centre-backs easily dealt with, or Hutchinson's long throws. Without Cooke there was no subtlety, no vision. A thoroughly unattractive game was won by a Kenny Burns goal before half-time, the Scot commenting 'it was unbelievable. I had all the time in the world. You don't expect that against a First Division side'.

In the end, Birmingham had five players booked, whereas Chelsea had none. Garland accused the Midlanders of intimidation, but maybe they just wanted to win it more and, for them, the end justified the means. Hutchinson had damaged a toe in the first minute and, in character, bravely battled on. The press was unsympathetic, highlighting the fact that Chelsea only had one shot on target, woeful finishing, a lack of talent and craft, the absence of a general and the failure to create chances. A 'dreadful', 'pathetic', 'terrible', 'humiliated' (take your pick) Chelsea simply were not good enough. A calamitous result. An upset Mears, seeing an abyss yawning in front of him, admitted 'this is a financial blow. We needed a cup run. We were terrible. Now it's a case of hanging on to a First Division place so we can start again next year'.

The *News Of The World* continued in similar vein. Under a 'Crisis At Stamford Bridge' headline, they wrote 'hard-up for both money in the bank and talent in the team, the prospect of a fight against relegation must send cold shivers down every Chelsea spine...I can't see a big crowd turning up for the next game even if they let them in for free'. Given that the next home game was against Birmingham in a fortnight, the correspondent was almost certainly correct.

Cooke, missed so much against Birmingham, had impressed Scotland manager Willie Ormond again against Leeds and, to his absolute delight, he was back in the Scotland squad. 'What an amazing turn-around. I can hardly believe it...I feel 22 not 32'.

So Chelsea ended the month in a parlous state. Out of both cups, with an appalling home record (though with the sixth best away record in the division) and no cash to improve the squad. They were in nineteenth place, worryingly close to the drop :-

16th Arsenal	p26 23pts
17th Tottenham Hotspur	p27 23pts
18th Birmingham City	p27 23pts
19th Chelsea	**p26 22pts**
20th Carlisle United	p27 19pts
21st Leicester City	p26 17pts
22nd Luton Town	p26 16pts

A good February and the gap to twentieth place might indeed become significant. A poor run and a footballing and financial nightmare would be harder to avoid.

February 1975

February offered four winnable League games, and Chelsea certainly had to win them. An away game at twenty-first placed Leicester City, another at Sheffield United. Home games against Birmingham City and Newcastle United. Not the hardest four games to play in a month, given that none of the opponents were in the top ten.

It did not help Ron Suart's cause that the injury jinx of the past two seasons reared its ugly head again. In the run up to the game he had six players – Ian Hutchinson, Chris Garland, Micky Droy, Peter Houseman, John Dempsey and Ian Britton – on the injury list. Hutchinson, ever the brave heart, was prepared to play at Filbert Street with a broken toe. He could not have a painkilling injection but was prepared to play in a special boot if at all possible, but in the end, this was impossible. None of the six were fit to play so Suart, desperate, called up youngsters John Sparrow, Steve Finnieston and Tommy Langley.

Full-back Sparrow had played eight games the previous season and Langley had made his debut at home to Leicester earlier that season. In the end striker Finnieston made his debut alongside Bill Garner, and Sparrow came into a makeshift side. Luckily, veteran maestro Charlie Cooke was fit, replacing John Sissons, who never wore a first-team shirt again. Leicester, in worse trouble than Chelsea and without a League win in three months, took the lead through Chelsea old-boy Keith Weller, a goal controversial enough to have Garner, Steve Kember and Ron Harris all booked for protesting it was offside. Kember's 88th minute headed equaliser was very welcome.

Chelsea's hero was Harris, who played on despite a cut under the eye early on, which later required five stitches, carrying a sponge to staunch and mop up the blood. Harris's centre-back partner David Hay played on with a thigh injury likely to rule him out of the Scotland side. Sparrow and Finnieston did well, as did fellow youngster Ray Wilkins, now established in the side at eighteen. Suart felt 'teams who survive a relegation battle...are those who refuse to allow the pressures to affect their normal game. We proved in an important game that we have this quality'.

Sparrow had been a success playing for the England Youth team in Canary Islands and later that month he, Ray Wilkins and Langley were all named in the England Youth squad. It was the first time for well over a decade that Chelsea had been so well represented at that level.

Before the Birmingham game, Chelsea Chairman Brian Mears had opened the 'sumptuous executive restaurant' in the £2 million East Stand with a reception. After 13 home games, Chelsea's crowds were actually 4.3% up year on year but still achingly below the 35,000 target.

Harris played with his stitches and Hay had recovered from last week's injury. Hutchinson declared himself fit to play, despite pain from his broken toe. A 2-1 win, a massively welcome third League victory at Stamford Bridge that season, was greeted with such enthusiasm by the crowd that, according to the *Daily Telegraph*, 'one could be forgiven for assuming they had won the championship', a mix of relief and joy. That crowd, a mere 18,144, was just over half that for the FA Cup game two weeks earlier.

The win put them ahead of Birmingham for the first time that season, and ahead of Tottenham. The dressing room at half-time was like a casualty ward - Hutchinson had, in addition to his broken toe, a fractured finger and was swallowing pain killers. Kember had stomach trouble and was vomiting. Philips had a black eye and Locke had ankle and calf injuries. It was to the enormous credit of the team that they battled so hard with such an array of injuries and illness. Wilkins, man of the match, scored his first first-team goal after a wonderful Wilkins-Locke-Hutchinson-Kember-Wilkins move. Substitute Langley, on for Locke, scored the winner on his seventeenth birthday with ten minutes left, after an enormous Sparrow long throw.

The *Daily Telegraph* wrote how the new generation were 'restoring some of the fan's faith in the future'. They argued that the youngsters (Sparrow, Wilkins and Langley in their teens, Locke and Finnieston twenty) contributed more to the victory than the elders (Phillips, Harris, Hollins, Hay, Kember, Hutchinson and Cooke), who the paper felt were clearly suffering from anxiety.

News broke in the week that Garland was being made available for transfer, the fee expected to be in the region of £100,000, the same as he arrived for three-and-a-half years earlier. Suart explained 'it's felt in the best interests of the club and the player that he's made available for transfer. For various reasons he hasn't settled as well in London as anticipated. There's been no disagreement between the club and the player. The decision to release him has been taken reluctantly ... He has been troubled with injury every season since he joined'. He had scored just seven League goals in his last 43 games, so was hardly prolific, though, as supporter Geoff Kimber remembers, he was a willing trier. He told the *Daily Mirror* 'I've never showed my potential at Chelsea. If I have to make an excuse it is because living in London has changed me ... there is something false about living here. I prefer the country way'. One theory was that cash raised by selling him could be spent on Millwall goalkeeper Bryan King.

The following week, at Sheffield United, Chelsea missed a chance to pick up a valuable point when Hollins missed another penalty, this one saved by Jim Brown, in a 2-1 defeat. Garner scored Chelsea's consolation goal. He, Droy and Hay were all booked as Chelsea continued their robust approach but Droy, playing well, went off with a knee injury that was to keep him out for over a month. Suart felt that Chelsea were the only team in it, but they still managed to lose. Hutchinson was sufficiently badly injured that he could not play in the first-team for six weeks, a significant loss.

Chelsea were now six points above twentieth place Carlisle United, a reasonable buffer with thirteen games to go, and a 3-2 home win against Newcastle convinced some that Chelsea had turned a corner and safety was not far away. Finnieston, in because Hutchinson and Garner were unfit, scored his first League goal, Cooke and Hollins, with a penalty, netting the other. Chelsea almost threw it away when, with the score 3-2, Malcolm MacDonald had a penalty saved by Phillips. Stamford Bridge became 'a boiling cauldron of sound', celebrating a vital and exhilarating victory.

Tommy Baldwin returned from Manchester United, even though his loan period still had two weeks to run. He only played two first-team games and five Central League games. Suart said it was clear United were not interested in retaining him. Martin Chivers was out of favour at Tottenham, and Suart and McCreadie watched him play for Tottenham reserves, but Suart made it clear 'we are not interested' in buying a player past his peak.

Bernard Joy, in an optimistic *Evening Standard* article headlined 'The Bridge Is Rich With Talent And Hope', believed 'Chelsea will keep their First Division place and will be one of the top teams in the country in two or three years' time'. He praised Ray Wilkins, Locke, Sparrow, Finnieston and Droy – the forerunners of 'an upsurge of talent which promises to bring the glory days back to Stamford Bridge'. 'The youngsters have not let the team down'. Suart enthused 'they are not hiding. They want the ball. They were accepted by the seniors right from the word go'.

Chelsea were now seven points clear of the bottom three positions at the end of February. The table looked more positive than it had for a while :-

16th Chelsea	*p30*	*27pts*
17th Birmingham City	*p31*	*26pts*
18th Arsenal	*p29*	*25pts*
19th Tottenham Hotspur	*p32*	*24pts*
20th Leicester City	*p29*	*20pts*
21st Luton Town	*p30*	*20pts*
22nd Carlisle United	*p31*	*19pts*

A good March and they would probably be, to all intents and purposes, out of trouble. A bad one and the trapdoor still loomed.

March 1975

A trip to Liverpool was always a cause for trepidation and that season was no exception. The Anfield side were in fifth place, still in with a chance of winning the League title. Ron Suart stuck with the same side that had beaten Newcastle and was rewarded when Ian Britton put Chelsea ahead. Steve Heighway's equaliser was matched by a simply superb Steve Finnieston chip from 25 yards that left Liverpool goalkeeper Ray Clemence dumbstruck. Even now, Finnieston regrets that his goal was not televised. Peter Cormack equalised with two minutes to go, but though Chelsea were massively disappointed not to win, in reality it was still one of their best performances of the season.

David Hay had not been bought as a centre-back but certainly performed well there, striking up a strong partnership with Ron Harris. Chelsea were now six points off the bottom three and another eight points, possibly less, would probably be enough to keep them up. The run-in was not an easy one and included a potentially vital trip to relegation rivals Tottenham, but there seemed no reason why enough points could not be picked up to ensure safety.

The *Daily Mirror* ran a lengthy feature on club finances that week, claiming two out of three League clubs were in the red and pointing out that many of the people running clubs and the game itself seemed less than competent to do so. They pointed out that Chelsea had scorned the opportunity to make Stamford Bridge a multi-sports stadium, missing out on revenue opportunities and the chance to provide community facilities. They did confirm the Executive Boxes had sold out that season, a considerable achievement given the travails of the team, but referred to 'Chelsea's conspicuous lack of success' which had led to the East Stand often being not much more than half full. Chairman Brian Mears reiterated 'we had a great team and we needed the ground facilities to go with it. Now we have the stand, we need the team to go with it'. The article alluded to Mears having plans to put Stamford Bridge's eight acres to more use but was cagey about explaining exactly how. The article concluded that if Chelsea went down, Mears 'could be praying for the revenue of a mini sports complex'.

The tough games continued, the next was a home game against title contenders Derby County. The club decided that one way to attract bigger crowds was to introduce some razzmatazz, so booked the 'Marching Mizzous' a 280-strong troupe of musicians and dancers from Missouri to play before the game and at half-time. The attendance was hugely disappointing given the quality of the opposition, 22,644, so the crowd-pulling experiment had failed.

Peter Daniels and Alan Hinton put Derby ahead before Hollins pulled one back, all inside five second-half minutes. Chelsea tried but could not force an equaliser. A wake-up call for Ron Suart and Eddie McCreadie that although blooding youngsters may be necessary given the constraints at the club, almost inevitably they would struggle against quality opposition. Hay, continuing at centre-back, was about to start a suspension, a headache Suart could have done without.

The Marching Mizzous? Their speciality was 'traditional English song' *It's a Long Way to Tipperary*, which they played long and loud. After initially being greeted with 'what a load of rubbish' and 'go home, you bums' they apparently won the East Stand over, if not The Shed, and 5,000 fans supposedly stayed behind after the game to watch another display. After Hollins pulled the goal back, the band spent the past 25 minutes behind Derby goalkeeper Colin Boulton's goal, drums and cymbals creating a right racket in a futile attempt to spur the team on to an equaliser.

Supporter David Gray remembers the occasion well. 'The club had arranged for the band to play at half-time. Fair enough, but because it was tipping down with rain the band stayed sitting in the condemned upper North Stand and played from there. But what followed was surreal...during the second half the band decided to strike up and thus we had the spectacle of two English teams battling in the mud and rain whilst a band, complete with baton-twirlers, played the *Monty Python* theme! How badly I wanted the stand to finally collapse there and then. It is indelibly etched in my mind'.

Transfer-listed Chris Garland was sold to relegation rivals Leicester City, 24 hours before the transfer deadline closed on March 13th. The club received what they paid for him, £100,000. His was a signing that never quite came off, though it was hardly his fault that Sexton stuck him out on the wing, or that he never got the chance to build up a long-term striking partnership. The income was not used to buy Bryan King from Millwall, as many assumed would be the case, and was banked. Chelsea had watched defender Phil Dwyer and forward Derek Showers of Cardiff in recent weeks, but nothing came of that and so troubled Chelsea spent precisely nothing that season after the summer purchases of Hay and John Sissons.

In recognition of his magnificent service and tremendous loyalty, Peter Bonetti was given a free transfer, and was now free to negotiate with another club before he went to America for the summer, to play for

St. Louis Stars. His release without a transfer fee being required reflected what he had done for the club and would enable him to negotiate a decent signing-on fee. It was to the credit of the club that they made this magnanimous gesture when they were in such a financial mess. 'The Cat', as he was known, is without doubt one of the very best goalkeepers Chelsea have ever had, though his star had waned that season and he had only made eight first-team appearances. Manchester City were immediately interested in him.

Unable to improve his squad, and with Hay suspended, Suart tried to make the best of it for the trip to Wolverhampton Wanderers, two points and two places above Chelsea. He paired John Dempsey, who had not started a first-team game since January, with Harris at centre-back, bringing back Garner for the departed Garland up front and keeping a frustrated Kember, captain earlier that season, on the bench. Wolves gave midfielder Willie Carr his debut after his signing from Coventry City for a bargain £80,000. Carr had a debut to remember, and the 21,649 crowd would not easily forget it, either.

Carr ran the game as he wished, Chelsea had no answer to the power and running of Steve Kindon, John Richards gave his usual effective display against Chelsea and the visitors were utterly humiliated. 3-1 down at half-time, Wolves scored four more in an embarrassingly easy second-half display. Six different Wolves players scored with Richards, inevitably, bagging a pair. Kenny Hibbitt, one of the scorers, exclaimed 'I have never found scoring so easy against any Chelsea team. It was like driving a bus down the M1'.

After Chelsea's biggest defeat for over seven years, a 'dazed' Ron Suart spoke to the *Sunday People*, praised Carr and Kindon and explained 'everything they hit went in, everything went against us...but you can't make excuses'. He told the *Daily Mirror* 'I am not trying to whitewash Saturday's defeat. It was a blow to our pride. But we have been playing well, and to make wholesale changes would not solve any problems'. The *Sunday People* felt Chelsea finished almost like a rabble, even though Garner did get them a goal. Chelsea fans unkindly taunted Phillips, who had little chance with five of the goals, with 'bring back The Cat' but he was not solely to blame, the problem was rather deeper. Whether Chelsea's tactical plan was not revised to consider the arrival at Molineux of Carr is not clear.

Supporter Richard Pigden remembers the day vividly, including an encounter with legendary Blues supporter Mick Greenaway. 'This was only my second away game outside of London. Every time Steve Kindon got the ball it looked like Wolves would score, he absolutely ran riot. When we got back to the train station I think we were all in shock, we had made quite a bit of noise on the way back but it went pretty quiet once we were inside Wolverhampton station. My most vivid memory was of Greenaway walking up and down the station platform, then up and down the aisle once we got on the train muttering 'seven ****ing one' over and over again. Luckily we were not on Match Of The Day or The Big Match'.

Howard Sole, a supporter whose father Gordon's Chelsea scrapbooks have been so useful in the author's research, tells another tale about that journey home. 'I was on the service train back to Euston with quite a good away following as one would expect from a trip to Wolves. The train stopped at Birmingham New Street, and Peter Osgood and another Southampton player got on, they had been playing Aston Villa away. News of his presence on board spread like wildfire all down the train. When we arrived back in London, whilst walking up the ramp from the platform to the ticket barrier line, Ossie was surrounded by a good number of fans chanting his name. As he went through the barrier he was lifted up in the air and carried part way across the concourse. I can remember that whilst he was in the air he was waving his arms about and requesting to be put down'. Gone but clearly not forgotten.

Suart, under real pressure, promised no panic changes but had three days to lift the spirits of his stunned team before a visit to QPR, sailing along in tenth place and, for the first time ever, the top team in West London. Dempsey, who had a dreadful game at Molineux but was not fully fit, was replaced by Marvin Hinton, 35-years-old and playing only his fifth game of the season. Charlie Cooke, Chelsea's best player that season, was left out for Kember, to toughen up the midfield. Langley, Sparrow and Ray Wilkins were pulled out of the England Youth squad that week, Suart keeping faith with the youngsters. Phillips kept his place and had a fine game, beaten just once, by Dave Thomas early on. Chelsea fought hard, played well and demonstrated real character but could not equalise.

Suart gave his latest defiant post-match interview, telling the *Daily Mirror* 'We'll definitely stick with these youngsters for the rest of the season. I've no doubt at all about their ability to get us clear of the relegation zone ... They were tremendous against QPR and we were unlucky to lose. If we can hold on this season - and we will - things look really good for the future'. He felt the senior players deserved credit for the way they had helped the kids and praised the supporters, who 'have given them every encouragement'.

After three defeats in ten days, Chelsea's position suddenly looked a lot more precarious. As they went into the home game with Middlesbrough on Saturday March 22nd, the table made unhappy reading :-

16th Birmingham City	*p34*	*30pts*
17th Arsenal	*p32*	*28pts*
18th Chelsea	**p34**	**28pts**
19th Leicester City	*p33*	*26pts*
20th Tottenham Hotspur	*p34*	*24pts*

21st Luton Town   *p33 22pts*
22nd Carlisle United   *p34 21pts*

Chelsea also had the worst goal average in the Division except for Luton Town. Middlesbrough were fourth, in with a chance of winning the League, an outstanding achievement by manager Jack Charlton and one that must have had Brian Mears looking on jealously.

The match programme announced that the imaginatively-named 'Chelsea's', the new Executive Club restaurant, held 275 and was available for hire. It glossed over the latest humiliation with a glib 'the least said about what happened at Wolverhampton last Saturday the better'.

Suart, in a decision that can only be described as 'brave', played an unlikely striking partnership of seventeen-year-old Langley and experienced midfielder Kember. Hay came back after suspension to partner Harris. A 2-1 defeat was bad enough, but a spiritless, clueless performance was of equal concern. Even Boro full-back Terry Cooper's dismissal, for disputing a throw-in, could not inspire Chelsea. The young players were understandably struggling, the *Kensington Post* referring to 'Chelsea's pathetic apology for a team of promise' and 'complete rubbish', fearing the youngsters 'did not have the talent' to avoid the drop.

The Observer reckoned 'Chelsea are at sea in a sieve'. They referred to 'apprehensive spectators' and saw how 'jitters took hold'. Cooke, as ever, tried to create chances but criticism of the team was unsparing, and it was clear that more games like that one would, in all probability, mean Second Division football the next season. Chelsea were still four points ahead of the bottom three, but Tottenham had a game in hand and their manager Terry Neill, impishly, observed that 'Chelsea could still save us from relegation'. To make matters worse Leicester had moved ahead of Chelsea and, worse, Chris Garland had scored a hat-trick for them.

A midweek testimonial at Woking, for loyal Chelsea staff Harry Medhurst and Dick Spence, gave a run out to a few untried youngsters – goalkeeper Derek Richardson and strikers Teddy Maybank and Trevor Aylott – as well as forgotten man Tommy Baldwin. The serious business, though, continued at West Ham on the Saturday, the last match in a nightmarish month that started well at Anfield but then fell apart. At Upton Park manager Suart, gambling furiously, made yet more changes. Ray Wilkins, Britton and Sparrow were dropped, Suart plumping for experience despite messages a week earlier about sticking with youth.

The much-changed team played better than since Anfield at the start of the month, which was not difficult, and deserved their shock, but very welcome, 1-0 victory. Droy scored the only goal with a diving header.

The final game of the month attracted a surprisingly large, and very welcome, crowd of 35,005 for the visit of Ipswich Town, third in the table and with a real title chance. Youth product Steve Wicks made his debut at centre-half as Droy was injured. Suart played Hinton as sweeper behind an unlikely back three of Locke, Wicks and Harris. Hinton was arguably the first sweeper in English football, Tommy Docherty using his cool composure to great effect there a decade earlier. A dreary afternoon ended in a 0-0 draw, probably unsatisfactory for both sides, though Chelsea had to hang on at the end so were probably the happier of the two sides.

The match programme pointed out that Chelsea were bottom of the Trident TV Fair Play League. Top were Liverpool with 458 points, Chelsea were bottom on 951 points, more than 100 below the next club, Manchester City. Five players had been suspended (two of them twice) compared with none the previous season. Editor Albert Sewell observed that 'clearly, for the good of the club's image, there needs to be a vast improvement next season'. The reality was, though, that Chelsea had to compensate for their lack of quality by showing fierce commitment, a poor disciplinary record an almost inevitable by-product of this.

16th Coventry City	*p37*	*34pts*
17th Arsenal	*p36*	*32pts*
18th Chelsea	**p37**	**31pts**
19th Leicester City	*p36*	*29pts*
20th Tottenham Hotspur	p37	28pts
21st Luton Town	p37	26pts
22nd Carlisle United	p37	23pts

Three points off the bottom three with five games to go. Stoke City and Tottenham away and three home games, Manchester City, Sheffield United and Everton. Eight points would mean certain safety, five would probably be enough.

April 1975

Stoke City had had the hex over Chelsea in recent seasons, particularly in the League Cup, and had not lost in their previous nine encounters. Charlie Cooke was out ill and what Chelsea lacked in his absence was flair. Stoke had plenty, in the shape of Chelsea old-boy Alan Hudson, who 'turned the relegation screw' as the *Kensington Post* put it. In a one-sided 3-0 defeat Chelsea were uncertain at the back, uninspired in midfield and lacked potency up front, though these were not new criticisms.

To ruin Chelsea's weekend still further, both Leicester City and Tottenham won, so Chelsea were but a point ahead of their North London rivals, with a significantly worse goal average. Four games to go, three at home and a trip to Tottenham in a fortnight that was already taking on monumental proportions. Though Suart was still confident of staying up, he surely realised that even if they did manage to, another season of struggle was almost inevitable. The Chelsea board probably realised the same, but the implications of dropping down to Division Two were so appalling that even another season of struggle was a significantly more attractive proposition.

A week to lick their wounds then an eminently winnable home game on Saturday April 12th against mid-table Manchester City, a side with one away win all season, the worst record in the division. Ian Hutchinson had been out of action for two months with a broken toe, a broken finger and a hamstring strain. In that time, their six-point over the bottom three had been whittled down to one, and they had only won two matches. Suart, welcoming him back, enthused 'there are few of his type around these days. With his courage he is always upsetting defences whether he is scoring or not'.

West Ham had beaten Ipswich Town in an FA Cup Semi-final replay at a full Stamford Bridge in front of over 45,344 supporters, 6,000 more than Chelsea's best of the season, against Liverpool back in August. That replay brought in receipts of £72,771, more than double the Chelsea record of £34,150 from that Liverpool game. In the crush, a barrier pole became loose on the North Stand terracing, so the club announced that a section of the North Stand terrace would be cordoned off against Manchester City. Chelsea Secretary Tony Green assured supporters 'one pillar started crumbling...there was no question of anything collapsing'. Except, perhaps, hope.

The *Daily Mail* asked chairman Brian Mears whether Stamford Bridge was doomed to become the Hillsborough of the South – used for Semi-finals but never full for home games? Mears was astonished. 'I see no analogy in our stadium and that of Hillsborough. But, very much more to the point, I see no connection between how the team has been performing and the ground it performs in. People talk as though we had a choice – to spend money on the team or the ground – and then made the wrong decision. I swear that has never been the issue. There has not been a single instant when the needs of the team and the stadium were in conflict. We are fourth from bottom and the next few weeks are vital. But whatever happens I KNOW we were right to re-build the Bridge. I am concerned about the present but not frightened of the future'. *Daily Mail* journalist Brian James felt Chelsea made the right choice, that the youngsters would fill the stadium. He did not consider the potential scenario of having to sell those youngsters to keep the club afloat.

Cordoning off a section of terracing was unlikely to cause a crush elsewhere given recent gates, especially when only 26,249 turned out to support their side in a critical game, nearly nine thousand less than for the Ipswich match twelve days earlier. The match programme stated the obvious. 'Not so many weeks ago we felt we were making our League position safe, but a sequence of only four points from the last eight games, coupled with a run of three victories by Tottenham ... has so changed the situation that we are now fighting for our First Division lives'. The club advised readers that striker Tommy Langley and winger Clive Walker had signed professional forms and that two reserves were off to America for the summer, John Sissons to Florida and Tommy Baldwin to Seattle Sounders.

Asa Hartford scored for City before half-time and Chelsea were too unimaginative and too unpenetrative to do anything about it. A defence of Locke, Hinton, Droy and Harris hardly had pace written all over it. The front six of Hollins, Kember, Hay, Cooke, Hutchinson and Houseman hardly had creativity or goals written all over it. Worse, some of the players seemed to have given up the ghost. Suart had chosen experience over youth as he thought they would handle the inevitable tension better, and it had simply not worked.

The *Fulham Chronicle's* 'Chelsea Fail Again' headline said it all, and the article itself stuck the knife deeper. 'Even Chelsea's most committed supporters can have little sympathy with the relegation-haunted Stamford Bridge club after their most recent defeat...Seemingly half-asleep Chelsea deserved no more than they got. Nothing...Chelsea, with a midfield overcrowded with work-horses where they needed a few thoroughbreds'.

The Observer referred to a 'desperate atmosphere' at a critical match. They picked holes in individuals and the team, in both quality and attitude. 'The rot in Chelsea's fortunes, the decay in their standards, had accelerated so abruptly that it was in danger of poisoning the morale of the team in the last crucial few weeks of the season...a lack of individual and collective co-ordination. Some were unbelievably bad. It was depressing to find Hay in this category. Kember and Hollins, for all the latter's effort, rarely achieved more than a scuffling contribution in midfield. Droy looked clumsy. Cooke's influence remained peripheral. Hutchinson had been away from the First Division so long, you could almost hear his hinges creak'.

In Hutchinson's defence he was not match-fit, but the others had little excuse. In a critical game they simply had not stepped up to the mark. Rodney Marsh underlined the shambles. 'Unbelievably bad, weren't they? It was almost impossible for us not to win it'. The only solace for supporters was that Tottenham lost at Burnley. The *Sunday Telegraph* built up the 'Dramatic Relegation Showdown' the following week. They observed that 'Chelsea are panicking' and noticed an 'air of despair around Stamford Bridge'.

Cooke and Hay were pulled out of the Scotland squad to allow Suart to experiment in a Monday night friendly at Fulham in aid of the Police Dependents Trust, *after* the appalling off-duty murder of local PC Stephen Tibble. Both players were unhappy with the decision, which smacked of punishment for their contribution to a dreadful Chelsea showing. 12,000 turned up at Craven Cottage, Chelsea winning through a goal from young striker Teddy Maybank.

The *Evening Standard* reported an un-named Chelsea player as saying 'we are worried what wages the club will be able to afford if we go down – especially those players whose contracts end this summer. The gates will drop in the Second Division but the overheads, particularly the new stand, will still be there...all at Chelsea are concerned about their long-term wages'. It is doubtful whether many supporters had much sympathy with senior players who, in some cases, seemed to have accepted relegation as inevitable.

The Daily Mirror published a picture of the directors against Manchester City, sitting one behind the other, looking very uncomfortable by a 'Chelsea Leave Brian In Torment' headline. 'He (Mears) is already showing the signs of strain ... he sat in the directors' box like a man in the electric chair ... smoked nearly 30 cigarettes ... made a million references to his watch'. He told them 'I still will not accept relegation, but this is the most worrying time since I have been at Chelsea. The club to me is a way of life. To go down would be a life sentence ... The most worrying thing is that Tottenham are scoring goals. We aren't'.

Mears was obviously, and understandably, feeling the pressure, but his comments to the *Daily Mail* bordered on the hysterical. The headline ran 'Stay Away From Chelsea, Mears Warns "Shirkers"'. They argued that if the team played with as little spirit and urgency at Tottenham in Saturday's showdown then Chelsea would surrender survival. 'I will just have a long talk with Suart and McCreadie and between us we will tell a few other people that anyone not interested in 100 per cent effort can stay away from the club. Too many people are passing the buck...some players have lost their appetite for the game. There is too much shirking of responsibility. I know my responsibility as chairman. I will not concede relegation. But if we go down, we must go down fighting. That is the least we owe our supporters, who have been tolerant and never sunk to shouting abuse at the team or us'.

The *Daily Mail* thought Mears was likely to advise staff of the economies necessary if the team go down, but nothing would interfere with the massive rebuilding of Stamford Bridge, of which the new £2 million stand was only a start. 'We know that if we go down, we will lose a lot of our support. They will not go anywhere else. They will simply not come back until Chelsea are back at the top'. A heavy pruning of staff and players seemed inevitable.

There is something distasteful about the way he referred to 'Suart and McCreadie' as though he was their commanding officer and banged on about 'shirkers', like factory manager Terry-Thomas in the satirical 1960 labour relations film 'I'm Alright, Jack'. Nobody could doubt Brian Mears commitment to, or love for, the club but outbursts to headline-hungry journalists were hardly the way to present a calm, positive front to supporters and opponents. Change was urgently required. Well, change was certainly delivered.

On the Wednesday, McCreadie was appointed Team Manager, with Suart moving up to General Manager. The Scot immediately promised the club would stand or fall by its youth policy. Appointing the dynamic, driven McCreadie certainly gave the whole club an immediate jolt of energy and focus. Whether he could turn things around in the three games left remained to be seen, it was a huge task for a man taking the helm for the first time. Suart, to his great credit, saw developments in a positive light, at least publicly. 'The reaction from the team will be the exact reversal of what outsiders might think. It is a terrific appointment and has my full backing. There was no aggro at all. It was mutually agreed and both Eddie and I knew when the decision was made last October that today's events would eventually happen'.

Suart's move to General Manager was covered in a revealing interview with the Scot in *Eddie Mac, Eddie Mac*. He makes it clear he stressed to Suart the need to include youngsters at the expense of the experienced players, to build for the following season given that relegation was likely. He says that he (Suart) 'was personally at the end of his time and really couldn't cope anymore with our terrible situation and the pressure of it...we both agreed that he should step down'. The board agreed that McCreadie should be appointed with immediate effect.

The *Daily Telegraph* led with a 'McCreadie Sure He Can Rally Chelsea' headline. 'I'm going to make these players believe in themselves and the club ... We've got some great youngsters coming through and they're going to take over. There are going to be a lot of changes – new faces, a new approach. My directors are behind me: we've thrashed out what was to be done and we'll do it. A new era is starting, and I won't rest until we have a team worthy of the club'.

The Sheffield United programme a week later the club gave the official view. 'When we made our appointments in October it was contemplated that at a later stage Ron Suart would become General Manager and Eddie McCreadie Team Manager. That stage has now been reached, and these appointments take effect from today...To former coach Eddie, in the task of pulling Chelsea together on the field, and to Ron, alongside him, we wish the best of luck - immediate and long-term'. Suart had tried valiantly but, given the resources at his disposal it was no surprise that, after a decent run in late 1974 and early 1975, results deteriorated.

McCreadie's popularity with the supporters was always high in his playing days and this swell of goodwill undoubtedly helped him, given the magnitude of the task he faced, both short and longer-term. In addition, supporters undoubtedly had their views on who was to blame for the club's current predicament, and the new manager was certainly not seen as one of the guilty parties.

The changes were not only in the managerial hot seat. McCreadie kept to his promise of drastic changes by making Ray Wilkins, at eighteen years and seven months, captain for the key Tottenham game, replacing Hollins, who was stripped of not only the captaincy but also his place in the team. The proud new manager told the *Daily Telegraph* 'I have picked the best team at my disposal. There had to be a shake-up after last week's display against Manchester City, and I can promise our fans they will see a big improvement. John Hollins has been a loyal and devoted Chelsea captain, but he accepts that he has been having a bad time. Ray Wilkins is not just captain for this match – he is the captain for the future. At eighteen he is very confident and capable, a player years ahead of himself'.

In a 2018 interview with the *Daily Telegraph* McCreadie enthused 'Butch was a player I wanted to rebuild the team around. I remember when I told him he was to be my captain, him saying to me: 'You think I can do it?' I never had a moment's doubt'.

Wilkins commented 'it makes me feel very proud. Despite the position we are in, this is a great club and I hope I can help'. Young striker Teddy Maybank made his debut at White Hart Lane and in addition to Wilkins, Sparrow and Britton were recalled. Out went Hollins, Hinton, Kember and Houseman. Of the old guard from the glory days of 4-5 years earlier, only Harris, Hutchinson and Cooke remained in the side. The *Daily Telegraph* pointed out it appeared to be a last, desperate throw of the dice, and thought it an odd moment to carry out their plan. The *Daily Mail* reported that McCreadie had told his players that 'the days of established men automatically staying in the squad are over'.

McCreadie denied that the appointment of Wilkins and Maybank's debut was a gamble. He told the *Evening Standard* 'I know the impact these decisions will have on the older players…it is never nice, or easy to understand, when you are dropped'. Wilkins added 'I was startled when I was told I had the job'. He was playing five-a-side when McCreadie approached him, took him to one side and told him he was captain. 'John Hollins and the rest of the lads have wished me luck'. McCreadie emphasised that 'it would be a tragedy if decisions today made him (Hollins) lose respect for me. He knows what I am doing is for the club'. He reiterated that Hollins had often been playing while injured. The paper rightly called it 'harrowing times' for the club.

The *Fulham Chronicle* argued that 'relegation, I fear, will be economically calamitous for Chelsea. If they go down, I cannot see them fighting their way back immediately, either. They need to avoid defeat or are almost certainly doomed…I have little confidence in their chances'. They pointed out that Chelsea had scored twice in six games and those goals were by defenders Sparrow and Droy. 'Chelsea's preponderance of too-similar midfield grafters cost them dear against Manchester City…By a misguided transfer policy and over-dependence on youngsters, they have contributed massively to their own downfall'.

McCreadie insisted he was picking the best team at his disposal. He reiterated 'I did what had to be done' and said Kember was substitute as he had lost a bit of form. A shocked Hollins told the *Daily Mirror* 'it appears I don't figure in his (Eddie's) plans. I'm certain it is all over for me at Chelsea. I'm only 28 and feel I've got a lot left to offer'. Wilkins had been out of the team for a month and admitted 'I've no illusions about the Tottenham clash. Everything depends on it'.

Peter Bonetti given a free transfer after 612 first-team appearances, showed his absolute loyalty to Chelsea. 'I still have a target with the reserves – to help them win the Football Combination...I'm as fit now as the day I joined Chelsea and I'll carry on playing until I'm no longer good enough'. Despite Phillips' occasional heroics, how McCreadie must have wished he had a Peter Bonetti circa 1970 in his team.

The League table on the morning of the match reiterated the criticality of the game :-

16th Leicester City	p40	35pts
17th Arsenal	p38	34pts
18th Birmingham City	p39	34pts
19th Chelsea	**p39**	**31pts**
20th Tottenham Hotspur	p39	30pts
21st Luton Town	p40	30pts
22nd Carlisle United	p40	26pts

Just four players who started the season in the first-team (Locke, Droy, Harris and Hay) lined up so the changes had certainly been rung. It seems surprising that three of the back four survived given the abject nature of some of their displays, but McCreadie did exactly not have many alternative defenders to choose from when he put out the following side :- *Phillips; Locke, Droy, Harris, Sparrow; Britton, Hay, Wilkins, Cooke; Maybank, Hutchinson.*

The game kicked-off ten minutes late due to supporters fighting on the pitch. The gates had been locked and police were struggling to cope with the crowds trying to break them down. It remained scoreless for nearly an hour before Alfie Conn gave Tottenham the lead. Wilkins missed a glorious chance to equalise, Steve Perryman grabbed a second and fight as they did, Chelsea could not dent the Tottenham defence. *The Observer*, under a 'Noose Tightens On Chelsea' headline, felt that McCreadie's team changes had improved the style and effectiveness of play and the balance of the team. The new manager was defiant to the last. 'The same team plays on Wednesday (against Sheffield United). I'm proud of the boys. They stimulate the older players. With this spirit we'll remain a First Division club'. Wilkins wept in the dressing room. 'We're not giving up. We must beat Sheffield United'. The *Sunday Telegraph* felt that the 'spirited and encouraging display suggests that all is not lost. If they do go down, they have the nucleus of a side to return'.

Tottenham required three points from two games to be sure of survival. They were a point ahead of Chelsea with a better goal average, but had Arsenal away and Leeds United at home, hardly easy games, to come, so there was still hope.

McCreadie indeed fielded the same side against The Blades, making Garner substitute instead of Kember. Chelsea simply had to win to put pressure on, as Tottenham next played on the Saturday, at Arsenal, when Chelsea were playing their final game at home to Everton. Tottenham's final game, at home to Leeds, was the following Monday, and Chelsea had to make them need something from that game. McCreadie, through the press, asked the crowd to make more noise but with only 23,380 present a raucous atmosphere was difficult.

Maybank's first first-team goal after six minutes, from a Hutchinson throw, gave Chelsea a 1-0 half-time lead but they could not grab a second the pressure grew, and it was no surprise when Keith Eddy equalised fifteen minutes from time. Locke had to go to hospital with concussion, depriving his side of the pace and energy he brought to the right flank. Chelsea pressed but to no avail. 1-1 it was. The young team got a sympathetic reception from the crowd at the end. Mears was chain smoking in the director's box. McCreadie, who enthused 'they all did me proud, but we didn't win', doing the same in the dug-out.

Hollins told the *Daily Mail* 'after being at the club so long, and knowing the players well, it is difficult not to feel for them, out on the pitch. I will be willing them to win and stay up…The sooner I can get fixed up at a new club the better'. The *Sunday People* had reported that Hollins, Houseman, Dempsey and Hutchinson would be put up for sale and that Kember and Phillips might put in transfer requests.

Chelsea, Luton Town and Tottenham were all level on 32 points, but Tottenham had two games left, Chelsea and Luton but one. Luton, whose goal average was superior to Chelsea's, were playing Manchester City. Victory for Tottenham or Luton on the Saturday would end Chelsea's twelve-year stay in the top division, so Chelsea had to better both rivals results to have any chance of avoiding the drop.

As the Everton game approached it was clear that Locke's concussion was going to prevent him playing. The manager was clear in his strategy. 'I am sticking by the Chelsea babes…I believe in myself. I can't do otherwise with the fine squad of players I've got'. He moved Hay to right-back, brought in Hinton for the injured Droy, and picked Kember in Hay's midfield place. The manager praised both his squad and the supporters. 'They can see what I'm doing, rebuilding a great side'.

The match programme was solemn and realistic. 'Fate is more in the hands of others than ourselves. We would like to express sincere appreciation of your loyal support during the last eight months and look forward to seeing you back at Stamford Bridge in August'.

In the event, the game was a bit of an anti-climax. Wilkins gave his side the lead and Hutchinson hit the bar, but a Phillips error let Bob Latchford snatch an equaliser. Chelsea, again, gave their all but it was not enough. Although Tottenham lost at Arsenal, Luton drew with

Manchester City. McCreadie embraced each of his men as they walked off, relegation confirmed.

The reaction of Mears and McCreadie straight after the game was to send twelve bottles of champagne to the dressing room. The manager told the *Daily Mirror* 'it's going to be a busy summer. Obviously, there are things here that are wrong. When next season starts, they will have been put right ... The only thing the other Second Division sides will be chasing next season is dust'. He told the *Daily Mail* 'I shall need to buy new players. There are one or two positions where we must improve'. Mears, somewhat surprisingly given the parlous finances, commented 'depending on who Eddie wants to buy, we can always find that little bit extra. If we can do well on the field, I believe our supporters won't let us down'.

Supporter Geoff Kimber recalls a 'strange, celebratory atmosphere in The Shed at the end of the game' and the *News Of The World* reported that the underground train after the game was full of 'sad, silent kids'. McCreadie was bullish to them, too. 'We can win the Second Division championship. We'll come straight back. I'm not sad. This club will be back – we have the finest youngsters in the country. There will be a lot of changes on and off the field. There's a lot to be done and I feel like starting now. Chelsea are a big club. We think big and we will bounce back.' Mears again defended the new East Stand, saying that the club had not got their priorities wrong. 'It remains to be seen whether the fans stay with Chelsea in the same numbers'. Indeed. A crumb of consolation was that when Chelsea last went down, in 1962, average crowds the following season went up over 8% from 27,013 to 29,376, though those crowds were watching an exciting, promotion-chasing side and there was no guarantee this would be the case again, despite McCreadie's fighting talk.

Cooke was voted the *Player Of The Year* for the second time and received his award the evening after the Everton game, which must have been a strange event for players and supporters alike. Chelsea won the Football Combination, the farewell involvement of Bonetti who was leaving on a free transfer.

In the *Sunday Telegraph*, John Moynihan wrote 'Chelsea dropped down into the Second Division for the fourth time in their eccentric history...now the post-mortems will begin'. He felt crowds potentially as low as 15,000 could be financially catastrophic for the club, saddled as they were with the debts incurred in building the East Stand.

The final Division One table confirmed what, frankly, had been likely for some weeks. If they had drawn at Tottenham, Chelsea would have stayed up, but they didn't and in the end finished in 21st place.

16th Arsenal	*p42 37pts*
17th Birmingham City	*p42 37pts*
18th Leicester City	*p42 36pts*

19th Tottenham Hotspur	*p42 34pts*
20th Luton Town	*p42 33pts*
21st Chelsea	**p42 33pts**
22nd Carlisle United	*p42 29pts*

Season Review

So a truly disastrous season, on and off the pitch, came to a sorry end. A season where a farmyard of chickens came home to roost. Underinvestment in players over three or four years. Over-reliance on an experienced cadre of senior players. The promotion of too many youngsters, too soon, at a stage of the season where it would have been a miracle if they had made any difference. 25 different players used, only six unchanged teams in 48 matches. *Rothmans Football Yearbook*, in its summary of the season, argued Chelsea had 'suffered a financial as well as an emotional tragedy'. As supporter Brian Gaches observes, the team were simply not good enough anymore.

It was arguably time for Dave Sexton to move on, but the unwillingness to select a non-Chelsea candidate, allied to the erroneous assumption that Frank Blunstone would jump at the opportunity to manage his old club, left the club in a tight spot. Ron Suart was a loyal club man, and undoubtedly did all he could, but the lack of quality in the squad, allied to the economic pressures that made avoiding relegation an imperative, meant he was operating with both hands tied behind his back. Eddie McCreadie was a genuinely inspirational manager, but it was too little, too late.

The lack of anything approaching a regular goalscorer was undoubtedly a significant factor. No Chelsea player had scored more than twelve goals in a League season since Osgood's eighteen in 1971-72, a lifetime ago in Chelsea terms. That the rarely-fit Hutchinson led the list with seven spoke volumes. Twenty-two goals in twenty-one home games was little short of pathetic. Good goalscorers were not necessarily cheap, but they were available. Had the team possessed a 15-20 goals-a-season man then relegation may have been avoided.

Similarly, the defence was simply not good enough. With the departure of David Webb, apart from Locke no member of the back four, regular starter or otherwise, consistently rose above the mediocre as 72 goals were conceded, equal worst in the division. The weaknesses had been there for some time, cash to address the issue had not. In retrospect, relegation probably became inevitable the day Webb left for Loftus Road.

One win in sixteen games in the autumn. One win in twelve games in March and April. Both runs illustrating the inability of the side to gather enough points. If Chelsea had stayed up it would almost certainly have been the prelude to another season of struggle, so maybe it was better to lance the boil, take the punishment and pain of relegation and move on. Eight points from their last fourteen games cemented why the team could have no complaints about the drop. As supporter Terry Cassley painfully remembers, though the support hoped and believed the players were good enough to turn things round, the brutal truth was that they were not. They got found out and paid for it.

The challenge for McCreadie would be to clear out most of the old guard, personally hard for him as he had known some for over a decade, relying on youngsters to try and take Chelsea straight back up again. Despite his confident public statements, this would undoubtedly be a massive task.

Average League crowds actually picked up 5.4% against the low base of the previous season but, at 27,380 were well below what was required to address the ever-growing debt problem devouring the club. Anyway, to hit the 35,000 break-even figure they would have to see a highly unlikely increase of 28%. They were also below those of Middlesbrough, Birmingham City and West Ham, clubs that historically Chelsea comfortably beat in terms of attendances.

Close Season

The Monday after relegation was confirmed the *Evening Standard* reported that, of the professional staff of 36 players (an extraordinary number in 1975), McCreadie was likely to put at least six on the list. Bonetti was already on it, and could be joined by Garner, Hollins, Baldwin, Dempsey, Sissons and Houseman. The *Daily Telegraph* added Kember to that list but emphasised the need for a carefully controlled clear-out so not to denude the club of experience. Mears admitted 'we would have had to streamline the staff, relegation or not'. Despite the chastening effect of the drop, he was confident Chelsea would 'bounce back in style in twelve months' time' with the young players maturing.

A couple of testimonials at Aldershot and Tonbridge and the season was over. Now for the clearing out, the rationalisation and the rebuilding. The clear-out of experienced players was pretty comprehensive, but the fire-sale mentality meant that cash raised was less than it would have been had the same players been sold a year earlier. Peter Houseman, a truly loyal servant to the club, went to Oxford United for just £30,000. Tommy Baldwin, available for £75,000 eighteen months earlier, went to Gravesend and Northfleet on a free transfer. Marvin Hinton went to Barnet, John Sissons ended up at Cape Town City, both with no fee involved.

Steve Kember went to Leicester for £80,000, less than half what Sexton had paid for him four years earlier and £45,000 less than the original asking price. Garner was listed but remained at the club. John Hollins, another one-club loyalist, went to QPR for £85,000 – a bargain for their manager Dave Sexton given that Chelsea were originally asking £175,000. Scott Cheshire, a man with an almost unrivalled knowledge of

Chelsea, argued in *Chelsea An Illustrated History* that Hollins was allowed to leave when he should have been leading the Blues through a difficult transition period, but it is clear that McCreadie wanted a clear break from the past. Cheshire also argued that Hay never fulfilled his potential and, though that is true, that was more down to injury than failings on the player's part. Hay delayed a necessary cataract operation in 1974-75 to aid the relegation fight, which undoubtedly affected his game.

On June 1st the *News Of The World* reported that Tony Green was being moved from his club secretary role but might be offered another role at Chelsea. Ron Suart could apparently have become secretary as well as general manager. In the end, Green left the club, Suart remained as general manager and in November 1975 club loyalist Christine Matthews was listed in the programme as administrative secretary. No board member stood down and no new members, who might have introduced sorely needed capital, were introduced.

Season Overview 1974-75

League Appearances
(inc sub) (top 11 players) – Harris 42, Locke 41, Cooke 39, Hay 34, Hollins 34, Phillips 34, Kember 31, Droy 26, Houseman 24, Garland 22, Hutchinson 22

League Goals (5+) – Hutchinson 7, Garner 6, Cooke 5, Hollins 5
League Clean Sheets – Home 5. Away 1
Biggest League Win – 3-1 v Coventry City (A) 24/08/74
Worst League Defeat – 1-7 v Wolverhampton Wanderers (A) 15/03/75
Final League position – 21st

League Record –
Home W4 D9 L8 F22 A31. *Away* W5 D6 L10 F20 A41. Pts 33

Hat-Tricks – None
Sending Offs –
Steve Kember v Manchester City (A) Division One 05/10/74;
John Dempsey v Everton (A) Division One 19/10/74

Biggest Home League Crowd – 39,461 v Liverpool 31/08/74
Smallest Home League Crowd – 11,048 v Coventry City 13/11/74
Average Home League Crowd – 27,380
Cup Performances – *FA Cup* 4th Round. *League Cup* 3rd Round.

Chelsea League Debuts – Steve Finnieston, David Hay, Tommy Langley, Teddy Maybank, John Sissons, Steve Wicks

Player Of The Year – Charlie Cooke

CHAPTER SIX
'A Monument To Wishful Thinking'

As supporter David Gray puts it, referring to early 1974, 'a multitude of strikes and a three-day working week had meant the building of the East Stand came to a virtual standstill and the escalating costs brought years of hardship for the club that so nearly brought us to our knees'. As the *Daily Telegraph* said shortly after relegation, 'the stadium became a £2.5 million albatross hanging round their necks'.

In *The Mavericks*, Rob Steen argued that the European Cup-Winners' Cup win was the worst thing that could have happened to Chelsea – because it gave Mears and the board ideas above their station. This seems a valid argument. Chelsea, historically a selling club, never had the revenue stream or assets to fund a development of the scale originally mooted. The wildly ambitious development plans might have stood a chance if the team kept performing and winning trophies but injury, loss of form, lack of money, disciplinary issues and mundane purchases prevented that. As supporter Geoff Kimber recalls 'none of us really knew that at the time but it slowly dawned on most of us that the financial difficulties and the downfall of the team were intrinsically linked'. Indeed.

Stamford Bridge certainly required development, it is the way it was done that was the problem. As supporter Terry Cassley says 'it was the right thing to do - the ground was old, it needed developing in some form or another. The West Stand had been built but that was just a roof and some seats on the existing terracing.' He agrees that the board 'overreached themselves' but points out that 'hindsight is a wonderful thing'.

Picking out exactly what happened regarding the progress of, and finances supporting, the East Stand construction is not an easy task. There are also a few urban myths surrounding the project, and the proposed redevelopment of the rest of Stamford Bridge, that seem to have little basis in reality. Sources used here include *Chelsea The Real Story* by Brian Mears and *The Bridge* by Colin Benson.

In *Chelsea - The Real Story*, written in 1982, Mears opined 'I must say that in no way do I regret the building of the new stand. There is also no way that the near collapse of the club was due to mismanagement by the directors. I firmly believe that had the stand been completed by the start of the 1973-74 season, as expected, the nightmare would not have occurred. I will go out on a limb and say that if the fifteen-month deadline had been met, Chelsea would still be sailing high in the First Division ...

Of course I made mistakes, but surely there is nothing a chairman can do if there is a strike or a picket line. The stand is magnificent ... Sadly it will be remembered for the wrong reasons'.

Having no regrets is one thing, but to say that 'there is also no way that the near collapse of the club was due to mismanagement by the directors' is pushing things a bit, given that those directors made the key decisions regarding appointment of architects, contract structure and finance.

In *The Chelsea Yearbook No. 5*, published in Summer 1974, a very pertinent question was asked. 'Will it be completed by the end of the 70s, the original target? Only time - and money- will tell'. In *The Mavericks* Ian Hutchinson hit the nail on the head from a player perspective. 'The plans were far too ambitious. Brian Mears is a lovely fella, but he seemed to be out of his depth. There was a mass exodus, just to get the money to pay for this stand'.

It is not clear at what point the plans to develop the rest of the ground were formally abandoned, but by Summer 1974 it must surely have been clear to the board that sufficient funding was unlikely to be available in the short or medium term. The club suffered a perfect storm of 'declining revenue, increased cost and fading team' – one role of a board is surely to create effective strategies to avoid such a situation. The fact is they couldn't, and the club took many years, and a lot more pain, before they recovered.

Journalist and avid Chelsea supporter Giles Smith, on the Chelsea website, told how *Times* writer Geoffrey Green described the new stand as having 'blossomed like a sunflower on the East side of Stamford Bridge'. Unfortunately, everything in front of that sunflower then seemed to wilt. Smith made the point that by 1975 grand architectural expansionism was no longer really on the cards for anyone, let alone a Second Division football club.

Britain's economy hit relegation form in the early 1970s, with a building strike among many delays to the construction, and the new stand was delivered late and over-budget. The strike undoubtedly impacted on the late delivery of the stand and accentuated the acute economic pressures the club were subsequently under. In *Kings Of The King's Road*, Clive Batty tells how the club cut corners on the East Stand, meaning a short-term saving but expensive remedial action in the years ahead. Supporter Brian Gaches remembers the promises of hot air being blown through holes under the East Stand seats, a feature that was never completed. The *mightyleeds* website, in a feature on the shambolic August 1972 game, called the plans 'almost fatally ambitious' which was close to the truth.

In *The Bridge* Colin Benson, who had worked at the club, is scathing about the board. 'In committing the club to one of the most imaginative and expensive redevelopments in the game, the directors were to bring the club to the brink of extinction...there must be serious question marks placed against some of the decisions they (the board) subsequently made'.

Mears made it clear in *Chelsea – The Real Story* that the board of directors were always unanimous that if players were sold simply for money then the entire structure of the club would tumble down, though that lofty ideal soon became heavily compromised. He insisted that Osgood and Hudson were sold to back the manager, though admitted that that transfer income allowed the club to stave financial crisis off, reducing the bank overdraft.

The Bridge recounts how the contractors had invoked the penalty clause because of the delays and cost over-runs. He points out that Mears had to negotiate deferred payments to the builders but was juggling with them, Barclays Bank and other creditors. Cash flow was critical with interest payments at £2,000 a week. There were still defects with the new stand such as water penetration and drains, and the GLC had yet to issue a public safety certificate. Contractors had unsurprisingly made little or no effort to remedy the defects or complete the building because of the debts owed. Mears reckoned that East Stand costs mushroomed from an original estimate of £1.2m to an actual cost of £2.5m.

Chelsea were incurring costs of around £10,000 a week without the stand costs and interest payments factored in, the club were at the limit of their bank overdraft and unable to identify other sources of funding. Unsurprisingly, the Football League and Football Association would not bale out Chelsea as it would set a precedent.

The 1974 loss was (according to *The Bridge*) £58,000, a year later it has grown to £209,000 and in 1976 to £365,000. These losses were after the likes of Osgood, Hudson, Webb, Hollins, Garland, Houseman and Kember has been sold.

Season-ticket revenue increased in 1974-75 because of the improved facilities but a disastrous season meant low attendances with a commensurate negative impact on income. If the break-even League crowd figure for 1974-75 was 35,000 (it may well have been higher) then that would have equated to a total attendance of 735,000. The actual total League attendance was 160,000 short of that. If the assumption is that most of those attending were standing spectators then, at 50p a head, that is a shortfall for 1974-75 of £80,000. Including a decent number of potentially seated spectators among the absentees, that figure would rise to £100,000 or more. Even if the club had had two lengthy and lucrative cup runs and had indeed raised £100,000 from the FA Cup as Mears hoped, it was hard to see breakeven being remotely approached.

Given this, it is impossible to see how the club hoped to pay the debt off in a reasonable time based on gate receipts and the efforts of Chelsea Pools. The latter, though a worthy initiative, raised around £170,000 in the five seasons up to summer 1975. Nice to have but making little dent in the East Stand costs, let alone the wider redevelopment plans. Weekly prize money started at £400 in August 1970 and rose to £600-£700 but never went much higher. On that basis, the estimated income a season probably never rose above £35,000, well below the £100,000 target. Worse, the revenue began to fall off when it was most essential, presumably a by-product of falling gates and a failing team.

Mears admitted in *Chelsea – The Real Story* that the post-relegation summer of 1975 was very bleak, given it was obviously harder to sell season-tickets and executive boxes in Division Two. He recognised that the supporters, who four seasons earlier had cheered the team home from Athens, were completely bemused. 'They needed someone to blame and I took the brunt of their anger', though, to be honest, it was a few more years before crowd hostility towards him really crystalised. As the Kensington Post worried some eighteen months earlier, the stand indeed became 'a monument to wishful thinking'.

The mess got even worse in 1975-76. On 24th October 1975 the board agreed to appoint a receiver, but Barclays Bank could not do so for technical reasons. The club owed the taxman, the VAT man, the bank and the builders. Martin Spencer of Stoy Hayward got a year's moratorium from the major creditors in June 1976. In the end, most of the major creditors settled for twenty pence in the pound.

Mears admitted in *Chelsea – The Real Story* 'in summer 1976 we went to the bank and told them Chelsea were finished...We were all under pressure but responded superbly to the situation'. McCreadie's young side missed promotion in 1975-76 but despite the continual financial strictures they achieved it in glorious style the following season, as detailed extensively and authoritatively in *Eddie Mac, Eddie Mac*. The players agreed to a pay cut, there were 'Cash For Chelsea' buckets at games and collections were made on special trains. The supporters did this willingly but, in retrospect, having to resort to this type of desperate fundraising to pay the bills spoke volumes about the incompetence at the top of the club.

CHAPTER SEVEN
In Hindsight

Brian Mears and The Chelsea Board

In *Chelsea – The Real Story*, Brian Mears expounded his ethos on how a club should be run. The problem was, he was acting as though Chelsea were a wealthy club, and had significant money to spend on hospitality, whereas by 1973 the reality was very different. He was clearly keen and happy to entertain VIP visitors and wrote 'Chelsea's hospitality was always superb and that is one aspect of being chairman that I tried to maintain...My father had always welcomed people to Stamford Bridge with open arms and I certainly tried to carry on that tradition. I enjoyed the luncheons before and sipping champagne in the boardroom afterwards. To me, the more people were attracted to the club the better because it meant we were doing well, we were an attractive proposition and, yes, I was honoured. I have always tried to maintain that image, even when results suffered, and we lurched from one crisis to another during the 1970s. I should like to think that when I was chairman of the club, we always had style. The doors were always open'.

Reading this quote, it is hard to avoid getting angry that his focus on image, and impressing visiting directors and other worthies, continued when the club were in desperate trouble and the team was crying out for investment. While this fine dining and mutual backslapping was going on, a dwindling support was watching a dwindling team in a stadium that from a terrace supporters' perspective was little short of a disgrace in terms of facilities.

Mears praised the Cobbold brothers on the Ipswich board, legendary for their lavish hospitality, for 'their (unique) sense of fun and style'. Chelsea official historian Rick Glanvill tells a revealing story about the Chelsea chairman and his board. 'Brian Mears told me that there was virtually a hospitality 'arms race' between the boards at Chelsea and Ipswich, each trying to outdo the other with their boozy opulence. It seems to have gone completely out of control, especially when elsewhere at the clubs, money was tight. Brian said one time that Cobbold told him to bring something extravagant to Portman Road and his chef would cook it. So he bought a huge fresh salmon and showed it to Cobbold who, half-cut, insisted, 'You'll have to cook that yourself.' So he did.'

As to whether the Chelsea board should have invested their own funds when things began to go wrong in 1973 and 1974, Mears was unequivocal. 'At Chelsea we always felt that if we had to shovel our own money into the club, we would have been mismanaging the situation. The club should stand or fall on its own achievements'. Given this attitude, it is a great shame that the board was not expanded to take on the likes of wealthy businessman Raymond Bloye. He tried to join the Chelsea board, and became friendly with Peter Osgood, but found an uninterested closed shop and eventually gave up and bought into Crystal Palace.

The impression is given that Chelsea was run like the fiefdom of the directors, more concerned with retaining power and enjoying the trappings of their position, than getting hard-nosed and wealthy businessmen on board, thereby putting the club on a significantly sounder footing, though inevitably ceding some control. They struggled regarding the stadium redevelopment, taking enormous risks with the club's financial future and, through poor contract and project management, created an environment where over-run and overspend was always on the cards.

The board were not responsible for the building strike or the Three-Day Week, but the country was in an increasing mess, economically and industrial relations wise, by Spring 1972 when the plans were made public, so it was at the very least naïve to not at least devise contingency plans in the event of problems. Plan A was optimistic in the extreme and there was no Plan B. Brian Mears, whose car sported a CFC11 number plate, loved Chelsea and it undoubtedly tore him apart to see the club struggle so massively and so publicly, but he and his colleagues must bear much responsibility for the decline.

They were responsible for the decision to rebuild Stamford Bridge at a time of gathering economic crisis, and they seemed either oblivious to the potential risks, or blithely accepting of those risks. Advisers unwisely structured contracts such that much of the risk was with the club, which was fine if everything had proceeded smoothly. However, so many major construction projects have problems in terms of time or funding, or both, that not sharing the risk more effectively was naïve.

In *Rhapsody In Blue*, official Chelsea historian Rick Glanvill recounted that Osgood's opinion was that the players liked Mears, accepting he was not the best chairman in the world but that as a person he was terrific. In *The Working Man's Ballet* Alan Hudson had a slightly different take on the chairman, arguing that Mears was educated to exert authority and expect respect.

According to the late John Phillips in a stunning story recounted in *Kings Of The King's Road*, such was the chairman's lack of self-awareness he did not cotton on to a 1974 Christmas party performance being a veiled insult by the players. In the book, the goalkeeper recounted how he and four other (sadly unnamed) players put on a spoof pantomime with Phillips playing Brian Mears as a clown and a teammate portraying his cousin Leslie as an alcoholic. They held a spoof board meeting, sacking manager Ron Suart, and referring to Leslie's outburst to the team after the Stoke cup-tie. Far from hauling the five over the coals, the chairman bizarrely commended them for their team spirit. Phillips thought 'you stupid prat, can't you see what we're saying' but apparently he genuinely thought the sketch affectionate as opposed to openly critical. This story indicates that, by this stage, a number of the players were singularly unimpressed with the board.

Dave Sexton

Interviewed in 2018, John Boyle emphasised that Sexton was 'a very decent man, and a wonderful tactician, who did not enjoy confrontation'. That seems a very apt and succinct summary. He was clearly an outstanding coach and tactically was right at the top of the class. Winning the FA Cup and Cup Winner's Cup in two seasons, with a side containing very few regular internationals, is evidence of this.

Supporter Brian Gaches was a fan of the manager but makes a salient point. 'I liked him because he always used to give us a wave in The Shed from his vantage point high up in the East Stand! The bottom line was he won silverware and got his team playing fantastic attacking football. His obvious fault became his failure to flex his man-management approach, to recognise that the likes of Osgood and Hudson required different handling to players like Harris and Bonetti.

In *Kings Of The King's Road* both Micky Droy and John Dempsey praised Sexton's coaching. In a 2018 interview on the Chelsea website, Dempsey eulogised about Sexton. 'He was a really outstanding coach who was years ahead of his time. He used to go abroad, particularly to Holland, look at training methods and techniques the coaches used there, and then would come back and try and implement these new things he had seen'.

In *Chelsea's Cult Heroes* Ron Harris felt that 'some of the players fell out with Dave. One or two new faces came in and they didn't work', referring to Garland, Garner and Weller. This is arguably the case with the first two, but maybe Harris's opinions on Keith Weller were clouded by their alleged fall-out.

If Sexton had been given the funds to rebuild in Summer 1972, when it was clear the side was not good enough to challenge for the title, or indeed at any stage in the next two seasons, then things might have turned out very differently. Sexton's evident frustration with flair players, plus that lack of funds, meant a transformation after 1971 from 'the beautiful game' to 'industrial football', from shirkers to workers. Understandable to a degree, and probably creating a more harmonious off-field environment, but at the expense of on-pitch excitement.

Energetic midfielders were one area where Chelsea were relatively well-off in Summer 1974, but Mears (according to Jimmy Hill) bought David Hay above Sexton's head when the priorities should have been replacements for some or all of Eddie McCreadie, David Webb, Peter Osgood and Alan Hudson. Sexton was placed in an impossible position, then sacked when the chickens started to come home to roost on the pitch as well as off it.

Supporter Geoff Kimber's memories of Sexton sums up the view of many fans from that era. 'I had the upmost respect for Dave Sexton. He really turned around the team after Tommy Docherty's sacking. We went on a largely unbeaten run after spending the first part of the season in the relegation zone and even ended up qualifying for the Inter Cities Fairs Cup. He was obviously a great coach and Chelsea played some of their best football ever under his watch. He was like chalk and cheese compared to The Doc. What really stuck in the mind though was winning the 1970 FA Cup. It's sometimes hard explaining to modern football fans how significant this was. When Sexton engineered winning the cup it was probably the biggest achievement in Chelsea history, even more so than winning the League in 1955'.

Dave Sexton was one of the unwitting victims of the Stamford Bridge redevelopment, though maybe his time had gone. Given everything he did for the club, and the dignity and class with which he conducted himself, he deserved better. He has to be recognised as one of the greatest managers in Chelsea's history.

Ron Suart and Eddie McCreadie

Suart was a very loyal club man, and worked hard as Sexton's assistant, but was placed in a very difficult position when his boss was sacked. The side was not good enough, and he would have been all too aware of the shortcomings, the urgent need for injections of new blood. He was tasked with bringing promising youngsters into the team, but suddenly flooding a side with raw talent is fraught with danger, as was shown when McCreadie, in a last throw of the dice, made the seismic series of changes at Tottenham in April 1975.

McCreadie was popular with the squad, relentlessly positive and a crowd hero from his playing days. As Suart's assistant he was a counterpoint to the latter's taciturn personality but had no time to waste in making his own mark. Making the Tottenham changes was certainly brave, and it is unarguable that the side that played against Manchester City were collectively mentally shot so change was essential, but even Brian Clough would probably have struggled to turn things around at that stage of the season.

The Team

It is an unarguable fact that the team declined sharply, in every area of the pitch, between winning in Athens and relegation four years later. Peter Bonetti and John Phillips, especially the former, were both quality goalkeepers and any shortcomings in the team were rarely due to goalkeeping inadequacy. Bonetti's bravery led to a couple of very nasty injuries, which impacted on his mobility and his perceived weaker distribution was one factor in his dropping after Christmas 1973. John Boyle felt Bonetti was 'a wonderful goalkeeper, brave and agile', and was criticised unfairly for his kicking, as his throws were superb, hard and accurate. Phillips was more than adequate as cover, though his confidence appeared to go during the traumatic 1974-75 season.

Full-back was a different matter. The emergence of Gary Locke as regular right-back in the 1972-73 season was a significant plus, the first youth product to gain a regular place since Alan Hudson three seasons earlier. Locke's athleticism, reliability and technical ability were of great benefit to a struggling side and meant Sexton could sell Paddy Mulligan. Left-back was however more problematic, Eddie McCreadie's injuries meaning that Ron Harris, who lacked pace and distribution, spent long periods in the role. Sexton did look on a number of occasions to buy a quality left-back but, again, money was a serious constraint.

Centre-back was an equally fraught position. Combinations of John Dempsey, David Webb, Harris, Marvin Hinton and, later, Micky Droy were increasingly found wanting. Injury took its toll on Dempsey, Hinton's style never really found favour with the manager and Harris, for all his fighting qualities, had his limitations at centre-back. If Chelsea really wanted to be a top First Division side then, in retrospect, they should have bought a top-class partner for Webb in 1972.

Sexton's enthusiasm for signing Steve Kember is hard to understand given he already had Alan Hudson and John Hollins as midfield lynch-pins in his preferred 4-2-4 system. The manager's solution, marginalising Hudson by pushing him wide, did not work consistently and starved the centre of midfield of a ball-player with incisive passing ability. Hudson and Kember's League goalscoring records were mediocre – Hudson scored 10 in 145 League games for Chelsea, Kember 13 in 130 games – leading to an over-reliance on Hollins for goals from midfield. He scored a superb 11 in the League in 1971-72 but only netted 14 over the following three seasons. Adding this to the less-than-prolific strikers (see below) and it is no wonder the side struggled.

In *Chelsea's Cult Heroes* Harris stated that he felt Ray Wilkins was only half the player Hudson was, which seems extremely harsh, especially as they were not the same type of midfielder. Sexton and Ron Suart were both very supportive of Wilkins, who became both the main playmaker and the captain very young. The older and more experienced players backed him, despite Harris's reservations.

As has been pointed out elsewhere in this book, Sexton's preference for playing midfielders and forwards on the wing once he had sold Charlie Cooke, rather than buying a quality winger, mystified then and mystifies now. It wasted and aggravated Hudson, while playing the likes of Bill Garner and Chris Garland out wide was never likely to work. Peter Houseman was an out-and-out winger, and a very good one, so moving him to full-back at the start of 1974-75 and replacing him with the injury-prone, past-his-best John Sissons was never likely to work. Very decent wingers were available in that period, but Chelsea were not in a monetary position to make a move for them.

The team sorely lacked a consistent goalscorer in the Jimmy Greaves and Bobby Tambling mould. 11, 9 and 7 goals should not have been enough to be Chelsea's leading League scorer from 1972-73 to 1974-75. Apart from Osgood in 1971-72, no Chelsea player appeared in the list of top ten Division One scorers for the four seasons under review. In 1974-75 Midfielders Kenny Hibbitt and Bruce Rioch both scored 15+ Division One goals, as did wingers Alan Foggon and Leighton James. Chelsea's leading scorer that season, Ian Hutchinson, netted just seven.

Peter Osgood's League goalscoring record was inconsistent and he was not as consistently prolific in the later years of his first spell at Chelsea as his reputation might suggest (18 in 36 games in 1971-72, 11 in 38 games in 1972-73 and 8 in 21 games in 1973-74). To be fair, he undoubtedly missed his partnership with Hutchinson, they were only able to play together as a partnership a paltry seven times after February 1971. Hutch's unavailability for most of the next three seasons had an enormous impact on the side. If that proven combination had been able to continue, Chelsea would almost certainly have been a more prolific goalscoring team. Identifying and buying a partner for the idiosyncratic Osgood would not have been easy but would have increased the chance of Chelsea remaining a top side as opposed to a team on the slide.

The striking combinations Sexton tried rarely came off. In under four years he had gone from a top-class front three of Osgood, Hutchinson and Keith Weller (used regularly in 1970-71 until Hutchinson's injury) to a less-than-startling trio of Garland, Garner and Sissons (used against Carlisle in August 1974) none of whom would have got near the 1971 side. Tommy Baldwin, Garland and Garner were moved around the forward line, never looked likely to set the world alight goals-wise and would have struggled to find a place in any top team at that time.

Yes, he was unlucky with injuries but Sexton, in retrospect, probably showed too much loyalty to his experienced players. As editor Albert Sewell pointed out in a match programme, the average age of the team against Coventry in November 1974 was 28. Sexton had failed to bring young players through, quickly jettisoning the likes of Mike Brolly, Peter Feely and Tommy Ord. Baldwin, Dempsey and Hinton were loyal, certainly, but the manager did not deem them of sufficient quality for a regular first-team place and might have been better moving them on, creating squad space for youngsters. Locke and Droy came through to gain regular places but were the exceptions in an ageing squad that was unlikely to improve.

Chelsea used an average of 25 players a season over the four seasons under review, compared with 18 for Liverpool and Derby County. Injuries might account for some of this discrepancy, but it is also clear that Sexton struggled to identify his best side.

Number of players wearing each shirt (League and Cups)											
Shirt	1	2	3	4	5	6	7	8	9	10	11
1971-72	4	4	5	3	3	4	9	8	2	7	5
1972-73	3	5	4	3	4	6	9	4	4	12	7
1973-74	2	4	6	3	2	4	6	7	7	7	6
1974-75	2	3	5	3	5	5	5	6	7	8	5

The above table indicates the extent of the problem Sexton had in picking a settled side. Nine different players wore the Number Seven shirt for two seasons running and an astonishing twelve were picked at Number Ten in 1972-73, making any sort of consistency and understanding very difficult to develop.

The regular teams, in terms of most League games played in each season, were as follows :-

1971-72 - Bonetti; Harris, Dempsey, Webb, Mulligan; Hollins, Kember, Hudson; Cooke, Osgood, Houseman. Sub Boyle.
1972-73 - Bonetti; Hollins, Harris, Webb, McCreadie; Kember, Hudson, Houseman; Garland, Osgood, Garner. Sub Locke.
1973-74 - Phillips; Locke, Droy, Webb, Harris; Hollins, Kember, Houseman; Garland, Osgood, Garner. Sub. Hudson.
1974-75 - Phillips; Locke, Droy, Hay, Harris; Hollins, Kember, Cooke; Garland, Hutchinson, Houseman. Sub R. Wilkins.

Only club loyalists Harris, Hollins and Houseman appear in all four sides. In terms of a composite side over the four seasons, again based on appearances, the side would look like this :-

1971-75 - Bonetti; Locke, Harris, Webb; Hollins, Kember, Hudson; Cooke, Garland, Osgood, Houseman. Sub Droy.

Another indicator of a lack of quality at Chelsea during the early 1970s was the lack of regular internationals in the squad. Until Hay arrived, none of the side had regular call-ups to international squads over that four-year period, suggesting a lack of real quality in the side. Rivals like Arsenal, Liverpool and Leeds had squads full of internationals, but Chelsea did not. Hudson and Osgood may have been excluded by Sir Alf Ramsey for reasons other than ability, but it is still a sorry reflection on the side. Chelsea's diminishing TV appearances, as highlighted in Appendix F, is another barometer of the reducing appeal of the transformation from flair to functionality.

Sexton's use of substitutes in League games was selective. In

1971-72 he used ten, in 1972-73 eighteen, in 1973-74 thirteen and in 1974-75 nineteen. Given the number of injuries he suffered, it is clear that tactical changes were at a premium. Whether he had the quality in the squad to make in-match changes, especially with just one substitute allowed, is debatable but given the regular mediocrity of the side it seems surprising he did not ring the changes during games more often.

The reserve side used 67 players over the four years under review. Many were either experienced players out of the side or recovering from injury, and the player with most Chelsea reserve appearances over that period was club loyalist Marvin Hinton. Others were youngsters on the way up, who made the grade in the first-team. A third group of 24, though, were those who never played for the Chelsea first-team. Of these, sixteen never played League football at all. The 24 included Keith Lawrence and Mike Sorensen who both played over 60 reserve games without getting a first-team chance, which given how mediocre the first-team was, seems unfair. They could hardly have done worse than some of those in the side.

In summer 1971 the club had the ambition to compete with the very top teams in England, if not Europe. The decision to redevelop the ground was openly predicated on the team building on the cup successes of 1970 and 1971. The decline that followed, with a lower League position every season between 1969-70 and 1975-76, a relegation, continued cup failure after 1972 and an absence from lucrative European football proved calamitous in terms of the impact on crowds. If Chelsea had carried out a ruthless rebuilding of the side after Athens, and primarily focussed spending on the team not the ground, history might have been very different.

Arsenal, Tottenham and Everton all declined during the early 1970s, and Tottenham went down in 1977, but none fell so far, or so fast as Chelsea and none were under the strictures Chelsea suffered. Chelsea's record against the top team was woeful. From 48 games against sides who finished in the top six in those four seasons, Chelsea picked up just 24 points, a clear indicator of the gulf in class.

In a 2007 interview with Peter Watts in *Time Out* magazine, Charlie Cooke gave an honest appraisal of how things went wrong. 'We were underachievers, and that was our own fault. We underachieved on the big occasions – we were dreadful in the FA Cup Final against Tottenham in 1967, and we lost to Stoke in the League Cup Final in 1972. We were out of control, wild and crazy, we egged each other on with the drinking culture. I have regrets. From this perspective, it was a lot of nonsense'. The same player told *The Scotsman* in 2016 'there was a crazy social scene at Chelsea: it was stupid, uncontrolled childishness'.

Certain player lifestyles were an increasing problem and concern. Sexton fell out with players whose egos often outweighed their performances on a Saturday and whose energies in their social lives often surpassed their energies on the pitch. His belief that professional footballers should put football first and everything else, apart from family, nowhere hardly struck a chord with key members of his squad. Hard-working, consistent players were his preference, but whereas other top managers balanced that approach with an element of flair, accepting an element of inconsistency, Sexton increasingly mistrusted such players. Steve Sherwood, talking to the *Daily Mail*, recalled how he had been used to seeing Peter Osgood and others hiding in bushes behind Epsom racecourse to avoid Dave Sexton's long training runs. The arrogance of Osgood talking about starting the season slowly and Hudson having to crash diet was indicative of the gulf between manager and these players.

Transfer Activity

The purchases Sexton did make after the glory of Athens, as the financial position at the club tightened, were not of the quality necessary to make the next step towards a consistent challenge for the title. His need for a prolific striker, a right-winger, a quality centre-half and a left-back (once McCreadie's injuries became a significant factor in his availability) was obvious to many observers, but the constraints, allied to a certain stubbornness, meant a continued reliance on those who were not quite of the required quality, for all their loyalty and endeavour.

The fact that none of the players Sexton brought in between the victory in Athens and him leaving the club, with the exception of Hay, were (or became) internationals also indicates a lack of ambition to make top signings. Departures Weller, Mulligan, Osgood and Hudson were all (or were to become) full internationals. The incoming Garland, Kember, Garner and Sissons were not. The decline in quality in the side was evident.

Supporter Peter Gray recalls the signings of Garland, Garner, Kember, Hay and Sissons. 'Even at the time I was not struck by any of these signings. They were not as good as the players they replaced (Osgood, Hudson, Weller, Webb) and didn't improve the side at all'. As supporter Terry Cassley says, he was 'completely underwhelmed' by the signings. As supporter Brian Gaches points out 'These (Hudson and Osgood) were the STAR players in Chelsea, the game-changers, world class on their day they were capable of producing magic which few players could do, and Chelsea were blessed with two in the same team. (Selling them) broke the heart and backbone of the great team in my opinion. The declining performance on the pitch reflected that'.

Taking as an example the need for a regular scorer, especially once Osgood's days were numbered. Malcolm MacDonald cost Newcastle United £180,000 in Summer 1971. He rewarded them with 76 League goals in four seasons. Bryan 'Pop' Robson joined Chelsea in 1982 when he was past his best. Had they signed him from West Ham a decade earlier, instead of him moving to Sunderland for £145,000, then the 63 goals the scored in four seasons would have been invaluable to Chelsea.

John Tudor, Billy Dearden and Bob Hatton were all regular early 1970s scorers and, in all likelihood would have been club leading scorer had they played at Chelsea. None cost a fortune. All would almost certainly have been more effective than Garland, Garner or an injury-scarred Hutchinson up front. Perhaps most damning of all, in August 1972 Frank Worthington moved from Huddersfield Town to Leicester City for £80,000, less than a month before Chelsea bought Bill Garner for £20,000 more. Worthington had already proved himself in Division One, at only twenty-three was already a charismatic crowd-pleaser, and within two years was playing for England.

The signing of David Hay was a statement of intent and a brave move given the state of the club. Had Hay stayed fit and had the succession of managers been clear which his most effective position was, then he could have made a significant difference to an ailing side. It is certainly arguable, though, that the needs to strengthen the defence and find a regular goalscorer were greater.

Looking at newspaper valuations, from a hard-hearted perspective the sales of Osgood, Hutchinson and Baldwin at the peak of their individual markets would have brought in a significant sum. The club originally valued Osgood at £300,000 (against a sale price of £275,000 including add-ons), there was interest in Hutchinson at £200,000 and Baldwin at £80,000. A total of £580,000 against an actual recouped value of £275,000. The terrible luck Hutchinson suffered with injury, and Baldwin's intransigence when it came to potential moves, impacted here. In addition, if Hutchinson had not been unavailable for such prolonged periods, the need to spend £100,000 on Garner would have been largely negated. Had Garner agreed to move to Tottenham for £200,000 in summer 1974, the club would have made a significant profit on him and Sexton may have been able to use at least some of the funds to strengthen the squad. Whether it would have been spent where it was required, or would have disappeared into the club coffers, is of course a moot point.

The sale of Weller for the same price as they paid for Garland weeks earlier demonstrates this point perfectly. Chelsea seemed unable to identify young talent, available relatively cheaply, and develop it. A whole host of promising youngsters moved to bigger clubs at comparative knockdown prices. Chelsea watched impotently as the likes of Ray Graydon, Don Givens, David Cross, Jim Bone and Steve Coppell each moved for £50,000 or less. Looking at those prices, the signings of Garland and Garner look even less smart. If funds were not there for major purchases then signing promising youngsters from lower divisions, cheaply, was surely the way ahead. Chelsea did that to a degree, but arguably chose the wrong players.

As has been detailed elsewhere in this book, the stadium redevelopment plans took financial precedence over the team. Initially that meant selling Weller to cover a hole caused by the purchases of

Garland and Garner. Whether the side would have been better if Weller had stayed and the other two had not been bought is a moot point, but he had without doubt proved himself a highly effective member of Sexton's team. Certainly, if that had been the case and Hudson had remained in the centre of midfield, the player would have been happier and more productive and, quite possibly, settled.

The following summer, the priority given to financing the redevelopment meant not buying top players to address the clear weaknesses in the side. Selling Cooke and Mulligan to Crystal Palace made an element of sense, as much of the income was used to buy a striker, though buying a proven First Division striker rather than Garner from Division Three would probably, in retrospect, have been a better bet. The balance, which disappeared into the nascent black hole of the club finances, would have been perfect to put towards a proven winger. By early 1974, economic pressures meant selling the most valuable players and not replacing them. Looking at the three years from that perspective, it is no surprise that the team declined from title contenders to relegation fodder in such a short period of time.

Although loyal club servants, there was a strong argument that moving on John Dempsey, Marvin Hinton, John Boyle and Baldwin by Summer 1973 would have saved on wages, brought in some much-needed income and also allowed youngsters earlier and greater opportunities in the reserves.

As Appendix D shows, over the four seasons the club made a surplus on transfers of £469,500, a significant sum. Given there was almost the feel of a post-relegation fire sale in the quantity and speed of disposals, transfer income could have been significantly higher. The surplus could have been used to improve the team, but for the demands of the East Stand. Dave Sexton's loyalty to the club meant he never publicly complained, but in reality, he was managing with one hand tied behind his back.

Attendances

The decline in Chelsea's crowds in the early 1970s was a significant contributory factor to the ever-increasing crisis the club found itself in. A few salient analyses, shown in Appendix E, highlight the stark decline both in absolute terms and compared to other Division One clubs. Crowds throughout top-level football were generally falling but not to the extent Chelsea's were.

After four successive seasons where Chelsea had one of the top six average crowds in the League, from 1972-73 onwards the situation was suddenly very different. A 23.3% decline in average crowds was shocking, especially when the average fall across the whole division was only 3.4%. The further decline of 12.6% in 1973-74, against a divisional average of 6.5%, was further evidence that the club had lost a significant proportion of its hard-core support. The board must have been tearing its hair out looking at the decline, unable to fund the signings necessary to revitalise the team and attract back the missing thousands. They could hardly stop building the stand and were therefore caught between a rock and a hard place.

The number of large crowds (over 35,000) slumped from fourteen in 1971-72 to an abysmal one just two seasons later whereas the number of small crowds, under 25,000, increased from one to seven. To lose 13,000 supporters a game in two seasons, allied to the decline on the pitch, belied any thought that Chelsea were competing at the higher echelons of the game by Summer 1974. There was a real danger that they were becoming a 'shadow' big club, trading on past glories as a mediocre team played in front of mediocre crowds.

If the East Stand had opened on schedule, in August 1973, then that might have had a short-term impact on crowd size, and would have increased revenues, though not by a significant amount and not on a permanent basis. To most absentee supporters it would have been the performances of the team, and the cost of admission, rather than the lack of a new stand, that kept them away.

Analysis of Chelsea's away crowds is also interesting. They declined 19.3% between 1971-72 and 1974-75, against an average divisional fall of 8.7%. This would indicate that supporters of other clubs were also finding them a less attractive team to watch.

The fall in gate revenues would have hurt the club, even without the East Stand albatross. By the summer of 1975, facing further reductions in attendances as a result of relegation, the picture was very bleak indeed. It was to be another 26 years before the 1975 35,000 average attendance target was actually reached.

The Supporters

In an interview in the *Daily Mail* in early May 1975, the week after relegation was confirmed, Chelsea supporter Derek Glasspool explained why he had stopped going to watch them regularly. He opined that since Hudson, Osgood and Webb had left 'we were left with a lot of faceless wonders'. Cooke was worth watching but he felt they had to get Osgood back. 'Maybe a couple of the new kids really are stars'. The shift from flair to functionality, from mercurial to mundane, undoubtedly affected the size of the crowds. Loyalists kept going but many casual supporters drifted away. Glasspool used to sit in the North Stand and when that was knocked down, those who sat there were distributed around the ground, losing the camaraderie that had been built up over the years.

Supporter Brian Gaches makes an interesting point on the difference between home and away crowds. 'Even allowing for the obvious impact of the East Stand rebuilding I remember the contrast really being obvious between the fantastic away support Chelsea continued to have during the bad times, whereas the home attendances and vocal support fell away quickly once the rebuilding started and the team's performances fell away from the highs of the early 70s. I believe it was in this period that Chelsea's great away support that stood out through the 70s and 80s really became engrained into Chelsea culture'.

In *Chelsea's Cult Heroes* Leo Moynihan felt both locals and glory hunters stopped going and there were far less away fans visiting Stamford Bridge because of potential trouble. John Dempsey, in a 2018 interview on the Chelsea website, felt the support 'was tremendous. As well as huge numbers at home we would take thousands away, really good support. When your name was read out before the game, you would give (The Shed) a wave and they would cheer, which brought a tingle to you, your hairs would stand on end'.

The core home support, especially in The Shed and The North Stand, remained loyal, but there were not enough of them. It took the glorious promotion season of 1976-77 to bring the crowds back, but even that was a false dawn as crowds dwindled until the restorative, redemptive 1983/84 promotion season under John Neal. The latent support was always there, but the absence of star quality, and lack of any success, meant the new stand, and the rest of Stamford Bridge, was regularly less than half full.

Had the board's dream been realised the new stand would have been full, a team of stars would have been playing attractive, winning football and the funds to pay for the rest of the redevelopment would have been rolling in. Sadly, that dream became a nightmare. Despite the best of intentions, and all the fine words about the team and the ground, the 1971-75 era at Chelsea is largely remembered for decline, failure and a gathering sense of chaotic foreboding. Off the pitch, the East Stand saga dominated the club strategically, financially and administratively. On the pitch, the sale of hugely popular, if high-maintenance, creative players presaged an unwelcome switch to functional football. The support deserved better.

APPENDICES

Appendix A
Player Profiles August 1971 – April 1975
(every player with 20+ appearances between 1971-72 and 1974-75)

Tommy Baldwin
53+1 League games 1971-72 - 1974-75, 19 goals
(182+5 games, 74 goals in Chelsea League career)
Signed from: Arsenal, September 1966 (swap for George Graham)
Chelsea League Debut: Manchester City (A), 1/10/66
Left for: Gravesend & Northfleet, June 1975
England U23 International

Peter Bonetti
84 League games 1971-72 - 1974-75
(600 games in Chelsea League career)
Signed from: Junior, April 1959
Chelsea League Debut: Manchester City (H), 2/4/60
Left for: Retired, June 1979
England International

John Boyle
30+3 League games 1971-72 - 1974-75, 0 goals
(188+10 games, 10 goals in Chelsea League career)
Signed from: Junior, August 1964
Chelsea League Debut: Leeds United (A), 23/1/65
Left for: Leyton Orient, December 1973
Scotland Youth International

Ian Britton
42+4 League games 1971-72 - 1974-75, 3 goals
(253+10 games, 33 goals in Chelsea League career)
Signed from: Junior, August 1971
Chelsea League Debut: v Derby County (H), 30/12/72 (as substitute)
Left for: Dundee United, August 1982
International appearances: none

Charlie Cooke
97+5 League games 1971-72 - 1974-75, 10 goals
(289+10 games, 22 goals in Chelsea League career)
Signed from: Dundee, April 1966
Chelsea League Debut: West Ham United (A), 20/8/66
Left for: Crystal Palace, September 1972
(re-signed Jan 1974, left for Memphis Rogues July 1978)
Scotland International

John Dempsey
56+2 League games 1971-72 - 1974-75, 1 goal
(161+4 games, 4 goals in Chelsea League career)
Signed from: Fulham, January 1969
Chelsea League Debut: Southampton (A), 1/2/69
Left for: Philadelphia Fury, March 1978
Eire International

Micky Droy
70+2 League games 1971-72 - 1974-75, 3 goals
(263+9 games, 13 goals in Chelsea League career)
Signed from: Slough Town, October 1970
Chelsea League Debut: Wolverhampton Wanderers (A), 13/2/71
Left for: Crystal Palace, March 1985
International appearances: none

Chris Garland
89+3 League games 1971-72 - 1974-75, 22 goals
(89+3 games, 22 goals in Chelsea League career)
Signed from: Bristol City, September 1971
Chelsea League Debut: Coventry City (H), 4/9/71
Left for: Leicester City, March 1975
England U23 International

Bill Garner
57+4 League games 1971-72 - 1974-75, 20 goals
(94+11 games, 31 goals in Chelsea League career)
Signed from: Southend United, September 1972
Chelsea League Debut: West Ham United (H) 9/9/72 (as substitute)
Left for: Cambridge United, November 1978
International appearances: none

Ron Harris
161 League games 1971-72 - 1974-75, 3 goals
(646+9 games, 13 goals in Chelsea League career)
Signed from: Junior, November 1961
Chelsea League Debut: Sheffield Wednesday (H) 24/2/62
Left for: Brentford May 1980
England U23 International

David Hay
34 League games 1971-72 - 1974-75, 0 goals
(107+1 games, 2 goals in Chelsea League career)
Signed from: Glasgow Celtic, July 1974
Chelsea League Debut: Carlisle United (H), 17/8/74
Left for: Retired in 1979 through injury
Scotland International

Marvin Hinton
34+4 League games 1971-72 - 1974-75, 1 goal
(257+8 games, 3 goals in Chelsea League career)
Signed from: Charlton Athletic, August 1963
Chelsea League Debut: Ipswich Town (A) 12/10/63
Left for: Barnet, June 1975
England U23 International

John Hollins
160 League games 1971-72 - 1974-75, 25 goals
(465 games, 48 goals in Chelsea League career)
Signed from: Junior, July 1963
Chelsea League Debut: Stoke City (A) 4/3/64
Left for: QPR, June 1975
(re-signed June 1983, retired June 1984, joined coaching staff)
England International

Peter Houseman
90+7 League games 1971-72 - 1974-75, 6 goals
(252+17 games, 20 goals in Chelsea League career)
Signed from: Junior, December 1962
Chelsea League Debut: Sheffield United (H) 21/12/63
Left for: Oxford United May 1975
International appearances: none

Alan Hudson
81 League games 1971-72 - 1974-75, 4 goals
(144+1 games, 10 goals in Chelsea League career)
Signed from: Junior, July 1978
Chelsea League Debut: v Southampton (A), 1/2/69
Left for: Stoke City, January 1974
(Re-signed August 1983, left for Stoke City February 1984)
England International

Ian Hutchinson
34+5 League games 1971-72 - 1974-75, 13 goals
(112+7 games, 44 goals in Chelsea League career)
Signed from: Cambridge United, August 1968
Chelsea League Debut: Ipswich Town (H), 5/10/68
Left for: Retired through injury, July 1976
England U23 International

Steve Kember
125+5 League games 1971-72 - 1974-75, 13 goals
(125+5 games, 13 goals in Chelsea League career)
Signed from: Crystal Palace, September 1971
Chelsea League Debut: Sheffield United (A), 25/9/71
Left for: Leicester City, July 1975
England U23 International

Gary Locke
89+1 League games 1971-72 - 1974-75, 1 goal
(270+2 games, 3 goals in Chelsea League career)
Signed from: Junior, July 1971
Chelsea League Debut: Coventry City (A), 30/9/72
Left for: Crystal Palace, February 1983
England Youth International

Eddie McCreadie
42+2 League games 1971-72 - 1974-75, 1 goal
(327+4 games, 4 goals in Chelsea League career)
Signed from: East Stirling, April 1962
Chelsea League Debut: Rotherham United (A) 18/8/62
Left for: retired November 1974, joined coaching staff
Scotland International

Paddy Mulligan
33 League games 1971-72 - 1974-75, 1 goal
(55+3 games, 2 goals in Chelsea League career)
Signed from: Shamrock Rovers, October 1969
Chelsea League Debut: Manchester City (H), 20/12/69 (as substitute)
Left for: Crystal Palace, September 1972
Eire International

Peter Osgood
95 League games 1971-72 - 1974-75, 37 goals
(286+3 games, 105 goals in Chelsea League career)
Signed from: Junior, August 1964
Chelsea League Debut: Leicester City (H) 23/10/65
Left for: Southampton, March 1974
(re-signed Dec 1978, retired Dec 1979)
England International

John Phillips
79 League games 1971-72 - 1974-75,
(125 games in Chelsea League career)
Signed from: Aston Villa, August 1970
Chelsea League Debut: Blackpool (A), 24/10/70
Left for: Brighton and Hove Albion, March 1980
Wales International

John Sparrow
20 League games 1971-72 - 1974-75, 1 goal
(63+6 games, 2 goals in Chelsea League career)
Signed from: Junior, June 1974
Chelsea League Debut: Burnley (H), 13/3/74
Left for: Exeter City, January 1981
England Youth International

David Webb
106 League games 1971-72 - 1974-75, 7 goals
(230 games, 21 goals in Chelsea League career)
Signed from: Southampton, February 1968
Chelsea League Debut: Manchester United (A), 2/3/68
Left for: QPR, May 1974
International appearances: none

Ray Wilkins
24+3 League games 1971-72 - 1974-75, 2 goals
(176+3 games, 30 goals in Chelsea League career)
Signed from: Junior, October, 1973
Chelsea League Debut: Norwich City (H), 26/10/73 (as substitute)
Left for: Manchester United, August 1979
England International

Appendix B
Total League Appearances and Goals 1971-75

Total League Games

Player	App	Sub	Goals	Goal Ratio
Harris	161	0	3	0.02
Hollins	160	0	25	0.16
Kember	125	5	13	0.10
Webb	106	0	7	0.07
Cooke	97	5	10	0.10
Osgood	95	0	37	0.39
Houseman	90	7	6	0.06
Garland	89	3	22	0.24
Locke	89	1	1	0.01
Bonetti	84	0	0	0.00
Hudson	81	0	4	0.05
Phillips	79	0	0	0.00
Droy	70	2	3	0.04
Garner	57	4	20	0.33
Dempsey	56	2	1	0.02
Baldwin	53	1	19	0.35
Britton	42	4	3	0.07
McCreadie	42	2	1	0.02
Hutchinson	34	5	13	0.33
Hinton	34	4	1	0.03
Hay	34	0	0	0.00
Mulligan	33	0	1	0.03
Boyle	30	3	0	0.00
Wilkins R	24	3	2	0.07
Sparrow	20	0	1	0.05
Sissons	10	1	0	0.00
Finnieston	9	0	2	0.22
Brolly	7	1	1	0.13
Wilkins G	6	0	0	0.00
Langley	5	3	1	0.13
Bason	4	0	0	0.00
Sherwood	4	0	0	0.00
Maybank	3	0	1	0.33
Ord	3	0	1	0.33
Feely	2	1	1	0.33
Smethurst	2	0	0	0.00
Weller	2	0	1	0.50
Potrac	1	0	0	0.00
Wicks	1	0	0	0.00
Own Goal			2	

Appendix C
1971-75 Season-By-Season Overall Record

	1971/72	1972/73	1973/74	1974/75
League	Division One	Division One	Division One	Division One
Home				
Won	12	9	9	4
Drew	7	6	4	9
Lost	2	6	8	8
Goals For	41	30	36	22
Goals Against	20	22	29	31
Points	31	24	22	17
Away				
Won	6	4	3	5
Drew	5	8	9	6
Lost	10	9	9	10
Goals For	17	19	20	20
Goals Against	29	29	31	41
Points	17	16	15	16
Total				
Won	18	13	12	9
Drew	12	14	13	15
Lost	12	15	17	18
Goals For	58	49	56	42
Goals Against	49	51	60	72
Points	48	40	37	33
Position 1st Sep	15	5	22	13
Position 1st Oct	18	6	16	18
Position 1st Nov	13	4	17	17
Position 1st Dec	9	5	13	20
Position 1st Jan	10	8	18	18
Position 1st Feb	9	13	18	19
Position 1st Mar	10	11	17	17
Position 1st Apr	9	11	11	19
End of season	7	12	17	21
Played in League	23	28	25	25
Most League Appearances	Hollins 42 Harris 41 Webb 41	Harris 42 Hollins 42 Osgood 38	Hollins 42 Webb 37 Kember 37	Harris 42 Locke 41 Cooke 38+1
Most Lge Goals	Osgood 18 Hollins 11 Baldwin 10	Garland 11 Osgood 11 Garner 7	Baldwin 8 Osgood 8 Garner, Kember 7	Hutchinson 7 Garner 6 Cooke, Hollins 5
FA Cup	Round 5	Qtr. Final	Round 3	Round 4
League Cup	Runners Up	Semi-final	Round 2	Round 3
Europe	ECWC 2nd R	n/a	n/a	n/a
Ave Lge Crowd	38,783	29,722	25,983	27,396
Highest Lge Crowd	54,763 v Man Utd	51,102 v Leeds Utd	40,768 v Leeds Utd	39,461 v Liverpool
Lowest Lge Crowd	23,443 v Stoke City	18,279 v Coventry	8,171 v Burnley	11,048 v Coventry
POTY	Webb	Osgood	Locke	Cooke

Appendix D
1971-75 Transfer Activity

1971-72 / 1972-73

	Player	Other Club	Players In	Players Out
71-72			£	£
Jul-71	Ian Britton	Juniors	0	
Jul-71	Gary Locke	Juniors	0	
Jul-71	Kevin Barry	Margate	2,000	
Sep-71	Chris Garland	Bristol City	100,000	
Sep-71	Steve Kember	Crystal Palace	170,000	
Sep-71	Derek Smethurst	Millwall		35,000
Sep-71	Keith Weller	Leicester City		100,000
Oct-71	Mike Brolly	Kilmarnock Star	1,000	
Dec-71	Alan Dovey	Brighton		1,000
Dec-71	Steve Finnieston	Juniors	0	
Mar-72	Jim Davis	Juniors	0	
Mar-72	Stewart Houston	Brentford		15,000
Mar-72	George Price	Juniors	0	
Tot 13			**273,000**	**151,000**
72-73				
Jul-72	Graham Wilkins	Juniors	0	
Sep-72	Brian Bason	Juniors	0	
Sep-72	Bobby Brown	Juniors	0	
Sep-72	Charlie Cooke	Crystal Palace		85,000
Sep-72	Bill Garner	Southend United	100,000	
Sep-72	Paddy Mulligan	Crystal Palace		75,000
Oct-72	Tommy Ord	Erith & Belvedere	1,000	
Nov-72	Laurie Craker	Watford		0
Dec-72	Alan Taylor	Alfreton Town	1,000	
Jan-73	Tony Potrac	Durban City		0
Feb-73	Peter Feely	Bournemouth		1,000
Tot 11			**102,000**	**161,000**

Appendix D (continued)
1971-75 Transfer Activity

1973-74
Loans were introduced for First Division clubs in 1973/74

Date	Player	Other Club	Players In £	Players Out £
1973-74				
Jul-73	Jimmy Davis	Charlton		0
Jul-73	John Spong	?		0
Jul-73	Barry Bolton	Juniors	0	
Jul-73	Keith Lawrence	Juniors	0	
Jul-73	David Lucas	Juniors	0	
Jul-73	Steve Perkins	Juniors	0	
Jul-73	Michael Sorensen	Juniors	0	
Aug-73	Ken Swain	Wycombe Wand.	500	
Oct-73	Ray Wilkins	Juniors		
Nov-73	Tommy Cunningham	Juniors	0	
Dec-73	John Boyle	Orient		0
Jan-74	Charlie Cooke	Crystal Palace	17,000	
Jan-74	Alan Hudson	Stoke City		240,000
Feb-74	Ray Lewington	Juniors	0	
Feb-74	Teddy Maybank	Juniors	0	
Mar-74	Peter Osgood	Southampton		275,000
May-74	Keith Lawrence	Brentford		0
May-74	David Webb	QPR		100,000
May-74	Steve Wicks	Juniors	0	
May-74	Alan Taylor	Reading		0
Jun-74	Mike Brolly	Bristol City		0
Jun-74	Tommy Ord	Rochester L'cers		0
Jun-74	John Sparrow	Juniors	0	
Total 23			**17,500**	**615,000**

LOANS 73-74

Jul-73	10/73 John Boyle to Brighton
Jul-73	11/73 Tommy Ord to Bristol City
Jul-73	11/73 Steve Sherwood to Millwall
Jul-73	12/73 Steve Sherwood to Millwall ended
Jul-73	12/73 John Boyle to Brighton ended
Jul-73	12/73 Tommy Ord to Bristol City ended
Jul-73	1/74 Steve Sherwood to Brentford
Aug-73	2/74 Keith Lawrence to West Brom
Oct-73	3/74 Keith Lawrence to West Brom ended
Nov-73	5/74 Steve Sherwood to Brentford ended

Appendix D (continued)
1971-75 Transfer Activity

1974-75

Date	Player	Other Club	Players In £	Players Out £
1973-74				
Jul-74	David Hay	Celtic	225,000	
Jun-74	Barry Bolton	Dordrecht		0
Aug-74	Bobby Brown	Sheffield Wed.		0
Aug-74	John Sissons	Norwich City	50,000	
Nov-74	Eddie McCreadie	Retired		0
Mar-75	Chris Garland	Leicester City		100,000
Mar-75	Tommy Langley	Juniors	0	
Mar-75	Clive Walker	Juniors	0	
May-75	Peter Houseman	Oxford United		30,000
Jun-75	Tommy Baldwin	Gravesend & Northfleet		0
Jun-75	John Hollins	QPR		80,000
Jun-75	Marvin Hinton	Barnet		0
Tot 12			275,000	210,000
		Total	667,500	1,137,000
Total	Transfer	Surplus	£469,500	

LOANS 74-75

Jul-74	8/74 Steve Sherwood to Brentford
Jun-74	10/74 Steve Finnieston to Cardiff City
Aug-74	11/74 Tommy Baldwin to Millwall
Aug-74	11/74 Tommy Baldwin to Millwall ended
Nov-74	12/74 Steve Finnieston to Cardiff C. ended
Mar-75	1/75 Tommy Baldwin to Man. Utd
Mar-75	1/75 Tommy Baldwin from Man. Utd ended

Additional Notes For Guidance:

Where disparity exists on reported fees, the most commonly reported version has been used.

For purchases from non-league clubs, in the absence of data a nominal fee of £1,000 has been given.

The sale of Steve Kember to Leicester was in July 1975 so is excluded from this Appendix.

Appendix E
1971-75 Chelsea Home Attendance Analysis
1969/70 to 1974/75

	69/70	70/71	71/72	72/73	73/74	74/75
Total League Crowds	847,173	830,469	814,552	624,520	545,651	574,976
Average League Crowd	**40,342**	**39,546**	**38,788**	**29,739**	**25,983**	**27,380**
Ave. Increase / (Decline) On Previous Season	2,729	-795	-758	-9,049	-3,756	1,396
% Increase / (Decline) On Previous Season	7.3%	-2.0%	-1.9%	-23.3%	-12.6%	5.4%
Average League crowd across all 22 clubs			31,324	30,258	28,294	27,238
Ave. League Crowd in Division 1 Ranking	4th	5th	5th	12th	12th	10th
Home League Crowds over 35,000	15	13	14	6	1	3
Home League Crowds under 25,000	1	2	1	6	7	10
Average Away League crowd	**34,772**	**34,957**	**34,465**	**31,035**	**30,527**	**27,815**

The section on attendances in Chapter Seven draws heavily on this analysis.

Relevant data is taken from *Through The Turnstiles, Chelsea: The Complete Record* and the *Bounder Friardale* website.

Appendix F
List of Games Televised: *Match Of The Day* / The Big Match

The Big Match listings taken from:
https://forums.digitalspy.com/discussion/499101/lwt-big-match-listings
Match Of the Day listings taken from:
https://sites.google.com/site/motdlistings/home/1965-66

Thanks to Rodney George for his listing of televised Chelsea games, which was invaluable.

All Division One games unless stated. *The Big Match* games shown are the main games, i.e. those shown in London. No comprehensive list could be found of games shown on other ITV regions. No comprehensive listing could be found of midweek domestic or European cup games shown.

1971-72 (17 games)
14/08/71   Arsenal 3 v Chelsea 0 – MOTD
21/08/71   Chelsea 2 v Manchester City 2 – TBM
04/09/71   Chelsea 3 v Coventry City 3 - TBM
02/10/71   Chelsea 3 v Wolverhampton Wanderers 1 - TBM
09/10/71   Liverpool 0 v Chelsea 0 – MOTD
16/10/71   Chelsea 1 Arsenal 2 - TBM
27/11/71   Chelsea 1 Tottenham Hotspur 0 - TBM
11/12/71   Chelsea 0 v Leeds United 0 - MOTD
22/12/71   Chelsea 3 v Tottenham Hotspur 2 (LC) – BBC
01/01/72   Derby County 1 v Chelsea 0 - ITV
05/01/72   Tottenham Hotspur 2 v Chelsea 2 (LC) - ITV
15/01/72   Blackpool 0 v Chelsea 1 (FAC) – MOTD
29/01/72   Chelsea 4 v Everton 0 – TBM
26/02/72   Orient 3 v Chelsea 2 (FAC) – MOTD
04/03/72   Stoke City 2 v Chelsea 1 (League Cup Final)
01/04/72   Ipswich Town 1 v Chelsea 2 - ITV
08/04/72   Chelsea 2 v Crystal Palace 1

1972-73 (20 games)
12/08/72   Chelsea 4 v Leeds United 0 – TBM
19/08/72   Derby County 1 v Chelsea 2 - MOTD
26/08/72   Chelsea 2 v Manchester City 1 – TBM
02/09/72   Arsenal 1 v Chelsea 1 - MOTD
30/09/72   Coventry City 1 v Chelsea 3 - ITV
21/10/72   Tottenham Hotspur 0 v Chelsea 1 - MOTD
28/10/72   Chelsea 1 v Newcastle United 1 - MOTD
04/11/72   Liverpool 3 v Chelsea 1 - ITV
11/11/72   Chelsea 1 v Leicester City 1 - TBM

13/12/72	Chelsea 0 v Norwich City 2 (LC) - BBC
16/12/72	Wolverhampton Wanderers 1 v Chelsea 0 - MOTD
30/12/72	Chelsea 1 v Derby County 1 – TBM
13/01/73	Brighton & Hove Albion 0 v Chelsea 2 (FAC) – TBM
20/01/73	Chelsea 0 v Arsenal 1 – TBM
03/02/73	Chelsea 2 v Ipswich Town 0 (FAC) – TBM
17/02/73	Leeds United 1 v Chelsea 1 - ITV
24/02/73	Sheffield Wednesday 1 v Chelsea 2 (FAC) – TBM
17/03/73	Chelsea 2 v Arsenal 2 (FAC) – MOTD
20/03/73	Arsenal 2 v Chelsea 2 (FAC) - BBC
31/03/73	Crystal Palace 2 v Chelsea 0 – TBM
28/04/73	Chelsea 1 v Manchester United 0 – MOTD

1973-74 (9 games)

25/08/73	Derby County 1 v Chelsea 0 - MOTD
01/09/73	Chelsea 1 Sheffield United 2 – TBM
08/09/73	Liverpool 1 v Chelsea 0 - MOTD
06/10/73	Queens Park Rangers 1 v Chelsea 1 – TBM
03/11/73	Manchester United 2 v Chelsea 2 - ITV
17/11/73	Arsenal 0 v Chelsea 0 – TBM
15/12/73	Chelsea 1 Leeds United 2 – TBM
05/01/74	Chelsea 0 QPR 0 (FA Cup R3) – TBM
09/02/74	Chelsea 1 v Manchester City 0 – MOTD

1974-75 (11 games)

17/08/74	Chelsea 0 v Carlisle United 2 - MOTD
07/09/74	Middlesbrough 1 v Chelsea 1 - ITV
14/09/74	Chelsea 0 Arsenal 0 – TBM
21/09/74	Ipswich Town 2 v Chelsea 0 - ITV
26/10/74	Chelsea 3 Stoke City 3 – TBM
09/11/74	Chelsea 0 Leicester City 0 – TBM
16/11/74	Newcastle United 5 v Chelsea 0 - ITV
30/11/74	Leeds United 2 v Chelsea 0 - MOTD
21/12/74	Chelsea 1 v West Ham United 1 - TBM
19/04/75	Tottenham Hotspur 2 Chelsea 0 - TBM
26/04/75	Chelsea 1 v Everton 1 - MOTD

It can be surmised that from 1973 onwards, Chelsea were a less attractive proposition to TV executives.

BIBLIOGRAPHY

Books

Some of these books have been used extensively in research, others for background or specific fact checking. Many are out of print, but all are worth seeking out and reading.

Barker, Kelvin; Johnstone, David; Meehan, Mark; Smith, Neil & Worrall, Mark *Eddie Mac, Eddie Mac* London. Gate 17. 2017.

Batty, Clive. *Kings Of The King's Road.* London. Vision Sports Publishing. 2007.

Benson, Colin. *The Bridge.* London. Chelsea Football Club. 1987.

Cheshire, Scott. *Chelsea – An Illustrated History.* Derby. Breedon Books. 1997.

Cooke, Charlie with Knight, Martin. *The Bonnie Prince – My Football Life.* Edinburgh. Mainstream Publishing. 2006.

Dutton, Paul & Glanvill, Rick. *'Chelsea - The Complete Record.* Liverpool. deCoubertin Books. 2015.

Glanvill, Rick. *Chelsea – The Official Biography.* London. Headline. 2005.

Glanvill, Rick. *Chelsea Football Club – The Official History In Pictures.* London. Headline. 2006.

Glanvill, Rick *Rhapsody In Blue – The Chelsea Dream Team.* London. Mainstream Publishing. 1996.

Harris, Harry *Chelsea's Century.* London. John Blake Publishing. 2005.

Hockings, Ron. *100 Year of the Blues. A Statistical History Of Chelsea Football Club.* London. The Hockings Family. 2007.

Hudson, Alan *The Working Man's Ballet.* London. London Books. 2017.

Hugman, Barry J. *Football League Players Records 1946-92.* Taunton. Tony Williams Publications. 1992.

King, Martin & Knight, Martin *The Special Ones*.
London. London Books. 2006.

Mears, Brian with MacLeay, Ian. *Chelsea – Football Under The Blue Flag*. Edinburgh. Mainstream Publishing. 2001.

Mears, Brian with MacLeay, Ian. *Chelsea – The 100-Year History*. Edinburgh. Mainstream Publishing. 2004.

Mears, Brian and Woolnough, Brian. *Chelsea – The Real Story*
London. Pelham Books. 1982.

Moynihan, John. *The Chelsea Story*.
London. Arthur Baker. 1982.

Moynihan, John. *Soccer Focus*.
London. Simon & Schuster. 1989.

Moynihan, Leo. *Chelsea's Cult Heroes*.
Derby. Knowthescore Books. 2005.

Osgood, Peter with King, Martin & Knight, Martin. *Ossie – King Of Stamford Bridge*. Edinburgh. Mainstream Publishing. 2002.

Rollin, Jack (Ed). *Rothmans Football Yearbooks 1971-1972 to 1975-1976*

Sewell, Albert *The Chelsea Football Book*.
London. Stanley Paul & Co. 1970.

Sewell, Albert *The Chelsea Football Book No.2*.
London. Stanley Paul & Co. 1971.

Sewell, Albert *The Chelsea Football Book No.3*.
London. Stanley Paul & Co. 1972.

Sewell, Albert *The Chelsea Football Book No.4*.
London. Stanley Paul & Co. 1973.

Sewell, Albert *The Chelsea Football Book No.5*.
London. Stanley Paul & Co. 1974.

Smith, Neil with Johnstone, David *Where Were You When We Were Shocking?* London. Gate 17. 2018.

Steen, Rob *The Mavericks.*
Edinburgh. Mainstream Publishing. 1995.

Tabner, Brian. *Through the Turnstiles.*
Middlesex. Yore Publications. 1992.

Westcott, Chris. *Upfront With Chelsea.*
Edinburgh. Mainstream Publishing. 2001.

Magazines and Programmes

Chelsea FC Magazines (various)
Chelsea FC home programmes (1970-75)
Chelsea FC away programmes (1970-75)
Foul – The Alternative Football Paper (1972-75)
Goal Magazine (1971-73)
Shoot Magazine (1971-75)
Time Out (various)

Newspapers (accessed via the British Library Newsroom)

Various 1969-76 editions of *Daily Express, Daily Mail, Daily Mirror, Daily Telegraph, Evening News, Evening Standard, The Guardian, Irish Examiner, News Of The World, The Observer, The Scotsman, The Sun, Sunday Express, Sunday Mirror, Sunday People, Sunday Telegraph, Sunday Times, The Times* plus local newspapers *Fulham Chronicle, Kensington News* and *Kensington Post.*

Websites

www.bounder.friardale.co.uk
(for results, scorers and season summaries)

www.chelseafc.com
http://www.the42.ie *(for Paddy Mulligan interview)*
https://thefoxfanzine.wordpress.com/2009/10/02/the-chris-garland-interview/
www.mightyleeds.co.uk *(for report on August 1972 Chelsea v Leeds game)*
www.worldfootball.net *(for leading scorers and other club appearances season-by-season)*
www.11v11.com *(for League tables during seasons)*
https://forums.digitalspy.com/discussion/499101/lwt-big-match-listings *(for The Big Match listings)*
https://sites.google.com/site/motdlistings/ *(for Match Of The Day listings).*

Other Sources

Chelsea scrapbooks compiled by Gordon Sole, and kindly lent by his son Howard.

London Borough of Hammersmith & Fulham archive.

GATE 17
THE COMPLETE COLLECTION
(OCTOBER 2019)

FOOTBALL

Over Land and Sea - Mark Worrall
Chelsea here, Chelsea There - Kelvin Barker, David Johnstone, Mark Worrall
Chelsea Football Fanzine - the best of cfcuk
One Man Went to Mow - Mark Worrall
Chelsea Chronicles (Five Volume Series) - Mark Worrall
Making History Not Reliving It - Kelvin Barker, David Johnstone, Mark Worrall
Celery! Representing Chelsea in the 1980s - Kelvin Barker
Stuck On You: a year in the life of a Chelsea supporter - Walter Otton
Palpable Discord: a year of drama and dissent at Chelsea - Clayton Beerman
Rhyme and Treason - Carol Ann Wood
Eddie Mac Eddie Mac - Eddie McCreadie's Blue & White Army
The Italian Job: A Chelsea thriller starring Antonio Conte - Mark Worrall
Carefree! Chelsea Chants & Terrace Culture - Mark Worrall, Walter Otton
Diamonds, Dynamos and Devils - Tim Rolls
Arrivederci Antonio: The Italian Job (part two) - Mark Worrall
Where Were You When We Were Shocking? - Neil L. Smith
Chelsea: 100 Memorable Games - Chelsea Chadder
Bewitched, Bothered & Bewildered - Carol Ann Wood
Cult Fiction: (Chelsea under Sarri) - Dean Mears
Liquidator: A Chelsea Memoir - Mark Worrall

FICTION

Blue Murder: Chelsea Till I Die - Mark Worrall
The Wrong Outfit - Al Gregg
The Red Hand Gang - Walter Otton
Coming Clean - Christopher Morgan
This Damnation - Mark Worrall
Poppy - Walter Otton

NON FICTION

Roe2Ro - Walter Otton
Shorts - Walter Otton

www.gate17.co.uk